What is the chief end of you?

A STUDY FOR CONTEMPORARY CHRISTIANS : WESTMINSTER SHORTER CATECHISM

BLACK BEAR BOOKS

Let's find it!

H U I   S A N G   H W A N G

What is the chief end of you?

by Huisang Hwang
Translated by Haeyoung Joo
Proofread by Casey Malarcher
Designed by Y. W. Kim
Illustration by Culture Code

Printed in Republic of Korea
Published by BlackBearBooks Korea, #801, Worldcup-Ro 190, Mapo-Gu, Seoul-Si, 03938

ISBN-10 8996738980
EAN-13 9788996738985

Scripture quotations are taken from the Holy Bible, New International Version (NIV).

http://blackbearbooks.blogspot.kr
blackbearbooks2011@gmail.com

「이 도서의 국립중앙도서관 출판예정도서목록(CIP)은 서지정보유통지원시스템 홈페이지(http://seoji.nl.go.kr)와 국가자료공동목록시스템(http://www.nl.go.kr/kolisnet)에서 이용하실 수 있습니다.(CIP제어번호: CIP2018009495)」

To Those Who Are Going to Church Every Week
With Unresolved Questions of "Why?"

CONTENTS
PART 1

Chapter 1 | **THE CHIEF END OF MAN** Q1   16

Chapter 2 | **THE BIBLE** Q2~3   28

Chapter 3 | **GOD** Q4~6   42

Chapter 4 | **GOD'S DECREE** Q7~8   56

Chapter 5 | **THE EXECUTION OF HIS DECREE: CREATION** Q9~10   64

Chapter 6 | **THE EXECUTION OF HIS DECREE: PROVIDENCE** Q11~12   78

Chapter 7 | **THE FALL** Q13~19   90

Chapter 8 | **CHRIST, THE MEDIATOR** Q20~22   114

Chapter 9 | **THE OFFICES AND ESTATE OF CHRIST** Q23~28   132

Chapter 10 | **EFFECTUAL CALLING** Q29~31   154

Chapter 11 | **THE BENEFITS OF MEDIATION: THE COMMUNION IN GRACE** Q32~35   170

Chapter 12 | **THE BENEFITS OF MEDIATION: THE COMMUNION IN GLORY** Q36~38   188

CONTENTS
PART 2

Chapter 13 | **MORAL LAW** Q39~44   206

Chapter 14 | THE TEN COMMANDMENTS PART 1 (1ST ~ 4TH) **LOVE GOD** Q45~62   220

Chapter 15 | THE TEN COMMANDMENTS PART 2 (5TH~10TH) **LOVE NEIGHBORS** Q63~81   248

Chapter 16 | **FAITH, REPENTANCE, AND THE MEANS OF GRACE** Q82~88   284

Chapter 17 | **MEANS OF GRACE: "WORD,"** SACRAMENTS, AND PRAYER Q89~90   300

Chapter 18 | **MEANS OF GRACE:** WORD, **"SACRAMENTS,"** AND PRAYER Q91~97   306

Chapter 19 | **MEANS OF GRACE:** WORD, SACRAMENTS, AND **"PRAYER"** Q98   328

Chapter 20 | **THE LORD'S PRAYER** Q99-107   336

A SUMMARY OF THE SHORTER CATECHISM PART 1&2   359

Author's Note

How can we build a strong foundation of faith?

It is such a blessing to be more than a church-goer. Being a believer (not merely a church-goer), we don't have to depend on the faith of our parents and the sermons that make us feel guilty, and even the long-lasting habit from childhood. If you have built your faith on any of the above, sooner or later, your church-going will become a ritual, a dreadful one.

Many of the problems modern day churches have brought on themselves are caused by the fact that they don't have a universal curriculum from which they can nurture the converts and raise their children. Without a universal curriculum that most churches gladly agree on, some have chosen to focus on knowledge while others focus on life application. Needless to say, without a universal curriculum either the pastor's leadership style or theological background will come to dictate the church education and the congregation growth.

A long-standing ancient problem

Churches in the past created numerous catechisms, their official curriculum, and used them to educate their parishioners. For example, in the 16th century, Elector Frederic III, sovereign of the Electoral Palatinate, commissioned the composition of a new catechism (which came to be known as the Heidelberg Catechism) to promote religious unity in his territory. Then he regulated for parents to teach their children, for teachers their students, and for pastors and catechizers their parishioners for religious unity.

Another well-known catechism, Westminster Shorter Catechism, was created in the 17th century. Back then England was in the middle of the English Reformation. And it was none other than the prosecutions Presbyterians experienced under the reign of King James I and Charles I that made them acknowledge the need of a common confession of faith (a byproduct of catechisms), by which they expected to clarify from the right theology of the Reformation matters of church governance and matters of life. With such a purpose, they summoned the saints to Westminster Abby in July of 1643, and their meetings, over a period of six years, produced the confession of faith along with Larger and Shorter Catechisms. The Larger Catechism, made of 196 sets of questions and answers, was designed primarily for adults and prospective ministers while the Shorter Catechism, made of 107 sets, was for the new converts and children in church. And this book is about the latter, the Westminster Shorter Catechism.

It is unfortunate that this precious jewel has come to lose its place in church education in the modern years of church history. The most common response to catechism-based church education is that it is so old-fashioned that it does not speak to today's needs. For this reason, it is not right for us to hold onto the catechism. Yet this is not true. Instead of abandoning it altogether under the excuse of its so-called irrelevance, we should come up with more creative and effective methods of teaching it. The contents of the catechism cannot be irrelevant, for it is written to communicate the eternal word of God, and His word is never irrelevant.

Then what benefits can we expect from this so call old-fashioned material? (1) Catechism based church education will bring a more balanced and systematic education to your church, for catechism itself maintains a great balance between theology and life application on the chief end of man (to glorify God and enjoy Him forever). And for this reason, (2) catechism based teaching is more likely to be followed in the practical life of the learners. When our life is examined under its chief end and its application is provided in detail, learners will be more likely to attempt to apply what they have learned in the catechism. (3) Lastly, it will enable the learners to effectively defend their faith and successfully avoid many heresies, for the essence of Christian faith is so clearly listed and elaborated in the catechism. From the above, believers will be made able to initiate and maintain a beautiful life as God's children, not as a duty but out of a willing heart.

And this book is designed to deliver all the benefits of the above to readers. Read the questions and statements below, and if you come to find any of them apply to you, then I highly recommend you read this book.

Who is this book for?

☐ I have been a church-goer since my childhood. Now that I am a grown up, I come to question if church-going is really necessary? Can't I just stay home and worship God by myself?

☐ I don't want my colleagues, business partners or customers to know that I am a Christian.

☐ It has been only two years that I have been coming to church because of my wife. And now she wants me tithe. Do I have to do this only for the sake of peace at home?

☐ I have a friend. We used to go to Sunday school together, but he says he has "quit" church. But his questions have not. My problem is that those questions have repeated themselves for ten years. I am getting tired of them.

☐ I am not denying God; I believe in Him. But I hate church. I am not going. Period.

☐ My husband is not a Christian and is really good at pointing out the things that churches are doing wrong. I wish I could know what to say to him.

☐ I am afraid I might run into those guys "two guys in a suit," and I don't have what it takes to defend my faith.

☐ He is literally the busiest one in my church. However, I have never seen him smile.

☐ I have tried my best to understand my pastor's sermons. But I wasn't able to.

☐ If asked, "Are you saved?" then I would answer, "Yes." But I do not know how to live my life.

☐ In no way do I look like God's child. Just look at my life!

☐ Why do I come to church? I'm dragged by my mom, harassed by phone calls from friends and pastors, or out of boredom, that is why.

☐ I have a friend to lead to Christ, but I cannot explain what Christianity, the Bible, and Christian teachings/doctrines are.

☐ I know that Christianity has earned a bad reputation, but I have nothing to say to change that. How unfortunate!

☐ Now I'm serving as a Sunday school teacher (or some other form of serving), but I wish I knew more.

☐ There were some moments during sermon I wanted to stand up and ask some questions.

☐ I have been going to church for a long time, yet I don't see many changes in my lifestyle or character.

☐ My children have begun to ask questions like "Why do we have to pray?" and "What is baptism?" Oh, I wish I could be a parent with good answers.

☐ I have tried to teach myself Christian teachings/doctrines, but all of the resources I could find I could not understand. I could not go beyond the first chapter.

The features of this book and ways to make the most of it

1. This book provides the Map so you may see the whole structure of the Shorter Catechism.

The whole map of the Shorter Catechism
It is provided by the App: WSC MAP(iOS only).

By locating the particular question and answer in it, you will be able to see the trees up close.
https://itunes.apple.com/kr/app/wsc-map/id796395687

Summarized map of Shorter Catechism (p. 16-17)
Having only the questions, this partial map will help you to see the forest from afar.

2. This book implements various ways so you may follow the logical flow of the original text.

It separates phrases and clauses, and positions them in a hierarchical way. This is to help you to more clearly see the original structure of the catechism. Before each question and answer set, a partial map is provided, which consists of the near questions and answers. This is to help readers to identify their current location. And various diagrams are presented to help readers to organize the concepts.

3. This book thoroughly covers each topic in order to enable readers to rightly interpret the concept and accordingly apply it to their lives.

It provides <Application and Sharing> in order to connect the teaching to the life of the reader. <Studies in Depth> and <Special Material> enrich the understanding of readers. And <Thomas' Question> covers various questions and provides answers.

Both the Catechism and Bible references (KJV) were used as they were in the original text, the final work of the Westminster Shorter Catechism written in 1648.

It is worth noting the Shorter Catechism does not find its base only on the referenced Bible verses, but rather on the entire Bible. However, referenced verses for respective questions show how the writers of the Catechism interpreted and quoted the Bible. You may find some of the referenced verses inappropriate for the question, but even so in such cases please reserve your judgement. We only partly know the intent of the writer; thus it should be read with careful research and prayer. (Regarding this, you may visit the following website for further help. http://www.shortercatechism.com)

Let the Larger Catechism explain the Shorter Catechism

This study chose not to list difficult names of various theologians or theological terminology, but rather put its focus on the text itself. As the titles suggests, the primary difference between the Shorter Catechism and the Larger Catechism is its length. The Larger Catechism includes more detailed explanations and applications; hence, this study chose to mainly utilize the Larger Catechism to interpret the Shorter Catechism.

Helpful Tips for Leaders

1. What is helpful for the study of catechism is the background knowledge on church history.

For there is only a paper thin difference between Church history and catechism (church doctrines) history. This is not to suggest readers need to become familiar with difficult names of various theologians. Rather it suffices to consider for specific expressions what kind of arguments were introduced and on what grounds.

2. Let the learners discover things for themselves.

a. Let them read the material and write what they have learned from it (reading) before the study.

b. After the study let them share what they have learned.

c. And let them help with each other's questions.

The leader should not burden himself/herself as if he/she must be able to answer all the question students will bring. Rather, leaders should limit their role to carefully follow students and encourage them.

3. Draw out as many questions from students as possible and keep a record of them.

Use this to help your students see how they are growing by being able to answer their questions by themselves as they study the catechism further. Offer them the opportunity to witness their own struggle and growth due to their study, and this opportunity will surely inspire them.

AS YOU PLAN THE STUDY:

It is suggested to plan six months to a year to study the entire Shorter Catechism of 107 questions. Those who fail to secure enough time tend to neglect the study of the Ten Commandments, and this does great disservice to the lives of the readers.

SHORT-TERM STUDY PLAN	PLUS
Chapter1~3	Supplement Lessons
Chapter4~7	Drawing Map
Chapter8~12	Review summary of Part 1
Chapter13~15(5th~7tb)	Supplement Lessons
Chapter15(8th~10tb)~16	Drawing Map
Chapter17~20	Review summary of Part 2 & End-Of-Book Party !

Supplemental Lessons

Specially the Ten Commandments and the Lord's Prayer in particular are closely connected to our daily lives, and thus after studying these respective units, watching related movies, documentary films, or theatrical productions and having follow-up discussion could be beneficial to motivate readers.

Mapping

After drawing a map yourself, compare yours with the one provided in the book or the WSC MAP. This will give you a chance to evaluate your understanding.

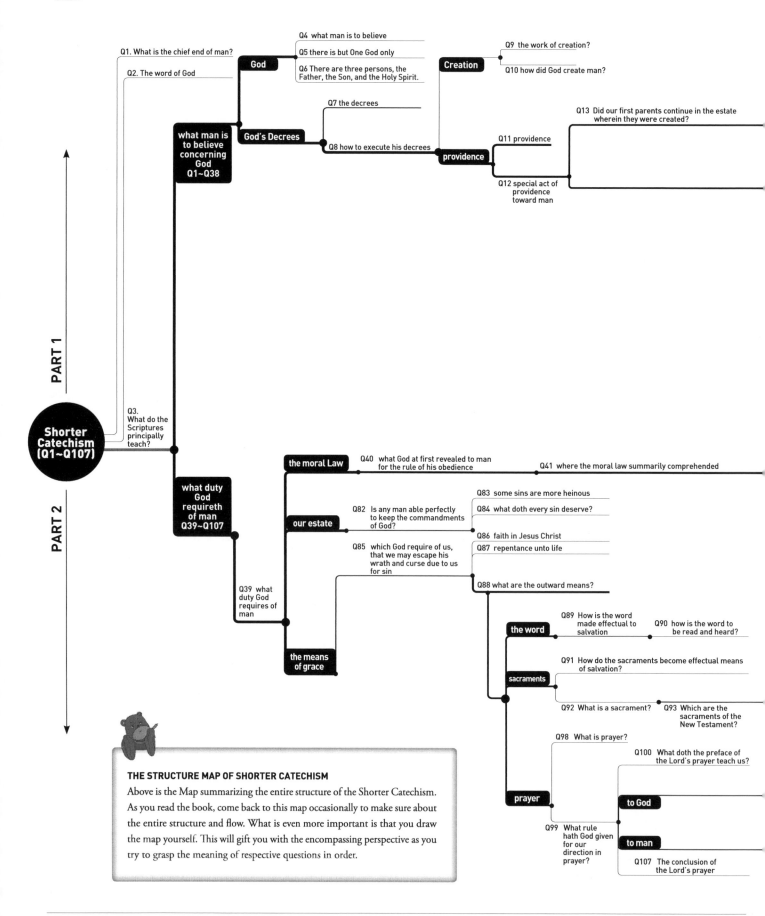

THE STRUCTURE MAP OF SHORTER CATECHISM

Above is the Map summarizing the entire structure of the Shorter Catechism. As you read the book, come back to this map occasionally to make sure about the entire structure and flow. What is even more important is that you draw the map yourself. This will gift you with the encompassing perspective as you try to grasp the meaning of respective questions in order.

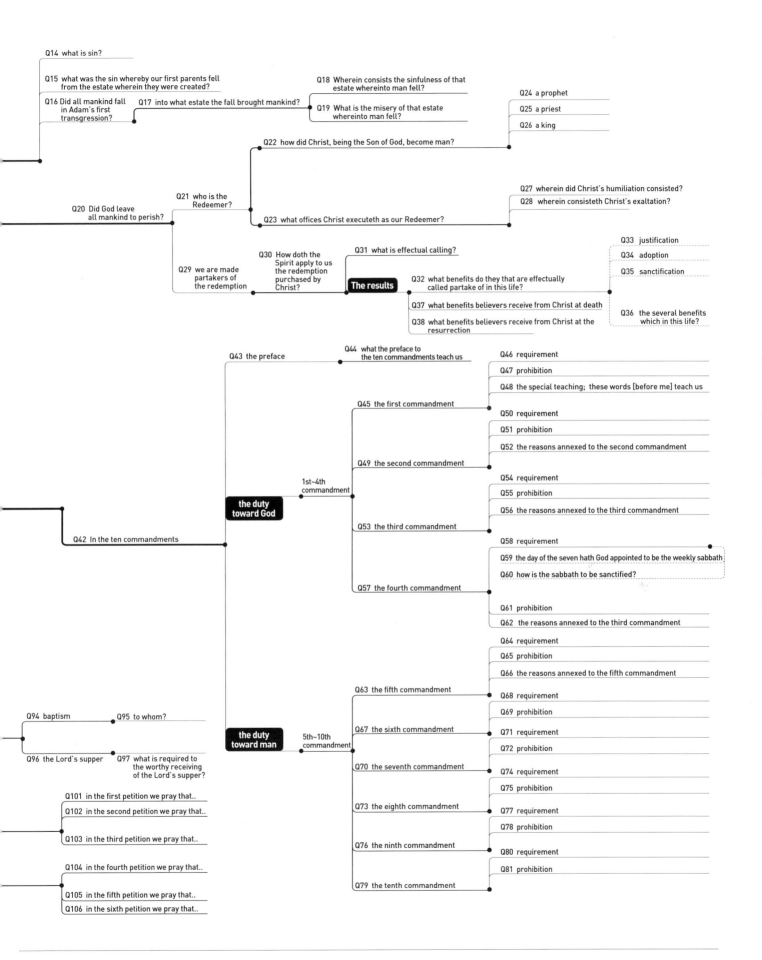

Q14 what is sin?

Q15 what was the sin whereby our first parents fell from the estate wherein they were created?

Q16 Did all mankind fall in Adam's first transgression?

Q17 into what estate the fall brought mankind?

Q18 Wherein consists the sinfulness of that estate whereinto man fell?

Q19 What is the misery of that estate whereinto man fell?

Q24 a prophet

Q25 a priest

Q26 a king

Q22 how did Christ, being the Son of God, become man?

Q27 wherein did Christ's humiliation consisted?

Q28 wherein consisteth Christ's exaltation?

Q20 Did God leave all mankind to perish?

Q21 who is the Redeemer?

Q23 what offices Christ executeth as our Redeemer?

Q29 we are made partakers of the redemption

Q30 How doth the Spirit apply to us the redemption purchased by Christ?

Q31 what is effectual calling?

Q33 justification

Q34 adoption

Q35 sanctification

The results

Q32 what benefits do they that are effectually called partake of in this life?

Q37 what benefits believers receive from Christ at death

Q38 what benefits believers receive from Christ at the resurrection

Q36 the several benefits which in this life?

Q43 the preface

Q44 what the preface to the ten commandments teach us

Q46 requirement

Q47 prohibition

Q48 the special teaching; these words [before me] teach us

Q45 the first commandment

Q50 requirement

Q51 prohibition

Q52 the reasons annexed to the second commandment

Q49 the second commandment

Q54 requirement

Q55 prohibition

Q56 the reasons annexed to the third commandment

Q53 the third commandment

Q58 requirement

Q59 the day of the seven hath God appointed to be the weekly sabbath

Q60 how is the sabbath to be sanctified?

1st~4th commandment

the duty toward God

Q57 the fourth commandment

Q61 prohibition

Q62 the reasons annexed to the third commandment

Q42 In the ten commandments

Q64 requirement

Q65 prohibition

Q66 the reasons annexed to the fifth commandment

Q63 the fifth commandment

Q68 requirement

Q69 prohibition

Q67 the sixth commandment

Q71 requirement

Q72 prohibition

the duty toward man

5th~10th commandment

Q70 the seventh commandment

Q74 requirement

Q75 prohibition

Q73 the eighth commandment

Q77 requirement

Q78 prohibition

Q76 the ninth commandment

Q80 requirement

Q81 prohibition

Q79 the tenth commandment

Q94 baptism

Q95 to whom?

Q96 the Lord's supper

Q97 what is required to the worthy receiving of the Lord's supper?

Q101 in the first petition we pray that..

Q102 in the second petition we pray that..

Q103 in the third petition we pray that..

Q104 in the fourth petition we pray that..

Q105 in the fifth petition we pray that..

Q106 in the sixth petition we pray that..

THE GROUND OF SHORTER CATECHISM

Q1-Q3 constitutes the premise of the whole catechism. For any discussion to be constructive there should be an agreement to which all parties involved could refer as they freely share their thoughts and concerns. If not, things will come to naught.

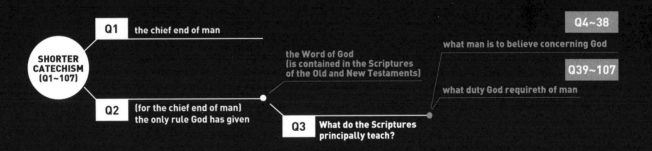

The above shows what we are to learn in the following chapters. Q1 and Q2 cover the fundamental premise for this study while Q3 summarizes the entire catechism.

Q1 | THE CHIEF END OF MAN

"WHAT IS THE PURPOSE OF MY LIFE?"
"WHO AM I?"
"WHY AM I HERE?"
"WHAT IS THE LIFE WELL-LIVED?"

Here is the beginning of the Shorter Catechism.

There is only one "first" question in the whole catechism. Despite its brevity, it opens up a whole discussion which makes it all the more important. It may sound familiar. Yet this must not be an excuse for you to overlook this question. Give your close attention to it as if you were to digest it one word at a time.

Give yourself enough time to reflect. It will be also helpful for you to discuss this question with others.

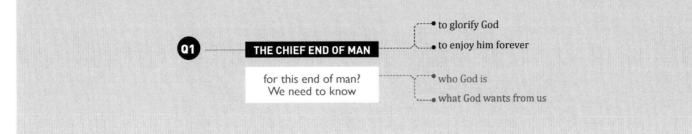

Q1 — THE CHIEF END OF MAN
- to glorify God
- to enjoy him forever

for this end of man?
We need to know
- who God is
- what God wants from us

Q1 What is the chief end of man?

A1 Man's chief end is

to glorify God, [1,2]

and   to enjoy him forever. [3]

1.
1 Corinthians 10:31

Whether therefore ye eat, or drink, or whatsoever ye do, **do all to the glory of God**.

2.
Romans 11:36

For of him, and through him, and to him, are all things: to **whom be glory for ever. Amen**.

3.
Psalms 73:25-28

Whom have I in heaven but thee? and there is none upon earth **that I desire beside thee**. My flesh and my heart faileth: but God is the strength of my heart, **and my portion for ever**. For, lo, they that are far from thee shall perish: thou hast destroyed all them that go a whoring from thee. **But it is good for me to draw near to God: I have put my trust in the Lord GOD, that I may declare all thy works**.

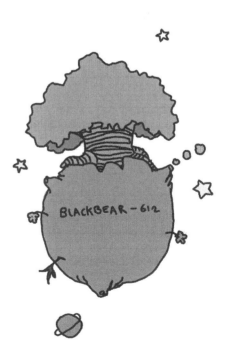

BLACKBEAR - 612

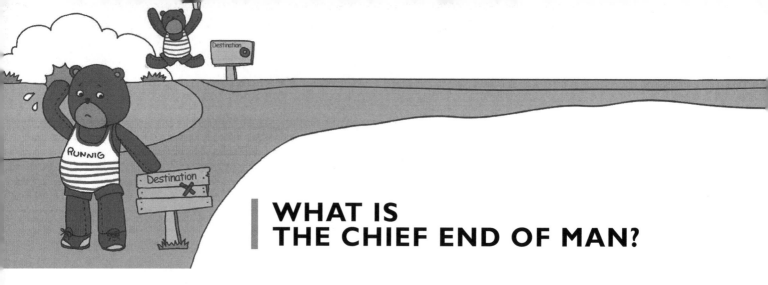

WHAT IS THE CHIEF END OF MAN?

THE MEANING OF THE FIRST QUESTION

This is the first question of the Shorter Catechism. It is asking for the chief, the highest, the first, primary, and the top end. Why does the Shorter Catechism choose to open up its discussion with this particular question? For any writing or book, the first line is just as important as its title or preface. Whenever we are about to begin an important discussion, we ponder, "How can I begin?" This applies to the Shorter Catechism as well. Before taking up its full speed, it establishes the premise of the whole discussion setting its course. If it is done in a wrong direction, any effort will contribute only to future frustration.

Rephrased, this question can be as straightforward as "Why do you live?" This is an important question in a way that it intends to enlighten the value of one's being and identity. Everyone must be able to give an explicit answer to this question.

Let's take a closer look. This question bases its argument on the premise that there is a purpose for everyone. Some may respond, "Do we really need a purpose?" "Can we not just live day by day without it?" For them, it is hard even to accept the premise that there is a purpose for everyone. In reality, many a people live in such state. However, without accepting this premise, it is impossible for us to move on. The Shorter Catechism builds its argument on the premise that without a purpose there is no meaning to any being.

There are two opposing views on this matter. The following table presents the stark difference between these two. It is due to their premises. How they view the absolute truth brings a great chasm between two. The Shorter Catechism through its first question claims that without a purpose there is no value in any being, and if I exist then so does the purpose of my life.

	BIBLE	ATHEISTS/MATERIALISTS
POSITION	There is absolute truth.	There is no absolute truth. The world exists by itself.
PURPOSE	Being created by the Creator, unlike other creatures, man is given a special purpose and reason. *"Fearing God is the whole duty of man" (Eccl 12:13).*	No one gives the purpose of life; rather, we have to find it ourselves. In our own eyes, we find what is the best for us. *"This is my life. It is for my happiness and satisfaction!"*
CHARACTERS	In order to make any life worthwhile, there must be an absolute purpose to life.	You and I are different and so are the purposes of our being.

THE POSITION OF BIBLE	VS	THE POSITION OF ATHEISTS AND MATERIALISTS
There is absolute truth. **We must pursue this truth.**		**There is no absolute truth!** **The world exists by itself.**

What makes any life worthwhile is its purpose. Life's purpose gives us the reason to wake up in the morning with excitement, and without it everything will become meaningless in the end. The Bible teaches that, unlike other creatures, man is created with a special purpose and reason. We are to live according to this purpose, pursuing the truth.

The writer of Ecclesiastes called this "the whole duty of man". *"Fear God and keep his commandments, for this is the whole duty of man." (Eccl 12:13)* Without knowing this purpose, whatever we do remains just temporary and will make everything more meaningless. *"'Meaningless! Meaningless!' says the Teacher. 'Utterly meaningless! Everything is meaningless.'" (Eccl 1:2)*

They believe there is no creator, and that only existence itself has meaning. This leads to another conviction that there is no given purpose for any man. For them, the purpose is not what someone can give but what we find—which is our own happiness and satisfaction. One's purpose is what we find looking the best in our own eyes.

Where does that lead us? This leads us to relativism, which argues that the preference of others and mine are different, and so are the purposes of our existence. This is no surprising end, given everyone is looking for what is best for me. In the eyes of relativism, there is no absolute truth. Absolute truth, according to relativism, is none other than what I think is the best for me. Thus, everyone in this world ends up with his or her own truths.

WHAT IF THERE IS NO PURPOSE?

We become anxious. Since there is no standard, there is no the answer to life. There is no reason to wake up in the morning with excitement. People come to set their own standards and work hard for them. Money, love, happiness, freedom, good deeds, sacrifice, justice, family are some examples. It is needless to say that these possess certain values in themselves. However, they have limits. Even though we come to achieve some of these, they will fail to satisfy us and we will continue to worry.

Everything becomes meaningless. Being captured by relativism, which claims "Only you have the value and you make the choice for yourself," you will be led to nihilism. Your efforts in anything will only increase this sense of meaninglessness for you.

THERE ARE TWO KINDS OF WORRIES!

The person with purpose	They worry to find a way to fulfill their purpose. This is healthy.
The person without purpose	They worry constantly not knowing what they are doing. This goes to back to the root of their being, making them anxious.

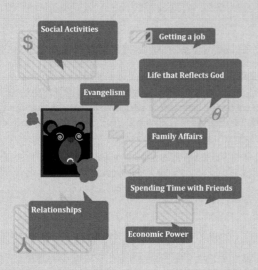

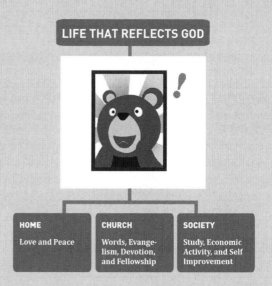

WHY THE "CHIEF" END?

This means, for any man, there is a primary end that we must seek in our lives as the first (the most primary) and the best (the most worthwhile). This chief end stands above all other ends and is the most important and ultimate end.

This implies that there are other ends and approves of them. However, in comparison, these must be the means for something more worthwhile. The chief end teaches that there is an ultimate and more important end in the midst of all the other ends.

As seen below, each can be an end at its respective stage. However, they remain a means to the overall end. The first question of the Shorter Catechism penetrates all of 107 questions. This seemingly simple and easy question which has been so far discussed comprises a significant agenda. How one responds to this question will change everything. Now, it is time to take a closer look at its answer.

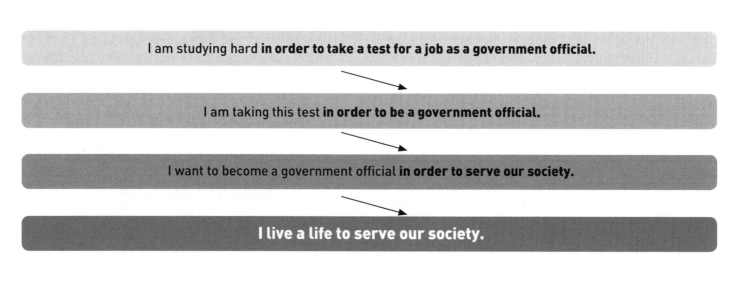

I am studying hard **in order to take a test for a job as a government official.**

I am taking this test **in order to be a government official.**

I want to become a government official **in order to serve our society.**

I live a life to serve our society.

1. TO GLORIFY GOD

This answer teaches that there is a connection between my life and God's glory. God is God, and we are humans. This is why the concept of "God's glory" and "my life" are easily misunderstood as different as day and night. However, this answer teaches that one of the ends of my life is to glorify him. In other words, I must live for God's glory.

I glorify God by testifying and demonstrating only him throughout all areas of my life. This means I find the ground of my being, life, thoughts, and behavior in Him, as not only acknowledging but praising His goodness, kindness, mercy, eternity, and holiness. On top of that, I never stop thinking about what would please Him while taking that as the priority of my life. Through everything in this world, I come to realize that God is the creator, and as one of the created ones, I acknowledge Him as my personal Lord and creator. I call on only to His name, and praise, give thanks to, and love Him alone, and obey His pleasing will. In everything, I acknowledge and fear Him. This is to realize and acknowledge that it is all because God has given me His grace that I am breathing, eating, sleeping, working, and even writing at this very moment.

WHAT MAKES THIS ANSWER UNIQUE IS THAT IT BRINGS THE FOCUS ON GOD.

The focus of my concern is not on me. The question was about man's end; however, the answer brings God's glory to the table. This is quite unexpected. We are always self-centered, and easily assume that our lives belong to us. Believers are not an exception. They too are humans. That is why we need to constantly remind ourselves that "No, everything is given by God" and try to demonstrate Him throughout everything.

I should make all of my choices by the standard, "What would please God?" This standard comes before any other, as helping us live according to man's end as believers. We do not make our choices to make things more comfortable or better for us or our families. These cannot be the standard of our choices. This is what sets apart God's people from others.

People may offer various answers to the question, "Why do you live?," but all these answers can come down to one, "For my happiness." However, the answer of the Shorter Catechism, "to glorify God," confirms that the focus is not supposed to be on my happiness. The concept, "What is good for me is good," is so prevalent these days that the pursuit of one's happiness came to replace the absolute truth and became the ultimate goal for many. This idea finds its place even among believers.

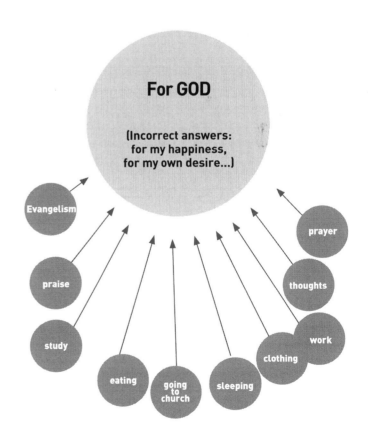

For GOD

(Incorrect answers: for my happiness, for my own desire...)

Evangelism · prayer · praise · thoughts · study · work · clothing · eating · going to church · sleeping

There is not much resistance against this particular end of life, "To live happily!" There seems to be no harm. However, the Shorter Catechism's answer places its focus on God.

Not even a truth, "Good triumphs over evil," which other religions teach, can be the standard. With regard to the question, "What kind of 'good' does that refer to?," their answers vary depending on their culture or region. **However, our answer must not be temporary and variable like theirs. It must come from the everlasting God.**

Other religions also attribute supreme worth to their god. However, what their god wants from his people is for them to go out to win a war for him or offer him their treasures. It rarely goes beyond the level of punishing those who go against his will. Meanwhile, Christianity teaches the life whose focus is on God, and that is how we glorify our God.

Why does our faith have to be like this? It is because **I am not my own, but belong—body and soul, in life and death—** to my faithful Savior, Jesus Christ. Because I am not my own, I live for God, my master, and for His glory. The Bible teaches "honor God with your body" and this refers to all areas of our lives. Thus, we have to not only take good care of our health but also strive to acquire the required knowledge.

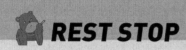 **REST STOP**

"What is your only comfort in life and death?"

This is the first question of the Heidelberg Catechism, which was written in the 16th century, a critical time period, in a region called Heidelberg in Germany. And the following is its answer.

"That I am not my own, but belong—body and soul, in life and death—to my faithful Savior, Jesus Christ."

What we daily face is the other "absolute" truth, "That I am my own." No one would appreciate the idea that he is not his own. It is crystal clear that Christian faith is different from this world. Also those who believe in and follow such a truth think differently from the world. It is obvious that this world cannot ever take people like us as its own. The life itself is different. For a believer, life means so much more than going to church every week, confessing the Bible as God's words, and believing in the miracles of the Bible.

"Do you not know that your body is a temple of the Holy Spirit, who is in you, whom you have received from God? You are not your own; you were bought at a price. Therefore honor God with your body." (1 Cor 6:19-20)

the cover of the first edition of the Heidelberg Catechism (1563)

Heidelberg Castle

"THE PURPOSE OF MY LIFE IS TO GLORIFY GOD"

This unique confession comprises the unique way that our faith understands this world. Christianity teaches us to abandon things of the world and to fix our eyes on the things of heaven. However, other afterlife-believing religions do the same. They also teach believers to abandon worldly things. Then, what makes Christian teaching unique? While acknowledging the things of this world, Christianity speaks to those who do not see beyond it and are clinging to such things: "Surely this is not all. There is something more worthwhile."

At the same time, Christianity offers the proper standing (worth) to the things of this world. The purpose of man is to glorify God. When it is misunderstood, it is predictable for people to take all things in this world as worthless and to quit their jobs and abandon housekeeping all together for the sake of church work. It is never right to mix the chief end with other ends, which could be the means for the chief end, so we must prioritize. In such a case, faith may appear to command them to choose only one out of many ends, and this is a grave mistake.

What does the right faith command us? It commands that we see things in a realistic view. What I am doing at this moment is also an important end for me. However, I have to be aware of the ultimate aim I am heading toward through this end. This is the right attitude.

> Christianity encourages, often promotes, worldly success, our works, and other values. If they remain as the means before the chief end, God's glory, and if the procedure is also right and blameless, they could glorify God. This is how we live our life toward the end of man. When this is confused, our life's value and God's glory will be destined to go separate ways. We will end up living a completely different life in church and in the world—a dualistic one.

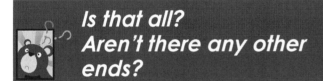

Is that all? Aren't there any other ends?

Of course, there are many other ends. Career, family, eating, and sleeping for the simple purpose of survival are a few examples. However, they are secondary to the greatest end, the chief one. "Why do I have to get a job?" "To which end, do I eat, exercise, and sleep?" What we learn from these questions is that all have one important end in them.

For many people this important and ultimate end is none other than their happiness. Despite being expressed in various ways, what they have in common is "the pursuit of happiness." However, the Shorter Catechism brings "God" into this answer. There are many ends in life, but before the end of glorifying God and enjoying him forever, they cannot remain as the ends in and of themselves but only become comparative means.

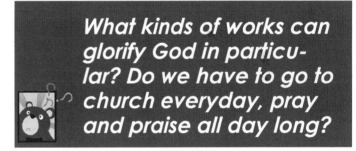

What kinds of works can glorify God in particular? Do we have to go to church everyday, pray and praise all day long?

It is not through religious activities that we glorify God and enjoy him forever. Neither our specific role nor work will do this job. This simply means that we are to make our efforts in all areas of our lives. Not only in church but also in home and society, we place God at the center of our words and behaviors and enjoy him all the days. We have to be consistent whether we are in church or in world. It is the same with our life whether in church or in other general areas. We have to live by the same principle.

For deeper understanding: Lectures in Calvinism by Abraham Kuyper

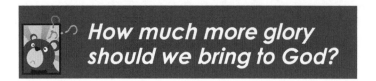

God is already glorious enough by Himself. It is not that we make Him more glorious by glorifying Him or by doing something for Him. Man is not able to add or take away any of His glory. Thus, we are not to think as if God were in need of or waiting for us to bring more glory to Him.

Then, why should we bother to say that we have to glorify God? It is because God wants us to live such a life. God wants us to glorify Him by demonstrating Him who is already glorious enough by Himself throughout our lives.

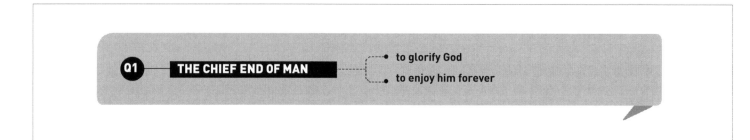

Q1 THE CHIEF END OF MAN
- to glorify God
- to enjoy him forever

2. TO ENJOY HIM FOREVER

The second part of the answer to the first question teaches that the chief end of man is to enjoy God forever. It seems quite off the topic at first. "To enjoy God forever?" It is hard even to wrap our heads around the concept. To enjoy him? How can this be the end of man?

To enjoy God forever with all our heart means to focus only on Him with all our thoughts, heart, and mind, to wait and desire His will and action, and in all events actively and voluntarily (willingly) to follow His will. This must not be done temporarily or on a whim, but continually throughout our life and even after that.

Think of someone you truly love. To enjoy someone is in other words to love that person. When we are in love, we become joyful. If there is someone we truly love, just the thought of that person makes our heart full of pleasure, joy, and desire to be always with him or her making it hard to think of anyone or anything else. We begin to wish to do whatever that person wants, and it gets easier to understand him or her. Also we desire to belong to and share everything with him or her.

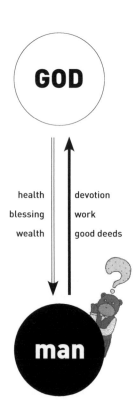

GOD

health   devotion
blessing   work
wealth   good deeds

man

The relationship between other religions' gods and their people

It is not just a sentimental expression that we enjoy God forever. It is to love God himself and being with him. When we truly love him, we begin to have certain feelings and according to this answer that is "to enjoy him."

"Love is neither a reward nor a contract."

Love is not a reward that I give to God because he did something for me. This could be quite similar to the love between men. When we say that we truly love someone, this means that we love that person just as he or she is regardless of his or her money, upbringing, or social status. This is the lesson many TV shows try to teach. In the same manner, when we love God, we enjoy him without turning our eyes to His gifts, blessing, or what I want in this world. It differs from the way other religions see their gods. They come closer and devote themselves to their god only to get something from him. Our God is more than that.

To enjoy Him forever means in all circumstances that we enjoy getting to know Him, obeying His words, seeing His words be done, and loving our neighbor as we love Him.

This teaching, to love God is the chief end of man, is incompatible with any common thoughts. No religion, no philosophy teaches the end of man in this way.

For deeper understanding: God's Passion for His Glory by Jonathan Edwards and Desiring God by John Piper

'To glorify God and to enjoy Him forever'—Isn't this only the interest of God? How can this be the chief end of man? Man needs the end for himself.

Believe it or not, this is a philosophical question. Any answer like "because the Bible tells us so" would not be so helpful. We need to see the premise hidden in the question itself.

Here is the premise hidden in the question: "It is good for God that I glorify him and enjoy him forever, but for man this is just a burdensome duty." This is not true, for it is also good for man. Only God is the supreme good and satisfaction to man. Sine only God is our creator and truly good, the greatest blessing for man is to enjoy Him. Since God is the standard of good of this world, what glorifies Him is also the greatest blessing for man. God created man that he may not find ultimate satisfaction apart from God himself. In other words, man's ultimate satisfaction lies only in God. Other things just fall short to bring complete joy to man. Nothing else but God can give the eternal and true blessing. Anything else is just temporary and momentary.

Another answer to why God gave such an end to man is found in His love. God never does anything only to annoy us by setting unnecessary rules. He is good and merciful, and is now asking us, His own creatures, to love with Him. Being the most supreme being, He comes down to us, mere creatures, asking "let us love" as if we were His equals. This is the love between two completely different beings. This simple fact, to glorify God is the end of man, should not make this relationship between God and man contractual, duty-bound, master and servant like, condition based, and burdensome. It must be the end we pursue willingly and cheerfully.

For deeper understanding: Chapter 1 of Magnalia Dei by Herman Barvinck

Herman Barvinck (1854-1921)
A Dutch reformed theologian and a pastor

A GOD-GLORIFYING LIFE IS ALSO A BLESSING FOR ME

People tend to consider God as a completely separate being distant from human life. Drawing a line between spiritual things and material things, eternal/shining things and worthless/filthy things, heavenly and earthly things, people may appear to be exalting God, but in reality they drive Him out from their world rejecting Him. They might be thinking, "In order for me to live as I see fit, He must be out of the picture all together."

Yet the Shorter Catechism's first answer teaches that to glorify God is the end of my life. I may used to have considered my life just as secular and worthless, but now I am able to glorify God with this everyday life. Whether I eat or drink or whatever I do—these are not irrelevant things but through these I can demonstrate God's glory. This is the answer of the Shorter Catechism.

It makes us bold. Whichever test we take, when its purpose rightly stands on God's glory, we will be able to see the test as one of many. This is how we bring the various ends of our lives to their rightful place, saying "This carries much worth." If this is true, even in the case of failure, we will not be utterly frustrated or disappointed but be able to try again or desire another way. The means is one of many open doors, and when one door shuts, another opens.

This is easier said than done. Under trial, it is hard for anyone to see what is unseen to his eyes. In such a case, only the seen becomes the end, making it more challenging for us to see the things beyond, and in the end we become fearful and obsessed. For example, high school seniors, for whom the college admission has become the ultimate end, will be so frustrated and down hearted should they need to make an extreme choice when they do not get the result they wished. (*This is particularly true with Korean students who spends most of their lives for this one chance—there is only one test offered for college admission each year in Korea—to prove themselves for a prestigious college.) Also trial comes without warning, and this can place anyone in a panic making him or her run about in confusion. That is why we are not to forget but dwell on Q1 of the Shorter Catechism.

This part will be dealt more in detail through Q11.

Discussion Questions

❶ "The chief end of man is to glorify God and to enjoy him forever." Why is this particular truth so important?

❷ What must we do in specific to glorify God?

❸ What has been your "chief end" so far?

❹ What do you think "to enjoy God" means?

❺ Pascal once mentioned, "There is a God shaped vacuum in the heart of every man which can be filled only by God." What do you think this mean?

❻ Given this study, how would you explain who a believer is?

❼ After reading Rom 11:36, 1 Cor 10:31, and Ps 73:28, summarize today's study.

❽ In what sense does this chapter give us the reason to be grateful?

Celcius Library in Ephesus, Turkey

Once enjoying prosperity, now it is in ruin,
yet it continues to remind us of Apostle Paul's confession,
"I consider my life worth nothing to me,
if only I may finish the race and complete the task the Lord Jesus has given me
the task of testifying to the gospel of God's grace."

Q2~3 | THE BIBLE

"HOW DO WE KNOW GOD'S WILL?"
"ISN'T THE BIBLE A MYTH?"
"THE BIBLE SAYS ONLY BE GOOD. THAT'S ALL, ISN'T IT?"
"ISN'T THE BIBLE TOO OLD TO BE RELEVANT TO OUR LIVES TODAY?"

You may have asked the questions above.
Isn't there a principle that can resolve these seemingly unending questions once and for all? The previous question was about the chief end of man.
Now it is time to learn what we can do—the way to such an end. This chapter also belongs to the premise of the Shorter Catechism.
God gave man his end and also the way to that end in detail, and that is what we are going to study through the second question. Both the end and the way came from the same God. Now let's take a look.

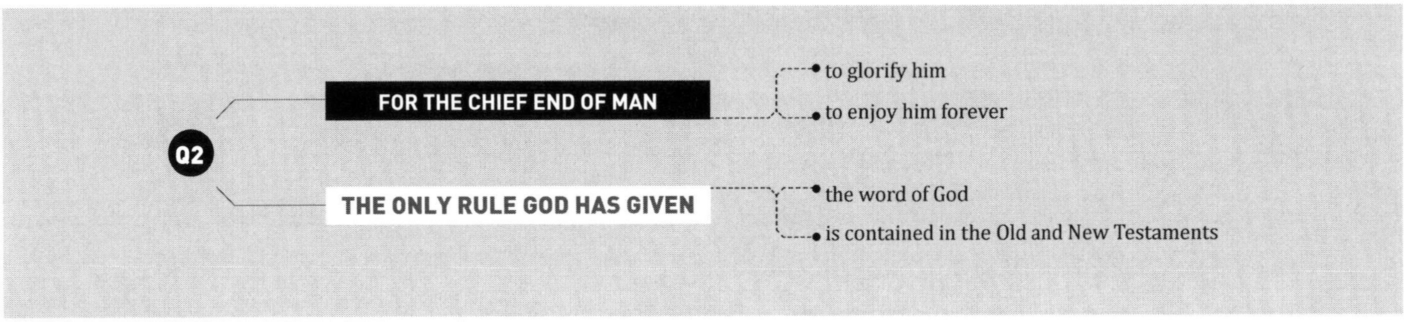

FOR THE CHIEF END OF MAN
- to glorify him
- to enjoy him forever

THE ONLY RULE GOD HAS GIVEN
- the word of God
- is contained in the Old and New Testaments

Q2 What rule hath God given
to direct us
how we may glorify and enjoy him?

A2 The word of God, which is contained
in the scriptures of the Old and New Testaments, [1,2]
is the only rule to direct us
how we may glorify and enjoy him. [3]

1.
2 Timothy 3:16

All scripture is given by inspiration of God, and is profitable for doctrine, for reproof, for correction, for instruction in righteousness.

2.
Ephesians 2:20

And are built upon **the foundation of the apostles and prophets, Jesus Christ himself being the chief corner stone.**

3.
1 John 1:3-4

That which we have seen and heard declare we unto you, **that ye also may have fellowship with us**: and truly our **fellowship is with the Father, and with his Son Jesus Christ**. And these things write we unto you, **that our joy may be full**.

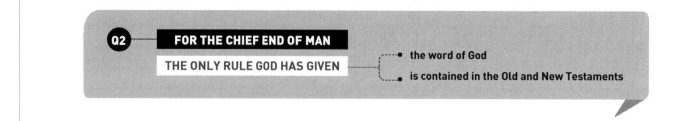

Q2 | FOR THE CHIEF END OF MAN
THE ONLY RULE GOD HAS GIVEN ---- • the word of God
                                 • is contained in the Old and New Testaments

THE ONLY RULE GOD HAS GIVEN

The previous question, Q1, asked what the chief end of man is, and its answer was God. What follows is, "Then, how can we do so?" It is the 'how' question.

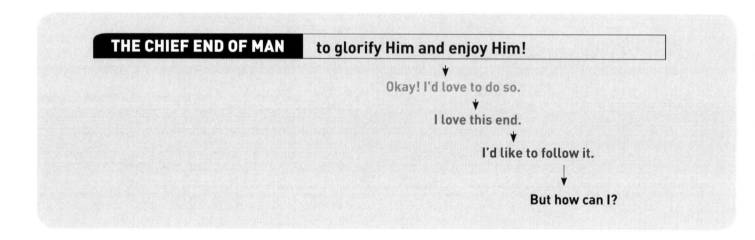

THE CHIEF END OF MAN | to glorify Him and enjoy Him!

↓

Okay! I'd love to do so.

↓

I love this end.

↓

I'd like to follow it.

↓

But how can I?

Is it an appropriate question?

Q1 has taught us the end of man, and now can we just go ahead live our lives after our own wills?

It is an appropriate question, for we do not know how. We do not gain the knowledge of God simply by having more time and experience. The knowledge of God belongs to another realm. What this question implies regarding the way we could glorify God and enjoy him is this: "Man neither knows nor is able to figure this out by himself." It remains true despite the world's claim, "Man can achieve anything." Q2 takes the form of question; however, what it communicates is that God has given us a certain "rule." This simple interrogative sentence presents the core difference between Christianity and other religions. For us to glorify God and enjoy him, He had to give us the rule to direct us. In other words, without that rule it is impossible for us to glorify or enjoy Him.

Why is that? Christianity is a religion which finds its foundation on God's revelation. Religion is commonly known as the search for the origin of things. People explore or pursue the fundamental truth of man and the world through religions. Here, man remains to be the main agent. This presupposes that man can find anything if he only puts his mind to it.

However, **we cannot get to know God unless He reveals Himself to us.** God, from the beginning, transcends the realm of man, and due to our limits, we are unable to comprehend the infinite God.

We may initiate the exploration, but it is destined to fail. Just like the blind men and the elephant, we cannot ever grasp the totality of the truth. Thus, the only way that man gets to know God is through His revelation to us. We can understand Him only as much as He illuminates Himself to us.

How can a man get to know God?
God has to reveal Himself!

THE RULE IS GIVEN

God revealed Himself to us, and it is done through His rule. Q2 is asking, "What is this rule?" The answer is, "It is the word of God, the revelation." Another question may follow, "Then, where is it?" This word of God is contained in the Old and New Testaments. And this is the only rule for us.

What is the rule? It is the law, something that we must keep. God has directed us, "This is how you get to know me." and "This is how you glorify and enjoy me." There is no other way. According to the Bible, when we neglect and violate this rule, God's wrath will be provoked. (Gal 1:7-9, Rev 22:18-19) What about you? Do you easily agree?

"Why do we have to keep the answer of the Bible as my 'only' rule? Do I have to? Aren't we being close-minded insisting there is only one rule in this wide world?"

These kinds of thoughts may sound quite natural, amicable, and reasonable. Most people would not easily agree that the Bible is given as the only rule all must keep. There are many other rules, and some of them look even wiser. This will seem even more so with those who take the Bible not as God's words but as something written by humans.

The Bible is completely different than other writings. Other wisdom and rules also belong to God's common grace. But they have limits. They could be useful for us to live our lives and help our neighbors, yet they fall short to be the rule for the chief end of life seen is Q1.

HOW THE COMMON MAN THINKS OF THIS IN GENERAL

"The rule for the end of life comes through one's conscience and ethics. Religion is simply the effort to deal with these as offering its studies and practices."

"Christianity is just one of many religions. Its formality is not important, but us being more good and civil is important."

"The Bible is just one of many sacred books. It is absurd to say that the Bible is the only rule for the end of life. There are many other ways."

We frequently hear the above. However, the answer to Q2 of the Shorter Catechism, just like Q1, is quite different from what other religions suggest. So it is from what the common man understands how he or she moves towards the end of man. That is why this proclamation, God gave us the only rule and it is contained in the Bible, remains to be another important premise of the Shorter Catechism.

For enlightenment, some employ study or self-discipline. Others strive to reach a certain state through overcoming their suffering. There could be those who wander searching for various experiences and a great teacher. Therein lies a conviction that someday we will find what we are looking for. However, the Shorter Catechism makes it clear, "Look in the word of God. There is the answer!"

This answer can appear as narrow-minded and self-righteous. Some may ask, "Then, what are all other studies for?" "Despite their efforts to find the truth, if they fall short to be the rule of life in and of themselves, then are they all useless?" The following additional explanation might be helpful.

	GENERAL REVELATION	GENERAL REVELATION
WHERE	The natural laws and all creation (Conscience, ethics, studies, and art are examples.)	Bible
PURPOSE	To offer the knowledge of God	To offer the true knowledge of God
DISTINCTION	Insufficient knowledge	Sufficient knowledge

GENERAL REVELATION

Given through the natural laws and all creation

It is not just the Bible but the general laws in this world and science that teach us there is the creator of this world. The ultimate purpose we were supposed to aim for through all these studies is to know God through them.

While studying biology and geology, we are supposed to head toward the enlightenment and proclamation of "Ah, God created and He exists." It is also true with psychology and sociology. Besides these, general social laws, ethics, love, encounters, and et cetera all have to eventually lead us to the knowledge of God.

However, these are not enough. There are indeed many great scholars and bright people, yet their intelligence does not guarantee a deeper knowledge of the Bible and God. This is because their efforts are geared to the general revelation, and they do not acknowledge the Bible as God's word. Unlike us, they fail to discover the special revelation given in the Bible.

SPECIAL REVELATION

Given for a special purpose

The special revelation offers the true knowledge of God. This is not only complete but also sufficient knowledge about both God's work and the blessing it carries. And this revelation is contained in the Bible.

It was before the time of the Bible that God often came down in the clouds speaking directly to his people, but today God speaks only through the Bible. The only channel through which we now receive the true knowledge of God is the Bible. We find God's revelation, which teaches us the rule to glorify God and enjoy him, only in the Bible.

What if we use the special revelation to interpret the general revelation? Then wouldn't we be able to understand the natural laws and all creation in better ways?

> *I know many unbelievers who are more conscientious and morally righteous than believers. They may continue to live until they die without knowing the rule we just learned. Then how are we supposed to see their lives? They are just so good!*

It is unfortunate they would live out their entire lives just as they are. Conscience and ethics offer enough for this life on earth. Due to their moral life, they could even gain respect and praise from other people, and perhaps leave their names in history. The lives of many saints in the past are examples. However, from the perspective of God, a life that does not know, much less does not live according to God's rule, is far from fulfilling the chief end of life. Compared to other people at large, his life may appear much more worthwhile; however, given the standard in Q1 of the Shorter Catechism, this life is not so much so. No matter how great or lowly one's life is (even to the point that throughout a man's entire life all he cared about was his own stomach) without reading this textbook of life, life without God is meaningless. On the other hand, even though one has nothing to boast about in his social standing, achievements, wealth, and reputation, if he loved God's word, acknowledged who He is through His word, glorified and enjoyed Him, in the eternal perspective, such a man's life will be much better than that of a saint.

Yet **it is all through God's grace** that we come to understand all of this. God is the one who lets us see things in this way. It is next to impossible for us to see things with an eternal perspective.

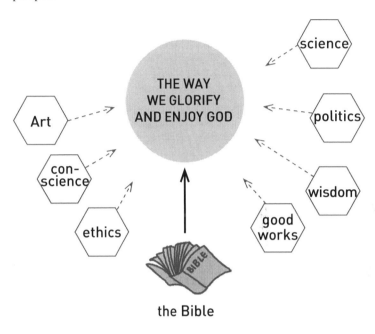

the Bible

> *Is it only through the Bible we get to know God properly? Then, what about those who refuse to listen to God's words and shut His words out altogether?*

If they continue with such an attitude, they would not be able to know God. Of course, if God wills to preach His words to them, He will open their minds and let them hear. The key principle is that hearing God's words must precede truly knowing God. That is worth repeating. Without hearing God's word, it is impossible that we get to know God properly.

> *Then, what about those who cannot read the Bible at all?*

You may have the blind in your mind. However, the Bible is accessible through various means, and this includes visual and sound aids. In the meantime, we have to work together to help those who have such an inconvenience to get access to the Bible.

What about those who are young or without the intellectual ability to understand the Bible?

At times there come people who insist they have heard God's words apart from the Bible.

If one is in a state where he cannot well understand what he is reading and there is a limit to his understanding, we can help. Or it might be very challenging for him to understand God's word in its entirety. Either way, we should not despair. This will be discussed more in detail later, but even our faith and confession in fact is the gift of Holy Spirit, who also works in that man's heart. Thus, even without knowing everything, we should believe that they are in God's pleasing will. This is also related to the matter of infant baptism. We will get a chance to study this in a much later part—the latter half of Part 2. At present, we have more wisdom to build, and hopefully through the study of the Shorter Catechism, we will be able to find the answer.

Once again it is through the word of God what we encounter and get to know God. It is either one of the following situations if one insists he received direct revelation in the wilderness apart from the Bible. It is either a lie or a pitiful self-illusion. Even if it were true that he has received a message different from the Bible, this is not from God and has neither authority nor benefit. Such claims have been rejected throughout the 2,000 year long church history without any exception. This has been repeated countlessly in the past and always proven wrong, and there is no reason for us to reconsider.

WHAT ARE CONSCIENCE AND ETHICS?

"If the word of God is the only rule and we are to follow only that, then what about conscience, ethics, and the moral teachings of our parents and teachers like 'be good' or 'do not lie'—Can they not be the rule at all? How are we supposed to understand all of this?"

What would be a proper place for conscience and ethics? What is the origin of our conscience? In any human society, we find ethics and conscience. Then, who made these? How much of it is made by man, and how much of it is the rule given by God?

God made ethics and conscience and gave them to man. Human society did not come to have these without any giver or event. God created man himself and then gave conscience into his heart. All people, even those who do not believe in God, have conscience and ethics. The origin of our conscience and ethics is none other than God.

We are created in God's image and innate with God-given conscience. For those who are known for their consciousness and moral righteousness, people love to give the special name of saint, pay their respect, and even desire to resemble such people. Yet without knowing God and believing in Him, no matter how virtuous he is, he brings no worth to God. Conscience and ethics, by their nature, have limits. Even the doctrine of compassion in Buddhism belongs to the area of conscience and ethics—a general revelation. Through it, such people were supposed to get to know God and His law, which came from none other than God.

The problem is that we are putting conscience and ethics to the wrong use. In reality, conscience and ethics fail to be the sufficient rule for us. People demand blind obedience from weaker ones by abusing the good rule to honor one's parents and elders. The rule, not to steal, lost its original intention, and the good system like private property is also misused for an evil purpose. All kinds of brutal ways are adopted by the strong to take more from the weak, and having done so through the loophole, they find no shame in their behavior. This is even more apparent with those who are conversant with the law and economy. Education in conscience and ethics also carries its limits. Everyone has their own standards to judge conscience based on how they teach and learn.

THE LIMITS OF CONSCIENCE AND ETHICS

① Our conscience and ethics are not established by an objective standard. For this reason, these cannot offer a sufficient ground for us to serve God properly. If we serve God, following our own conscience and ethics, then it is not the truth. We are all brought up in different surroundings. Only judging based on our up-bringing, even the same behavior will appear differently—sometimes as conscientious (morally righteous) and other times not. Thus, man's conscience and ethics cannot be the truth.

"The truth will set you free." This connotes that **only the word of Jesus is the unchanging truth, and only when we believe and follow this word will we indeed be able to believe Him without any error**. And this is a free life.

② Beside, we are fallen and this makes us imperfect and quite immature. We cannot utilize our conscience and ethics well enough. Many around us strive to find the truth and oftentimes go extra miles. However, such attempts are never enough. They only come back to the place of futility and vanity. And people do not appreciate this truth. In order for us to glorify God and enjoy him, we have to acknowledge our limits and humbly follow the God-given rule, which this world refuses to admit.

"Aren't we more than this? We have sent people to the moon. We are now exploring the limits of this universe. Someday, we will be able to analyze God. Seek, and we will find. Our ability is infinite, and someday we won't even need God."

However, according to the Bible, these attempts are futile.

Man's pride brings man-centered and haughty ideas. And our ethics, conscience and recent advances in science are polluted by this pride. This is also true for many Christians. They do not consider the Bible as God's word, but as containing only a part. This justifies some of us making a choice about what to accept and not from the Bible as fitting to our circumstances. This is rebellion against the only rule.

Today this line of thought is prevalent among many people. For this reason, the second question of the Shorter Catechism plays an important role correcting our fundamental understanding of the Bible.

"ONLY WHEN GOD ALLOWS, WE CAN COME TO KNOW"

The rule to glorify God and enjoy him—it is contained in the Bible. Only when we take the Bible as the only rule will we be able to glorify and enjoy him properly.

Without learning the Bible, no matter how well educated we are in this world, how morally righteous, or how well mannered, we will not be able to move towards the chief end of man. In other words, the more we read and learn from the Bible, the more we will be able to glorify God and enjoy him.

In this sense, we become all the more grateful that the Bible is not human writing but God's word.

If we did not know how to live and what truth is, having the standard of right and wrong, we would have been left groping in the dark. Yet God, creating men, did not leave us alone saying, "Now serve me. As far as how you do it, just be creative." If so, we would have had no answer. In great bewilderment, we would have wasted our entire lives. Thankfully, God has given us the rule.

As mentioned, Q1 and 2 are the premise for the entire catechism. Without an agreement to these, we cannot move on. Q3 begins to deal with the Bible. Indeed, there is not a single question or answer in the Shorter Catechism that we can gloss over without careful examination. We have to study each one of them holding it as dear as a precious jewel.

Q3 **WHAT DO THE SCRIPTURES PRINCIPALLY TEACH?**

- What man is to believe concerning God
- What duty God requires of man

Q3 What do the scriptures principally teach?

A3 The scriptures principally teach
what man is to believe concerning God,
and
what duty God requires of man. [1, 2]

1.
2 Timothy 1:13

Hold fast the form of sound words, which thou hast heard of me, **in faith and love which is in Christ Jesus**.

2.
2 Timothy 3:16

All scripture is given by inspiration of God, and is profitable for doctrine, for reproof, for correction, for instruction in righteousness.

"IF THE BIBLE IS THE ONLY RULE AND WE ARE TO LIVE ACCORDINGLY, then what is it? What is that rule in the Bible?"

Q1 dealt with the end of life, and Q2 taught that the only rule given for us to achieve such an end is the Bible. Then we have to know what the Bible teaches in detail. It is obvious that Q3 now deals with the above question.

This also divides the structure of the Shorter Catechism into two. For this reason, this book is comprised of parts one and two.

Regarding the principal teaching of the Bible, people may offer their own views—a book with wisdom for life, the way of salvation, an introduction to Jesus, the blessings of life, the history of Israel, and so on. For the most part, they are right. However, regarding the principal teaching of the Bible, the unbiased and formal answer is offered through Q3 of the Shorter Catechism. You may use this answer when asked a similar question.

Key teaching of the Bible

MAN ← GOD	GOD → MAN
What man is to **believe** concerning God =Knowledge	What **duty** God requires of man =Practice
Catechism part one (Q1-38)	Catechism part two (Q39-107)

Part 1: Q1-38   What man is to believe concerning God
Part 2: Q39-107   What duty God requires of man

This is what the scriptures mainly teach. "What is the Bible about?" There could be various responses to such a question, yet the answer of the Shorter Catechism would be the most ideal one.

1. WHAT MAN IS TO BELIEVE CONCERNING GOD

The Shorter Catechism emphasizes the knowledge concerning the object of our faith. Knowledge is essential to faith. When one believes without knowing what he believes in, it is called blind faith. Faith without firm ground leads us to worry, to be unable to articulate what we believe, and to be shaken even by little trials.

2. WHAT DUTY GOD REQUIRES OF MAN

True faith works in a way that we listen to the object of our faith and do according to His requirements. It does not force us to do anything out of a dutiful mindset. Also it does not require any actions apart from our faith. These two, faith and actions, are not disconnected. They should not be seen in a dichotomous way as two separate matters, but in an inseparable one in a sense of what we believe and the proper practice and application of what we believe. The former is the root of the latter and the latter is the fruit of former. In other words, we have to know who God is prior to listening to Him and doing according to his requirements. We are not supposed to listen to any strangers without being cautious.

We have to know whom we follow and love and what He likes, for only then His character will touch us, we become thankful for His work, and we desire to voluntarily follow Him. This is true obedience and a truly free faith.

This will make us ask, "Now, what should I follow?" and this is the sign we are at last ready to accept God's direction with a cheerful heart. And this is our happiness. Without knowing, even the desire to follow is of no use. Our life is none other than the ongoing process of an obedient life. This is also what Q1 of the Shorter Catechism referred to in specific.

The importance of Bible translation

Because the Bible is the essential element for us to get to know God, the global efforts to translate and distribute it is very imperative. There remain minor ethnic groups without their own written language, and for that reason some efforts reach even to creating a written language for them. It is a vital mission of the Church to strive to the ends of the earth so that all may be able to read the Bible.

Q2 OF THE SHORTER CATECHISM

God himself gave us the rule to glorify and enjoy him, and taught this through the Bible. This is a significant teaching in Christianity. Christianity is a religion that receives everything from God. We do not work for our spiritual awakening or reach the level of mastery through our constant efforts. Everything is given as gifts. God gave us not only our being but also the way we are to live including its end, way, and even process.

This brings us to the place of gratitude. What we are about to learn in the following sections must lead us into thanksgiving. The end of our study of the Shorter Catechism is supposed to be gratitude toward the one who gave these as gifts. The more we get to know God, the more grateful we become, full of grace and joy. For this is the best gift for us.

Q3 OF THE SHORTER CATECHISM

The answer to Q3 has two parts in it, and they are closely related. The former, "What man is to believe about God," will be dealt with in Q4-Q38, and this part is mainly about the triune God, His work, and its consequences. This will be Part One of the Shorter Catechism.

The latter, "What duty God requires of man," will be dealt with in Q39-107, and this part will teach us what God, whom we have learned through Part One, wants us to hold to and follow. This will include also the teaching of what kind of help God has provided for us to live in such a way. This will be Part Two of the Shorter Catechism.

Another way to say that we get to know God and believe properly is to say that we get to know what God requires of us and further obey Him. These are the same truth.

The conclusion of this chapter comes down to the answer to the first question of the Shorter Catechism. What we learn from the Bible is to glorify God and fully enjoy him forever. The focus of our lives is on God.

> We should continue to ponder the premise of Q1-3 throughout our entire lives. It is one thing to "know" these answers and another to "believe". It may seem that we agree to all of these now, yet we will be troubled and anxious along the way. However, do not despair. The Shorter Catechism will offer us not only assurance but encouragement.

Discussion Questions

❶ For man to know God's will, why is the Bible necessary?

❷ Regarding the key teaching of the Bible, how would you answer now?

❸ Can the Bible be the answer to every problem at home and in society? Share your opinions.

❹ What, in a word, is the gift God gives us through the Bible?

❺ In what sense does this chapter give us the reason to be grateful?

SHORTER CATECHISM PART 1

Now begins the Shorter Catechism more in full scale.
While studying the Shorter Catechism, be always mindful of where you are in the context of whole Catechism, which may
require constant reviews on what has been taught in previous chapters. Through Q1 and Q2, we have learned 1) about
man's end and the rule for such an end, 2) and God's Word is that rule. Through Q3, we were also told that the Bible,
God-given rule, mainly teaches two things, which in turn formulate two great streams in this Catechism. From now on,
we will be tracing the first stream out of two.

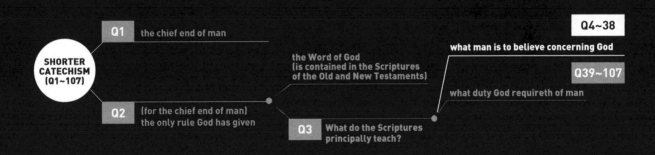

The above shows what we have been learning so far in the form of mindmap.
The Shorter Catechism Part 1, Q4-Q38, teaches, "What man is to believe concerning
God." This will include various topics—God, creation, providence, man, sin/fall, Jesus
Christ, salvation, and life/death—and will present how closely all of these are connected.

"WHO IS THIS GOD ANYWAY?
IS HE THREE OR ONE? IT SEEMS ONLY A WORD PLAY."
"HOW IS THIS GOD DIFFERENT FROM OTHER GODS?"
"IS GOD MERCIFUL?
HE SEEMS ONLY TERRIFYING TO ME.
WHY DOES EVERYONE RECOGNIZE THE SAME GOD
IN MANY DIFFERENT WAYS?"

For man to attempt to understand God altogether is like for a little child to pour the water of the sea into a hole by the means of a ladle.

This chapter opens up Shorter Catechism Part 1, which teaches, "What man is to believe concerning God."

If Shorter Catechism Part 1 is to be divided into two, they should be:
Teaching concerning God Himself (Q4-6)
Teaching concerning God's decree (Q7-38)
In other words, we will be learning about God in Q4-6 and the decree of such a God and its execution in Q7-38.

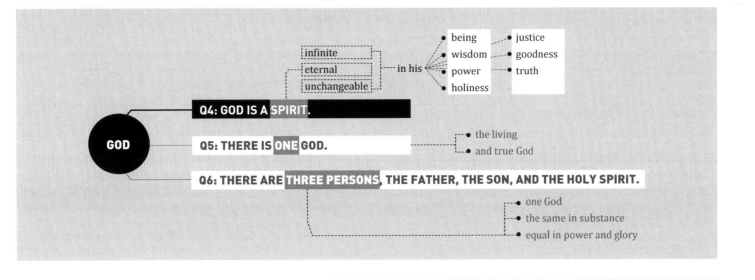

Q4 What is God?

A4 God is a Spirit,[1]
  infinite,[2] eternal,[3] and unchageable,[4]
  in his being,[5] wisdom,[6] power,[7] holiness[8]
  justice, goodness, and truth.[9]

1.
John 4:24

God is a Spirit: and they that worship him must **worship him in spirit and in truth**.

6.
Psalms 147:5

Great is our Lord, and of great power: **his understanding is infinite**.

7.
Revelation 4:8

And the four beasts had each of them six wings about him; and they were full of eyes within: and they rest not day and night,

2.
Job 11:7-9

Canst thou by searching find out God? canst thou find out the **Almighty unto perfection?** It is as **high as heaven**; what canst thou do? **deeper than hell**; what canst thou know? The measure thereof is **longer than the earth, and broader than the sea**.

saying, Holy, holy, holy, Lord God Almighty, which was, and is, and is to come.

3.
Psalms 90:2

Before the mountains were brought forth, or ever thou hadst formed the earth and the world, **even from everlasting to everlasting, thou art God**.

8.
Revelation 15:4

Who shall not fear thee, O Lord, and glorify thy name? **for thou only art holy**: for all nations shall come and **worship before thee; for thy judgments are made manifest**.

4.
James 1:17

Every good gift and every perfect gift is from above, and cometh down from the Father of lights, with whom is **no variableness, neither shadow of turning**.

9.
Exodus 34:6-7

And the Lord passed by before him, and proclaimed, **The Lord, The Lord God, merciful and gracious, longsuffering, and abundant in goodness and truth**, Keeping mercy for thousands,

5.
Exodus 3:14

And God said unto Moses, **I AM THAT I AM**: and he said, Thus shalt thou say unto the children of Israel, **I AM hath sent me unto you**.

forgiving iniquity and transgression and sin, and that will by no means **clear the guilty; visiting the iniquity of the fathers upon the children, and upon the children's children**, unto the third and to the fourth generation.

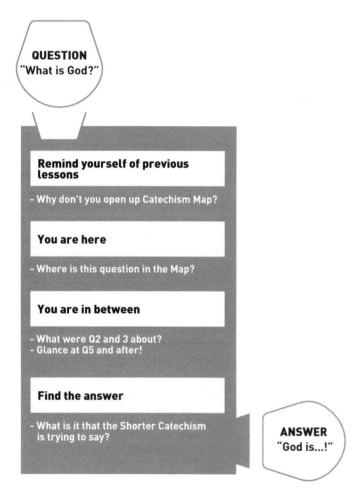

QUESTION
"What is God?"

Remind yourself of previous lessons

- Why don't you open up Catechism Map?

You are here

- Where is this question in the Map?

You are in between

- What were Q2 and 3 about?
- Glance at Q5 and after!

Find the answer

- What is it that the Shorter Catechism is trying to say?

ANSWER
"God is...!"

Q4 is about who God is. It is asking: How can we identify God, define God?

This appears quite simple yet tough to answer. What makes this question interesting is that it uses "What" instead of "Who." It is probably due to the underlying belief of this Catechism, which is that we cannot ever directly know "Who God is" but only "What He is like" through His attributes. It confirms our limits, which we have learned in previous chapters.

Q5, the following question, is similar. "Are there more Gods?" For some, this may sound over-the-line bold and even daring. Who would ask such a question in church? Yet the Shorter Catechism does so, for this is an important question and can be dealt with only by such boldness. Otherwise, it will remain unexplained causing many to get confused. Even though boldness is required on our part, we have to maintain such an attitude especially with the important and fundamental questions, for this is the best way to get a good answer.

Now, what should we do to give a right answer to this question, "What is God?" There is something to be made sure beforehand. What should be understood first in order for us to give a right answer to this question? The reminder from previous chapters would be valuable at this point. What kind of preparation is required here? It is in the humble acknowledgement, "We can know only when God teaches." That was the heart of Q2. We have also learned its reasons. For this is a different kind of knowledge. This is entirely different knowledge from the general scientific and philosophical exploration of any other beings.

THE KNOWLEDGE OF GOD

God is not an object we can analyze and then figure out. Not an object we can analyze by our mind, grasp by our hands, and measure by any other means. We can neither understand Him by our minds nor touch Him by our hands. How can finite beings comprehend the infinite one? This is a special knowledge that deals with a being greater than our minds and our knowledge.

Q4-6 must be understood in the context of previously instructed Q2-3. This is the knowledge we cannot ever grasp on our initiative; rather, it becomes available only when God reveals it. This is the knowledge entirely different from what we gain from our daily lives or in school. It is not a matter of the degree of the knowledge—how much we know, but the nature of it. It is not the knowledge of intelligence and an encyclopedia, but of blessing and eternal life.

Q3 has taught that the Bible speaks about God. Now Q4 is asking, "Then, who is this God?" Missing the connection between these two, will leave one without an answer. "How can I know who the most high God is?" One may throw up his hands in despair. However, God made it possible for us to get to know Him. He revealed Himself. He teaches. This is the point that we have to continue to remind ourselves of while tackling Q4. Because we do not have an answer, we come to the Bible. For this reason, we find all the answers of the Shorter Catechism in the Bible. We can get to know God through the Bible.

What is more important is that this simple fact—this great, marvelous, and noble One reveals Himself to us--, should deeply touch our hearts. The Bible opens itself with the introduction of God. "In the beginning God created the heavens and the earth." It is the explanation of creation with which the Bible begins. It did not begin with information on God Himself—how He comes to exist, where He came from, and what He likes; rather He is explained in relation to our world. This is an intense proclamation: "I made all things in this world and you as well." And He did so without feeling any burden or trouble. He did it all only with words. God is as amazing as this, and this God created us. He also is our Father, who is the most high yet at the same time close to us.

This should make us all the more grateful. Does this give you enough reason to give thanks and worship? As we tackle Q4, this balance is required. If not, we may end up falling into many wrongful ideas about God.

WRONGFUL IDEAS ABOUT GOD

When God is deemed "too far away"...

Agnosticism	"Nothing is known or can be known of the existence or nature of God."
Deism	This accepts the existence of a creator on the basis of reason but rejects belief in a supernatural deity who interacts with human kind.
Atheism (Materialism)	Disbelief or lack of belief in the existence of God. ("Nothing exists except matter and its movements and modifications.")

When God is deemed "too close"....

Polytheism	The belief in or worship of more than one god.
Pantheism	It identifies God with the universe, or regards the universe as a manifestation of God.

GOD IS A SPIRIT, WHICH IS INFINITE, ETERNAL, AND UNCHANGEABLE

What is infinite, eternal, and unchangeable? His being, wisdom, power, holiness, justice, goodness, and truth are so.

As the answer to the question "What is God?" it gives **God is a Spirit** before anything else. Then the additional explanation follows. He is the infinite, eternal, and unchangeable Spirit. Then, what is so? His being, wisdom, power, holiness, justice, goodness, and truth are all infinite, eternal, and unchangeable.

These attributes of God are so different from ours--changeable, limited, and weak in many ways--that they could sound strange and foreign. **Some may even doubt their significance.** Yet they are crucially significant. For God's attributes are closely connected to what will be explored in the following chapter of God's decree.

Just as God's attributes are good and perfect, God's work is also good and perfect. Just as God's attributes are unchangeable and just, God's work is also unchangeable and just. Sometimes due to our lack of understanding and limited perspective, His work could appear unjust to us. He seems to be capricious and teasing, and this could make us doubt whether His work is indeed just. At those times, we have to remind ourselves of God's attributes. Even though God appears to be doing some wrongful deeds in our eyes and we cannot understand such deeds of His, this reminder can help us be assured "This is not who He is. We must be wrong." This is how we have to see the works of God at all times.

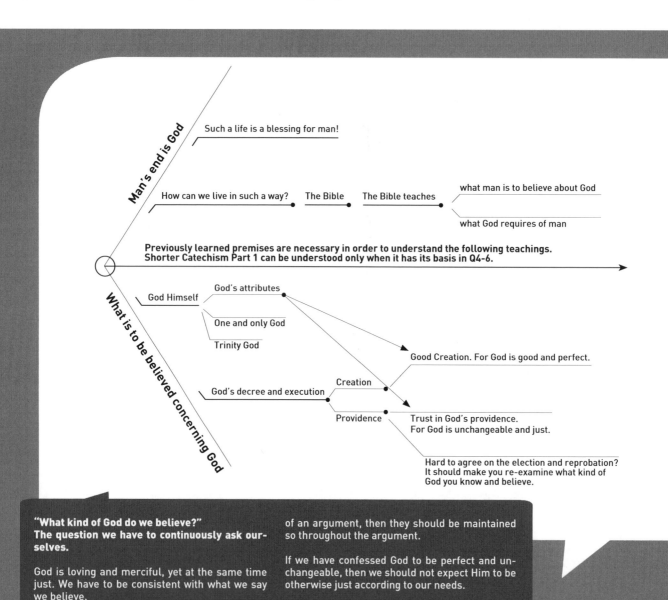

Man's end is God
Such a life is a blessing for man!

How can we live in such a way? — The Bible — The Bible teaches — what man is to believe about God / what God requires of man

Previously learned premises are necessary in order to understand the following teachings. Shorter Catechism Part 1 can be understood only when it has its basis in Q4-6.

What is to be believed concerning God

God Himself — God's attributes / One and only God / Trinity God

God's decree and execution — Creation — Good Creation. For God is good and perfect.

Providence — Trust in God's providence. For God is unchangeable and just.

Hard to agree on the election and reprobation? It should make you re-examine what kind of God you know and believe.

"What kind of God do we believe?" The question we have to continuously ask ourselves.

God is loving and merciful, yet at the same time just. We have to be consistent with what we say we believe.

If certain premises were agreed in the beginning of an argument, then they should be maintained so throughout the argument.

If we have confessed God to be perfect and unchangeable, then we should not expect Him to be otherwise just according to our needs.

An example is found in prosperity gospel. It preaches a different God from the Bible.

Does God have eyes, nose and ears like us?

God is for sure intimate with us. Despite this, there is an enormous gap between God and us. We have body, but He is a Spirit. God, unlike us, does not have a visible form. These are only figurative expressions—his eyes, his hands, and his foot.

Then what does 'man being created in God's image' mean?

Because man is a being entirely different from God, is there no similarity whatsoever? No. Words like wisdom, power, and truth are used for man as well. 'Man being created in God's image' does not mean that his eyes, nose, and mouth resemble God's; rather, man's intellect, emotion, volition, harmony, love, beauty, and order take after God's attributes.

Does God hate, feel jealous, and get angry? We find such expressions in the Bible many times.

Not in the same way man does. God transcends such feelings. He created the world with words, and it does not make sense such a God does not have enough power over man's heart that He feels jealous or upset. Such expressions in the Bible are to describe God's ways to have Himself known to us. They are the examples of God's intimate ways coming to us. Even though there is nothing that limits Himself, He comes to His creatures in intimate ways, as if He were just like one of them, and reveals Himself in a way that we can understand Him. This is called "accommodated revelation." He accommodates Himself to the level of our eyes like we do with our little children.

Is it true that God neither grows weary nor sleeps?

This is another example of accommodated revelation. Since man attempts to comprehend God's infinity with his finite perspective, he falls into the need of such expressions. When being imagined in man's image, God must grow tired, sleep, and get angry. But He is entirely different from the creatures. He was not created, but from the beginning all things have found their origin in Him. Even the name we use to call Him we cannot define.

That is why God's name is *"I Am Who I Am." (Exod 3:14)* There is no creature that has infinite, eternal, and unchangeable attributes. According to the thermodynamic laws of physics, all matter in this material world is finite, and as time passes it becomes chaotic. This is the truth. Yet this is not applied to God. He never sleeps and is eternal. We get tired because lactic acid is built up in our muscles disrupting oxygen exchange, yet none of this is applied to God who is a Spirit.

If God was alone before the creation, he must have been lonely. Is that why He created man? To fellowship with him?

This is also a misunderstanding. Man feels lonely when he is alone. It is because he feels the lack. Yet is there any lack in God? God's attributes say otherwise. He does not have any lack in Himself; thus, God does not feel lonely. He rather has the utmost contentment in Himself. The purpose of creation was for God's glory and it was done according to His free will, not because He wanted to fill any lack in Himself.

Come to think of it, God created even this thing called "the beginning." It is so because God created time itself. God probably sees the history of this entire world from the beginning to the end at a single glance like a film editor sees all cuts of a film at a single glance. For Him, a thousand years would be just like a day. He sees even the things to be done in the future as if it were now done with the editing and ready to be released.

The more we think about God, the more we get confused. It is due to the limit of our minds. We may imagine God in an ideal and abstract way. But such imagining should not be enough to gratify our curiosity. We'd better follow one step at a time as the Bible teaches about God.

Just bear with me a little more. :)

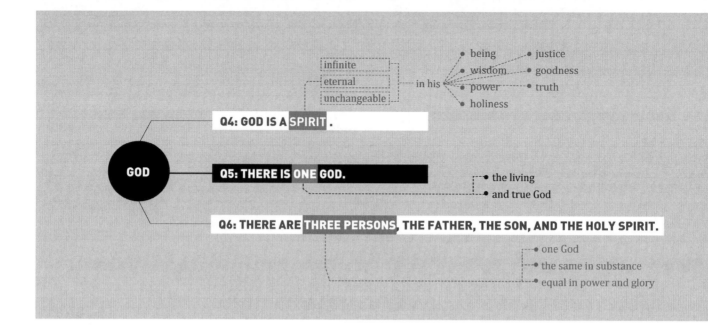

Q5 Are there more Gods than one?

A5 There is but One only,
        the living and true God. [1,2]

1.
Deuteronomy 6:4

Hear, O Israel: **The Lord our God is one Lord**.

2.
Jeremiah 10:10

But **the Lord is the true God, he is the living God, and an everlasting king**: at his wrath the earth shall tremble, and the nations shall not be able to abide his indignation.

There exist many gods in this world. Listening to the explanation of Q4, God's amazing attributes and His distinction from the creatures, it now raises the question whether there are more gods like Him. It may sound quite absurd for some, given the existence of many gods throughout human history, yet this is rather a natural and expected question.

What is funnier is the answer. "There is but One only, the living and true God." In other words, there are many dead, empty, and false gods. **These are man-made false gods. Many religions of this world have their own gods. However, Q5 makes it very clear.** "There is but One only, living and true God." This God deserves so much more than other kinds of gods. This is why we should know God and serve Him not like other gods.

No one would be willing to admit their god as not living or true. Believing their god is living and true, people used to call on their god to prove that he is more powerful than others. Yet with the advent of human reason and the development of sense of identity, such religions have gradually gone out of the picture. Mainly because they did not work. No matter how hard they called on their god, it did not work. At first, they

may have thought, "Oh, I should try harder," yet still being challenged, they finally came to deny the existence of god at all.

But that does not mean men were able to remove God from their hearts altogether. God placed the sense of God in everyone's heart with the intention of helping them to find God Himself. Yet being fallen, men rather used this in vain as mistaking the absurd as the true god and seeking after it. One way or the other this sense of God kept men striving to find alternatives, for example mysterious forms of energy. This has been repeated throughout history.

This has gotten even more absurd these days as men came to gradually take the place of God. Mysterious "cosmic energy" acclaimed through the book and movie The Secret is a typical example. We can be like god only if we cultivate ourselves and come to understand the truth. What a vain thought that we could be an infinite, eternal, and unchangeable being! It is not that we have any chance at this, but we have to be on guard against such a profane thought.

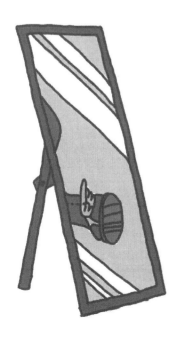

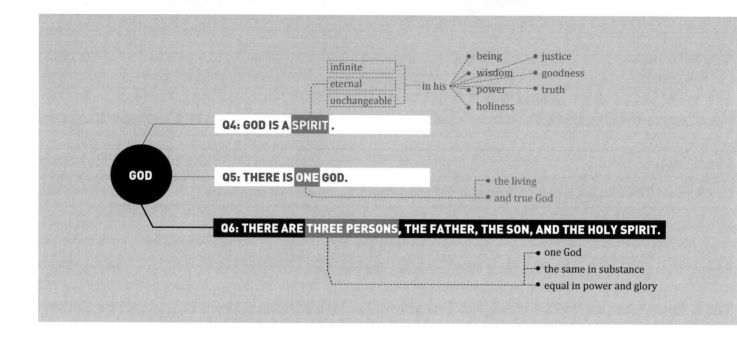

Q6 How many persons are there in the Godhead?

A6 There are three persons in the Godhead;
the Father, the Son, and the Holy Ghost;
and these three are one God,
the same in substance,
equal in power and glory.[1,2]

1.
1 John 5:7

For there are three that bear record in heaven, the Father, the Word, and the Holy Ghost: and these three are one.

2.
Matthew 28:19

Go ye therefore, and teach all nations, baptizing them in **the name of the Father, and of the Son, and of the Holy Ghost**.

Tough Question! All of sudden, this question brings up unfamiliar terms. They, especially Godhead and persons, may sound strange for many. What do they mean?

Godhead	It means God's holy nature and substance.
Persons	The word person came from persona (Latin), and it means an independent person with his own volition and reason.

Tough is not only the question but the answer as well. These three—the Father, the Son, and the Spirit—are one God. How are we supposed to understand this seemingly contradictory sentence?

EXPLANATION A

One way to explain the words in question is that God's holy substance (Godhead) is absolute and being shared, but persons (personas) are relative and not being shared. It may sound difficult. Let me try an easier way. Being a man and being a father are distinct matters. Yet a person can be a man and at the same time a father. As far as the substance goes he is a man while as far as the relation to his son goes he is a father. In the same way, being God and being the Father, the Son, or the Spirit are distinct matters. As far as Himself goes He is God while as far as the relation to each other goes He is the Father, the Son or the Spirit.

Then what do we make of the answer that these three persons are one God? Through the previous question, Q5, we have learned that God is one and only. Yet Q6 teaches that the Father, the Son, and the Spirit are distinct persons. The Father, the Son, and the Spirit are one, yet at the same time possess their own unique personalities. These three persons are equal as God. In other words, they are distinctive, yet equal. This is what God through the Old and New Testaments has taught about Himself.

This is often mistaken as if three persons were actually one but are only seen in three different forms (modes). This is not true. There are three independent persons yet one substance, and as far as the relation to each other and ministry go, they hold equal power and glory. To repeat, three persons are the Father, the Son, and the Spirit, yet there are not three Gods but one.

EXPLANATION B

This is how God reveled Himself. As we have learned in previous chapters, man should go to the Bible to understand God. In other words, the Bible is the reference book for us to go to for any description of God. And the Bible forces us to accept God in Trinity. The Bible explains God as one, yet does so as if there were three. However, it concludes there are not three Gods but one. What should we make of this?

In fact, no one can understand this perfectly. Due to the limit of our language and space-time, we cannot comprehend a greater God who transcends all of us. It is true that we cannot understand, yet we can just accept what the Bible speaks as the truth. This makes the difference. This is for sure an incomprehensible mystery, yet we can go as far as the Bible speaks and explains. The doctrine of Trinity is not an exception. The Church throughout history has come to understand the Bible in a more comprehensive way and put such an understanding in the form of doctrine.

This is the principle by which we understand God. We have to admit our limits in understanding Him and be content to understand Him only as much as we are taught. This is the only way we get to understand Him. At the diaper stage, babies can never understand the hearts of their parents. Having no interests in their parents, they only make their demands, for example food and the change of diapers with crying and fussing. This perfectly mirrors us. Given such a level of understanding, the best we can come up with concerning God through the Bible, our minds and languages are found in Trinity.

Thus, in some ways, it is perfectly normal that we do not understand the Trinity in a complete way. If it were neatly understood, then something must have gone wrong. If He were neatly understood, He must not be God any longer. Yet, it is now clear that we can and have to come to know God as far as the Bible takes us. Otherwise, we may fall into agnosticism that claims God can never be known so we had better stop paying any attention to getting to know Him.

WRONGFUL IDEAS ON TRINITY

Tritheism	Godhead is really three separate beings forming three separate gods.

Monarchianism	There is one God as one person, the Father. Modalism belongs to this category. (Modalism teaches that God is one person who has revealed himself in three forms or modes.)

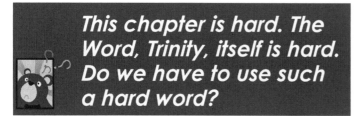

This chapter is hard. The Word, Trinity, itself is hard. Do we have to use such a hard word?

In fact the word trinity is not found in the Bible. Men coined this term, and it has limits and room for error. Yet this word is incredibly helpful for us to understand God and keeps us from arrogance by which we stubbornly try to define God as we desire. Actually the word, trinity, has appeared in the process of correcting the errors from history of early churches and is functioning even to this day as the barometer preserving the true knowledge from numerous heresies and discerning the truth from lies. To break away from this doctrine of trinity is to do so from Christianity itself (both protestant and Roman catholic). This doctrine is central to our faith.

Both the Apostles' Creed and the first question of the Heidelberg Catechism are structured according to the Trinity. (Refer to the next page.)

Q1. What is your only comfort in life and death?
A1. That I am not my own, but belong with body and soul, both in life and in death, to my faithful Saviour Jesus Christ.

The Structure of THE APOSTLES' CREED

The Structure of THE FIRST QUESTION OF HEIDELBERG CATECHISM

I believe in God the Father Almighty, Maker of heaven and earth,

THE FATHER

He has fully paid for all my sins with his precious blood, and has set me free from all the power of the devil.

THE SON

and **in Jesus Christ,** His only Son our Lord, who was conceived by the Holy Ghost, born of the Virgin Mary, suffered under Pontius Pilate, was crucified, dead, and buried; He descended into hell, the third day he rose again from the dead; He ascended into heaven, and sitteth on the right hand of God the Father Almighty; from thence He shall come quick to judge the live and the dead.

THE SON

He also preserves me in such a way that without the will of my heavenly Father not a hair can fall from my head; indeed, all things must work together for my salvation.

THE FATHER

I believe in the Holy Ghost; The Holy Catholic Church; The Communion of Saints; The forgiveness of sins; The resurrection of the body; And the life everlasting. Amen

THE HOLY GHOST

Therefore, by his Holy Spirit he also assures me of eternal life and makes me heartily willing and ready from now on to live for him

THE HOLY GHOST

OUR MINDS CANNOT CONTAIN THE PERSON AND WORK OF ETERNAL GOD

Our minds cannot contain the person and work of eternal God. Even the great theologian, Augustine, who has contributed much to the doctrine of the Trinity, said, "For man to attempt to understand God altogether is like for a little child to pour the water of the sea into a hole by the means of a ladle." Yet this simple truth that we cannot understand God should be another evidence for how great and marvelous our God is.

If God revealed Himself only in a form of the Father, the Son, or the Spirit, then we might have ended up with an imagination of our own. That is why God has revealed Himself in the form of the Trinity so that we may understand him without errors. Of course the highest God did not have to come down to us using our way of knowing, which can make us wonder.

Why? There is no other answer than His great and amazing love for us.

Thus, this doctrine of Trinity should lead us into deeper gratitude and more praise towards God, who cares for us. Yet at the same time, it should warn us against imagining God apart from the teaching of the Bible.

Discussion Questions

❶ Before how have you understood God?

❷ "The heavens, even the highest heaven, cannot contain you." (2 Kings 8:27) Explain what this verse means.

❸ Why would you say you believe this hard-to-understand doctrine of Trinity?

❹ Reminding yourself of what you have been learning, discuss the right attitude of worship.

❺ In which sense, does this chapter give us the reason to be grateful?

St. Peter's Cathedral, Geneva in Switzerland

This cathedral visible between two buildings is well known as the church where John Calvin(1509-1564), the great protestant reformer, gave his sermons. International Museum of the Reformation and The Calvin Auditorium stand adjacent to the cathedral.

"THIS WORLD IS SUCH A MESS. WHAT IS GOD DOING?"
"GOD CREATED US JUST FOR FUN AND IS NOW SITTING BACK DOING NOTHING."

In the previous chapter, we have learned about God. Yet there is more to learn about Him. What could this be?

For a person to be known, there should be more than a distant observation. What that person wants, has done in the past, and what kinds of interests he has must be factored in to understand him deeply. When we are in love, we want to know him better, and this extends even to his upbringing and works in the past. For the same reason, in order to know God better, we have to learn His decree. Teaching God's decree and execution, the Shorter Catechism makes sure that its focus remains on encountering the loving and true God on a personal level instead of getting more information about an abstract God.

Systematic understanding is especially important here. With the structure map of shorter catechism, be always mindful of where you are. The remainder of the Shorter Catechism Part 1 will be explained in this chapter, God's Decree.

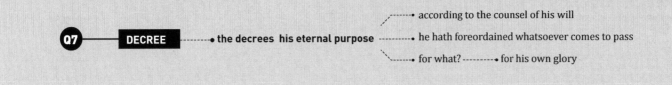

Q7 What are the decrees of God?

A7 The decrees of God are, his eternal purpose,
       according to the counsel of his will,
       whereby for his own glory,
       he hath foreordained whatsoever comes to pass. [1,2]

1.
Ephesians 1:4, 11

According as he hath **chosen us in him before the foundation of the world**, that we should be **holy and without blame before him in love**......In whom also we have obtained an inheritance, being **predestinated according to the purpose of him who worketh all things after the counsel of his own will**.

2.
Romans 9:22-23

What if God, willing to shew his wrath, and to make his power known, endured with **much longsuffering** the vessels of wrath fitted to destruction: And that he might make known the **riches of his glory** on the vessels of mercy, **which he had afore prepared unto glory**.

It says the decrees of God are His eternal purpose. Let's stop for a minute to take a careful look of the word purpose. From our conception, it is one thing to have a purpose and another to have a plan. If things go wrong with the plan, it is so with the purpose. Yet, God is able to bring His purpose as it is; thus, His decree is purpose, plan, and execution all at the same time. According to His attributes, His plan also is unchangeable, perfect, and eternal.

Also it says His decrees are according to the counsel of God's will. For those who find the word counsel strange, the Trinity which has been taught in the previous chapter would be helpful. This counsel is among three persons of God. Yet this is entirely different from the counsel among men. When we gather in counsel, it is to make up for our shortcomings, yet God does not have any shortcomings to make up for.

As previously taught, God's counsel belongs to the area which we have a hard time to understand. Regarding God's decrees, there is much we cannot even argue for or against. Yet we can understand as far as the Bible leads. Meanwhile the purpose, scope, and object of God's decree are clear enough. Its only purpose is the glory of God Himself, and its scope and object covers everything. Everything God had in His mind and executes happens and comes to pass.

FOREORDAINING WHATSOEVER COMES TO PASS

This definition of Q/A7 is indeed amazing! We know by experience we cannot have our way all the time. Thus, it is not strange that many people would not want to admit God has such a plan. Yet the Bible makes it clear enough that everything is in God. Out of God's decrees, nothing can occur or come to pass. There is nothing that occurs by itself or comes to pass just by chance. This includes everything that is good and bad in our eyes, even the advance of science and the mistakes of men. Not only my salvation, but also my failures, sin, Satan's temptation, all the evils and the absurdity of this world, poverty, disease, grief, global warming and the destruction of the environment. To trace it back to the beginning, God included in His decrees even Adam's taking and eating the fruit. (Gen 3:6)

This should generate many questions. In fact it is a hard truth to swallow that God included even the work of Satan and the sin of men in His decree. Saying so, it seems God can be blamed for sin. Only if He did not allow it, there would be no problems. Then, why did He? Questions abound.

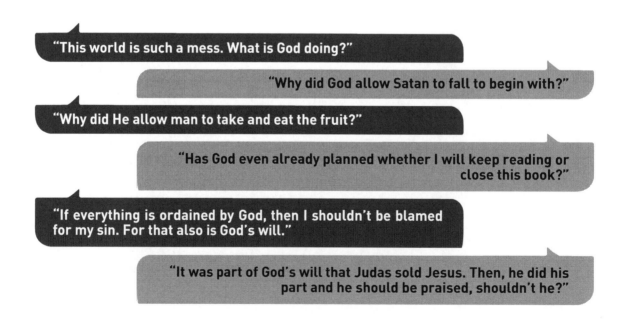

"This world is such a mess. What is God doing?"

"Why did God allow Satan to fall to begin with?"

"Why did He allow man to take and eat the fruit?"

"Has God even already planned whether I will keep reading or close this book?"

"If everything is ordained by God, then I shouldn't be blamed for my sin. For that also is God's will."

"It was part of God's will that Judas sold Jesus. Then, he did his part and he should be praised, shouldn't he?"

We need to clarify the concepts beforehand. Let's begin with the meaning of these two words, "will" and "plan." How are they different from each other?

In order to accomplish something, we make a plan. Would this plan include only what we want or what we do not want as well? For sure it should include both. For us, what we want (our will) and what we plan are different concepts.

Let's say we want to build something, yet there is something on the site which requires destruction beforehand. Destruction was not in my will (what I want), yet it must be now included in the plan. Another example can come from the Bible. It was not the master's will to pull up the weeds. What the master wanted was the wheat. Yet he planned to leave the weeds, worrying about pulling up the wheat together. This can be applied to the matter of sin and the fall as well. The fall is not what God wanted at all. Yet it was allowed not because God did not have any other options; rather, it was intended as part of God's good plan.

Along with unresolved issues, this may remain ambiguous. This part is hard to understand. This has been so throughout history, and for that reason, many heresies have appeared on this matter. Misunderstood decrees make men **only the puppets** or **God dualistic**. The best way to resolve this is in humility to admit that this transcends our understanding. Instead of being obsessed by any logical explanation, it would be much more helpful to see the actual ways of decrees being executed. For that reason, this will be dealt with in more detail in Q11, providence, and Q13, the fall. For this part to be correctly understood, a comprehensive understanding of God's providence and men's fall, which also belongs to God's providence, is required.

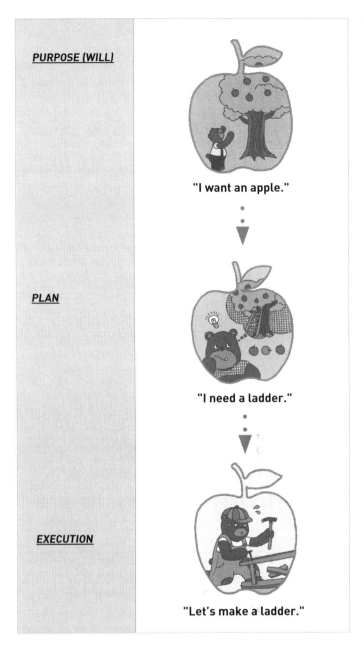

DECREES AND PREDESTINATION

These two should be used distinctively. Decrees contain predestination. (Refer to the diagram.) The particular decrees about men and angels are called predestination. God predestined to elect some angels and men and give them eternal life while passing others, and this belongs to God's decrees. For detailed information, refer to the Larger Catechism Q13. In this book, this will be dealt with in more detail in providence, Q11-12.

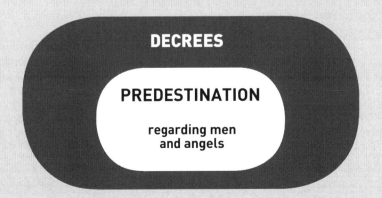

To what extent does God's decree cover?

"Is it true that God's decrees cover everything?"

"Isn't it that God foreordained only the macroscopic matters, and we are left to our will with the details?"

For such questions, what Q4-6 have previously taught regarding who God is and what we know about His attributes must be brought together. God is an absolute being. He is omnipotent and omniscient. If this were not overlooked, many misunderstandings could be prevented. If God, without knowing what would come in the future, only acts according to the circumstances, He would not be an almighty God. Rather, He would be just like any of the Greek and Roman gods.

Then, couldn't it be that He knows what would come in the future yet does not intervene? Or He made us just for fun and is now sitting back doing nothing? We also have learned such ideas were all wrong. He is not the designer of a meticulous watch who now sits back and does nothing. He is now working with us, knows when we sit and get up, is the source of our thoughts, and reproaches and rejoices with us.

Even a single breath of a sparrow continues only because God allows. Seen in such a perspective, the thoughts above cannot go along with God's attributes the Bible teaches.

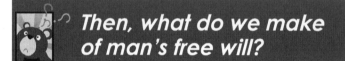

Then, what do we make of man's free will?

If God ordained everything, then what is this mental activity in which we think, worry, judge and determine?

This is the activity of reason God has given to every man in general. With the help of reason, we think, sing, read, and eat. It appears completely free on our perspective whether we pick up a spoon or not. Yet God, who governs this entire universe, uses man's every free action to execute His decrees inevitably. It may seem we act as we wish, yet working on a higher level, God without limiting our free actions is able to accomplish His will. Some may ask, "How can freedom and inevitability work together?" Yet the antonym of freedom is force not inevitability. The antonym of inevitability is chance not freedom. God never forces us.

However, there is something that is much more important than such a logic and this should be included in the discussion at hand. "What does God wants from His people?" When we make up our minds for example about what to eat, which career to choose, and who to marry, God's attention is on by which standards we do so. And He wants us to move towards the direction and have thoughts He delights in. God's such will must be included in the discussion of man's free will.

Due to our fallen nature, we are incapable of doing what we know as good. Even the saved believers, apart from God's grace, would not be able to make the right decisions and live a life worthy of God's will. For that reason, the Bible encourages us to daily seek after God's grace, repent of our sins, and depend on God.

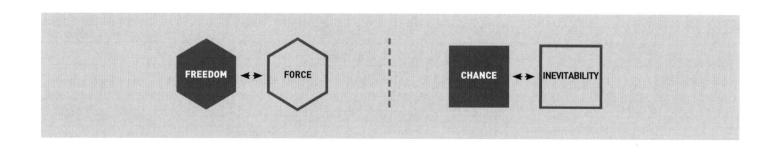

WHY DOES GOD WORK IN SUCH A WAY?

Because **He loves us.** God does not see us as and treat us like mere robots, but rather as respectable persons. Here is a question that can make this point. If God loved David (and He did), then why didn't He stop him from committing adultery with Bathsheba? He could have used His almighty power, for instance by working on his brain waves, to keep him from making such a mistake and preventing its treacherous consequences. Then all would have been OK. But that is not the way God loves believers. He calls His elects "His Bride," "His Children" and "His people." The relationship between God and His people is neither desolate nor mechanical. The means through which He shows His love are extensive and various. He sometimes steps right in and keeps us from sinning. Other times He waits while watching over the choices we make and letting nature run its course. One thing for sure is that He never condones our sins. He always brings charges against sins and rebukes them, and He sees that justice is done. On the other hand, when we keep on the good and righteous path, He takes great delight in us. He desires for our obedience and intimate fellowship with Him to continue. That is how God communicates His love with His Bride, His people, and His children. He wants us to abide in Him and grow holy.

This will be dealt with in more depth in the Fall of Man, Q13. For what caused man's free will to crumble was the Fall, giving all men a fallen nature. Without understanding such a context, things can be puzzling. Thus, it is suggested as you study Q7-19 not to go through them apart from each other but give your attention to the whole story which tells us a unified message.

Now it is time to move on to the execution of God's decrees.

Q8 How doth God execute his decrees?

A8 God executeth his decrees
in the works of creation and providence.

THE EXECUTION OF DECREES

A decree can be divided into the decree itself and the execution of it. And then the execution is divided once again into creation and providence. Q8 presents such a structure and outline.

Just like to the decree, all principles previously taught will be applied to its execution. In other words, in the process and ways of creation and providence, God also executes his decrees in the amount and ways that transcend the breadth of man's understanding. In mysterious ways, God, according to free and unchangeable counsel of His will, grants His blessings. Both creation and providence come from God.

God created all things and did not step back but preserves and governs them. The Shorter Catechism continues with more detailed information in the following. Q9-10 will cover creation; Q11-12 will cover providence.

Discussion Questions

❶ How is God's plan different from man's?

❷ If God ordained everything, what should we make of our autonomy and independence?

❸ When the doubt "Why is God working in such a way?" comes, what should we do?

❹ Explain the relation between what has been previously taught in Q4 and God's decree in Q7.

❺ In which sense does this chapter give us the reason to be grateful?

[Visualize by Mapping]

Make your own review by drawing a mindmap for the Q and As you have learned so far.

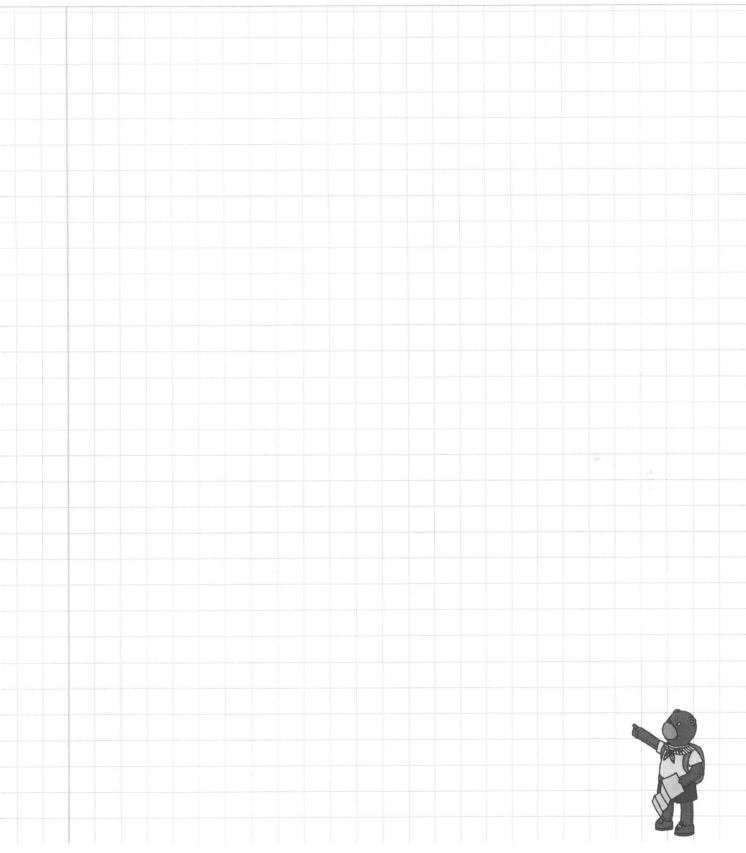

THE EXECUTION OF HIS DECREE: CREATION

"IN TERMS OF SCIENCE, CREATION IS NONSENSE.
DO WE STILL HAVE TO BELIEVE IT AS TRUTH?"
"ISN'T IT BECAUSE OF THE CHRISTIAN TEACHING TO RULE OVER CREATION
THAT OUR ECOSYSTEM IS BEING RUINED?"
"WHAT EXISTED IN THIS WORLD BEFORE GOD'S CREATION?"

The first of two executions we have studied in the previous section is about creation. The Bible seems to open up its whole discussion with the following proclamation. "Lift your eyes and look to the heavens: Who created all these?" Since the creation of the world, God's invisible qualities—his eternal power and divine nature—have been clearly seen. (Rom 1:20) Q9-10 of the Shorter Catechism focus on the question of creation especially that of us men.

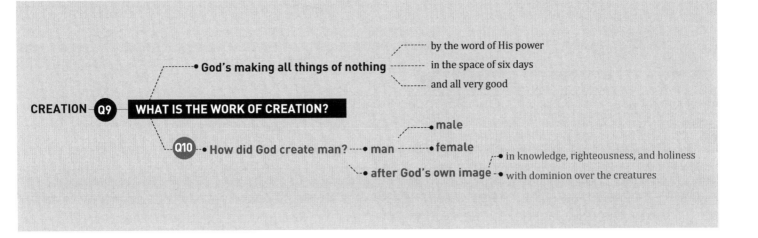

Q9 What is the work of creation?

A9 The work of creation is,
    God's making all things of nothing,
        by the word of His power,
        in the space of six days,
        and all very good.[1,2]

1.
Genesis 1:1-31
Throughout.

2.
Hebrews 11:3

Through faith we understand that **the worlds were framed by the word of God, so that things which are seen were not made of things which do appear**.

Q9 | WHAT IS THE WORK OF CREATION? ------- • God's making all things of nothing -------- • By the word of his power
• in the space of six days
• and all very good

We will be studying creation with Q9 of the Shorter Catechism.

Here is an important reminder regarding where this specific question about creation is situated in the entire Catechism. As mentioned above, creation belongs to the executions of God's decree.

THE EXECUTIONS OF GOD'S DECREE: CREATION AND PROVIDENCE

"[God] created all things, and by [His] will they were created." (Rev 4:11) We have to remember that creation is the work of God, and it belongs to God's decree. It may sound too basic to mention, but is important. For this reason, **creation is thoroughly planned and executed accordingly**. This world did not come into its existence just by accident without any intention. Rather, it has an end and direction.

The answer to Q9 reveals the level of God's work of creation. It is not about how well He made something, but simply states that **He created all things in this world from nothing**. This is the key definition of creation.

Besides, for creation's means, He neither received any help from other experts nor invested His time and ingredients. Instead, He used only the Word. And this is followed by the number of days of creation and its result being **all very good**.

What such descriptions teach us is the worth and the standing of this whole world before Him.

THE END OF CREATION: WHY DID GOD CREATE THE WORLD?

Compare two different positions on the end of creation.

1. THE MOST GENERAL VIEW OF PEOPLE

"It is because God needed something."
We invent or make something because there is a need. We make things to put them to use. This is the way most people see God's creation. Being alone, he was bored, lonely, and feeling empty, and that was why he wanted to fill the hollow space with this world. Just like we play with toys, it is often imagined that God created the world to play with it.

2. HOWEVER, THE BIBLE OFFERS A DIFFERENT VIEW.

As mentioned before, creation belongs to God's decree, and it is important for us grasp this idea for sure. Here is the reason. Creation is also part of God's decree and has its end. And the end of creation is the same as of God's decree. They are all for God's glory. Creation as well has its end in God's glory, and its way, procedure, process, and even the result are planned just according to the counsel of the will of the triune God. Providence, which will be dealt with in Q11-12, is not an exception. Providence is God's preserving and governing of creation so that all things work out just according to the original end of creation. The end of providence is also God's glory.

THE RESULT OF CREATION

What was this world like right after being created for the glory of God and according to the counsel of His will? It should have been very good given the fact that almighty God created it in six days with great care. We could only imagine how all very good it was, like the Shorter Catechism describes. The result was satisfactory. What does "good" mean, by the way? Looking around, such an expression does not touch our hearts right away. Is this world good? Can we say that everything is all very good? Not at all.

However, the world right after its creation was good, com-pletely different from what we now see and experience.

It is impossible for us to know how good it was in a complete sense, but we can imagine through the description of the Garden of Eden in the Bible.

The God-created world was all very good. Keep this in mind. The Shorter Catechism will reveal as you move along how important this simple truth is. How this all very good world has been changing, what has contributed to this change, and what follows such change, the Shorter Catechism will explain point by point.

Is evolution the antonym of creation?

Many tend to compare Darwin's theory of evolution with creation believing that these two are opposing views. This is not necessarily so. Evolution does not offer any explanation regarding the origin but only the process of how already existing things have been evolving. Evolutionists believe everything came to its existence just by accident. This is understandable given the fact that evolution has set its course not in quest of the origin of this world but situates its root in biology. (Charles Darwin's Origin of Species). While it is true that the premise of evolution sees the whole universe as a continuous process, it is not true that evolution theory has set its course to deny the validity of creation. The true antonym of creation is to be found in the realm of philosophy.

If necessary to name the theory that opposes creation, it would be possibility. For example, according to the Big Bang theory, which is often referred to by astronomers and physicists, there was a huge random explosion in the beginning and from this explosion the whole universe came to exist. Based on certain evidence, this theory itself is now being accepted as a scientific truth without any doubt. However, offering no conclusive explanation regarding its ultimate origin but only speculations, it also fails to explain what caused this big bang. For there is no one who has seen the beginning and no experiment that can be done to prove its validity. There is only a hypothesis which requires our faith. There is no answer for now, and this will be so in the future. <u>Any attempt to explain the beginning of all things apart from God is of no use.</u>

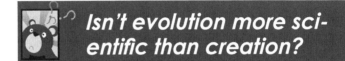

Isn't evolution more scientific than creation?

Science is systematic knowledge based on facts learned through verifiable experiments. In this sense, evolution is not scientific. An experiment itself is impossible. What is unknown is unknown.

We are not to use the power of our faith to turn a deaf ear to already proven scientific facts. It is easy to place creation against science. We tend to denounce science as if it were Satan himself opposing God. We also tend to claim what is written in the Bible as scientific truth without any condition. While the Bible recorded only the truth, it is not a science book. Creation in its nature is a mystery.

Science and faith must converse with each other. It is true that science is arrogant. Moreover, faith and science have their own premises and different conversational methods, and these create a huge gap between their viewpoints. However, <u>what science pursues is also truth.</u> The conversation between these two must be done with much discretion. Instead of denying each other's premises, they are supposed to come up with a conversational point.

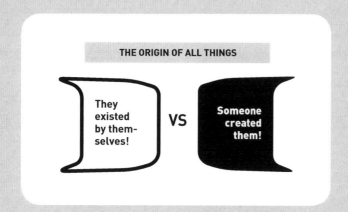

THE ORIGIN OF ALL THINGS

They existed by themselves! VS Someone created them!

The attempt to find the answer to the origin of all things has been an age-long struggle for humankind. The word itself, religion, reveals that it also attempts to find the root. Regarding the origin of all things, there have been two opposing viewpoints. One is "All things existed by themselves," and the other is "Someone created them." Of course there are mixed views such as "Someone took already existing things and created something else with them" or "Someone made a thing and it evolved by itself," yet, whether the matter was there by itself or someone created it is incompatible by its definition.

1. FIRST VIEW "ALL THINGS EXISTED BY THEMSELVES."

Materialism and idealism represent this particular view. These two have been long standing at the opposite sides of two opposing parties.

For **materialist**s, matter was first, is eternal, and has had the potential from the beginning as one entity. Everything comes from matter, and matter grows by itself and it only has meaning. Those who believe only what is seen belong to this category of materialism.

Idealism believes a power or force unseen to our eyes was the beginning of this world and all matter came from that force. Religious people whose interests are more aligned with the unseen spiritual world than matter belong this this category of pantheism.

These two positions have been coexisting in human history while its form and terminology continued to change—mind and matter, spirit and flesh, what is seen and what is unseen, psychological and physical, etc. Since human beings tend to place their interests beyond the matter of survival, throughout history pantheism rather than materialism appeared to gather more support for a longer period of time. However, with the dawn of the Renaissance after the Middle Ages, people seemed to prefer the position of materialism. Yet, the advance of modern science proved that these two positions after all are the same. The law of conservation of energy and the Einstein formula, $E=mc^2$, proved that matter and energy are the same, eventually making these previously conflicting positions, materialism and pantheism, less distinct. For example, after the Middle Ages, Western culture has preferred rationalism, in which people can choose to believe only what is seen, yet these days people show greater interest in Eastern philosophy like the energy of the universe and confuse themselves.

Here, we find, whether it is materialism or pantheism, these positions have had one voice all along despite their differing appearances. The core premises of these are: The origin and reality of all things is either matter or energy, they existed by themselves, and there is no other way than to believe this.

Listening to these core premises, we cannot help but ask, "Where did the first matter or energy come from?"

Can they answer this question? Their answer will be "We don't know." It is granted that we cannot either know or prove this.

The only thing we can offer is faith. "We do not know the beginning. Yet we will get to know it someday."

2. SECOND VIEW "GOD CREATED ALL THINGS."

From nothing to all things! The Bible teaches that someone made all things. It claims that all things in this world are God's creation. This world did not come to its existence and does not exist by itself, but only by God who called it from nothingness to all things. Creation of all things from nothing transcends the law of conservation of energy. Whether matter or energy, it did not exist before the beginning, and it came to exist only because someone created it. This creator must be from beyond this material world, transcending all things He created, and there is no one capable of this creation but the absolute and almighty God. What would be more fitting names than the absolute, the almighty, the sovereign, and the creator for this God who created all things?

All things exist—This is indisputable truth, and no one can deny it. However, as discussed above, there are two different views regarding the beginning of already existing things, and they both require our faith. Then, we have to ponder which view we would like to take as ours. This choice will determine the attitude of our life and the standard of good and evil. A philosophical approach is needed.

Atheism, which believes all things existed by themselves and there was no creator, will bring **an atheistic outlook on life and one's values**. For atheists, there is no absolute truth or values, but all things in this material world exist for themselves without any meaning. Man also came to his being by accident in the process of evolution, which does not give man any purpose or reason to pursue a life of any worth. All are futile beings! This deteriorates the ground of the sanctity of life and the absolute ground of morality and ethics. Also, it is inevitable that this will lead to relativism and nihilism. Everything is relative and came to its being by accident; thus, there is no way to prevent the idea that we are to live for food and pleasure and go back to dust when the time comes.

Meanwhile, the Bible bases its position of creation as attributing the meaning of all things' existence to the counsel of God's will, which created the world. God's decree brought creation, and the existence of all things and man is its by-product. Thus, **there is a purpose for all things, and the absolute standard and measure is none other than God's will.**

Especially man's value (which will be discussed in the following section of Q10 in more detail) carries more meaning in that God created man with dominion over other creatures, and also the morality and ethics of human society are not just for the convenience of man but from God's commandments given to us so that we may live according to his eternal will, which gives man evident value and direction. For that reason, we are to live according to His commandment with humility and joy by doing good and keeping ourselves from evil.

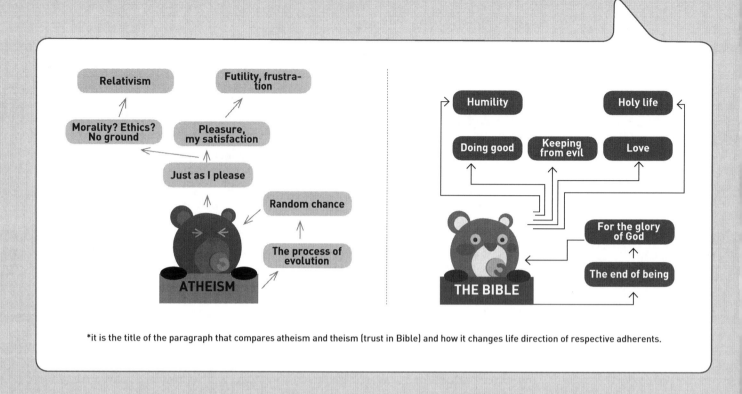

*it is the title of the paragraph that compares atheism and theism (trust in Bible) and how it changes life direction of respective adherents.

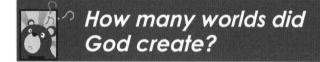

How many worlds did God create?

As far as the Bible says, God created only one world. Reincarnation in Buddhism teaches about a previous, present, and after life, and according to its teaching, this world repeats itself endlessly. "Good triumphs over evil" or the concept of karma could be an example. However, the Bible does not speak in terms of a previous and after world but of a time to create and bring to an end. According to the Bible, there is the beginning and the end. The end here does not connote a futile end where everything is destroyed leaving nothing behind, but the eternal rest prepared for God's people. The world we are living in has the destination of eternal rest with the beginning and the end having an obvious purpose.

Yet, regarding this world, there have been **many hypothetical ideas** suggested throughout human history, and they ended up being written down in numerous stories. Various myths about the origin of this world may appear interesting at first, but in fact they are absurd. Some go even further describing worlds of different dimensions than ours. People seem to love the idea of Middle Earth presented in the novel and movie The Lord of the Rings. As in the movie, Ghost Town, the story about ghosts who live around us without being seen could appear interesting. Harry Potter presents a fourth dimensional space called platform 9 ¾ where the students of Hogwarts School of witchcraft take the steam engine to Hogwarts. These are attractive and interesting subject matters for a movie or novel. Yet what if these are real?

Such beliefs will lead to pessimism in the end. Any attempt to find a solution of today's pain, irrationality, and insufficiency through the interest in other worlds is destined to face the question, "Then, what?" and the eventual conclusion is only despair and frustration. Isn't it strange that the movies The Thirteenth Floor, Inception, Contact, Avatar, The Matrix, and The Butterfly Effect depict gloomy and hopeless futures?

WHAT SHOULD WE DO WITH CREATION?

The Bible emphasizes, through this creation of all things, God's creation, we should be able to know God. (Refer to Rom 1 and Ps 19.) Nature is supposed to reveal God's power and wisdom, and our being is supposed to teach God's image and attributes.

Even what is unseen, such as personal relations, affections, love, and the wisdom we gain through various life experiences is supposed to help us get to know God. Creation is none other than the fundamental means for us to get to know God.

To grow in the knowledge of God through his creation! This is the original end of any study. By discovering and analyzing the principle of how this world works, the existence, attributes, and laws of all things of this world, we are supposed to discover none other than God himself. It is not enough that we exclaim, "Wow, what a beautiful, magnificent, and mysterious world!" It is not our end that by getting to know and study creation that we gather more knowledge, money, and fame for our own happiness.

It is beyond our imagination how much astronomers love the universe. Their passion is simply amazing. So is their work. They also spend enormous amounts of money for a device like a particle accelerator. However, it will be just a waste if they have set an inappropriate end of what they hope to discover through it all without knowing the original end of their study.

Deeper insight into the meaning of creation will be presented in the section for Q12.

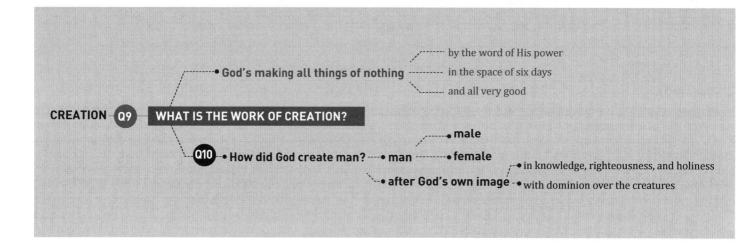

CREATION — Q9 — **WHAT IS THE WORK OF CREATION?**

- **God's making all things of nothing**
  - by the word of His power
  - in the space of six days
  - and all very good

- **Q10** — **How did God create man?** — **man**
  - **male**
  - **female**
  - **after God's own image**
    - in knowledge, righteousness, and holiness
    - with dominion over the creatures

Q10   How did God create man?

A10   God created man male and female,

after his own image,

in knowledge, righteousness, and holiness,

with dominion over the creatures.[1,2,3]

1.
Genesis 1:26-28

And God said, Let us **make man in our image, after our likeness**: and **let them have dominion over the fish of the sea**, and **over the fowl of the air, and over the cattle, and over all the earth, and over every creeping thing that creepeth upon the earth**. So God created man in his **own image**, in the **image of God created he him**; male and female created he them. And God blessed them, and God said unto them, **Be fruitful, and multiply, and replenish the earth, and subdue it: and have dominion over the fish of the sea**, and over the **fowl of the air**, and over **every living thing that moveth upon the earth**.

2.
Colossians 3:10

And have put on the new man, which is renewed in knowledge after the **image of him that created him**.

3.
Ephesians 4:24

And that ye put on the new man, which after God is **created in righteousness and true holiness**.

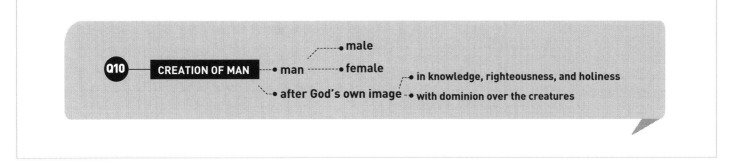

CREATION OF MAN: IN THE IMAGE OF GOD

While explaining the matter of creation, the Bible emphasizes the creation of man with much weight. The book of Genesis sets apart man's creation by putting more weight on it than other things on which it spends only one or two sentences. The story of man's creation can be found in Gen 2.

Man is created quite differently from other creatures, and this applies even to the procedure of man's creation. The Bible teaches that the creation of man was the climax of all creation and this world is created with a special focus on man. The creation of man was the heart of God's work of creation.

Man is the only creature that is created in God's image. No matter whether it came from a higher organism or resembles man, if it does not have the image of God then it differs from man. Why did God create only man in His own image? It is to place us over other creatures so that we may rule over them. Being creatures ourselves, we are yet given the status of ruler over other creatures. God is God to us, and in the same way we are kings to other creatures. We have to be aware of such a status of ruler over all creatures.

1. THE ATTRIBUTES OF GOD'S IMAGE:
holiness, righteousness, and knowledge

Q10 of the Shorter Catechism teaches that God created us in His own image. And this image of God is holiness, righteousness and knowledge. Q4 has taught us that God, being spirit, does not have a visible image. When we are created in His image, it does not mean that we have His visible appearance. Rather, we are created in His holy, righteous, and intelligent image. This is also what we, as the rulers of this universe, must possess.

Then, it is only fitting that if we examine ourselves, we find God's image in us—holy, righteous and with abundant knowledge. However, this is not the case. Why is that? Is it because our God-given image was imperfect as it was? Or since a long time has passed, did it just ruin itself?

It is because God gave us His own image perfectly as it is, but we lost it by sinning.

We are created in God's image.
"The image originally given to us"
"Now damaged and lost image of God"
We have to know the difference between these two. If not, we will be very perplexed. What is wrong with this world God created? Why did He make me like this? These questions by themselves are in error. God did not create anything as it is now. It was all very good.

This is one of the important reasons nonbelievers hate churchgoers. Hearing that we are created in God's image, nonbelievers jump to the holy and righteous image that we lost by sinning. That is why they speak ill of us believing we are two-faced people. Our words sound holy and righteous, yet our actions speak otherwise. This is reality. We do not have God's perfect image. That is why the Bible commands us to restore

God's image. We lost it, yet this is not supposed to be the end of the story. **We are in the process of being restored to God's image**.

Not knowing such a difference, nonbelievers only see the present state of ours and grumble, "Do not overrate yourself. You are not righteous and holy." In many cases, this is how we see ourselves as well. Surprisingly, this is a commonly misunderstood teaching.

We are saints, holy ones. But this does not refer to perfect holiness. Holiness is what God wants from us in His eternal will, and this is given to all including both churchgoers and others as our duty. It also is a blessing of life for us. The reason we speak for morality and justice is not because we have already attained them but because we believe this is a blessing for us.

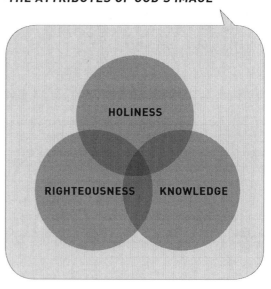

THE ATTRIBUTES OF GOD'S IMAGE

2. DOMINION

This picture roughly depicts the relation between God, creatures, and man. For convenience, this picture has only earth in it, yet the earth represents the whole universe including all creatures. Man is standing tall on this earth with God above him. Man is created to dominate and rule over the whole universe God created. He is the steward of God in charge of the whole universe.

A steward has to be familiar with his authority and duty. Things are not entrusted to him just for his pleasure. Neither should those things be neglected. It is not a good sign for a steward to incline towards either habit.

The authority to manage and rule over all creatures is given, and we are to take this calling in a serious manner. This is our responsibility. Yet, examining ourselves, we find that this is not the case. How are we exercising this authority? It seems like right after creation man exercised this authority well. The evidence is found in Adam naming all animals in the Garden of Eden. In order to name something, perfect knowledge about the object would have been necessary.

Compared to Adam, the first man, and his ability, we are now almost completely unable to perceive and understand the essence of any phenomena. Our eyes are almost blind to figure out the cause out of anything. For this reason, the more science advances and gets a handle on subjects like biotechnology and gene manipulation, the more wisdom and humility it should seek. Science must not be abused. It can be beneficial, yet without man's original ability, we mishandle science oftentimes.

For example, we attempt to cross breed different animals or plants, to create a new kind of species, or to manipulate genes in order to create a new kind of animal or plant.

Without the proper concept of bacteria in the past, doctors did not understand the use of properly cleaned medical equipment on their patients, and this resulted in spreading the same disease to many patients. This practice was repeated for hundreds of years. At first, it must have been an amazing discovery that by cutting out the affected area, patients can be made well again. However, without further knowledge, early doctors had to repeat their foolish mistake. Without the image of God, this is where man is destined to fall.

We have to admit our imperfect knowledge. A man would not make a good ruler if he insists on reckless behavior only based on momentary successes. This is not limited to fact-based sciences. Even in personal relationships, we hurt other people without even noticing.

Looking at the current condition of man without the original perfect image of God, we can only imagine how great our condition was before the fall. What we are to remember is that God created us in such a noble condition at first. We have to realize **how worthy we are and aim to restore this original condition**. We have to be aware of that the current condition is neither normal nor right.

However, this world does not say so. The current condition of man is just a point in the process of our billion-year-long evolution. Man is only different in the sense that he is at the front line of evolution. There is no God's image as from the Bible. Knowledge, holiness, and righteousness are not given by God but seen as social consequences. These are either coincidence or by-products of evolution, which the joined forces of men's hardwired survival instincts came to cause. Primitive men had no reason to form a social structure if there were not a need to protect themselves from wild animals, and that caused the beginning of today's complex and multi-faceted society according to this theory. The master-servant relationship is another example.

However, man of the Bible lives as a man from the very beginning. Man is entirely different from other creatures. He cultivates, forms a society, and marries, living entirely differently than beasts. Ants and bees can organize themselves, even forming groups and society, yet it is only due to the instinct given by God and completely different from the way of man.

3. MALE AND FEMALE: THERE IS A PURPOSE

Q10 specifically mentions that God created man male and female. It seems needless to mention, for it appears such an obvious truth. Here is the reason. Man is created male and female—This simple truth carries so much weight that it has to be mentioned in the catechism. This also emphasizes the institution of marriage through which male and female come together and form a family.

Man and woman, who were once complete strangers to each other, come together, fall in love, become one, make a family, and begin to walk toward a united goal—a miracle would be the only fitting description of this process. However, what is more important lies in the following questions: "What should this family do in the future?" "How does God see this family?" How significant these questions are! There are higher purposes than living happily ever after, eating well, living better, and having and raising a child together. Each family is given the purpose of man's creation which is the calling to manage all life and creatures.

This question is about the purpose of marriage. We tend to give the first one as our answer, yet it seems lacking in something. The second answer seems to be better to me, but what do you think?

Forming a family to be helpers to each other, man and woman should give their thoughts to life as stewards before God. Some young people tend to see marriage as the end of their work. They think they have completed their mission fulfilling their responsibility. However, marriage, followed by birth, childhood, and getting married, has its own challenge to advance in this world as a family. Man and woman, as helpers to each other, should encourage each other to mature for the purpose none other than making a family for the work of God. This is not only the purpose but sine qua non for a happy family. Without this purpose, it is certain that no family can experience a happy family life. At first it could be good, but before long everything will turn meaningless.

For this reason, life after one's wedding is more important. Which principle and purpose should our family follow?— There must be a sure founded answer to this question. The questions of which principle we would like to take to raise our child, which mind and attitude to serve church, which standard for economic activity, or whether to live in apartment or house, we should not decide just as we see fit. Since we are stewards, the servants of God, we should follow the commands of our master, and this is why husband and wife should discuss together what should be the focus of their family as suitable for the life of stewards.

In this sense, man's role as the head of a family becomes more significant. The primary role a man should carry in the family is to bring such discussions to the table, give guidance, explain, give hope to, and encourage the family members. A woman plays a significant role as well. When given a direction, she should not insist on the way of this world or even on going in the opposite direction.

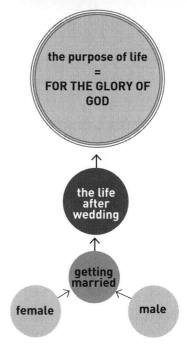

THEN, WHAT SHOULD WE DO?

Most people seem to be preoccupied with how they can feed themselves and their family. However, how big to us is what God has given us through creation? It is the entire universe. Just as big as this universe, we have to increase our mindset in size. To the size of this entire universe!

This is neither a euphemistic expression nor a meaningless slogan. How should we respond to the issue of natural resource and waste? What should we do with waste filling up the earth? We should dedicate our thoughts to come up with an environmentally friendly way to handle the waste issue with the ultimate goal to decrease its volume. I once heard "There is nothing to worry about. We can just send our waste into space." My response was, "Then, who will clean up space later?"

These may sound like comical notions, yet we need to seriously broaden our outlook to God's entire creation. Just imagine all of the world population of 6.5 billion people maintaining the original condition of wisdom Adam had before the fall. How well we would be ruling over this universe! God gave us both the ability and mindset at the beginning. Even though they are now damaged and thus have some limits, we have to try our best.

CHRISTIAN PERSPECTIVE IN ALL STUDIES

Given such a principle of creation, we have to include all areas of studies into our consideration. What are the things today's teenagers consider as a factor to decide which major to take? The first and foremost factor is whether it would offer them a better chance to get a job. What is better than this would be whether it is fitting to their interests, or in other words, whether they would be able to enjoy it in the long run. In this case, the end is self-actualization. If even more mature, they would consider how they could contribute to their neighbor. However, even this is a very simple consideration giving much room to grow to "how well I can rule over this world and entire universe" and "what I must do for this."

This can happen in various areas. We find irrationality everywhere, for example, in the economy, politics, culture, environment, and welfare system. Even government officials whose job is to legislate or administrate should give their thoughts over to what they should do for the will of God in the area God has called them to be his stewards. This means they have to search for the way to reveal God's sovereignty in a better way. For the purpose of raising such people of God, church education is given. This should be the aim of church education. It is not right for the Church to merely tell Bible stories to its students or aim to make them feel at home.

A Christian perspective in all studies may sound unfamiliar and unnecessary, making many people doubt whether these ideas belong to the world, but rather to the Church. However, this is not true. The Church and the world do not stand apart from each other, and God is not just the God of churchgoers. He, the Lord of all heaven and earth, created all men and applies the same law to all.

A global mindset may come in useful, and the following cases could be encouraging. Some, even in adverse conditions, try their best to prevent global warming, and others try to mitigate racism and conflicts worldwide. These works are no doubt strenuous and challenging. Yet being driven by their calling, such people continuously strive day and night. We may not undertake such a work simply due to our lack of ability, yet there is a way to participate. We can support correct policies and vote for the candidates who pledge such policies.

What brings such a perspective, then? It is from a Christian worldview. And the first step would be the Shorter Catechism. This mindset must be encouraged for both elementary and youth ministry students. The purpose of their study is not to make a lot of money in the future, but to live an accountable life as the rulers in this world and to grow up to be reputable men and women. Adults are not supposed to present getting good grades and the admission to a prestigious college as the highest aim for our future generation. That is the perfect recipe for rebellion.

Our children will not be satisfied with such things. What if we present to them the entire universe, encouraging them to have it all? I am afraid that we might have been crushing their dreams with our past lower aims, replacing higher aims with only worthless ones. What they need is reputable mentors who will challenge them to live and grow like them.

This teaching will be offered in Part 2 of the Shorter Catechism in more detail.

CONCLUDING THE CHAPTER

I hope you have been following well. We have learned God's decree and now its execution, which is creation and providence. And man is standing in the midst of this creation and providence. The following is how the Larger Catechism describes this part, which amazed me.

"Q17. How did God create man?
A17. After God had made all other creatures, he created man male and female; formed the body of the man of the dust of the ground, and the woman of the rib of the man, imbued them with living, reasonable, and immortal souls; made them after His own image, in knowledge, righteousness, and holiness; having the law of God written in their hearts, and power to fulfill it, and dominion over the creatures; **yet subject to fall.***"*

I could not help but dwell on the vey last part, "yet subject to fall." I will never be able to comprehend God's decree in a complete sense, yet this mysterious revelation of creation and providence offers us only a glimpse of his love. Giving us freewill, God waits for us with His long patience, and this love is indeed enough to overwhelm my little heart at once.

Being easily swayed by whims, we often say, "That was not love" or "What you and I had was not love." But God's love never lets go of our hands. No, it is not just our hands but our entire beings. He decreed to love us from the beginning, created us as the object of His love so that we may exist, called us into a personal relationship, yet in His power He never forces our submission from us, His creatures; rather, in his providence He actively changes us to love Him.

After realizing this, my love for God was at last able to move on to a higher place. This is God's creation and providence for this world and me. In His grand will, therein exist this entire world and me. Of course, so do you. We all are dwelling in the fullness and mystery of this love.

Discussion Questions

❶ What can we learn from the way God created all things?

❷ What does it mean that we are created in the image of God?

❸ How should we respond to the theories of modern science regarding creation?

❹ In what sense does this chapter give us the reason to be grateful?

"IF GOD DOES EXIST, WHY IS THIS WORLD FULL OF WARS AND DARKNESS ALL THE TIME?"
"EVERYTHING IS NOT GOING WELL WITH ME. EVEN MY HEALTH IS POOR.
GOD MUST BE PUNISHING ME FOR SOMETHING.
IF ONLY I COULD KNOW WHY. I AM HEAVY HEARTED WITH WORRIES."
"AFTER ALL, DOESN'T EVERYTHING HAPPEN JUST BY CHANCE?"

In two ways God executes his decree, creation and providence. We have discussed the former, and now it is time to look at the latter.

What if the creator, bringing all things from nothing, leaves what He created as they are? Will they remain the same? As time goes by, will they get out of order? Or will they advance to perfection? In contrast, if God does not leave them as they are, what kind of work would He be doing to his creatures? This chapter, while exploring the matter of providence, will answer such questions.

It is necessary that we remain in the context of the entire Shorter Catechism. Just like creation, providence also belongs to God's decree; thus, providence is also according to the counsel of God's will. Providence is not done randomly or carelessly and not a simultaneous response to the circumstances; instead, it is done just according to God's absolute and perfect will, which has been firm from beginning to finish. This must remain a mystery for us men who are limited in time and space.

What is more important is the purpose of study. We will get to know more of God through this study of creation and providence. And it is only to love Him more and give thanks for all He has done for us. Even with a clear understanding as far as our brains go, if not accompanied with thanksgiving and praise, such study is in vain. This study is supposed to help us exclaim in gratitude.

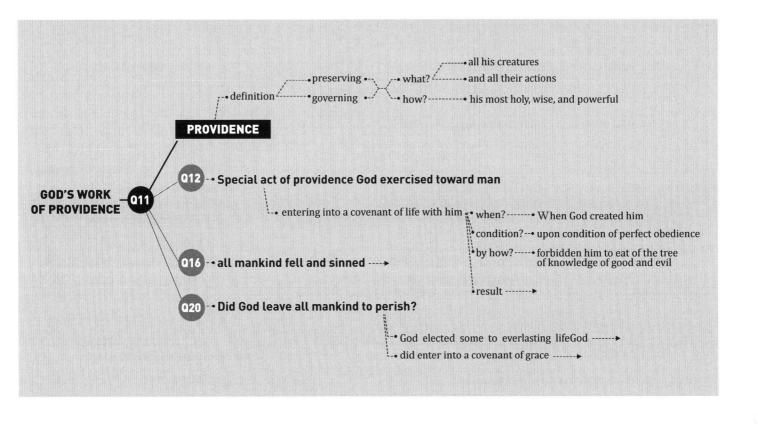

Q11 What are God's works of providence?

A11 God's works of providence are
      his most holy,[1] wise,[2,3] and powerful
    preserving[4] and governing
      all his creatures, and all their actions.[5,6]

1.
Psalm 145:17

The Lord is righteous in all his ways, and **holy in all his works**.

2.
Psalm 104:24

O Lord, how manifold are thy works! **in wisdom hast thou made them all**: the earth is full of thy riches.

3.
Isaiah 28:29

This also cometh forth from the Lord of hosts, **which is wonderful in counsel, and excellent in working**.

4.
Hebrews1:3

Who being the brightness of his glory, and the express image of his person, and **upholding all things by the word of his power**, when he had by himself purged our sins, sat down on the right hand of the Majesty on high.

5.
Psalm 103:19

The Lord hath prepared his throne in the heavens; and **his kingdom ruleth over all**.

6.
Matthew 10:29-31

Are not two sparrows sold for a farthing? and one of them **shall not fall on the ground without your Father**. But

the **very hairs of your head are all numbered**. Fear ye not therefore, ye are of **more value than many sparrows**.

Q11 TEACHES THE DEFINITION, OBJECT, AND WAY OF PROVIDENCE.

THE DEFINITION OF PROVIDENCE

There are two: to (a) preserve and (b) govern.
Remembering that God of providence is first and foremost God of creation may help us to understand what to preserve means. The one who created preserves, and only then any being can continue to exist. Other religions also teach that the creator preserves. Yet it is different from Christian teaching in the sense that our creator not only preserves but governs over all. Here to govern is not to assign an abstract principle and by that principle have all things run by themselves. Rather, this creator intervenes in person, getting in and working.

THE OBJECT OF PROVIDENCE

The objects are all His creatures and all their actions. Many tend to think God rules over only those who believe in Him as if God were limited to people of a certain religion. Yet this is absolutely not true. God created all creatures, and this includes both believers and nonbelievers.

THE WAY OF PROVIDENCE

The key teaching of preservation is that this is not a programming. God determines all our actions included among all His creatures, yet He governs in the way of preservation not known to us.

If God preserves and governs, then by which standard does He do so? In order to understand creation, it is necessary to consider its underlying purpose; This is exactly the same with providence. Indeed by which standard does God provide His care? Where does He place value? These are crucial questions, for it is an easily accepted belief that there is a principle by which this world runs. For nonbelievers, it is not God who provides His care, but there is a principle by which this world operates and by this principle all things move and run their course.

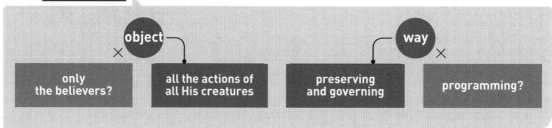

"Everyone has good times and bad times. After all, doesn't everything happen just by chance?"

There are sayings such as, "What goes around comes around," "Good triumphs over evil," and "Justice will prevail". The concept of good and evil has taken the place of the standard of all things, and the above sayings are quoted to express that the results of things that one has done, either good or evil, will someday have an effect on the person who started the events. These even seem to sound similar to "in all things God works for the good" from the Bible. Is it so? What does "the good" mean here?

GOOD: VIRTUOUS AND RIGHT?

The debate over what is good and what is right is not a matter of black and white, so still to this day, people carry their own standards. For example, according to utilitarianism, the truth aligns with "the greatest happiness of the greatest number," yet there exist many other positions different than this.
For deeper understanding: Chapter 1 of Magnalia Dei by Herman Barvinck

We have learned God himself is the standard of good. God's will being done, that is the good, and ultimately speaking, God himself is good itself. We have the concept of being good and right. We say someone is good when he is generous, helps other people, does not steal, keeps the current law, and does not hate. We take morality and ethics as man-made. However, we must acknowledge that the very concept of good is God-given. The reason we do not steal from others is because we know how to respect their belongings, and this comes from knowing how to value not only ourselves but others and ultimately, what God wants from us is is to "love your neighbor."

God's will being done is, in the end, good. For this reason, it is very appropriate to relate "in all things God works for the good" with the purpose of clarifying God's decree and providence, which is the execution of such a decree. God's providence can be used interchangeably with God's working for His good.

People tend to understand this as religious belief or wishful thinking in which they choose to believe that for everyone there are good times and bad times, yet in the end they all lead to the good. What was previously mentioned, "Justice will prevail" and "An evil may sometimes turn out to be a blessing in disguise" are examples. Struggling with the evil of this world and things that go against their will, nonbelievers eventually choose to rationalize life's events and move on.

The Bible teaches that God plans all things in this world, and through it all, He eventually accomplishes His pleasing will. All things in our past long history, the free actions we made as we please, and even the evil deeds done in our wicked minds, they all belonged to God's providence.

People in this world would have a hard time to agree to this teaching of the Bible, that God preserves and governs all his creatures and their actions including all the teachings of the Shorter Catechism from Q1. Man loves to see himself as an independent being feeling disdain for and uncomfortable with the idea that he is being governed and dominated. However, this is an undeniable truth. Given what we have been learning so far, providence must work in this way. The rationality of creation could be applied here as well. Given God's attributes, being perfect and unchangeable, it does not hold that God cannot preserve or govern. If so, this would nullify the absoluteness of God.

WHERE WILL YOU FIND YOUR STANDARD?

For a better understanding of this chapter, knowledge of the history and the course of philosophy is encouraged. Philosophy, in simple terms, is the answer to questions like "What is the right way for man to live out his life?" and "What is the truth?" Throughout the 5,000 year long history of civilization, numerous suggestions regarding the way of life were made and even recorded. However, there is no unified answer. If democracy were to be taken as an example, therein exist various opinions. There was even a point in time when dictatorships were considered good. Hitler could not have done anything if there were no support from the people. At that time, most Germans believed him to be right, his policy the best, and took an active role in supporting him.

Then, where will you find your standard?

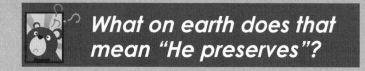

In the process of learning about providence, what challenges us is the concept of preservation rather than governance. This is because the latter is more familiar to us. We have been continuously governed. It was by kings in the past, and now even without visible kings, this still continues by the authorized ones whose power comes from social order and constitutions. But it is not a familiar concept to be preserved.

WHY IS THAT?

It is because we feel comfortable about existing by ourselves. Taking preservation for granted, we feel rather challenged by this concept. We may have gotten physically ill to the point of imminent death, yet we are still alive and well. We cannot survive without air and water even for a moment, but we have been preserved well enough, which make us confident that we can continue to be so without any trouble in the future. That is why God's preservation does not come and touch our hearts at once.

Yet it is close to a miracle when something exists and is preserved as stable as it is. An extreme example is a molecule, which is preserved by nuclear and electromagnetic force. What if all at once those forces disappear? This whole world might end up in smoke at just that moment. As we know, all matter can be split until it becomes very small sized fundamental fragments, which are called molecules. What comprises a molecule is atoms, and it was a long held belief that atoms were the most basic unit of chemical elements. Then it was speculated that atoms were tightly packed inside. Upon, splitting an atom, therein was found the atomic nucleus and many electrons going around that nucleus. Compared to the size of the nucleus and electrons, the space between these particles was amazingly huge. This reminds one of outer space. There exist countless planets in the universe, and what is between these planets? Is there something or not? There is but nothing.

NOTHING

Does this word "nothing" sound familiar? We have seen it in the study of creation. This is the same "nothing" which was used while explaining the creation from nothing. All things are made of atoms, and these are as empty as froth. The act of seeing is nothing more than light particles passing through this emptiness between the atoms of our eyes, but the reflected image made by the light bumps into the retina of our eyes. Receiving such stimulation, our brain restructures the form of objects making us feel like we see something. We are able to lift an object because the molecules of our skin cells, being filled with empty space, cannot pass through the molecules of the objects in our hands. This cross passing is hindered not because each particle is tightly packed but because there is the energy field working inside each atom that forms the matter of both parties. What is the purpose of all of this talk anyway?

If God deconstructed this law of physics, this world would go back to nothing right away. God created the law of $E=MC2$. That energy is mass, which is another way to say that energy is existence, is now accepted as an eternal truth, and it is God who created and set this law. Given He created, it is up to Him to de-create or change anything.

What if God changed this law? Then, we would go back to nothing. He called us into existence through creation, and if He did not preserve our existence, there would not be existence itself. If He let go, not only we but everything around us, the earth and universe, would disappear like the morning mist. This is what preservation in God's providence is.

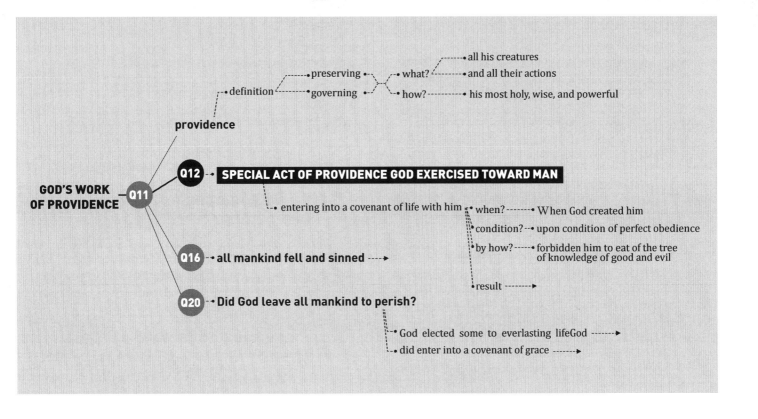

GOD'S WORK OF PROVIDENCE — Q11

providence
- definition
  - preserving
  - governing
    - what?
      - all his creatures
      - and all their actions
    - how? — his most holy, wise, and powerful

Q12 · SPECIAL ACT OF PROVIDENCE GOD EXERCISED TOWARD MAN
- entering into a covenant of life with him
  - when? — When God created him
  - condition? — upon condition of perfect obedience
  - by how? — forbidden him to eat of the tree of knowledge of good and evil
  - result — ►

Q16 · all mankind fell and sinned — ►

Q20 · Did God leave all mankind to perish?
- God elected some to everlasting lifeGod — ►
- did enter into a covenant of grace — ►

Q12 What special act of providence did God exercise
toward man
in the estate wherein he was created?

A12 When God had created man,
he entered into a covenant of life with him,
upon condition of perfect obedience;
forbidding him to eat of the tree
of the knowledge of good and evil,
upon the pain of death.[1, 2]

1.
Galatians 3:12

And the law is not of faith: but, The man that doeth them **shall live in them**.

2.
Genesis 2:17

But of the tree of the knowledge of good and evil, thou shalt not eat of it: for in the day that thou eatest thereof **thou shalt surely die**.

FROM HERE ON, THE SHORTER CATECHISM MOVES ON TO A NEW TURNING POINT.

SO FAR IT HAS DEALT WITH ECUMENICAL TOPICS, BUT NOW AT LAST IT BRINGS ITS FOCUS ON MAN.

As man was at the heart of creation, God offered a special providence to man unlike other creatures. He did not do it after the creation having an afterthought, but when He created man. (By this point, even without such a reminder, we have to be well aware that God's decree was established from the beginning and is unchanging. This truth remains throughout the context of the entire catechism.)

God's special act of providence is that He entered into a covenant of life with us. Further explanation is regards its condition and way. The condition was that we give God perfect obedience, and the means to measure that perfect obedience was to forbid us to eat of the tree of the knowledge of good and evil. The key point was our obedience, and eating of the tree of the knowledge of good and evil was just an indicator to judge our obedience.

What was at stake with this covenant? The pain of death was. This was the consequence resulting upon the violation of this covenant.

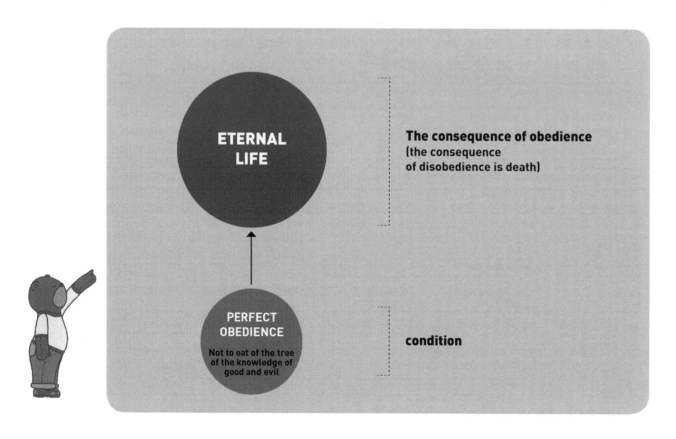

ETERNAL LIFE

PERFECT OBEDIENCE

Not to eat of the tree of the knowledge of good and evil

The consequence of obedience (the consequence of disobedience is death)

condition

THE EXECUTION OF DECREE

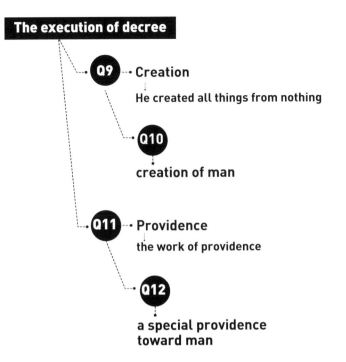

The execution of decree

- **Q9** Creation
  - He created all things from nothing
- **Q10**
  - creation of man
- **Q11** Providence
  - the work of providence
- **Q12**
  - a special providence toward man

We will now discuss the "execution" of God's decree. The execution of God's decree is divided into two topics, creation and providence, and regarding the former, the explanation of man's creation was previously provided. Now Q12 teaches there is a special providence toward man.

1. THE WORD, WITH (WITH HIM)

He entered into a covenant of life with man. Not with other creatures, but with man He entered into a covenant of life. The reason I have repeated myself twice here is because many tend to place the point in a very wrong place. Hearing about the covenant of obedience, they jump to the conclusion that God burdens man. "He could have just left man as free as he was created. What was it for that He came and made a big deal about eating a piece of fruit threatening man with his life? Isn't it a bit childish?"

The point is that **God has now entered into a covenant of life with man**. And the condition is nothing unbearable, only obedience which must be fair for all creatures. Unlike other creatures, God gave man the authority of dominion, and going further entered into a covenant of life with him—this is more important than that he commanded voluntary obedience from man—and entered into a personal relationship with him.

This is surely astonishing and honorable to the creatures with whom God entered into such a covenant. We were just dust; yet worse, nothing.

Previously we have learned about God's decree. As we have learned, we belong to this decree. However, it is not just that we belong to it, but we belong as special beings. That is what Q12 teaches—**God's special providence towards man**. Where we have to place our attention first and foremost is on the fact that He provides His care for man—that God, who lacks nothing and has no reason to be in need, enters into a covenant with us men.

Hearing this so often, many people take this idea lightly and for granted, but in fact, it is tremendously amazing. The Highest One made a personal relationship with men!

For those, **who think men are so great that even God is not out of their league, this concept would not be tolerable**. However, for those who came to realize how great God is and how lowly man is, this simple teaching resonates in their heart as an amazing and mysterious truth. If such a difference were truly known, the fact that He is speaking to us itself would make us feel indeed undeserving and grateful. Furthermore, it is not a commandment, but a covenant. This is the expression of God's love, which demands personal obedience from us. Such a relationship between creatures and God—the idea of such fellowship speaks for His exalting and loving us.

Would He enter into a covenant of life with other creatures such as lions, tigers, and ants, saying, "If you obey me, I will give you life?" No, He would not.

2. PERFECT OBEDIENCE?

Why did He demand obedience? In order to answer to this question, let us recall what we have learned regarding creation. Why did He create? As discussed, there exist many misunderstandings. Feeling bored and lonely, God created the world and men, but these men disobeyed him. Taking offense at this, God drove men out and forgot about them. The concept of creation was not supposed to be merely allegorical or symbolic like this example. What we are studying is not a fable or a legend. Its beginning is not supposed to sound like, "Once upon a time there was a tree…"

God created all creatures with an end in mind and especially made man as a special being. He enters into a special covenant with man whom He created. This special covenant demands perfect obedience. He offers the relationship of eternal life to us and even promises that He would enter into it with man.

Then, isn't this covenant good only for God, while for us, it is just an agreement that demands perfect obedience to the letter, like hell? God would not have named it a special decree if that were the case. **Obedience itself is good for the creatures**. It is a blessing for men to obey God, who is the greatest good and the fount of blessing. Freedom is not a blessing. Neither are rebellion, independence, and dominion. It was obedience that God originally demanded, and when it is being offered, this not only glorifies God but also becomes a blessing to us. Since God is the absolute good, morality, and perfection, it would be for our good to perfectly obey Him. In the same way, it would be to our loss if we offer evasiveness or partial obedience to Him.

The obedience God desires is none other than love. It is not obedience only given in fear against one's will, but the beautiful kind given in love towards the beloved one. Most religions believe as the following. They obey because they fear their god, which makes their obedience a reluctant one, or they desire something in return. This is calculating. They are making a deal with their god. "Why don't we meet in the middle? I will obey you, and you give me a bigger house." However, what our God desires from us is to love Him, and that is why He first showed His love for us, which was supposed to overcome us to the point that we willingly obey Him. Because He loves us, we cannot help but love Him.

Indeed God gave us a wonderful gift. That He entered into a covenant of life with us is much more important and amazing beyond any description than that He created us as the stewards of this entire universe. It is truly a special decree!

3. THE INCIDENT OF THE FRUIT

As the way of entering into a covenant of life with man, in order to guarantee such a promise, God gave the tree of knowledge of good and evil as the indicator of man's obedience. It was a test. "I will see whether you will obey Me or not through your not eating this fruit." Here some peculiar misunderstandings are found as well. In myths we commonly find some secret ways of gods that men should not come to know about, and this tree of knowledge of good and evil is seen as something like Pandora's box or a magic portion that would open such ways of the gods. "Isn't it because God did not like the idea of man coming to know good and evil that He forbade men to eat this fruit? Doesn't this make God evil?" Some may ask such a question. However, the tree is none other than a testing material, which is to show whether we will obey Him

or not. Thus, any curiosity about its nature or question of its components would be inappropriate. "What kind of tree was this, apple, sweet persimmon, or peach?" or "What kind of effect did it have that it carried such a result? It says their eyes were opened—What component of this fruit can possibly do that?" Rather, what is important is, with this least prohibition of not eating the fruit of this tree, man should have confessed his faith of obedience to God's word.

Without this concept rightly set in mind, our thoughts would go drifting. "He caused this trouble for nothing, by creating the tree." "Why does God want to test man to begin with? Trust should not have any strings attached. He could have left men as they were in the Garden to live happily ever after." You may have had these thoughts at least once. But this is not how we are supposed to see it. What God desired was not that we live in the garden being mere gardeners. The point was not whether we eat this fruit or not, but that we become the beings who perfectly obey Him. There must be our focus.

4. THE PAIN OF DEATH

This does not mean this fruit, being poisoned, was supposed to send Adam and Eve to death when it was bitten. As a matter of fact, Adam and Eve did not die immediately. Then, what did this death mean? Did God lie? Was it just a warning? Neither is true. Here, death means none other than that men fell into the state wherein they could not receive the eternal life God has promised on the condition of obedience. Death in the Bible means the separation of man from God. That they were driven out from the garden meant also the severance from God, thus death. Death is associated with leaving God, living against His will, and falling into the state wherein we cannot receive God's love.

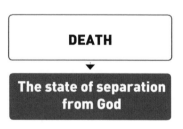

As might be expected, this pain includes the death of our body. (This will be discussed more in detail after Q13.) As discussed before, it is solely due to God's preservation that we exist; it is by God's sustaining power that our bodies stand That is why the death of our bodies also belongs to this pain. Science sees the death of our bodies as a great mystery. Life is mysterious, but what is more mysterious is why that life must come to an end at some point, and for many scientists, this becomes the subject of their study. Maintaining the perfect system up to a certain point from which aging takes over, our bodies finally die. When energy is introduced to our systems, our bodies cells reproduce themselves, and despite damage, they regenerate. Yet, strangely, all life dies. More than life being maintained, growing old and dying is more mysterious, and this breakdown of the system has come as pain from God, who created it at first.

Given this meaning of death, life and salvation must mean **we become moved from the place of pain and death to where God is with us**. This is not merely us being restored to where we were, but God has a place to bring us. This is not to the garden where Adam once lived before sinning, but to the place worthy of greater honor with Adam and the angels. This is God who saves us. This is the salvation we get to receive. Just as worthy, high, and loving as that.

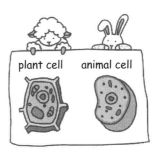

plant cell   animal cell

We will be learning in more detail regarding this after Q20.

We have an age old long problem. Learning about God's absolute sovereignty and providence, we find this conflicting against our will. If just one thing goes wrong, predestination falls into fatalism—this is the problem. In our mind, it can be continuously repeated that this is not fatalism, but in reality, we fail to find any distinction between these two. For this reason, many are discouraging the teaching of God's decree and providence. For them, it is just asking for trouble for us to confess and teach that God predestined everything. Today, this idea has now become a prevalent opinion. And we have been unable to argue against it. Yet this is not the right way to solve this problem. When we avoid the truth just because it is tough, it may seem that the problem is gone at first. However, before even a day passes, our conscience will testify otherwise letting us know that such should not be the solution to the problem.

What is truth? Truth is truth by itself.

We may never fathom all of its teachings and ways, and it may never become perfectly fitting to our eyes. No matter whether this world approves of it or not or whether we are able to understand it or not, regardless of our limits, truth remains unchanged and un-repudiated by itself. Truth testifies to itself.

What is grace?

Choosing the object of His grace, God did not consider its condition. Giving Christ, He foresaw the corruption of man, which was so great as to be unable to be greater, yet this did not stop Him from giving His grace. There is no, not even the slightest, personal righteousness. Yet planning to save men as holy and blameless beings, He chose to give Christ without seeing their faith, will, or goodness. There was any condition. This was a choice which finds its basis not on our mental activity or behavior but on God's will alone. It is God's sovereignty by which He hardens the heart which He hardens and saves whom He saves.

What is reward?

God is. The greatest reward for men is God and only Him. (Gen 15:1) "What can you give me?" While asking this question to God, Abraham had the answer he wanted to hear in the question. He wanted a son. For him, the thing he most wanted was a child, an heir. Knowing it all, God said, "Yes, I will give that. Not only Isaac but land—I do not trust you and you do not deserve any reward, but I will give you them all." And there is even more. Saying, "I am your reward," God let him know that He actually wanted to give himself to Abraham. He said he would give everything Abraham wanted and on the top of that Himself as a reward. Abraham received what he wanted, and that became a snare for him. He ended up receiving what God wanted him to have as the father of faith. Without even realizing it, he became the one who had already received. This is what a gift is. Given, regardless of the recipient's state or level, it glorifies the giver. This principle was passed down to the patriarchs of faith even to the time of Joseph.

For deeper understanding: The Doctrine of Absolute Zanchius by Jerome Zanchius

What is good?

What in specific does the providence, by which God works for the good, include? Can everything really be good for me? While living on this earth, do we get to experience and be assured of this without any doubt? Of course, the answer is yes. God clearly shows this. Using the entire life of Isaac, Jacob, and Joseph as the means, He has shown how He works for our good. Obviously this could be extremely challenging for the person directly involved. At the very moment of finally coming to realize that God has been conducting his life, he could breathe his last breath. Still he has received. He has received throughout his life. He has been chosen by God's grace and has been in His providence and still is.

It is indeed hard for us to completely comprehend **how deep the nature of His grace for the ones He loves is**. Yet this is an undeniable truth, which is working even at this moment. It may be true that we cannot prove this throughout our rather brief lives on the earth, yet the Bible, throughout its long-standing place in history, proves and repeatedly demonstrates this. Then, why is life so dim, hard to clearly see, time consuming, and painful? It is smelting. Only through hard means are we taught to become His people whom He wants us to be. It is His reprimand with the staff and rod. This is how the Lord gathers His people, and throughout their entire lives, He clothes and rears them—us—to be worthy of His calling.

***Smelting**: extracting metal from its ore by a process involving heating and hammering; strengthening one's body and mind through training
***Reprimand**: a rebuke or reproach for someone's fault or wrongdoing

We take free will for granted. However,

strictly speaking, there is no such a thing called free will. I no longer live, and it is not I who is doing any of my believing, having faith, and being saved. Nowhere is there free will in the sense that we expect it to be. Rather, free will only exists in the form that we receive God's grace from Him. Modern science has already proven that man's will is not free. Today we cannot claim man's will to be anything absolute. It may appear that we have come to know this only after the dawn of the 21st century, but the Bible has been teaching this from the beginning. We have to heed this word as a means of girding ourselves. Before God, man has no free will, and only God has His will. This God chose us—someone like us—only by His will so that we may keep His ways and seek His righteousness. This is for our blessing. While asking righteousness and love from us, God is saying, "This is good for you. Having nothing to do with me, this is good for you." Righteousness and love are blessings for us. What else is our blessing? What else can be a blessing for you?

Life, blessing, death, and woe

God uses all of these as His means to lead us so that we may accomplish His worth. God uses life, blessing, death, and woe as His means— that is right, even death is a means for God— so that we may take a role in accomplishing such a noble worth, and this is His providence. Even the existence of Satan is an instrument in God's providence. If God allows, He can mobilize any force. Before someone like Him, can we speak of our will and darken His counsel? Who can do such a thing? Is there anyone who ever saw the end of the universe? The end of universe is unknown. We can only imagine it, for even light and electric waves cannot reach it. Is there anyone who ever saw the foundation of the world? When a particle is being split repeatedly until it cannot be divided any longer, what comes out of it is nothing like a particle and it just scatters. Even a particle accelerator cannot do any more splitting. We do not know anything unseen. As might be expected, we can only make a prediction that something might be somewhere to some degree. We only see the possibility of things.

We need eyes to see and hands to touch. Can such a being say, "I don't know" or "This is wrong" only because something is not fitting to our eyes, ears, and brain? Can we say, "There is no predestination" or "the Bible is fiction" because we cannot understand and easily explain it? Can we dare to say, "God works, but I have to respond for Him to work" or "God and I work together" in order to keep our pride?

God came near to us and said, "I am your utmost reward." Upon giving everything, He called us to the place of grace where He gives the greatest thing as the actual gift. Then, what are we still looking for? We have already failed too many times in the past. Our eyes have been only on our own happiness, desires, and favored circumstances, and when these were not given at once, we blamed God grumbling that His arm is too short. However, this is not how eternal life is given. It is not given that lightly and cheaply. Before His will, which insists on giving us the qualifications to enjoy eternal life, His heaven, reward, and God himself, we cannot help but transferring all of our worth to Him. We must not take it as if it were noth-

Even death and misfortune were the means...

ing because it is given freely. If eternal life did not hold God's image in it, then what would be the meaning of it? If we have to live forever miserably, it is not a blessing but death and destruction—a place worthy to be called hell.

God is hiding the best thing from me. God is good, and He is now for me and doing some glorious work even though it is yet unknown to me. This is our blessing and reward.

"Now what I am commanding you today is not too difficult for you or beyond your reach. It is not up in heaven, so that you have to ask, 'Who will ascend into heaven to get it and proclaim it to us so we may obey it?' Nor is it beyond the sea, so that you have to ask, 'Who will cross the sea to get it and proclaim it to us so we may obey it?' No, the word is very near you; it is in your mouth and in your heart so you may obey it." (Deut 30:11-14)

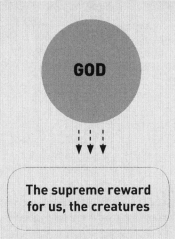

GOD

The supreme reward for us, the creatures

*This essay was written while listening to a sermon by the president of the Research Institute for the Bible and Reformed Theology, Prof. Young-Kyu Kim, and for the purpose of this book, the sermon has been summarized and modified.

Discussion Questions

❶ How would you define true obedience and true love?

❷ What would happen if we didn't believe in providence?

❸ If even sin belongs to God's providence, then didn't God create sin? Please explain it in your own words.

❹ Why is it a gift that God entered into a covenant with us?

❺ What did God want to reveal through this way of providence?

❻ In what sense does this chapter give us the reason to be grateful?

Q13~19 | THE FALL

"I GO TO CHURCH AND EVEN INVITED JESUS INTO MY HEART, BUT LOOK AT MY LIFE."
"I CANNOT HELP BUT HATE MYSELF."
"NONBELIEVERS SEEM TO LIVE BETTER."

What we are about study is quite strange. In the previous chapter, studying God's special decrees for us, our hearts were deeply touched by such an amazing providence and love, but something terrible and absurd now follows. Getting out of bed we find ourselves standing in the middle of a crime scene. Blood is dripping off of our hands. Q13-19 explains how that happened, what comes about by this, and what we should do. It is an extremely serious chapter.

So, let's make sure of the following before proceeding to the study of the Fall.

Q13-19 of the Shorter Catechism will cover the meaning and consequences of the Fall, which surely placed us in a dire situation. Here lies a very important yet easily overlooked truth: Even this Fall belongs to God's providence. It may puzzle you. Don't be discouraged, for this kind of reaction is natural. Just continue the study with the question in your mind. Of course, even after the completion of the book, the question can linger in your mind. Certainly this kind of question deserves a resolution, or it will cause other troubles along the way. The last thing anyone should do is to sweep it under the carpet and pretend it doesn't exist.

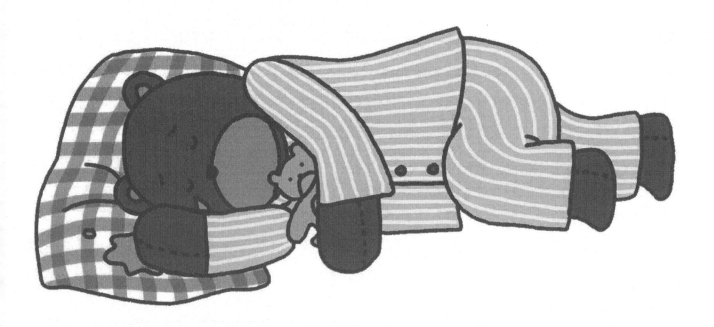

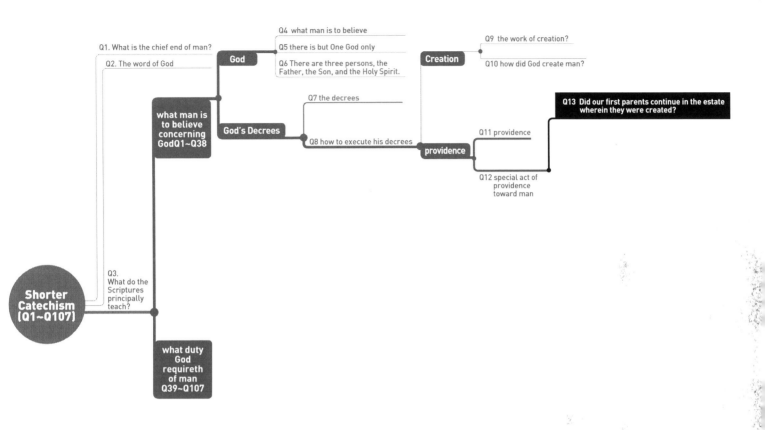

When the Shorter Catechism feels puzzling, you have to go back to what was previously studied. Q7 and what follows it must be understood in the light of God's attributes provided in Q4. Everything in God's decree must be seen in the context of who our God is, absolute and just, according to His attributes. What was previously studied and what follows are so closely intertwined they cannot be separated.

In order to fully grasp the Fall, we have to make the connection to what we have learned regarding Creation (Q10) and Providence (Q7). Let's recall what we have learned about Creation. What a glorious being man was created to be! Only when we recall the originally created state of man are we able to fully grasp how miserable the current state of man caused

by the Fall is. Where this Fall started and led us to, we should know. Another critical aspect of the Fall is death for man, which is nothing other than separation from fellowship with God.

Also let's recall what we have learned about Providence. Should the Fall belong to God's Providence, some may argue "Then it is God's will that we sin." This only comes from mistaking the difference between "God's Will" and "God's Plan." You may refer to the chapter on God's decree for a detailed discussion of this. Sin is nothing other than to leave God by one's own will. It is no more and no less than that, and the responsibility falls on the person, not God.

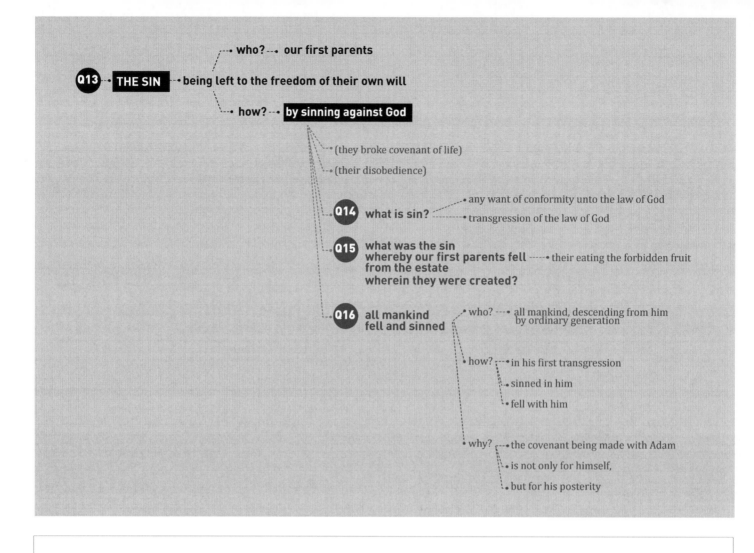

Q13 — **THE SIN**
- who? → our first parents
- being left to the freedom of their own will
- how? → **by sinning against God**
  - (they broke covenant of life)
  - (their disobedience)

Q14 what is sin?
- any want of conformity unto the law of God
- transgression of the law of God

Q15 what was the sin whereby our first parents fell from the estate wherein they were created? → their eating the forbidden fruit

Q16 all mankind fell and sinned
- who? → all mankind, descending from him by ordinary generation
- how?
  - in his first transgression
  - sinned in him
  - fell with him
- why?
  - the covenant being made with Adam
  - is not only for himself,
  - but for his posterity

Q13 Did our first parents continue
in the estate wherein they were created?

A13 Our first parents, being left
to the freedom of their own will,
fell from the estate wherein they were created,
by sinning against God.[1,2]

1.
Genesis 3:6-8, 13

And when the woman saw that the tree was good for food, and that it was pleasant to the eyes, and a tree to be desired to make one wise, **she took of the fruit thereof, and did eat, and gave also unto her husband with her; and he did eat**. And the eyes of them both were opened, and they knew that they were naked; and they sewed fig leaves together, and made themselves aprons. And they heard the voice of the Lord God walking in the garden in the cool of the day: and **Adam and his wife hid themselves from the presence of the Lord God** amongst the trees of the garden......And the Lord God said unto the woman, What is this that thou hast done? And the woman said, **The serpent beguiled me, and I did eat**.

2.
Ecclesiastes 7:29

Lo, this only have I found, that God hath made man upright; but **they have sought out many inventions**.

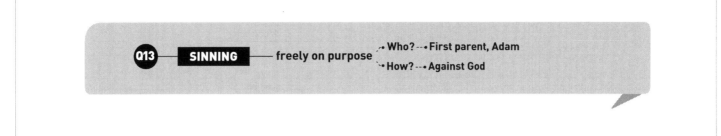

First of all, this question reports that our first parents did not remain in the estate wherein they were created but fell. And this fall came as they sinned against God. As previously taught, eternal life was promised on the condition of obedience; thus, this should be easily understood as contrasting concepts. Obedience brings the covenant of eternal life and rebellion brings death.

On top of this, this question reveals this fall occurred through no other reasons than their free act of their own will.

In this chapter, we will inspect the significant meaning that each of these three deliver. Then, through Q14-16, sinning itself will be explored more in detail. And through Q17-19, by the result of such a fall what we have become will be explored more in detail.

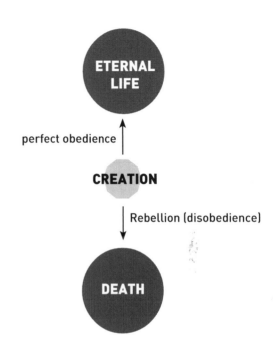

HOW DID Q13 MAKE YOU FEEL?

Q13 is closely related to Q12. There is a tremendous gap between what Q12 introduced, entering a covenant of life with God, and the real life of ours. This brings up a question. Did we remain in the estate wherein we were created? As expected, the answer is "No." We fell from the estate wherein we were created by sinning. What on earth were they in want of that led them to fall?

THE MEANING OF THE FALL

Regarding man's fall, there have been many explanations of various myths such as man fell because the gods, with the intention of keeping man from challenging them, gave a riddle which was utterly beyond man's intelligence or gave a test that an average man could not even dare to attempt. However, the explanation of the Bible is the opposite. The previously taught covenant of life was the test no man could fail, yet man failed. According to the Shorter Catechism, man sinned on his own, freely, doing wrong. It was not that they had no other choice but to take the fruit.

How many fruit trees would have been in the Garden? We can only imagine, but it must have been beyond count. They did not have to take the fruit of the knowledge of good and evil. For the Garden was the best place on earth, paradise; it might have had all the delicious fruit trees. Yet they had to go sin on purpose. God made this clear enough, "When you eat of it, you will surely die," yet they dared to eat. They sinned against God out of arrogance.

And they sinned on their own and freely. "Adam ate the fruit, but Satan tempted him to do so." "Satan must be blamed. Didn't you say that man was created good? Then, the origin of sin is Satan." We may want to shift the responsibility on Satan and get out of it insisting "Satan's temptation must have been too compelling to say no to." Yet, technically speaking, Satan is merely an instrumental cause. Even though Satan tempted, it is always "I" who take the fruit.

Adam was an outstanding man. He was so not only among people of today but also among anyone of human history. It was impossible for such a man not to understand God's warning, have a weak mind or an addiction, which compelled him to take the fruit. It was simply his arrogance, which made his own judgment more important that God's words and in the end have him fall into Satan's psychological temptation.

"When the woman saw that the fruit of the tree was good for food and pleasing to the eye, and also desirable for gaining wisdom, she took some and ate it. She also gave some to her husband, who was with her, and he ate it." (Gen 3:6)

We men came to eat the fruit because **we left the place of gratitude disregarding that we came to exist merely due to God's creation and this Creator entrusted us with the authority to rule over and manage the creatures, that such a high One spoke to us, "Obey Me and let us love" which should be such an honor for us, and that He even promised this amazing eternal life to be ours in the end overlooking how precious this covenant is.** This is the heart of man's fall.

If previous lessons are remembered, this could appear even more absurd. Be at a loss for words. Adam did not have any need to sin. Then, for what reason did he have to go against such a good God? Wasn't he supposed to have this gratitude that overwhelmed all of us while we were at the previous chapter? What on earth had happened to him? If it were a movie, it is such an unexpected turnaround of events. Everything was going so perfectly, flawlessly, peacefully, and all of sudden things have gotten entangled and messed up. They "fell from the estate wherein they were created." This is surely not enough of a description. From where to where did this fall happen? The answer is demanded.

This fall has been made to the place of death. Some may ask does this--that man went against God and fell--really matter? Yes, it does, for this means death. The place they fell to is not a place somehow livable by any means but a place of death. If the word were borrowed from creation, it is the place of nothing. The place that can break every bone in our body.

THE MEANING OF DEATH

What more words are needed? Death means the separation from the relationship with God. That is why Adam and Eve had to be kicked out from the Garden. They were not able to get along with God as before. That is death. "Gee... I can take that." If this is how anyone sees this, then he is in a serious condition. What is life? It is to be with God. On the contrary, death is to be separated from God. "Yet Adam did not die--at least physically. He did not die right after the fall, but lived to cultivate a vineyard, have children, and lived up to 900s." This is not the right way to see it. By this fall, humanity all together has gotten cut off from the relationship with God. Without God, there can be no meaning to any existence. One can be breathing, but it is not living. It is miserable not to be able to fellowship with God. That is how the Bible speaks about death.

This was the change not in some aspects but all. This change was as great as between life and death. If it were just the shift between some levels, then one may respond, "I can adjust to it." Yet this cannot be living at all.

The Fall in God's Providence

Then, a question arises, "How could this serious fall have happened?" We were just learning about God's decrees and providence, and out of nowhere, the fall emerged. It is quite disrupting. Everything, even including us, must be in God's perfect decrees. Then how could this fall, which looks like a fatal flaw, have happened? This question is quite natural.

Other questions are also viable.

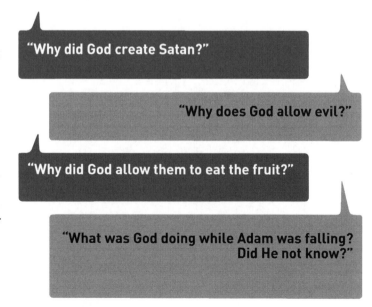

"Why did God create Satan?"

"Why does God allow evil?"

"Why did God allow them to eat the fruit?"

"What was God doing while Adam was falling? Did He not know?"

How can a man's fall glorify God? Being part of God's decree, it should glorify God, yet it seems quite hard to connect the fall and God's glory. "God could have left Adam and Even to live happily ever after, but He had to make the fruit of knowledge of good and evil." "If He really had to, He could have put a fence around it or made man unable to be tempted at all."

Answers to such questions have been given already in previous chapters. How did God create man? God did not create man as a robot or puppet.

A great example can be found in the love between a man and a woman. We oftentimes find in various movies and TV shows that in the name of love one treats the other as his possession and tries to take the freedom away from that person. He not only takes away the freedom but blocks all other possibilities from her, hoping that she loves him only. This cannot be love. **God did not love us like that**. If we were created in such a way that we were programmed to love God without any condition, then we would be just robots. Why is that? What is a robot? According to the three laws of robotics, a robot must obey the orders given to it. A robot is created to be only an instrument. God did not create us to be such a being. If you learned creation well, then it should not be hard for you to grasp. A being obeys whatever God says…? God did not want such a creature. He did not create such a being and have him to rule over the world. If He had, neither the Bible nor the law would be required for man to live.

God created us to be able to love Him voluntarily and personally. And this brings glory to God. It is so much more than the way materialism sees man or bioengineering makes a man-like robot. That God created man as a being who can disobey God makes His creation all the more great. This creation cannot even be compared to the three laws of robotics.

This is not only amazing but precious. This can be understood better when we are in love. You may have the experience of it. In love, there comes a moment that we want to force the other's brain, if possible, to reciprocate our love. But we come to realize soon enough that this cannot be love. The love earned by such a force would neither be precious nor exciting. It is great that God does not treat us like that.

When you acknowledge this, you will come to be more grateful for such a love of God. This may be one of the most important acknowledgements in our lives.

Q14 • WHAT IS SIN? • any want of conformity unto the law of God
• transgression of the law of God

Q15 • WHAT WAS THE SIN WHEREBY OUR FIRST PARENTS FELL FROM THE ESTATE WHEREIN THEY WERE CREATED? • their eating the forbidden fruit

Q14 What is sin?

A14 Sin is any want of conformity unto,
or transgression of,
the law of God.[1]

Q15 What was the sin
whereby our first parents fell
from the estate wherein they were created?

A15 The sin whereby our first parents fell
from the estate wherein they were created,
was their eating the forbidden fruit.[2]

1.
1 John 3:4

Whosoever committeth sin transgresseth also the law: for **sin is the transgression** of the law.

2.
Genesis 3:6,12

And when the woman saw that the tree was good for food, and that it was pleasant to the eyes, and a tree to be desired to make one wise, **she took of the fruit thereof, and did eat, and gave also unto her husband with her......and he did eat**. And the man said, The woman whom thou gavest to be with me, she gave me of the tree, and **I did eat**.

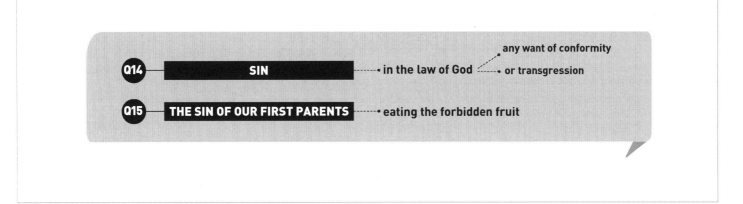

CLARIFYING THE CONCEPTS

Only appropriate to the gravity of the issue at hands, these questions sound quite pointed. They appear to be grilling us about what sin, the law of God, and what specifically their sin was. As examining the answers to each, we will be clarifying the concepts one by one.

THE DEFINITION OF SIN

What a unique definition! And this is also critical. This is surely different from the way morality and ethics define sin. That morality and ethics differ from the standard of God has been previously mentioned more than once, yet here through the definition of sin it gets to be clarified beyond any question in the future. Now, what is sin? Sin is any want of conformity unto or transgression of the law of God. Not only that we violate but also lack in God's law—that is all sin. The bar is set tremendously high.

THE LAW OF GOD

This definition introduces a new terminology, the law of God. If Q3 of the Shorter Catechism were recalled, the main teaching of the Bible could be divided into two. What was the second one? You may refer to p. 37. One was "What man is to believe concerning God", and the other was "What duty God requires of man." In Part 2 we will get into the second part more in detail.

Yet to say a little in advance, this law of God is revealed in the Bible in a general form and in the Ten Commandments more in a condensed summarized form. The ways we can love God and our neighbor are thoroughly described in them. This is the law of God.

SIN AND ITS DEFINITION

- any want of conformity unto, or transgression of the law of God.

THE LAW OF GOD

- to obey God's Word, which is revealed in the Ten Commandments in a condensed form.

THE SIN OF ADAM

- to eat the forbidden fruit.

- Violation of God's Words and disobedience.

- He relativized God, which resulted in the sin of arrogance. In this, he exalted himself before God.

Good question! We have seen how grave the problem of the fall is. The definition of sin has also been examined. Then, it can make some wonder what Adam did and how that can be called sin. The Bible explains this in detail, and Q14 puts this in order.

The sinful act of Adam was to eat the forbidden fruit. This is quite a famous story that everyone knows. The serpent tempted Eve, Eve ate the fruit and gave it to her husband, and her husband ate it too. This is how this beyond description, absurd, and pitiful incident happened, and through this disobedience the fall has occurred. Yet the heart of the matter was,

as previously mentioned, their disobedience. "God is so petty that He had to make such a big deal out of eating some fruit." This is not the right way to see this. The issue is not their act but disobedience. They deliberately violated God's words. That is how death came to all of us. Our relationship with God is destroyed, and there is no way that we can restore this relationship by our initiative.

Between man and man, we may be able to find many ways to restore a broken relationship. We can ask for forgiveness and actually earn it with pleasant words. Mutual agreement, proper compensation, or time can also bring restoration. Yet between the Creator and the creatures, the matter is not simple enough to be resolved merely with an apology. God has to offer a way to reconcile on His side.

A: Here Adam, being the husband and head, was given a special role and position of a representative. This will be dealt with in Q16 in more detail.

Q: Why is this called Adam's sin? Eve is equally responsible.

THE END OF THE BEGINNING:
From the Beginning to the End, everything was God's Plan.

In the structure of Catechism, the Fall of man falls into God's decrees in which sense all the events of past history could be described as inevitable. There is no IF in history, some have said. It is even more so when God's decrees, in which God foreordains whatsoever comes to pass, is taken into consideration. "What would have happened, if Adam didn't take the fruit? We would have been living in the Garden without any trouble." We entertain such thoughts either for fun or with shame. However, in the light of God's attributes, this kind of thought has no place to stand.

Keep in your mind that everything in the Shorter Catechism finds its reasons in God's attributes and decrees. Just as God Himself is eternal, unchanging, and perfect, so are His decrees. God had His decrees planned beforehand, and this includes even the fall of man. It is oftentimes mistaken that by Adam's fall God's plan has been frustrated, yet this cannot be so considering the nature of God's decrees.

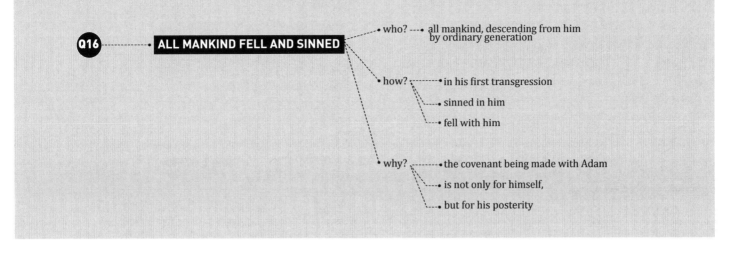

Q16 Did all mankind
fall in Adam's first transgression?

A16 The covenant being made with Adam,
not only for himself, but for his posterity;
all mankind, descending from him
by ordinary generation,
sinned in him, and fell with him,
in his first transgression.[1,2,3]

1.
Genesis 2:16-17

And **the Lord God commanded the man, saying**, Of every tree of the garden thou mayest freely eat: But of the tree of the knowledge of good and evil, thou shalt not eat of it: for in the day that thou eatest thereof thou shalt surely die.

2.
Romans 5:12

Wherefore, as by one man sin entered into the world, and death by sin; and so death passed upon all men, **for that all have sinned**.

3.
1 Corinthians 15:21-22

For since **by man came death**, by man came also the resurrection of the dead. For **as in Adam all die**, even so in Christ shall all be made alive.

ADAM'S SIN BEING IMPUTED TO ALL MANKIND

This explains how Adam's sinful act, which was previously dealt with, is related to all mankind. It is primarily because the covenant being made with Adam was not only for himself but for all mankind. Thus, in his transgression, all mankind sinned in him and fell with him.

In other words, Adam's sin is not his, but the sin of ours. Eve being tempted by the serpent ate the fruit before him, yet the Bible takes Adam as the representative and calls it Adam's sin, and in the same way we call all of our sins his. For this reason, the definition of sin and its basis from previous chapters should also be applied to us. We have become those who violated God's law and are left with no other countermeasures than death. Let's continue.

Q16 IS THE ANSWER TO THE QUESTION, "What does Adam's sin have to do with me?"

"I did not eat the fruit." "You made this covenant with Adam, not me. Please go to the one who is directly involved in this contract." Those who have gone to church for a long time would probably accept the idea "Adam's sin is ours" without resistance, yet there have been various complaints regarding this. "It is not right that the punishment goes beyond the person who sinned to his descendants. Here, God is being unfair." "This is so primitive. This is worse than guilt by association in which the third generation used to be held responsible and punished." This sounds quite reasonable.

Moreover, by this very principle--through this one man, Adam, sin has been imputed to countless other people--, through this one man, Christ, the salvation has become available to countless others. It is the same principle. By exalting Christ alone, all of those who should be saved by taking Him as their representative are to be exalted being united with Him and invited to this place of eternal happiness. If one continues to insist that he should be separate from Adam, then he has no other choice than being separate from Christ as well.

OUR REPRESENTATIVE, ADAM

The Shorter Catechism answers this question by offering an additional explanation of the characteristic of this covenant of Q12. God made this covenant not only with Adam but all mankind. Adam is the head of all mankind. In the past, a king was the representative of his people, and for that reason, the king's captivity meant the defeat of his people in war automatically. Also, in diplomatic matters, a decision made by a representative influences every person of his nation, and whichever nation you go to, the name of the country of your origin does not change. These can be helpful examples.

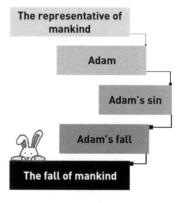

ADAM, THE REPRESENTATIVE

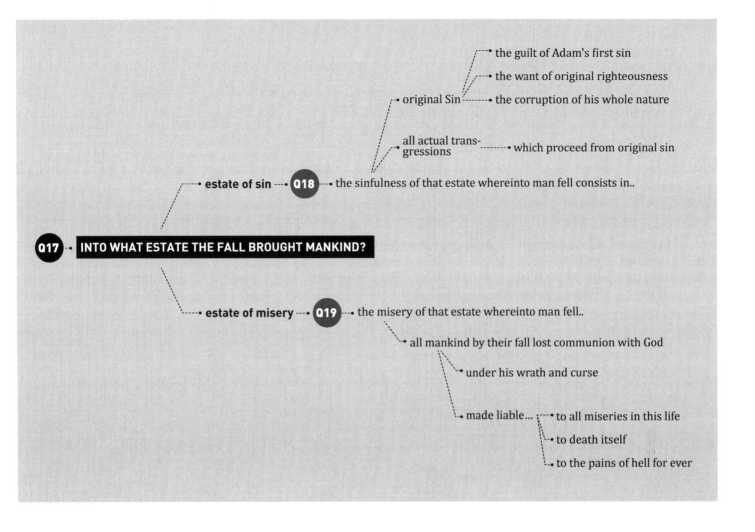

Q17 — **INTO WHAT ESTATE THE FALL BROUGHT MANKIND?**

- estate of sin — **Q18** — the sinfulness of that estate whereinto man fell consists in..
  - original Sin
    - the guilt of Adam's first sin
    - the want of original righteousness
    - the corruption of his whole nature
  - all actual transgressions — which proceed from original sin

- estate of misery — **Q19** — the misery of that estate whereinto man fell..
  - all mankind by their fall lost communion with God
  - under his wrath and curse
  - made liable...
    - to all miseries in this life
    - to death itself
    - to the pains of hell for ever

Q17 Into what estate did the fall bring mankind?

A17 The fall brought mankind
into an estate of sin and misery.[1]

1.
Romans 5:12

Wherefore, as by one man **sin entered into the world**, and death by sin; and so **death passed upon all men**, for that **all have sinned**.

THE ESTATE OF SIN AND MISERY

The wages of sin is death. According to the previous teaching, by Adam's fall, we fell with him. Now we should take this punishment of death. Then the question follows, into which estate did this fall bring us?

As the answer, two are mentioned.
The estate of sin and misery.

Logic requires more explanations on this topic of death, yet this question speaks only of the estate of sin and misery. It is because this is the very punishment of death. Being able to eat, speak, go some place and move around, we may feel as if we are living. Yet we are in this estate of sin and misery, which is death. One may feel alive, but it is only an illusion.

The Shorter Catechism Q1 taught about man's purpose. Apart from that purpose, there is no life to begin with. This is why many philosophers and saints have confessed that life is meaningless.

Atheism can lead people to nihilism, and the final destination of it is death. For them, life can be a living hell. If you do not know how miserable such a life is for the simple reason that you have not experienced it yet, then you should be grateful. It will be dealt with in more detail later, but the fear of death any man has is also given by God as the result of our sin.

Do not worry if you can't fully grasp the above now, for its understanding could come in an unexpected way as you reflect on what life is and where that life invites you to be later in the future. Because some things are only understood through seeing and tasting them yourself.

> **Clarifying the Terms**
>
> Regarding sin, we have encountered several related terms, for example, "sinning" in Q13 and "an estate of sin" in Q17. But these should be used distinctively. "Sinning" refers to the act of sin while "an estate of sin," "sinfulness" or "wickedness" is the result of such sinning.

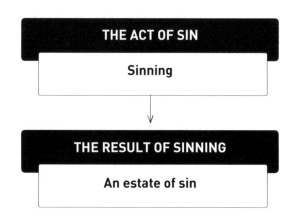

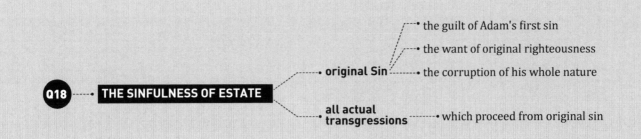

Q18 Wherein consists
the sinfulness of that estate whereinto man fell?

A18 The sinfulness of that estate whereinto man fell,
consists in the guilt of Adam's first sin,
the want of original righteousness,
and the corruption of his whole nature
which is commonly called Original Sin;
together with all actual transgressions which proceed from it.[1, 2, 3, 4, 5]

1.
Romans 5:12, 19

Wherefore, as by one man **sin entered into the world**, and **death by sin**; and so **death passed upon all men**......for that all have sinned: For as by one man's disobedience many were made sinners, so by the obedience of one shall many be made righteous.

2.
Romans 5:10-20

3.
Ephesians 2:1-3

And you hath he quickened, who were **dead in trespasses and sins**; Wherein **in time past ye walked according to the course of this world**, according to the prince of the power of the air, **the spirit that now worketh**

in the children of disobedience: Among whom also we all had our conversation in times past in the lusts of our flesh, fulfilling the desires of the flesh and of the mind; and **were by nature the children of wrath, even as other**s.

4.
James 1:14-15

But every man is tempted, **when he is drawn away of his own lust, and enticed**. Then when lust hath conceived, it bringeth forth sin: and sin, when it is finished, bringeth forth death.

5.
Matthew 15:19

For out of **the heart proceed evil thoughts, murders, adulteries, fornications, thefts, false witness, blasphemies**.

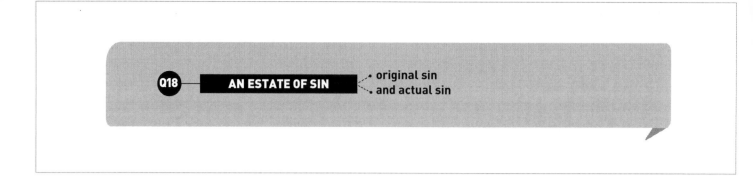

Q18 — **AN ESTATE OF SIN** — original sin and actual sin

This section thoroughly analyzes sin. Q18 may appear lengthy and complicated, yet if cut into pieces, it is not so overwhelming. According to the previous teaching, as the result of the fall, men were brought into an estate of sin and misery. Q18 deals with the first part, the estate of sin. One is original sin and the other is actual sin.

ORIGINAL SIN			ACTUAL SIN
the guilt of Adam's first sin	the want of original righteousness	the corruption of his whole person	all sinful acts, which proceed from the original sin

ORIGINAL SIN

It is explained in three different parts. These are three elements, which compose the original sin: guilt, the want of (original) righteousness, and the corruption of nature.

A. GUILT

Being sentenced "guilty," everyone has to assume this responsibility of sin. It works the same way as in court. This guilt cannot be put away just because I think of myself innocent. Everyone came to carry this guilt before God even though one is not under arrest/an injunction or convicted by the human court.

B. THE WANT OF RIGHTEOUSNESS

It has become hard to find any righteousness in men. Men cannot do what is righteous. The righteousness given to man as God's image at the creation is now lost. No matter how hard one tries, one cannot be righteous before God. All fall short of God's standard.

C. THE CORRUPTION OF NATURE

This means the actual corruption of sin. On the top of the verdict and the want of righteousness, we are now corrupt with rotten sin. This corruption of nature refers to the depravity of the whole person. All including intellect, emotion, and volition are now irrevocably corrupt.

ACTUAL SINS

To put it plainly, actual sins(all actual transgressions) sins are the sins we commit ourselves. Due to the original sin, original righteousness is lost and the whole nature of mankind is also corrupt, and this makes every deeds of any man only sinful. The numerous sins that Adam's prosperity could not have helped but commit is called actual sins.

Q18 of the Shorter Catechism explains that actual sins proceed from original sin. However, people refuse to acknowledge this. They think that we sin only by accident and do not even imagine that we are in an estate in which we cannot help but sin. According to them, man's current estate is just normal, and any lack or problems can be filled up and fixed. In such a milieu, the importance of education is often emphasized. For them, man sins only because he had not received proper education.

Others bring the structural problem to the table. Wealth is not evenly distributed, and this is why, for instance, a hungry man steals bread. They have a point, and it is more than right that we continue to improve social justice despite its cost. Yet we need to confront the fact that our nature, in which we may strive to deny and avoid that the original sin is causing our sinful acts, has also come as the result of sin.

The Bible indicts this fundamental problem of man very seriously. There is a fundamental cause in our sinful acts, and without it being fixed, we have no way to fix that sin. This tends to be one of the reasons people refuse to accept the Bible. Man despises to hear about sin. Especially his own. There is no man who would willingly respond "Yes, I am" to the accusation "You are a sinner." Yet this is so true.

WHY IS IT GOOD TO KNOW ABOUT THE FALL OF MAN?

When the fall is properly understood, it helps us understand others. This simple acknowledgment that man is sinful and imperfect due to the corruption of sin offers us the chance to examine our expectation towards others. The nature of man's hope in man himself is that despite current conditions with proper support man can surely better himself. Yet the Bible says otherwise, total depravity, and helps us not to expect anything good from man. It is ironic that this acknowledgement stretches the extent of our understanding and sympathy towards others and at the same time offers comfort to us in the moment of frustration in man and even in our social structures and politics.

Understanding the fall of man, we won't easily despair, fear, or be frustrated. We won't have any false hope either while always seeking after the alternative—to serve better in our own relationships and society that we belong to. We won't waste our energy while combatting with unnecessary conflicts. Instead we acknowledge evil and pursue truth all the more.

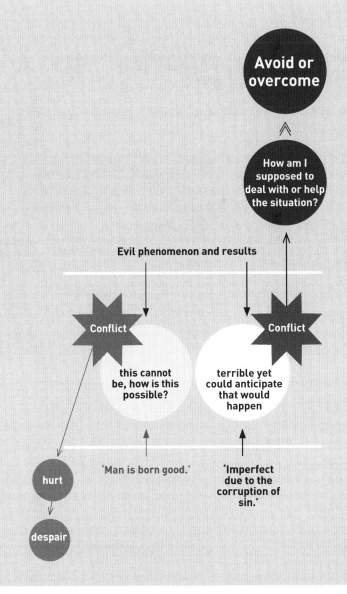

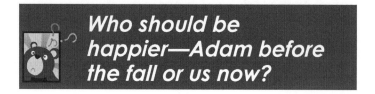

Who should be happier—Adam before the fall or us now?

God, creating us, not only made us very precious but also called us to be the highest steward among the creatures. On top of that, God promised to give us the place of eternal life.

Taking the above into consideration, Adam was an astonishing man. He was perfect in his intellect, emotion, and volition, and lived in a perfect living environment called the Garden of Eden. Before sin and the fall, he must have been as happy as he could possibly be. By contrast, we are weak in every aspect.

However, we do not have to feel jealous. We are those who have been saved and now are enjoying the new life. Inspite of this feeble condition of ours, imagining our future life in heaven offers so much expectation of eternal bliss.

Then what can we finally say about who should be happier between Adam and us? I hope this question would enlighten you in the understanding of the estate of Adam and ours. Also in the process, you would come to know the mystery of God's providence even a little better.

There is a fundamental difference between Adam's estate before the fall and ours now. What is this? Adam's estate was the one in which he was "able not to fall." On the other hand, ours is the one in which we are "not able to fall." If Adam did not have any interest in eternal life, and at the same time did not fall and thus stayed in the Garden, the best he could be was just a gardener. However, we are the elected who are invited to heaven to live in eternal fellowship with God. Had there been no difference between these two, we should be all the time anxious we might fall again. For this reason, we are for certain more precious and happier beings than Adam then. We had better not say any longer, "All could be better if only Adam did not eat that fruit. We could be now eating fruits and playing with the lions and having so much fun without any worries."

Then are we happier than even angels?

Of course. The Shorter Catechism does not include this topic, but the Larger Catechism deals with this quite in detail, explaining angels as the hired helpers of God. It is true that angels are great beings, but we are the children of God. In a pal-ace, who is higher between the prince/princess and the help? It is a no-brainer.

Also out of pure imagination, many come up with their own theories on angels. Some religions say that each man has his own guardian angel. Others say good people die and become angels in heaven. These are absolutely not true. God created angels distinctly only to have them work for Him. We must not overinterpret.

Then who is Satan? Is he God's rival?

This is the most critical misunderstanding to consider Satan as if he were an equal deity to God. This is what Zoroastrianism and Manichaeism think. They see the world as a confrontation between a good god and an evil god, yet nothing is further from the truth. Satan is none other than a fallen angel. He is the same as angel, and can never stand as a match for God or as an equal to Him. There is nothing equal to God, including Satan.

Rather, **Satan is just an instrument before God**. When he is no longer needed, his being will at once be eliminated. In Job, Satan comes to God asking for permission for every work of his. Even Satan is what God has work for Himself. He may do his best to conspire against God, yet even this belongs to God's providence and he is destined to exist and work only within the limit that brings glory to God.

On a concluding note, we are God's children. The value of angels cannot be compared to ours. We are much more precious than angels before God. How precious are we? God loved us even to die for us. God, having even the fall of men in His providence, brings men to a higher place that God wanted in the first place. (This will be covered after Q20 more in detail.) God allows even the work of Satan and the sin of our hearts and uses them for His glory—This is the power of God. It had been a constant wonder how my violation could glorify God, yet the simple truth above has resolved such a question. Even my violation becomes God's instrument to bring me to God and to the place of eternal life, and lets me praise such a great and amazing God of love!

"What is man?" Mankind has been offering countless answers to this question, and they can be categorized in two ways. One believes that man is born good and every man's heart is innate with the potential of being good. The other believes that man is born evil and what is seen as good in man is a mere acquirement.

What does the Bible say about man?

As explaining sin, the Bible also speaks about what man is and in which estate he is. According to the Bible, the current estate of man is sin without any countermeasures of his own.

"There is no one righteous, not even one; there is no one who understands, no one who seeks God. All have turned away, they have together become worthless; there is no one who does good, not even one." (Rom 3:10-12)

It may sound too resolute and outspoken. The Bible teaches total depravity, which is the extreme version of the latter from above. It is "total" because, being compared to God's righteousness, we are so depraved that nothing good can come out of us. We are without even the slightest chance to be saved-- this is dreadful, yet it is the reality of us depraved men. Because of sin, nature has become so corrupt that all men have died to righteousness. This is the way God sees us. How serious and terrifying!

- all mankind by their fall lost communion with God
  - under his wrath and curse
  - made liable...
    - to all miseries in this life
    - to death itself
    - to the pains of hell for ever

Q19 What is the misery of that estate whereinto man fell?

A19 All mankind by their fall lost communion with God,[1]

are under his wrath and curse,[2, 3]

and so made liable to all miseries in this life,

to death itself,

and to the pains of hell for ever.[4, 5, 6]

1.
Genesis 3:8, 10, 24

And they heard the voice of the Lord God walking in the garden in the cool of the day: and Adam and his wife **hid themselves from the presence of the Lord God** amongst the trees of the garden...... And he said, I heard thy voice in the garden, and I was afraid, **because I was naked; and I hid myself......So he drove out the man; and he placed at the east of the garden of Eden Cherubims, and a flaming sword which turned every way,** **to keep the way of the tree of life**.

2.
Ephesians 2:2-3

Wherein in time past ye walked according to the course of this world, according to the prince of the power of the air, the spirit that now worketh in the children of disobedience: Among whom also we all had our conversation in times past in the lusts of our flesh, fulfilling the desires of the flesh and of the mind; **and were by nature the children of wrath, even as others**.

3.
Galatians 3:10

For as many as are of the works of the law are under the curse: for it is written, **Cursed is every one that continueth not in all things which are written in the book of the law to do them**.

5.
Romans 6:23
For **the wages of sin is death**; but the gift of God is eternal life through Jesus Christ our Lord.

4.
Lamentations 3:39

Wherefore doth a living man complain, **a man for the punishment of his sins?**

6.
Matthew 25:41, 46

Then shall he say also unto them on the left hand, **Depart from me, ye cursed, into everlasting fire, prepared for the devil and his angels......And these shall go away into everlasting punishment**: but the righteous into life eternal.

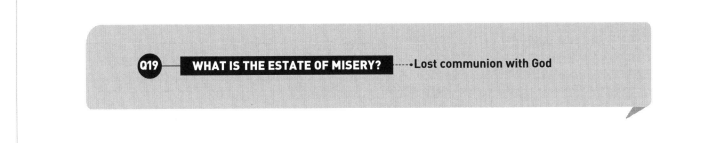

We are studying the result of the fall—the estate of sin and misery. Q18 has dealt with the former, and now Q19 covers the latter listing what consists of that misery. Inserting the preposition by this question first and foremost reminds us of what caused this misery. By the fall, we lost communion with God, and ultimately this brought us to the place of misery. What follow is the detailed contents of the misery written in four phrases.

For those who do not know it, they may think their life is full and have only standard fears about death as a way of avoiding the topic of the afterlife. Yet what the Shorter Catechism constantly reminds us of is that we are in this estate of misery not only during this life but also at death and even after. Even though it is not seen, God's wrath is far reaching and we are now under punishment. This is the misery.

God is not distant or far away being unable to locate the sinner, but He is right before us looking into the deepest part of our soul and the punishment reaches us even to our bones. This better be acknowledged now, if it has not already been.

The reminder, the cause of this misery is the lost communion with God, helps us recall that the supreme good of man is God and only God. We cannot find our rest in any other place. The Shorter Catechism constantly brings up Q1 as it proceeds.

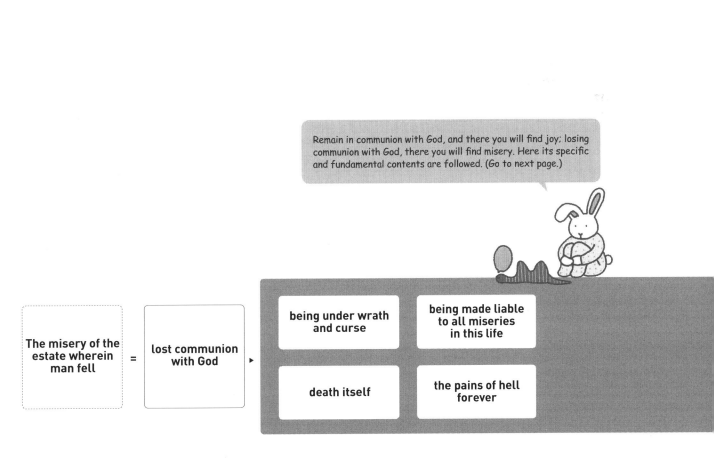

Remain in communion with God, and there you will find joy; losing communion with God, there you will find misery. Here its specific and fundamental contents are followed. (Go to next page.)

The misery of the estate wherein man fell = lost communion with God ▸ being under wrath and curse / being made liable to all miseries in this life / death itself / the pains of hell forever

LOST COMMUNION WITH GOD

1. BEING UNDER WRATH AND CURSE

Is there anything more sorrowful, miserable, and pitiful than that we are under God's wrath and curse after trading away the love of such a good God? Our Father God looks at us with His wrathful face, and we have no way to avoid His curse coming upon us. Nothing is more miserable than this. How horrific that this misery is currently influencing the fallen mankind!

2. BEING MADE LIABLE TO ALL MISERIES IN THIS LIFE

This is for everyone. There is no way to escape until the day we die. No one can say, "Enough is enough. No more miseries for me." Everyone in his own way continues to encounter miseries in this life. They come in various forms and ways. There is no exception even with those who appear to have it all in our eyes. Thus, when disaster, disease, and accident come our way, we should remind ourselves that they are God's penalty.

3. DEATH ITSELF

Every man dies. Yet even so, this is not natural. Death is a form of misery given to us due to the fall. Death is the worst punishment of all. Man is created worthy of eternal life. Thus, the death of our body is neither natural nor normal. This is something abnormal, which is given to us as punishment.

4. THE PAINS OF HELL FOREVER

Just the thought of hell should make every one resist to go to such a place. The images used for hell in both the Bible and other literature are so appalling. The Divine Comedy written by Dante is well known for its description of hell and, it includes various and endless pains. Every time we are reminded of this, we become petrified and ever more unwilling to go to this place.

Yet the significance of hell is not in such pains, for example, being bitten by snakes and thrown into fire, but in eternal severance from the fellowship with God. Just like heaven, hell is eternal.

ABOVE ARE FOUR THINGS THE MISERY CONSISTS OF IN REALITY.

Those, who do not know the above, cannot possess more than

a general understanding, and also cannot help but live without knowing that he is in an estate of misery. All they can hope for is a morally good life, in which they could bring up the following questions.

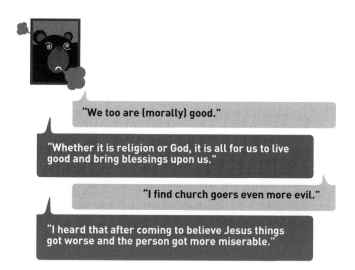

"We too are (morally) good."

"Whether it is religion or God, it is all for us to live good and bring blessings upon us."

"I find church goers even more evil."

"I heard that after coming to believe Jesus things got worse and the person got more miserable."

They could be right. Yet all of these are merely phenomenon. It is only to see what is being seen. "After coming to Christ, the whole family came to experience hardship; it is Buddha that gives you wealth." However, what the Bible points out is the essence, which is not being seen. No matter how much one gets to eat, possesses, and enjoys in life, if he is separated from God, then his life is miserable. This is equally true the other way around. After going to church, one's business has been a success and life blossomed, and when inviting others to church, such people tend to mention the blessings of wealth, long life, a peaceful mind, a united family, and the rest of body/mind. Yet these also are not the essence. We cannot say anything about one's relationship with God from only what is being seen.

BEING SEPARATED FROM GOD, LIFE IS ONLY MISERABLE

We have to be able to discern the essence. Even at this moment, God's warning and wrath are continuing. You may think that your life is intact and you are making the best of it while enjoying weekend get-aways and having your own way. Yet you have to immediately repent and turn around. As much as one has lived without God, he has lost his life and lived in a miserable state. Some may say "I wish I had spent more time in the world and come to believe in God in later years." I wish this were only a joke. The earlier we come to believe in God, the better it is for us. This must be acknowledged.

> **Is disaster a punishment?**
> **Disease, accident, or disaster occurs also to us, the saved. While we understand this as a punishment for non-believers, what should we make of this?**
> **Are we being punished because we also are under the wrath and curse?**

It needs not be a huge disaster or accident, but any trouble can cause Christians to wonder whether this might be punishment for their sin. If the trouble continues, it can make some even doubt whether God has abandoned them. Yet as moving along with the Shorter Catechism, we have to build a proper understanding of the issue of disaster. For nonbelievers, it could be a punishment caused by God's wrath and curse. Yet this is not so with believers any longer. It should be understood more as a gentle rebuke from God to help us do right. It may appear to be the same rod, yet they are completely different. It is the rod of love. Regarding this, we will get a chance to study more in depth in the section of sanctification.

> **Totally depraved man does not have any goodness in him?**
> **Is man a monster of entirely pure evil? Like Satan?**

"Total" should be understood as referring to scope rather than degree. This means every aspect of man has been corrupted by the fall. That is why sometimes even totally depraved man can do good deeds and be seen without any evil.

> **What about saints, (morally) good people, and philanthropists?**
> **If all men are depraved and all good comes only from God, then what do we make of the goodness of these people? Is it a counterfeit?**

on, God covers evildoers with goodness. Thus, no matter how saint-like one is, if God removes His grace from him, he remains as only a sinful man. Sin is that fearful.

God watches over believers with an exceptional care, yet provides general grace to all mankind. God does not govern this world while keeping sunshine from nonbelievers and giving only downpours on the way of nonbelievers. What would happen to this earth if God holds off sunshine from the dwelling places of nonbelievers? Or gives oxygen for believers and carbon dioxide for nonbelievers? This is not the way of God. If this were so, no one would survive. No society would be able to stand. God provides His general grace first to preserve this world to the day He wants and second due to His long patient fatherly heart. It must be acknowledged that we are only able to walk the street because of God's care.

It is not because they are good themselves but covered by God's grace. God allows goodness even though it is not perfect. In order to maintain this world, God can provide good character to evildoers. And we are the reason that He does so. In order to protect believers, and sometimes to prompt them to press

AFTER THE FIRST SIN AND THE FALL, NOW WHAT IS LEFT FOR US?

We just learned about the sin and fall of man, which at once should alert those who were paying attention, "We have to do something. Otherwise, we are all done for! We are all doomed!" "I cannot bear another minute not doing anything about who I have become because of the first sin and the fall." After hearing what Apostle Peter had to say, people were cut to the heart and said "Brothers, what shall we do?" And this is how we should respond to what we came to know—where we stand apart from salvation! Acknowledgement of who we are must lead us to crying out for help. Salvation belongs to those.

However, things are not that simple. For salvation is not something we can work for ourselves by putting our mind to it. There is absolutely no way. How come? Because we all are dead. Due to the fall of man, we all are made dead. What can corpses do for themselves? Nothing! Even though the way was made and we were invited, none of us the corpses can rise and come forward. Corpses have no means to do so—neither ears to hear nor limbs to walk. Our sinfulness is that grave and great.

There is no way from our side. Then what is left? The way from God's side. In other words, He has to come to us.

In that sense, the Shorter Catechism makes the perfect transition to Q20 *"Covenant of Grace"* where we find hope in His grace alone. If everything could be described as inevitable in His decrees, then regarding whatsoever is to come, we have to turn our eyes to Him alone. Any other means will come to naught.

Nothing can change the fact that Adam took the fruit in the Garden. However, that doesn't mean nothing can be done to reverse the tragic fate of man. What a comfort we have that there are more Q and As we can delve into!

There is nothing we can do! What should we do?

Let's head to the next question! We could find something there!

Discussion Questions

❶ Read 1 Sam 15:22 and discuss what "To obey is better than sacrifice" means.

❷ Why is Adam's sin ours? Why is it not only good for us but grace?

❸ Why is it important to know for sure that man is in a place of sin and misery?

❹ In which sense does this chapter give us the reason to be grateful?

[Visualize by Mapping]

Make your own review by drawing a mindmap for the Q and As you have learned so far.

"CHRISTIANS SAY THAT SOME ARE SAVED WHILE OTHERS ARE PASSED.
HOW CAN A GOD OF LOVE DO SUCH A THING?"
"JESUS SUFFERED, YET WASN'T THAT JUST A SHOW?
IF JESUS WERE GOD, EVEN HUNGER AND CRUCIFIXION COULDN'T HAVE HURT HIM."
"WHO ON EARTH DID JESUS SAVE? MANKIND STILL SUFFERS FROM DISEASE, POVERTY, AND
DISASTERS. NOTHING SEEMS TO BE DIFFERENT..."

Now we are about to study what salvation is.
"Jesus died on the cross for our sins and rose
again." Anyone who has gone to church has heard
this so many times that this may sound cliché.
Even nonbelievers know this. Yet this teaching
is so unclear for many that it is one of the most
vulnerable to the attack of heresies.

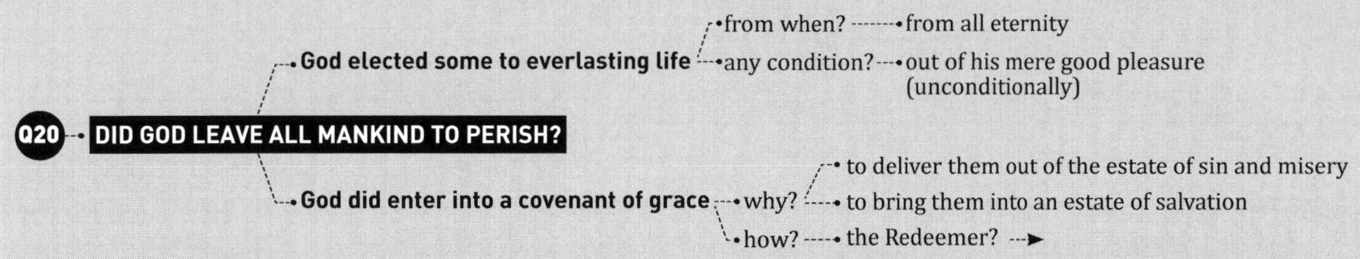

Q20 DID GOD LEAVE ALL MANKIND TO PERISH?

God elected some to everlasting life
- from when? ----- from all eternity
- any condition? --- out of his mere good pleasure (unconditionally)

God did enter into a covenant of grace
- why? --- to deliver them out of the estate of sin and misery
- to bring them into an estate of salvation
- how? --- the Redeemer? ➤

Q20 Did God leave all mankind to perish
in the estate of sin and misery?

A20 God having, out of his mere good pleasure,
from all eternity, elected some to everlasting life,[1]
did enter into a covenant of grace,
to deliver them out of the estate of sin and misery,
and to bring them into an estate of salvation
by a Redeemer.[2, 3]

1.
Ephesians 1:4

According as he hath **chosen us in him before the foundation of the world, that we should be holy and without blame before him in love**.

2.
Romans 3:20-22

Therefore by the deeds of the law there shall no flesh be justified in his sight: for by the law is the knowledge of sin. But now **the righteousness of God without the law is manifested**, being witnessed by the law and the prophets; Even **the righteousness of God which is by faith of Jesus Christ unto all and upon all them that believe**: for there is no difference.

3.
Galatians 3:21-22

Is the law then against the promises of God? God forbid: for if there had been a law given which could have given life, verily righteousness should have been by the law. But the scripture hath concluded all under sin, **that the promise by faith of Jesus Christ might be given to them that believe**.

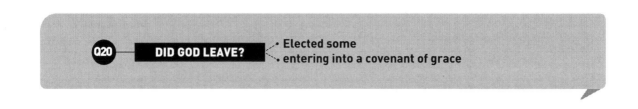

"DID GOD LEAVE ALL MANKIND TO PERISH?"

Being surprised by the fall previously taught, one burst out with this question of 20. Fortunately the answer is "No" and contains what God has done with this. First, God elected some to everlasting life and second, He entered into a covenant of grace. These were to deliver them out of the estate of sin and misery and to bring them into an estate of salvation. As the means of this, the word, a Redeemer, emerged. This is very fortunately the answer to Q20.

> ***Redeemer**: The word originates from the ancient slave market and refers to the one who by the payment gains the freedom of a slave.

Q20 follows Q19. What we have to be mindful of is that we just had our feet on the teaching of the fall. Learning the result of the fall, everyone must have groaned "Oh I so want to get out of this place." "Something must be done before it comes to an end as it is." In the context of such groans, Q20 emerged. "What if God left us just as we were? What if He did? Oh no…"

However, Q20 has something interesting. The focus of this question is not on "Then, what should we do now?" When any problem occurs, we tend to gather together to discuss "What we are to do." Yet this is not the way Q20 responded. Because we cannot. Why? Because we are dead, and that is why we cannot gather to discuss the countermeasures to this problem.

It has been mentioned several times before, yet it is worth repeating. For us to recognize our current estate without any error, let me once again reiterate.

What is being dead and living? In the estate of sin, we may be able to breathe but this is not living. "Because of the fall, now we have to live without God. It is unfortunate, but we can surely make lemonade with it." This is not how it works. With this severed relationship with God, we are dead.

In the same way, only when we live with God, we get to truly live. As creation has taught, we are created in God's image for us to love and live with God forever. However, as the fall has taught, such an image was destroyed which caused us to plunge into an estate where we cannot live with God. Being fallen, being severed from the relationship with God, and dead—this is what we have become. The fall has brought this enormous gap, which cannot be overcome and has made us completely unacceptable. It is so not only as God sees it but even from our perspective that things seem hopeless.

In this context, Q20 brings its focus onto God once again. It is not about "What we have to do now," but "What God has done." There is nothing we can do and we cannot do anything. Only God can do whatever and however for us who are left with no countermeasures.

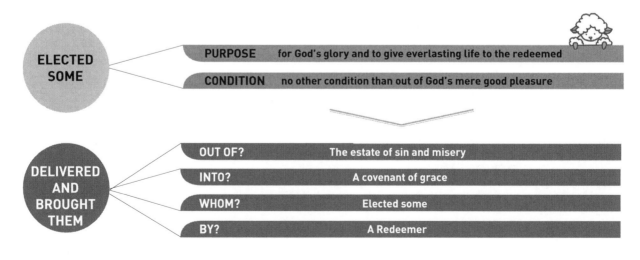

ELECTED SOME

PURPOSE — for God's glory and to give everlasting life to the redeemed

CONDITION — no other condition than out of God's mere good pleasure

DELIVERED AND BROUGHT THEM

OUT OF? — The estate of sin and misery

INTO? — A covenant of grace

WHOM? — Elected some

BY? — A Redeemer

"FOCUS"

On what are your eyes and interests? This is a very important question. Everyone is heading somewhere. We are just like an auto focus camera, which constantly works its lenses until it finds the focus. If possible, we have to bring our focus onto the right direction, which would bring the greatest blessing onto us.

Yet being only a word of slogan, this will have no meaning to it. **Truth requires concrete evidence in real life**. For example, we keep the Lord's Day holy. Why is that? Keeping the Lord's Day holy is a faith practice by which we make sure the focus is onto the right direction. The Lord's Day could be a symbol or a sample by which we present eternal rest on this earth. Eternal rest is the rest of the kingdom we are eventually heading toward and of a new heaven and a new earth where we will be able to see God face to face forever.

It does not merely mean that we get to be restored to the original state of creation being redeemed from the estate of the fall. Restoration to when man used to eat fruit and enjoy the company of orangutans? There should be much more to it than that. Going to church and having a full day of rest on Sundays are **to acknowledge with one's life that his focus is not on things of this world and he is living his life with the hope for God's Kingdom**. In such a context, keeping the Lord's Day holy could be the confession of faith and practice of one who is already a citizen of God's Kingdom. "God, You only are my rest and I am heading towards you." By keeping the Lord's Day holy, one gets to confess and prove his faith before himself, his neighbor, the entire world, and God in a practical way.

Our ultimate directing point should not be on the labor on this earth (all material things) but on the rest we have in life with God. It is not right that for six days we live for this world, and only on the seventh day we take the rest and offer that day to God. All seven days belong to God. We should re-examine what our focus, the chief interest and the end of our life, is.

HE DID NOT LEAVE

Fortunately God did not leave us. Q20 states two things. God elected some to everlasting life and entered into a covenant of grace. And its purpose was to deliver them out of sin and misery and bring them into an estate of salvation. That is the heart of Q20.

Mankind was at the point of being destroyed all together, yet God did not leave them as they were but out of His mere love and mercy brought them into the place of salvation. It was only out of His love and mercy. In fact, God once asked a question "Where are you?" toward the man who being fallen was avoiding God then, (Gen 3:9) and this question itself reveals God's grace.

Originally, we had to die all together because of sin, yet among them, God elected some. **This is eternal life that Q12 has previously taught**. Even though there has been the fall in between (Q13-19), God's special decree toward man is still being executed.

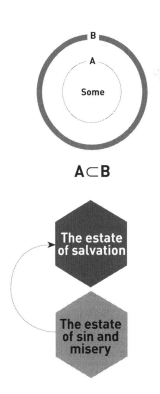

A ⊂ B

GOD ELECTED SPECIFIC OBJECTS OF HIS LOVE

It is necessary to understand the election in the context of what has been taught up to this point. Please recall what you have learned about God's decrees. Everything in this world is for God's glory. And this applies to our beings as well. God wanted us to give perfect obedience to Him. In other words, God called us to live with Him "in love." However, let alone giving perfect obedience, man right away sinned against God. Because God is just, He cannot abide with such sinning of man at all. The wages of sin is death. At the moment Adam disobeyed God, all men died spiritually. Yet God brought some to life.

ELECTION AND REPROBATION

Why did God elect only specific ones? For those not elected, it is so cruel. Yet this is not strange, given God's attributes.

A. BECAUSE OF HIS ATTRIBUTE OF JUSTICE, HE CANNOT ACCEPT SIN

Words, such as not being elected, being passed, or reprobation, offer us little sympathy; they throw us into a shock. Yet we have to admit even this brings glory to God. God promises eternal life on the condition of perfect obedience and makes it clear if one disobeys he should not receive eternal life, which is in other words death. That is why men die.

To understand this, God's attributes must be recalled. (Refer to Q4) God cannot babble nonsense, and eating the fruit was a frontal attack on God's words, which was hard to overlook. Just according to God's words and warning, His justice is being brought forth.

B. BECAUSE OF HIS ATTRIBUTE OF OMNISCIENCE AND OMNIPOTENCE, HE FREELY CHOOSES AND EXECUTES

God knows everything. Both the Bible and our life experience confirms that not everyone gets to be saved. If God wanted for all to be saved but only some got to be saved, then it defies God's attribute of omnipotence. Anything that omnipotent God wanted and planned will come to pass. That is how we can come to know God predestined those to be saved and those not, and saves them accordingly. *"And those he predestined, he also called; those he called, he also justified; those he justified, he also glorified." (Rom 8:30)* God saves the ones whom He predestined to save and does so unto the end.

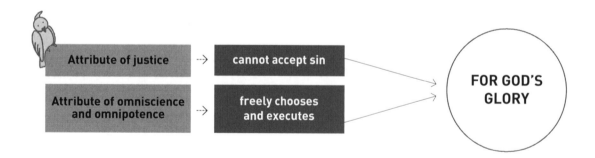

UNCONDITIONAL ELECTION

Then who gets to be saved and who does not? The answer is given: it is out of God's mere good pleasure. The criterion of God's election is purely on God's will and does not depend on us at all. Election is not made based on any condition of ours. God does not have any implicit conditions in His election--neither appointees nor rounds of election, but it is made out of God's mere will. Good people or bad people, those who have read the Bible once or twice, how much sin one committed during his life, and so on… these cannot be its condition.

In fact, there is nothing we can present as our merit before God. We may compare apples and oranges among ourselves, yet if we saw this world from a plane, things would look pretty much the same—What of ours can look good enough to God?

This is even more so if we are reminded that we are dead in our sin. There is nothing we can boast about.

However, such an intellectual understanding is not enough. This must bring an acknowledgement in us that this unconditional election reflects the depth of God's love. Election itself is love, yet that its condition is not on us but on God is also love. If the conditions were argued, the level of this election would be very low, and if this were all there was to it and this were God, then we would indeed be miserable. If God chose by weighing His gains and losses, then He must be very cruel. If it were up to us alone, then because of our inability, we must have fallen at once into despair. For we have nothing.

This should be more so to the intellectually immature who cannot hear and understand the Word. They will be shut off all together. Both those who do not have the ears to hear and the disabled who can neither understand nor make a rational judgment will be excluded from God's election, and this is just as cruel as the Spartans who abandoned their newborns if they did not appear strong enough.

God is not like that. God transcends the level we imagine; He is much deeper. All we could hope is for this election to be fair. Yet not knowing such a hope of fairness could cause a reverse effect on ourselves.

DID GOD INVITE ALL?

A different teaching from the Shorter Catechism has been widely spread. Being perfectly capable, God not only wants to save but actually invites everyone into salvation. If any man accepts such an invitation of God, he will be saved; if not, then there will be no salvation for him. Such an understanding calls for a closer look. "What if God invited one, yet he refuses?" Then God wouldn't be all-powerful. This God would not be the God we know through the Bible. In many tracts, it is recorded, "Everyone is invited. It is a done deal only if you accept Him. Now invite Him into your heart." Yet this is not actually true. What comes before man's acceptance is God's election—only those who are elected by God can come to accept Christ. Care is required on our parts.

Then, why did God elect only some? It is only out of His mere good pleasure. No other reasons are needed, and there is no better answer to it. Come to think of it, God might have wanted us to know what genuine love is. Genuine love always accompanies election. For example, we do not love all and choose only one to be our spouse and make a family with him or her. In such a sense, God's election has to make us all the more grateful. He did not pay any attention to our social status, intelligence, and appearance, but without any condition, He chose us.

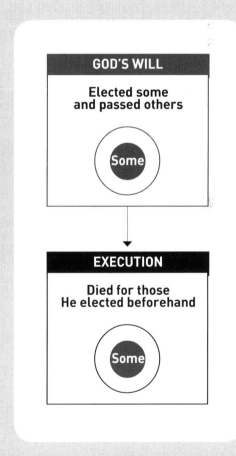

THE MEANING OF SALVATION

So far the election has been covered. Let us continue with the remaining answer of Q20. God elected some, delivered them, and brought them into an estate of salvation. What does this mean?

What is salvation? Some may offer only the literal meaning of it—being saved. Yet from where to where this has occurred is more important. In other words, from which estate to which estate has the change been made? This is not mere restoration to the previous estate. Salvation is more than a child walking with his mom, by mistake stepping into the mire, and his mom, being surprised, scooping him out at once, washing him off, and both getting back on the way.

As has been taught, the fall is death. Salvation is life. The distance between the fall and salvation is as far as between death and life. This is the matter of life and death. This is the change from the estate of the worst (the estate of death which has nothing worse) to the best (the place to be with God). It is not easy to bridge the gulf between these two. That is why a Redeemer appears in the end. You may recall the work "redeemer" originates from the ancient slave market and refers to the one who by the payment gains the freedom of a slave. Just like this, **a Redeemer delivered us from the estate in which we were destined to die and brought us into the place of life**.

This is also called mediation. To mediate is to reconcile this fatally severed relationship between men and God. By this Redeemer's blood and death made on behalf of men, our relationship with God is restored and maintained.

WHO IS THIS REDEEMER?

Then, who is this Redeemer who plays such a necessary and precious role of mediator for us. It may sound redundant, but we have to ask. Regarding what Q20 teaches, we cannot just take this for granted. Instead, we have to constantly ask questions of why after why. This is essential for accurate knowledge. And this also reflects the importance of the question at hand. This is what the Shorter Catechism continuously answers. For example, Q21 offers the answer to the question, "Who is the Redeemer?" quite in detail.

Here the foundation of our faith is reinforced through the expression of the Shorter Catechism.

What must be done for salvation? The main subject embedded in this question is "I". Another way to ask this question is "What should I do to gain salvation?" Yet there is nothing you can do. There is only the Redeemer.

In salvation, there is nothing, not even a little part, that I have done myself. It is given only through God's love and mercy!

Of course, the proper attitude of a believer who has been given such a salvation should be an active one. He is now responsible for a humble life only in God's love and mercy. He may fail every time, yet he must not quit. God predestined and gave the grace of salvation in which all the work appear to be done by God alone, yet in the meantime He demands faith from us and leads us to believe. Yet with such a demand, He gave His promised Spirit. Preparing all necessities, He made us believe and enabled holy obedience; for this reason, all we have to do is to confess that He has done it all and praise Him.

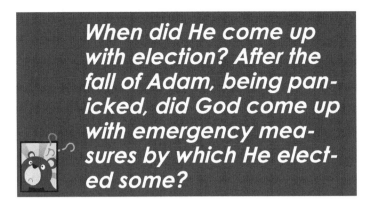

When did He come up with election? After the fall of Adam, being panicked, did God come up with emergency measures by which He elected some?

The Catechism's answer includes the phrase, "from all eternity." This is an unusual expression. Seen in our chronic time, the covenant of life with Adam was made at the time of creation, and the covenant of grace is after the fall as if it were a follow up measure impetuously trying to save him. Yet while learning about God's attributes, we were reassured that God knows the future like the past. Also from learning about God's decrees, we were reminded of God's notion of time. God is not restricted by time and place but rather transcends them. Whether it is the eternity before, the present, or the eternity after, He can plan, govern, and execute. The covenant of grace is also the plan from all eternity. If seen from our perspective, **this is before the fall of man**. Being offended by the fall, He did not come to elect only some; instead, from all eternity He elected those to be redeemed to have eternal life. Now many questions can follow. Let's take a look one by one. :)

If all are included in God's decrees, then did God also predestine those to be saved and those not?

Of course, it is also predestined. If all things in this world are predestined, then the matter of our salvation should be as well. In fact, this is the heart of God's predestination. Yet for our mind to understand this part, a deep understanding of sin and the fall must precede. Without the accurate knowledge of being dead, it would be tough to comprehend what being alive again means. The beginning is to acknowledge that, being dead, we deserved only death and were unworthy of election and mercy. This should be our starting point.

However, among those worthy only of reprobation, God, out of His grace, elected some. For this reason the elected become only grateful. There was no condition. We came alive not because we believed but because He elected, raised us from the dead, and enabled us to believe. Some may imagine as if God were cheering us on saying, "Come on! You can do this." And somehow this woke us up, and we came to say "Yes, I believe it," to which God responded, "Oh, this is good that you came to believe. Now come here, and I will save you." This is not how this works, simply because we were dead. For the dead, it is not even an option to listen and rise. It is completely inappropriate to see our salvation as if all deserved life yet God had to abandon some and to question His reason for this. If you have such a question, I'd recommend you to go **back to Q7**.

He is known to be God of love. Why does He not simply forgive everyone? Why does He require everyone to pay for their sins?

Because God is also God of justice. While we learned "What man is to believe concerning God," every question regarding God's attributes should lead us back to Q4. This is the hub. What comes in the first part of the Shorter Catechism will serve as the principles to which we can always go back.

The purpose is **to praise the glory of His justice**. To have man pay for their sins is to praise the glory of His righteousness. God of justice cannot condone any sins, and there should be no exemption.

"I am the LORD your God; consecrate yourselves and be holy, because I am holy." (Lev 11:44)

"For it is written: 'Be holy, because I am holy.'" (1 Pet 1:16)

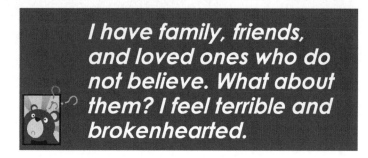

I have family, friends, and loved ones who do not believe. What about them? I feel terrible and brokenhearted.

You should. We all should. If God did not elect, there is nothing we can do. Yet, there is one thing that we should not forget. The heart of the covenant of grace is that He elected. And another part is that **this election is not known to us**. That is why we should not be rash at all.

"My family does not go to church… They are the children of wrath and in the estate of misery…" This is enough to make anyone feel hopeless. However, we have to remain hopeful that they might be in the process of God's salvation. Praying without ceasing in anticipation and hope, we have to share the gospel with them as the chances come. This may continue till the end of one's life without any success. They may fall into heresy and continue to live in misery. However, the end of one's life is not known to us (Refer to Q35), and this should make us hopeful. He may come to God only at the end of his life, yet God could use him in His own way for His church. We can pray for them reminding ourselves of that. For both the believers and nonbelievers, it is good for all humankind to be near to God. No matter who he is, we can pray he comes before God.

I am the only believer in my family. Should I not find reassurance in "You and your household will be saved"?

Acts 16:31 is primarily given to the jailer. The Bible should not be rashly generalized. We may anticipate and hope for such a blessing, yet it is very perilous to take the Bible, generalize it, and interpret it as we wish. The following verse (v.32) must also be figured into the context: "Then they spoke the word of the Lord to him and to all the others in his house." It is our responsibility to pass down what is passed down to us. Verse 31 can make us complacent, yet we have to be on guard with more fervent prayer as being faithful to our responsibility. This includes striving for a godly life, treating others well, and being the aroma of Christ.

In the perspective of God's Kingdom, all are considered as one member and brothers/sisters. Being a sample institution given for us to foretaste the coming kingdom while on this earth, our earthly family will transcend the current relationship or norm in the heaven. (Matt 22:24-30) This should make us feel less burdened, taking away such worries for example as, "I have to bring at least my own family to heaven." Rather, we can strive to establish the proper fellowship among all believers and the holy church. **If we begin to live a righteous life and such people gather to form a church enjoying their fellowship, then our family members who stay closest to us will be able to witness what heaven is like**. What it takes for them to see God through us is sometimes only a word or a small deed. When we follow God's Word in every aspect of our lives, our family comes to recognize and admit, "I wonder what makes him different. He is not like me." This would be the most aggressive form of evangelism.

As previously taught, it is through the Word that we glean the knowledge of God. The Bible teaches the Word and instructs us about God's will through the law. Thus, when we begin to live according to the law, people around us will see such a life and be able to experience the will of God. God's Word should be revealed through our lives.

"I will also make you a light for the Gentiles, that you may bring my salvation to the ends of the earth.'" (Isa 49:6b)

"But you are a chosen people, a royal priesthood, a holy nation, a people belonging to God, that you may declare the praises of him who called you out of darkness into his wonderful light." (1 Pet 2:9)

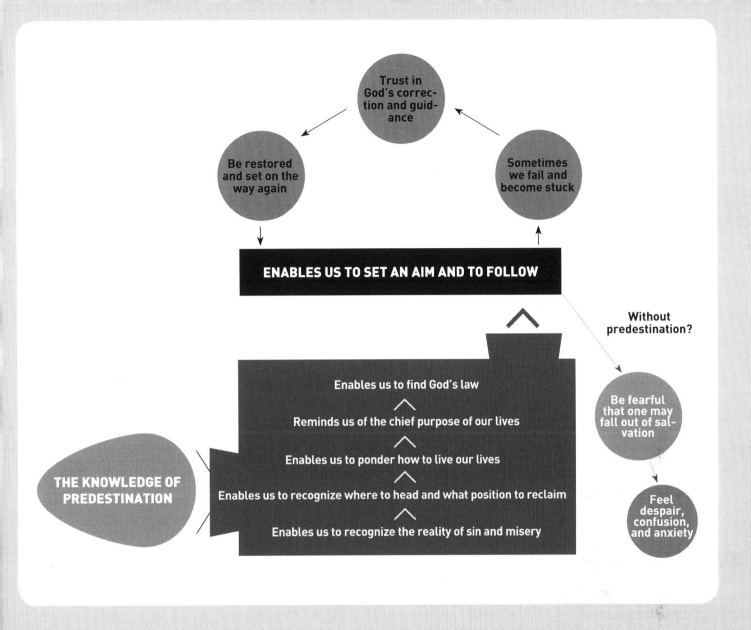

The Knowledge of Predestination:
- Enables us to find God's law
- Reminds us of the chief purpose of our lives
- Enables us to ponder how to live our lives
- Enables us to recognize where to head and what position to reclaim
- Enables us to recognize the reality of sin and misery

ENABLES US TO SET AN AIM AND TO FOLLOW

Trust in God's correction and guidance → Be restored and set on the way again → Sometimes we fail and become stuck → Trust in God's correction and guidance

Without predestination? → Be fearful that one may fall out of salvation → Feel despair, confusion, and anxiety

AN ALTERNATIVE TO PREDESTINATION?

If not for predestination, the matter of salvation falls into men's hands. The final say in salvation is found in the act of man's belief, and this makes man chief commander. This is exactly against the Bible. Remind yourself of the premises previously taught. God holds absolute power and His decrees are perfect and unchanging. This also applies to His election and salvation. God chooses those who would believe; He does not change His will just based on our decision or wait for our decision with great anxiety. This is clearly stipulated in many Bible-based creeds and catechisms.

All whom God chose will eventually come to believe. He chooses whom He loves and calls. Who can say "No" when He calls? Who can disobey when He commands? God is God, and we are not. We may think we can freely make our choices, even resist, yet working in all environments and circumstances, God takes all He chose and makes them believe Him in His providence.

We may never understand God's heart. We may never measure its depth. Suffice it to say that such a God called you and loves you.

For a deeper understanding, refer to The Cross of Christ by John Stott.

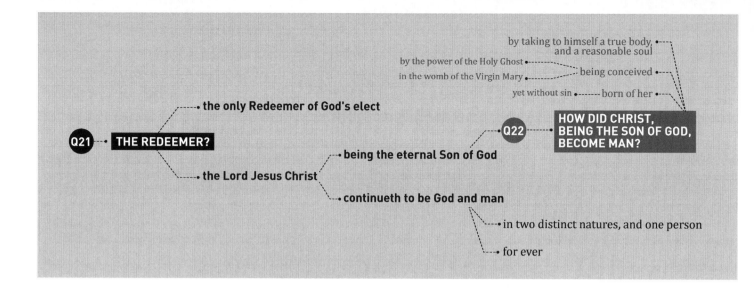

Q21 Who is the Redeemer of God's elect?

A21 The only Redeemer of God's elect is
the Lord Jesus Christ,[1]
who, being the eternal Son of God,
became man,[2,3] and so was,
and continueth to be,
God and man
in two distinct natures, and one person,
for ever.[4,5,6,7]

1.
1 Timothy 2:5-6

For there is **one God, and one mediator between God and men, the man Christ Jesus**; Who gave himself **a ransom for all**, to be testified in due time.

2.
John 1:14

And **the Word was made flesh, and dwelt among us**, (and we beheld his glory, **the glory as of the only begotten of the Father**,) **full of grace and truth**.

3.
Galatians 4:4

But when the fulness of the time was come, **God sent forth his Son, made of a woman, made under the law.**

4.
Romans 9:5

Whose are the fathers, and of whom as concerning the flesh Christ came, **who is over all, God blessed for ever. Amen.**

5.
Luke 1:35

And the angel answered and said unto her, The Holy Ghost shall come upon thee, and the power of the Highest shall overshadow thee: therefore also that holy thing which shall be born of thee shall be called **the Son of God.**

6.
Colossians 2:9

For in him **dwelleth all the fulness of the Godhead bodily.**

7.
Hebrews 7:24-25

But this man, because he continueth ever, hath an unchangeable priesthood.

Wherefore he is able also to save them to the uttermost that come unto God by him, **seeing he ever liveth to make intercession for them.**

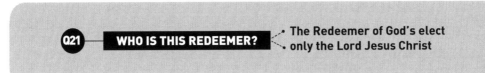

Everyone would have guessed Jesus Christ to this follow-up question, "Who is this Redeemer?" Then was this question necessary? This was to know this Redeemer more accurately. Is this Jesus God or man? Or neither? What in particular makes Him our Redeemer?

The answer is rather complicated. He, being Son of God, became man. What a mysterious saying! Even more mysterious is what follows that He continues to be so after the ascension and even after that.

What an unusual and special state He is in! Why does He have to be like this? Is there a particular purpose? We may wonder. Let us see more in detail.

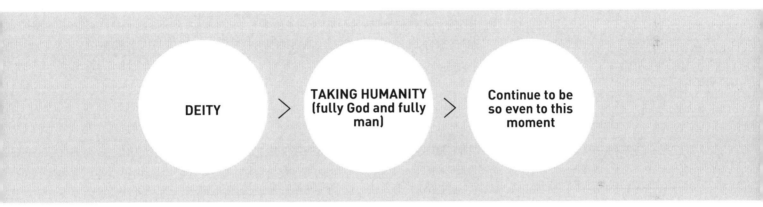

DEITY > TAKING HUMANITY (fully God and fully man) > Continue to be so even to this moment

THE SON OF GOD IS GIVEN FOR US

We have learned about redemption, and this is not performed on our part. It is not that we figure out our own way, but God has come to us. For this, God promised to give us a Redeemer who will redeem us. In such a context, Q21 poses the question "Who is this Redeemer?" And the answer to this question is the Lord Jesus Christ. Jesus Christ is our Redeemer and the only One.

Jesus Christ is a historical figure who existed.* As many have heard, it was about 2,000 years ago, Jesus came to the land of Israel, worked, was killed, rose again, and ascended to heaven. He was definitely a man. Yet He also is God. He is God the Son, about whom we have learned in the Trinity. Such a God came to us as a Redeemer. In His love, He laid Himself down. Man could not have done what He has done for us in His love. He is certainly a God.

For a deeper understanding, refer to The Case for Christ by Lee Strobel

JESUS + CHRIST

The name Jesus means "the One who saves His people from their sins." At first "His people" only referred the chosen ones from the Old Testament, yet later it came to be extended to the elect as we have learned in Q20. And the title Christ means "the anointed." In the past when kings and priests were appointed, oil had to be poured on their heads to proclaim that they are suitable for the office. This title in Jesus' name reveals His perfect suitability for the work of Redeemer who has to redeem us.

INCARNATION : THE QUALIFICATION OF THE REDEEMER

Now follows the qualification of our Redeemer. Q21 continues to explain that God, in order to truly save us, needs a Redeemer and this Redeemer has to pass very specific qualifications. This is also crucial to the question such as "Why can only Jesus be the mediator?" Here is also revealed the difference between what Christians believe and all other religions of the world that refuse to admit Jesus as the Redeemer.

This explains that the Redeemer is the eternal Son of God, and that He became man and continues to be so. What does "was so and continues to be" mean? Why does the mediator have to be both God and man? Why does He have to be God and man with both deity and humanity? This is tough to understand.

One qualification our Redeemer has to posses is that He must be fully man and fully God.

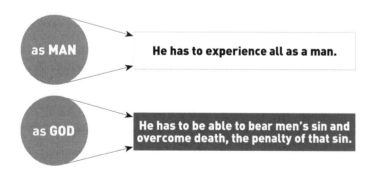

AS MAN:

Because He has to experience all as a man.
God loves man, yet how can a God love man who is only a creature. There is only one way to do this. God has to become a man. This was necessary for God to love man. After all, it was because of His love for us.

AS GOD:

At the same time, He has to be able to bear men's sin and overcome death, the penalty of that sin. As a man, it is impossible to endure God's wrath. It is impossible to conquer death and be resurrected.

> **Caution: This is two distinct natures but one person.**

After all, the qualification of the Redeemer has its single focus on this: that He must perfectly resolve our sin on our behalf yet at the same time plainly reveal the principles of God's love and justice. God demonstrated **His own love for us in loving us to death**. How great is God's love? He loved us to death. What more do we need to say?

"But God demonstrates his own love for us in this: While we were still sinners, Christ died for us." (Rom 5:8)

This is not so with other religions' gods. Their playground is completely separated from men's world. Would any of these gods die for man? Never! These gods rarely step into the world of men. If they do, it is only to satisfy their own greed or lust, which generally result in disaster. In other religions, it is usually a man who strives to be near to their god or become like him by overcoming their limits. In such efforts, all kinds of penance must be attempted. Oftentimes in extreme forms. Yet the way the Bible explains is love. God, having sympathy for us, came to us. More abounds His grace!

THIS CONTINUES EVEN TO THIS MOMENT

Okay, He sympathized once. Wasn't this enough so that He can keep humanity even to this moment in heaven? The Bible explains it is still for us to pray. Jesus did not take the form of man only for a while on this earth, but **even at this moment** He appears before God in the form of man **still praying for** **us** who due to weakness commit sins. Christ knows our weaknesses well.

For this reason, we always end our prayer saying "In the name of Jesus we pray." It is because of Him that our prayers could be lifted up to God. Indeed, nothing can be done apart from Jesus.

This will be dealt with more in detail in Q28, <Christ's exaltation>.

He could have loved us while remaining God.

God, because He loved us, became a man. This kind of explanation can frustrate some. Others can wonder whether such a complicated process was truly necessary for God to redeem us. Without becoming a man, God could have given us an assurance of His love. And this should have been enough.

The answer is "No." If God did not become a man, His love could not have been perfect. Of course it is not that God's love is not perfect; rather, it is that we, who are both weak and sinful, could not have come to believe such a love. It was to deliver His love that He became a man. It was to show His love and care for us. It was to truly **sympathize** with us.

To sympathize is to agree in heart and mind. Simply speaking, it is to feel what the other person feels and know what the other person knows. Here is an example. Who can be the best counselor? It is the one who has the same experience with the counseled. Because the counselor can effortlessly place himself in the shoes of the counseled.

Another example comes from parents-children relationship. We can come to understand the love of our own parents only after becoming parents ourselves. This is to sympathize.

Of course God created us. *(The LORD… who made you, who formed you in the womb, and who will help you—Isa 44:2)* In modern terms, God being the designer of the human genome map knows every detail about us. Yet He came down to the same level as us. It is indeed a great and amazing gesture of love which in turn makes everyone grateful.

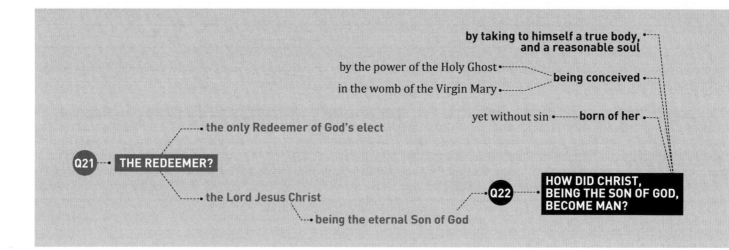

Q21 → **THE REDEEMER?**
- the only Redeemer of God's elect
- the Lord Jesus Christ
  - being the eternal Son of God

Q22 → **HOW DID CHRIST, BEING THE SON OF GOD, BECOME MAN?**
- by taking to himself a true body, and a reasonable soul
- being conceived
  - by the power of the Holy Ghost
  - in the womb of the Virgin Mary
- born of her
  - yet without sin

Q22 How did Christ, being the Son of God, become man?

A22 Christ, the Son of God, became man, by taking to himself a true body,[1, 2] and a reasonable soul,[3] being conceived by the power of the Holy Ghost, in the womb of the Virgin Mary, and born of her,[4, 5] yet without sin.[6, 7]

1.
Hebrews 2:14, 16

Forasmuch then as the children are partakers of flesh and blood, he also **himself likewise took part of the same**; that through death he might destroy him that had the power of death, that is, the devil......For verily he took not on him the nature of angels; but he **took on him the seed of Abraham.**

2.
Hebrews 10:5

Wherefore when he cometh into the world, he saith, Sacrifice and offering thou wouldest not, but **a body hast thou prepared me.**

3.
Matthew 26:38

Then saith he unto them, **My soul is exceeding sorrowful, even unto death**: tarry ye here, and watch with me.

4.
Luke 1:27, 31, 35, 42

To a virgin espoused to a man whose name was Joseph, of the house of David; and the virgin's name was Mary......And, behold, thou **shalt conceive in thy womb, and bring forth a son**, and shalt call his name **JESUS**......And the angel answered and said unto her, The Holy Ghost shall come upon thee, and the power of the Highest shall overshadow thee: therefore also that holy thing which shall be born of thee shall be called the Son of God.....And she spake out with a loud voice, and said, Blessed art thou among women, and **blessed is the fruit of thy womb.**

5.
Galatians 4:4

But when the fulness of the time was come, **God sent forth his Son, made of a woman, made under the law.**

6.
Hebrews 4:15

For we have not an high priest which cannot be touched with the feeling of our infirmities; but was in all points tempted like as we are, **yet without sin.**

7.
Hebrews 7:26

For such an high priest became us, who is holy, harmless, undefiled, **separate from sinners**, and made higher than the heavens.

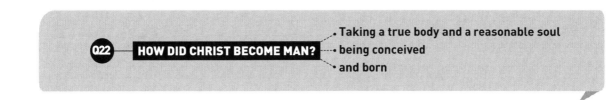

Things are getting complicated. Sentences are getting longer, and even worse, questions are now full of things tough to understand. It was tough enough that the Son of God became a man, but now He took a true body/a reasonable soul and one the top of that He was conceived by a virgin. This can be challenging for many. Yet through this chapter, you will get to see good reasons behind each one of these. God did not do any of these without reason.

We previously learned that we need a Redeemer, and here we get to carefully examine the qualifications of that Redeemer. Redemption is such a crucial matter to us that we need a perfect One for this to work properly.

Combining what we have learned in Q21 and Q22, let us delve in.

TRUE BODY AND REASONABLE SOUL

This highlights the fact Jesus came with the same humanity as us. He had a body just like ours and took on a rational and sensible soul. He became a man, not a ghost. He should not be imagined as a ghost coming into an empty body. It was neither a fraud nor magic, but truth.

In fact, this has caused many controversies throughout church history. For this reason, even after the Apostles' Creed, more creeds* had to follow to clarify things. These were to resolve suggestions such as "Jesus only appeared to be man" or "How can God take such a vulgar body?" If so, the pain of Jesus on this earth becomes a deception. If he did not, He just pretended to suffer.

1. Nicene Creed (325 AD)
2. Constantinople Creed (381 AD)
3. Chalcedonian Creed (451 AD)
4. Athanasian Creed (420-450 AD)

BEING CONCEIVED BY THE POWER
of the Holy Ghost, in the womb of the Virgin Mary…yet without sin

Jesus Christ had to be born as a sinless man. For this reason, He was not born in a conventional way yet was conceived by the Holy Spirit in the womb of the Virgin Mary. By the power of the Holy Spirit, Jesus was born with a sinless mind and nature.

This is a critical principle. What if someone, who has his own sin, wanted to redeem another? He would be unqualified. Only a sinless one can offer himself for another. A death-row convict so loved another death-row convict that he offered himself to die for him by pleading with the jailer, "I will take his place. Let him go." That is complete nonsense! Only the sinless One can be our Redeemer.

Discussion Questions

❶ Why did God choose us?

❷ How would you explain "God loved us first" relating it to previously taught Q13-19.

❸ List the qualifications of our Redeemer, and why do you think these are necessary for our salvation?

❹ "Believe and you will be saved." How can this be misleading?

❺ In which sense, does this chapter give us the reason to be grateful?

Westminster Abbey in London, UK

Westminster assembly was held in this building from 1643 to 1649. Westminster Shorter Catechism was written by the Scottish commissioners and the members of Westminster. Also, they produced important documents, like as "The Directory for the Publick Worship of God," "The Form of Presbyterial Church-Government," "Larger Catechisms," and "The Confession of Faith of the Westminster Assembly of Divines."

"HE COULD HAVE JUST FORGIVEN.
WHY DID HE HAVE TO MAKE THINGS SO COMPLICATED?"
"WHAT ABOUT THE BELIEVERS IN OLD TESTAMENT?
JESUS WASN'T EVEN BORN AT THAT TIME."
"THOSE WHO LIVED BEFORE JESUS COULDN'T HAVE HEARD OR KNOWN ABOUT HIM.
DID ALL OF THEM GO TO HELL?"
"IF JESUS STAYED WITH US AFTER HIS RESURRECTION,
ALL WOULD HAVE COME TO BELIEVE HIM.
DID HE HAVE TO GO BACK TO HEAVEN? IT IS SUCH A DISAPPOINTMENT."
"JESUS IS NOW SITTING AT THE RIGHT HAND OF GOD.
THEN, WHO IS WORKING NOW, ONLY THE SPIRIT?"

In the previous chapter, we have learned who the Redeemer is. Now it is time to learn what kind of work this Redeemer, Christ, does.

While learning about God, we have divided the study into two: the study of God Himself (Q4-6) and God's decrees (Q7-). This will be the same with the work of Christ. For this, two studies will be provided: What kind of work He has done (Q24-25) and in which state (Q26-28).

Q23 — WHAT OFFICES CHRIST EXECUTETH AS OUR REDEEMER?

offices
- a prophet — **Q24** →
- a priest — **Q25** →
- a king — **Q26** →

estate
- in his estate of humiliation — **Q27** →
- in his estate of exaltation — **Q28** →

Q23 What offices doth Christ execute as our Redeemer?

A23 Christ, as our Redeemer,
executeth the offices of a prophet, of a priest,
and of a king,
both in his estate of humiliation and exaltation. [1, 2, 3, 4, 5, 6, 7, 8, 9]

1.
Acts 3:21-22

Whom the heaven must receive until the times of restitution of all things, which God hath spoken by the mouth of all his holy prophets since the world began. For Moses truly said unto the fathers, **A prophet shall the Lord your God raise up unto you of your brethren**, like unto me; him shall ye hear in all things whatsoever he shall say unto you.

2.
Hebrews 12:25

See that ye refuse not him that speaketh. For if they escaped not who refused him that spake on earth, much more shall not we escape, if we turn away from him **that speaketh from heaven**: (Compare with 2 Corinthians 13:3)

3.
2 Corinthians 13:3

Since ye seek a proof of **Christ speaking in me**, which to you-ward is not weak, but is mighty in you.

4.
Hebrews 5:5-7

So also Christ glorified not himself **to be made an high priest**; but he that said unto him, Thou art my Son, to day have I begotten thee. **As he saith also in another place, Thou art a priest** for ever after the order of Melchisedec. Who in the days of his flesh, **when he had offered up prayers** and supplications with strong crying and tears unto him that was able to save him from death, and was heard in that he feared.

5.
Hebrews 7:25

Wherefore he is able also to save them to the uttermost that come unto God by him, seeing he ever liveth to make intercession for them.

6.
Psalms 2:6

Yet **have I set my king** upon my holy hill of Zion.

7.
Isaiah 9:6-7

For unto us a child is born, unto us a son is given: and **the government shall be upon his shoulder**: and his name shall be called Wonderful, Counsellor, The mighty God, The everlasting Father, **The Prince of Peace**. Of the increase of his government and peace there shall be no end, upon the throne of David, and upon **his kingdom**, to order it, and to establish it with judgment and with justice from henceforth even for ever. The zeal of the Lord of hosts will perform this.

8.
Matthew 21:5

Tell ye the daughter of Sion, **Behold, thy King cometh** unto thee, meek, and sitting upon an ass, and a colt the foal of an ass.

9.
Psalm 2:8-11

Ask of me, and I shall give thee the heathen for thine inheritance, and the uttermost parts of the earth for thy possession. **Thou shalt break them with a rod of iron; thou shalt dash them in pieces** like a potter's vessel. Be wise now therefore, O ye kings: be instructed, ye judges of the earth. **Serve the Lord** with fear, and rejoice with trembling.

Q23 functions as the overview of what comes ahead in Q24-28. Use the above mindmap to familiarize yourself with the overall flow of the Shorter Catechism.

The Shorter Catechism explains the work of Christ in three offices--prophet, priest, and king and in two estate--humiliation and exaltation. Through the last 2,000 year long history, the Church has been searching for an unbiased and better way to deliver this work of Christ--what Christ has done on this earth, and the doctrine at hand is heavily in debt to such an effort.

For both the disciples of Jesus and the teachers of the early church, the eyewitness accounts were probably more than enough; yet as time passed, a more formulated way has been needed in order to answer to the question related to the work of Christ.

"Why did He preach such sermons then?" "Why did He heal the sick?" "Why did He go up to the mountain to give that sermon?" "Why did He ride on donkey?" Attempting to answer such questions, people have come to see that He was working in these offices. Going even further, people have come to find that it was Jesus Christ for whom these offices had to exist.

His humiliation and exaltation also clarify that Christ did not work spontaneously following the needs around Him, but orderly following God's plan, which was established even before eternity.

OFFICES

Jesus Christ, our Mediator, works in three offices—prophet, priest, and king. In the following questions, Q24-26, these offices will be described in detail.

What is a prophet? Q24
What is a priest? Q25
What is a king? Q26

The descriptions above came from the Bible. Being mentioned in the Bible numerous times, these offices served as antitypes of those of Christ. Already in the Old Testament, these offices were used to represent Christ, and also in the New Testament, used by Jesus' disciples and apostles to describe Him. It was the same with many teachers in the history of the Church, for they also used these three offices in the process of describing the work of Christ.

What these offices share in common is that one had **to be anointed** for the responsibility. In previous studies, we have learned that the meaning of Christ is being anointed. (Q/A21) In such a context, Christ culminates all these three offices.

A more detailed description will be provided in the following questions respectively. For now, it is sufficient to say for the work of mediation, which was in need since the fall of man, and for the restoration of man's intelligence, emotion, and volition, these compartmentalized roles were required. Also the prophets, priests and kings in the Old Testament could not fulfill the work of mediation for the simple fact that they were merely human, yet Christ has come and fulfilled everything in a perfect way by Himself.

ANTITYPE:
It is a type that prefigures something in the future. Here, God gave the offices of prophet, priest, and king to the people of Israel, letting them work out the offices of forthcoming Jesus Christ in advance. It was through these antitypes, people of the Old Testament came to place their faith in Jesus Christ and be saved.

Some say that Christ imitated them. Yet this is quite the opposite. They were the antitypes of Jesus. Moreover, Jesus is incomparable to them. Christ fulfilled these three offices not separately but simultaneously. We needed Christ who could hold these three offices all together. For our entire being including not only our body and soul but also our head, heart and hands to be saved, we needed the Savior who could perfectly save. And Christ has fulfilled and completed this job for us.

ESTATE

In addition, our Mediator did not work without care but according to the plan ordained before eternity, and was perfectly obedient to the will of the Father. Such a process is described in the humiliation and exaltation respectively.

| Humiliation | Q27 |
| Exaltation | Q28 |

Jesus' offices were executed in these two estates given the record of the New Testament. Jesus' humiliation began with His birth and continued through His death. Yet He did not remain under the power of death, but was exalted through His resurrection and ascension. His work still continues even today. And He will come back in an exceedingly glorious appearance on the day He has set.

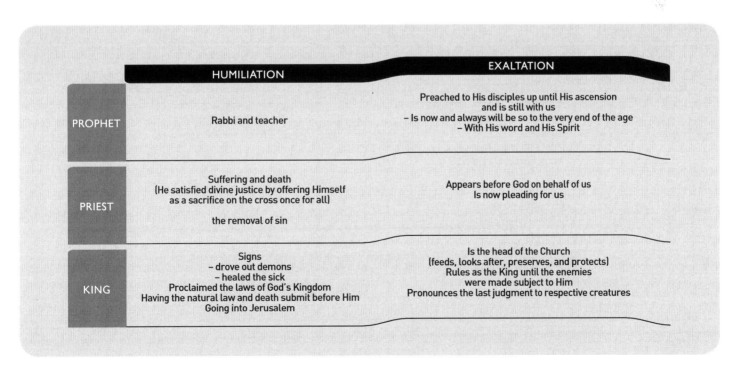

	HUMILIATION	EXALTATION
PROPHET	Rabbi and teacher	Preached to His disciples up until His ascension and is still with us – Is now and always will be so to the very end of the age – With His word and His Spirit
PRIEST	Suffering and death (He satisfied divine justice by offering Himself as a sacrifice on the cross once for all) the removal of sin	Appears before God on behalf of us Is now pleading for us
KING	Signs – drove out demons – healed the sick Proclaimed the laws of God's Kingdom Having the natural law and death submit before Him Going into Jerusalem	Is the head of the Church (feeds, looks after, preserves, and protects) Rules as the King until the enemies were made subject to Him Pronounces the last judgment to respective creatures

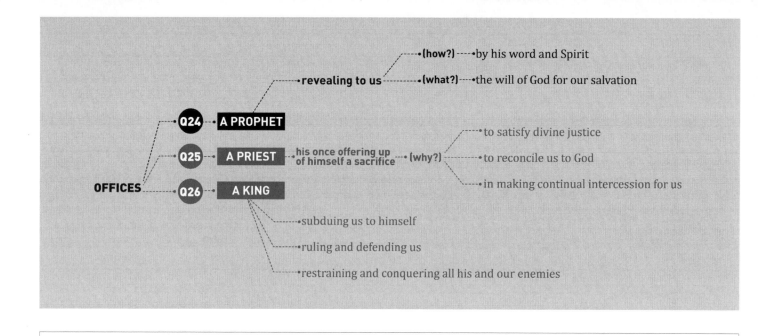

Q24 How doth Christ execute the office of a prophet?

A24 Christ executeth the office of a prophet,

in revealing to us,

by his word and Spirit,
the will of God for our salvation.[1,2,3,4]

1.
John 1:18

No man hath seen God at any time; the only begotten Son, which is in the bosom of the Father, **he hath declared him.**

2.
1 Peter 1:10-12

Of which salvation the prophets have enquired and searched diligently, who prophesied of the grace that should come unto you: Searching what, or **what manner of time the Spirit of Christ which was in them did** signify, when it testified beforehand the sufferings of Christ, and the glory that should follow. Unto **whom it was revealed**, that not unto themselves, but unto us they did minister the things, which are now reported unto you

by them that have preached the gospel unto you **with the Holy Ghost** sent down from heaven; which things the angels desire to look into.

3.
John 15:15

Henceforth I call you not servants; for the servant knoweth not what his lord doeth: but I have called you friends; for all things that I have heard of my Father **I have made known unto you.**

4.
John 20:31

But **these are written, that ye might believe that Jesus is the Christ**, the Son of God; and that believing ye might have life through his name.

RECALL THE PROPHETS YOU KNOW.
You may have recalled Isaiah and Jeremiah. Then, what kind of work did they do?

It is through the Bible we come to understand the kind of work prophets did. You may take them as spokesperson that shared God's words. They used to reproach the wickedness of their days, give out warnings to unclean kings and officials, and also declare God's words. They used to urge "Repent and turn from the wicked ways of this generation" and announce God's will. Their message used to include comfort from the Savior prepared for those who repent and turn around.

"The Kingdom of heaven is here," proclaimed the last prophet, John the Baptist. What would be the key of all these teachings? This is what Q24 of the Shorter Catechism clarifies. The work of all prophets was to teach the plan of God for our salvation. The greatest prophet, Jesus Christ, came and taught the same, yet in its finality. He revealed in a perfect form what other countless prophets have already mentioned. Our salvation was **the will of God**. And this is **revealed through His word and Spirit given to us**.

Christ and all other prophets who were the antitypes of Christ may have given many other teachings, yet all of them can be boiled down to this. They may have proclaimed fairness and justice, and rebuked the wrongful sacrifices and idolatry of their people, yet all of them should be concluded as this: to reveal the will of God for our salvation. Some may mistake being born again as the final end of their Christian walk. Yet this simple answer exposes that our Christian walk should go beyond and include pure worship before God and a life of confession and practice worthy of Him.

Then, were the offices of other prophets and of Jesus the same?

Yes, in effect they were. Christ, through the prophets of the Old Testaments, His antitypes, executed this office in the same way. Yet of course there was an apparent difference. While the prophets could have only repeated what God spoke, Christ could have directly spoken in His description of heaven. (See Matt 5-) It should have been so, given that He knows better than anyone.

As God Himself, He taught about heaven and the will of God, and this makes other prophets now needless. Christ is the prophet, the perfect and complete One. Knowing all the secrets of heaven, God Himself taught, and His teaching was able to bring people to a better understanding. It is not surprising that listening to His teaching they would have become amazed. "Wow, I have never heard such a teaching." "Who is this man?" (Matt 7:28-29)

Jesus revealed what the teachings of the Old Testament prophets truly meant. This encompasses the history of the Old Testament, the meaning of the law, the temple, the errors of the Pharisees, the meaning of suffering, and even the detailed ways believers were supposed to live in their own contexts. Jesus' teaching included what the law could not, and He taught with authority and excellence. As seen in "Give to Caesar what is Caesar's, and to God what is God's," "If any one of you is without sin, let him be the first to throw a stone at her," and the parable of the vine and the wheat. His teachings were surely unconventional, yet He successfully delivered the true meaning of other prophets' teaching.

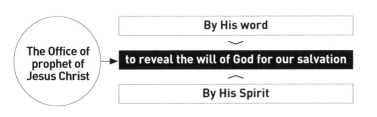

By His word
to reveal the will of God for our salvation
By His Spirit

The Office of prophet of Jesus Christ →

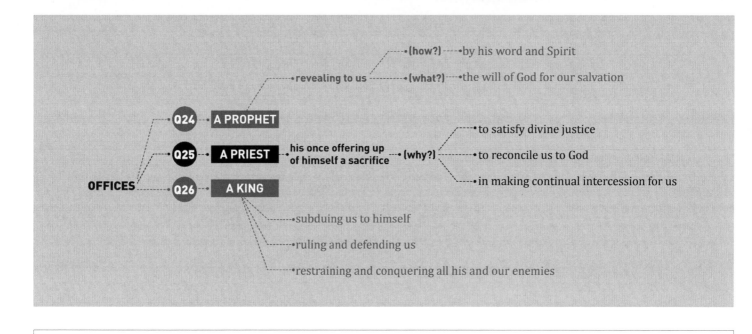

Q25 How doth Christ execute the office of a priest?

A25 Christ executeth the office of a priest,
 in his once offering up of himself a sacrifice
  to satisfy divine justice,[1]
 and reconcile us to God;[2]
 and in making continual intercession for us.[3]

1.
Hebrews 9:14, 28

How much more shall **the blood of Christ**, who through the eternal Spirit **offered himself without spot to God**, purge your conscience from dead works to serve the living God?......So **Christ was once offered** to bear the sins of many; and unto them that look for him shall he appear the second time without sin unto salvation.

2.
Hebrews 2:17

Wherefore in all things it behoved him to be made like unto his brethren, that he might be a merciful and faithful high priest in things pertaining to God, **to make reconciliation for the sins of the people.**angels desire to look into.

3.
Hebrews 7:24-25

But this man, because he continueth ever, hath an unchangeable priesthood. 25 Wherefore he is able also to save them to the uttermost that come unto God by him, seeing **he ever liveth to make intercession for them.**

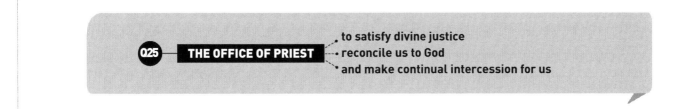

Q25 | THE OFFICE OF PRIEST
- to satisfy divine justice
- reconcile us to God
- and make continual intercession for us

RECALL THE PRIESTS YOU KNOW.
You may have recalled Eli, Nathan, or Samuel. Then, what kind of work did they do?

Priests used to make offerings and sacrifices before God on behalf of their people. They also used to make intercessions for their people. It was through the sacrifice that people used to use other animals to pay for their sins, and death being the wages of sin, the priests had to kill that animal by pouring out and burning its blood on the altar. Thus, the nature of their work was certainly brutal and filthy. People brought a lamb, ox, or dove to their priests, and the tough work fell on them. They had to cut the animal into two, take the inner parts out, pour out its blood, take all the fat from it, and in the end offer them up in the smoke. "God, take the life of this animal and forgive us." That was how they used to seek the forgiveness for their sins. Instead of the person who sinned, by sacrificing an animal in a gruesome way, they asked for their forgiveness.

mere act of killing an animal can neither resolve the fundamental problem of sin nor satisfy divine justice. Only through the death of Christ can the sin problem of all men be resolved.

Christ's body was torn and His blood shed on the cross, and He perfectly satisfied divine justice. He made the perfect priest, without leaving any need for other ones. In other words, He came to be a sacrifice Himself. It was man that had to die; yet God died instead demonstrating His love for us.

> The dreadfulness of sacrifice only reflects that of our sin. Its wearing repetition only highlights its incompetence. In the end, all of these lead us to Jesus Christ, who is the key to solving the problem of our sin. Sacrifice without Jesus Christ, our High Priest, is just as futile as that of other religions.

The Office of priest of Jesus Christ

- Making intercession (without ceasing even to now)
- Reconciling (as the result)
- Perfectly satisfying divine justice (by offering Himself)

This way had to be repeated every time and without an end. It takes only a little imagination to be taken aback when remembering the barbarous ceremonies ancient religions used to practice. A personal God should not prefer such bloody sacrifices, let alone forgive sins by such a practice.

The above is right, and such practices cannot forgive our sins. Sacrifice is meaningful only when it foreshadows Christ. The

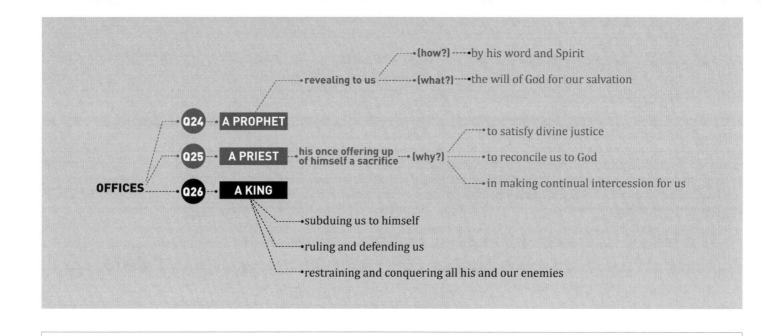

Q26 How doth Christ execute the office of a king?

A26 Christ executeth the office of a king,

in subduing us to himself,[1]

in ruling[2] and defending us,[3]

and in restraining and conquering all his and our enemies.[4,5]

1.
Acts 15:14-16

Simeon hath declared how God at the first did visit the Gentiles, **to take out of them a people for his name**. And to this agree the words of the prophets; as it is written, After this I will return, and will build again the tabernacle of David, which is fallen down; and I will build again the ruins thereof, and I will set it up.

2.
Isaiah 33:22

For the Lord is our judge, the **Lord is our lawgiver, the Lord is our king**; he will save us.

3.
Isaiah 32:1-2

Behold, a king shall reign in righteousness, and princes shall rule in judgment. And **a man shall be as an hiding place from the wind**, and a covert from the tempest; as rivers of water in a dry place, as the shadow of a great rock in a weary land.

4.
1 Corinthians 15:25

For he must reign, **till he hath put all enemies under his feet.**

5.
Psalm 110 throughout.

The Lord said unto my Lord, Sit thou at my right hand, until I make thine enemies thy footstool. The Lord shall send the rod of thy strength out of Zion: rule thou in the midst of thine enemies. Thy people shall be willing in the day of thy power, in the beauties of holiness from the womb of the morning: thou hast the dew of thy youth. The Lord hath sworn, and will not repent, Thou art a priest for ever after the order of Melchizedek. The

Lord at thy right hand shall strike through kings in the day of his wrath. He shall judge among the heathen, he shall fill the places with the dead bodies; he shall wound the heads over many countries. He shall drink of the brook in the way: therefore shall he lift up the head.

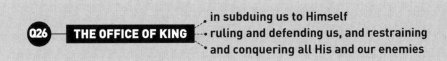

Q26 **THE OFFICE OF KING**
• in subduing us to Himself
• ruling and defending us, and restraining
• and conquering all His and our enemies

RECALL THE KINGS YOU KNOW.
You may have recalled David, Solomon, and Hezekiah. Then what kind of work did they do?

The role of kings in Israel was highlighted in the Old Testament, for their place among the world powers constantly forced them to go through wars. They were often overrun by the Philistines, threatened by the Ammonites, and stuck in between Babylon, Mede, Persia, and Egypt, which robbed them of any peaceful days. However, the kings of Israel disobeyed God, and the ultimate cost was the destruction of their nation. The people of Israel were taken captive and had to go through countless hardships. Through such experiences the Israelites came to expect the true King who would surely restore God's kingdom. "Only if such a King would come and free us from our oppression, then we can become even stronger than Rome." Their Messianic expectation grew stronger.

Yet the Kingdom Christ established was different from their expectation. Without being limited yet transcending the worldly office of king, Christ established the Kingdom above, which was the Church, the gathering of the elect. He offers saving grace of the mind and life of the elect and lets them obey. He forgives our sins, keeps and preserves us from numerous temptations. Also He helps us endure suffering to the end. Christ is the King of the kings.

How does God govern us? The government of this world is always with flaws. Hoping to see just government, some even resist a corrupt and immoral administration. Yet in most cases, the government of this world gives us only disappointment and distress. Yet God's reign is completely different. We are under His reign even at this moment. Yet when do we come to acknowledge that? We come to acknowledge that we are under His reign mostly when we practice His words. This gives us great joy, which no government of this world can offer.

Believers are those who keep the commands of our King while going beyond the laws of this world. It does not mean that we may disregard the laws of this world, rather going even further keeping a better one. Christ proclaimed the law of heaven. "If someone strikes you on the right cheek, turn to him the other also." "If someone takes your cloak, do not stop him from taking your tunic." These are examples of such unconventional laws.

Only those who keep this law in their lives will come to know its excellence. There is much joy and satisfaction embedded in this law. What about the law that commands us not to work but rest on Sundays? No one condemns us if we do not keep this law, rather they commend us; yet we dare to keep this law. In fact, listening to Christ's proclamation on the law of heaven, His disciples and audience must have been bewildered. For they did not have to live in such a way and no one forced them, yet Jesus continuously and in many different ways taught this law. And what we should do is to obey this law Christ has given us. In order to teach this law, Jesus had to go into Jerusalem riding on a donkey. Being different from any other king of this world, in humility, He came and taught.

The reign of Christ can be demonstrated in a visible form through His Church. Everywhere on earth, through the authority, order, and ministries of the Church, this has been confirmed. God appoints ministers and gives them the means of commandments and disciplines with which they can govern His Church. For believers who believe Jesus to be their King, they should **acknowledge and obey the authority of the ministers**.

Lastly, Christ reigns over the entire world. Even though many people in this world would resist and refuse to acknowledge this, it does not change the fact that He still reigns over this entire world. Despite numerous opponents, Christ remains the powerful ruler and accomplishes His purpose.

RULING AND DEFENDING US

We have seen the expression above in God's providence. (Q/A11) The only difference is the extent it covers: While providence covered every aspect of this world, here it has its focus particularly on us.

It is often overlooked, yet Christ's reign (His rule and defense) is practical, just like the reign of worldly kings and governments. The reason God demonstrates His reign in such practical forms is found in His love--for believers it is to have them understand His profound love toward them, and for nonbelievers their state and God's wrath toward them.

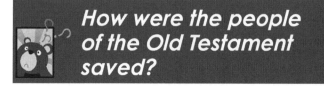

How were the people of the Old Testament saved?

The Old Testament is the time before Jesus. Learning that Jesus Christ is the only way to salvation, many people came to wonder how the people of the Old Testament were saved.

Just like us, it was only through Jesus Christ they were saved. Also through the law, they came to acknowledge how corrupt and hopeless they were, and in such an acknowledgement, they called on God's help. They practiced circumcision, Passover, and sacrifices, yet they did not believe they could keep the law without any flaw but acknowledged they needed God's help. Even while sacrificing, they were well aware that those animals could not bring their salvation, let alone they could keep the

law in its perfection. Confronting such a limit, it was for God's grace they offered these sacrifices. For them it was obvious that their sacrifices by themselves could not bring salvation.

Both in the Old and New Testament, salvation comes only by faith, which originates from God's grace not the work of law. The only difference between the Old and New Testament is whether Christ has come to the earth as a man or not. The Triune God has existed both in the Old and New Testament. Being the Creator of all heaven and earth and everything in it, being eternal, infinite and unchanging, God could not be confined in specific times and places. Thus, the Triune God equally existed both in the Old and New Testament, yet God the Son in the form of a man only came as Christ in the New Testament. Meanwhile this Christ has been foreshadowed in the Old Testament through circumcision, Passover, and sacrifice, and this is the difference between the Old and New Testament.

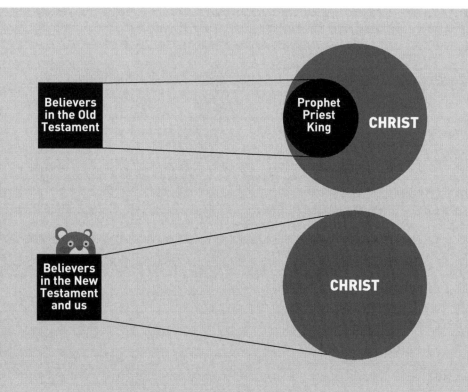

- Prophets, priests, and kings in the Old Testament represented the forthcoming Christ.

- Believers in the Old Testament, through these offices, were made to acknowledge Christ and were saved by placing their faith in Jesus who had not yet come. Today, we are saved by placing our faith in Jesus, who has already come. Christ is the only way to our salvation both in the Old and New Testament.

- From our perspective, Jesus surely came and exited only for a specific time of history, yet in God's perspective, which is over the entire history of humankind, all salvation comes only though Christ. There is no difference between the Old and New Testament.

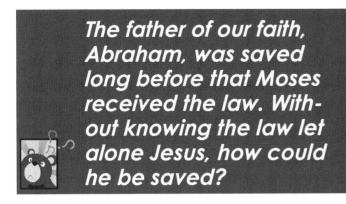

The father of our faith, Abraham, was saved long before that Moses received the law. Without knowing the law let alone Jesus, how could he be saved?

Good question! It is right that the law was given at the specific time of Moses, yet God's eternal moral law transcends time. Abraham also was saved by placing his faith in God. Rom 4:2-3 says, "If, in fact, Abraham was justified by works, he had something to boast about-but not before God. What does the Scripture say? 'Abraham believed God, and it was credited to him as righteousness.'" As far as our salvation goes, there is no ground whatsoever on our end, but it comes only through God's grace.

What about those who did not even get a chance to hear the gospel of Christ?

Your answer should include the acknowledgement that the gospel we know comes only through Christ. Yet the question above is worth more pondering, for the heart of the question is in fairness. "It is unfair. God should have given equal opportunities to all." Yet what is this opportunity? It is the opportunity through which "I" can come to believe, and therein is the trick. The salvation we have learned so far does not come through such a way. Salvation is God's unconditional election. Not only does it not depend on whether we come to believe, but also God is not obligated to give such an opportunity. (If necessary, the review of Q13-19 would be helpful.)

Insisting there were another way, we destroy the exclusivity of Christ despite its expediency.

Do not trade the truth with an easy and convenient explanation. Predestination is an undeniable truth, of which no one can steer clear. What is unfair is that we dare to mention the opportunity to believe, for we do not have any worth to be saved to begin with. We are saved not because of our belief but solely God's grace. And the way to such a salvation is through the only God-given Mediator, Christ. Some may complain "It is unfair, and God is overbearing," yet such responses will not change the biblical truth one bit. Such responses only come from the ignorance and rebellion of men. Thus, sharing the gospel, we should neither add nor subtract anything. We should share the gospel as it stands so those who hear from us will be set on the right course of faith.

An expedient way of faith is destined to fail. If one begins to doubt "there might be," then before long, he will be led to some other way than Christ and the Bible. Also he would not be able to see any reason for God to be the one and only, and every teaching of the Church would become meaningless for him. Here the premises of the Shorter Catechism Q1-3 are at the stake.

If you feel stuck at this, do not give up on yourself yet. Instead, allow and encourage yourself to move as far as the Bible leads you to and proceed to the following studies with prayer and hope.

[QUIZ] A TYPICAL MISUNDERSTANDING

"God must have prepared another way than hearing the gospel. We do not know what that is, yet God is powerful enough to do so."

Take a minute to find the error of the above and write that down in the following.

Our enemy is not the one who gives us personal troubles. Rather, we should take God's enemy as our enemy setting our personal biases aside. And the identity of this enemy is closely related to the original sin of man. Man began to oppose God by taking the fruit and disobeying His words, and it must not be belittled as the actions of a little child; rather, it was a significant event through which man by his opposition to God has become God's enemy. If we stayed in such a state, then we would have remained as His enemy and still be battling against Him.

Is God fighting against His enemies? Is there any chance He might lose?

This world is not caught in a battle between a good god and an evil god as is often described in movies. God is not fighting His battle against His enemies as their equal, and this makes our cheering needless. No one can be the match for God. God, who created the world only with words, can eliminate everything in it in an instant. He is just allowing in His providence the work of His enemies for a while.

Then, how are we supposed to understand spiritual battle? In God's allowance, His enemies may try to tear us down, and out of good desire we may try to fight with them. Yet even this fight belongs not to us but to God. (2 Ch 20:15)

Then, how can we discern who is our enemy?

Such discernment must be carefully made. Since our personal will cannot always be in sync with God's will, we may not claim any achievements by our works as God's will being done. Rather God's good will must be, and this is clearly stated in the Bible. It is easy to take what is good to my own eyes as God's will. Yet such a personal application and confidence must be avoided at all cost.

1.
Luke 2:7

And she brought forth her firstborn son, and wrapped him in swaddling clothes, and **laid him in a manger**; because there was no room for them in the inn.

2.
Galatians 4:4

But when the fulness of the time was come, God sent forth his Son, made of a woman, **made under the law.**

3.
Hebrews 12:2-3

Looking unto Jesus the author and finisher of our faith; who for the joy that was set before him **endured the cross**, despising the shame, and is set down at the right hand of the throne of God. For consider **him that endured such contradiction of sinners** against himself, lest ye be wearied and faint in your minds.

4.
Isaiah 53:2-3

For he shall grow up before him as a tender plant, and as a root out of a dry ground: he hath no form nor comeliness; and when we shall see him, **there is no beauty that we should desire him. He is despised and rejected of men; a man of sorrows, and acquainted with grief: and we hid as it were our faces from him; he was despised, and we esteemed him not**.

5.
Luke 22:44

And **being in an agony** he prayed more earnestly: and his sweat was as it were great drops of blood falling down to the ground.

----------• in his being born

----------• in a low condition made under the law

----------• undergoing the miseries of this life

----------• undergoing the wrath of God

----------• undergoing the cursed death of the cross

----------• in being buried

----------• in continuing under the power of death for a time

Q27 Wherein did Christ's humiliation consist?

A27 Christ's humiliation consisted in
his being born,
and that in a low condition,[1]
made under the law,[2]
undergoing the miseries of this life,[3, 4]
the wrath of God,[5, 6]
and the cursed death of the cross;[7]
in being buried,[8]
and continuing under the power of death for a time.[9]

6.
Matthew 27:46

And about the ninth hour Jesus cried with a loud voice, saying, Eli, Eli, lama sabachthani? that is to say, **My God, my God, why hast thou forsaken me?**

7.
Philippians 2:8

And being found in fashion as a man, he humbled himself, and became **obedient unto death, even the death of the cross.**

8.
1 Corinthians 15:3-4

For I delivered unto you first of all that which I also received, how that Christ died for our sins according to the scriptures; And that **he was buried**, and that he rose again the third day according to the scriptures.

9.
Acts 2:24-27, 31

Whom God hath raised up, having loosed the pains of death: because it was not possible that he should be holden of it. For David speaketh concerning him, I foresaw the Lord always before my face, for he is on my right hand, that I should not be moved: Therefore did my heart rejoice, and my tongue was glad; moreover also my flesh shall rest in hope: Because **thou wilt not** leave my soul in hell, neither wilt thou suffer thine Holy One to see corruption......He seeing this before spake of the resurrection of Christ, that **his soul was not left in hell**, neither **his flesh did see corruption.**

The thought of Christ's humiliation may fill your eyes with tears. It should. He suffered greatly because of our sin, and if you have gone to Sunday school from the early years, you must have at least one experience of being in tears as you participated in the Passion play or sang a gospel song.

Yet, there is more to find in Christ' humiliation than just sentimental value. This may require another look on its position in the whole Catechism. It finds its place inbetween God's special decrees of Q12 and the grace covenant of Q20. Given such a position, it becomes more obvious that God executed this with a certain purpose and meaning.

For this reason, Christ's humiliation offers hope rather than grief. The more its meaning becomes distinguished one after the other, the more it should touch our hearts and offer more reasons to be grateful. This also offers unwavering confidence and benefits. Now let us take a look point by point.

Q23 is about the estate in which Christ existed while He executed His three offices, and it is answered with His humiliation and exaltation. Q27 deals with the former before the latter, following its chronological order. Jesus Christ was first humiliated and then exalted. While studying this section, try to recall Christ's three offices.

WHAT DID CHRIST'S HUMILIATION INCLUDE?

The answer is listed following the preposition "in" and will be provided in the table below.

BIRTH	Nothing can be more humiliating than God in the body of man
THAT IN A LOW CONDITION	**AS A BABY:** He did not come as a knight in shining armor or a hailed hero, but as a baby that must have required constant care from a grown up. He must have worn diapers and also been fed. **IN POVERTY:** He was born in a manger. He probably had to help in His father's carpentry work.
MADE UNDER THE LAW	He was the Lord of the law, yet he had to submit to the law.
THE MISERIES OF THIS LIFE	He had to undergo all different types of the miseries of this life surely including diseases and even cold.
THE WRATH OF GOD	He had to bear what was due to us without any sin.
THE CURSED DEATH OF THE CROSS	The death which we have learned from the previous chapter, the separation from God... Tremendous pain which God Himself could not experience...
BURIAL	Being prepared by a rich man, His tomb might have been superbly nice, yet still was not a proper place for Jesus.
CONTINUING UNDER THE POWER OF DEATH	it was for three days.

People tend to take Jesus' humiliation lightly, yet the table above speaks otherwise. "Becoming a man," Can this be considered as a humiliation? This can be better explored with your answer to other questions, for example "What kind of a being is man?" or "What kind of a man am I?" For these questions could offer us a chance to revisit the limits and miseries of man and will bring us to a conclusion which may be subjective and different for each individual. And this makes the amount of grace, which the Son of God being humiliated in becoming a man brings to each individual, also subjective and different. If you have not had any particular complaints about yourself and consider yourself average or above, then this could be a difficult idea for you to comprehend, saying to yourself, "It would not have been such a bad thing that He became a man." Yet the Shorter Catechism reveals the cognitive limits of men and describes Christ's humiliation point by point.

This humiliation is beyond our imagination, transcending any concepts and symbols of men, mainly because the object of this humiliation was the Son of God, God Himself. While we were still sinners, He who knew no sin died in our place, and this misery and despair was so enormous that no man could come to understand it. This God we encounter through Christ's humiliation and the depth and abundance of His love and grace is indeed unfathomable.

This touches our hearts deeply and makes us all the more grateful. But why did He have to be this humiliated? God probably would offer the following words as His answer:

"And he died for all, that those who live should no longer live for themselves but for Him who died for them and was raised again." (2 Cor 5:15)

Grateful—that is all there is to say. For me, all other words fail.

Pilate's Court? Jesus was tried in Pilate's court, and Pilate was the legitimate judge of this world. In other words, he represented the judge of all men, and this prevents anyone from saying "When did I kill Jesus?"

Westminster Confession
Chapter VIII **OF CHRIST THE MEDIATOR**

IV.
This office the Lord Jesus did most willingly undertake;[Psalms 40:7-8, Hebrews 10:5-10, John 10:18, Philippians 2:8] which that He might discharge, He was made under the law,[Galatians 4:4] and did perfectly fulfil it;[Matthew 3:26, 5:17] endured most grievous torments immediately in His soul,[Matthew 26:37-38, Luke 22:44, Matthew 27:46] and most painful sufferings in His body;[Matthew 26:27] was crucified, and died,[Philippians 2:8] was buried, and remained under the power of death, yet saw no corruption.[Acts 2:23-24, 27, Acts 13:37, Rome 6:9] (the rest omitted)

The cover of Westminster Confession of Faith printed on 1647

ESTATE----•in his estate of exaltation----•Q28•-- **WHEREIN CONSISTETH CHRIST'S EXALTATION?**

•in his rising again from the dead on the third day
•in ascending up into heaven
•in sitting at the right hand of God the Father
•in coming to judge the world at the last day

Q28 Wherein consisteth Christ's exaltation?

A28 Christ's exaltation consisteth
in his rising again from the dead on the third day,[1]
in ascending up into heaven,[2]
in sitting at the right hand of God the Father,[3]
and in coming to judge the world at the last day.[4, 5]

1.
1 Corinthians 15:4

And that he was buried, and that **he rose again the third day** according to the scriptures.

2.
Mark 16:19

So then after the Lord had spoken unto them, **he was received up into heaven, and sat on the right hand of God.**

3.
Ephesians 1:20

Which he wrought in Christ, when he raised him from the dead, and **set him at his own right hand in the heavenly places.**

4.
Acts 1:11

Which also said, Ye men of Galilee, why stand ye gazing up into heaven? this same Jesus, which is taken up from you into heaven, **shall so come in like manner as ye have seen him go into heaven.**

3.
Acts 17:31

Because he hath **appointed a day**, in the which he will **judge the world in righteousness by that man** whom he hath ordained; whereof he hath given assurance unto all men, in that he hath **raised him from the dead.**

Q28 — WHAT IS THE ESTATE OF EXALTATION?

We may feel more comfortable with Christ's humiliation. Yet His exaltation is equally relevant to us. Let us take a minute and ponder, "Why does this question appear at this particular moment and place?" For this can be enlightening. We have been following the order of the Larger Catechism: the supreme good of man, revelation, God, God's creation and providence, decrees, fall and punishment, covenant and Mediator. And through the study of Mediator, we came to explore who God is, who man is, how fatal the separation between God and man is, and how God alone can bring restoration. And as we have learned from the previous study of His humiliation, God in His pleasure came and satisfied divine justice and showed his love for us.

Yet it takes more than His humiliation to complete this restoration. Christ's exaltation is also necessary. It is at this point we encounter the question, "What is the estate of exaltation?"

WHAT IS CHRIST'S EXALTED ESTATE?

Its answer consists of four elements. What does each mean? Why are His rising again and ascending considered as exaltation? Is it because its physical direction goes upwards?

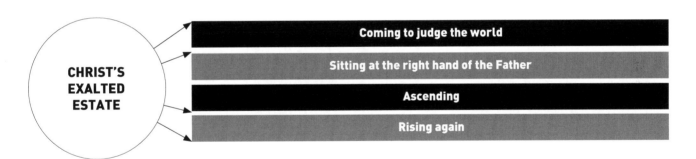

CHRIST'S EXALTED ESTATE

- Coming to judge the world
- Sitting at the right hand of the Father
- Ascending
- Rising again

RISING AGAIN : RESURRECTION

The heart of Christ's resurrection is in His victory over death. The wages of sin is death. For this reason, He had to rise again from the dead and satisfy God's justice by offering His blood.

Christ's resurrection is also of the body. The resurrection of only His spirit would not have been enough. We are made of body and spirit. Thus, by the resurrection of Christ, who is fully God and fully man, our whole person became freed from the authority of death.

Christ through His resurrection proved Himself to be the Messiah. Yet this was in no way the end. His resurrection was a leap into an entirely different state of life, the sure sign of Him being God's Son, and the beginning of His continual exaltation. Of course before eternity He was the glorious Son of God. He was so even in the estate of humiliation. Yet such a being was hidden in the form of a servant. Yet now after the resurrection, God has publically declared and proclaimed that He is now the Lord and Christ, Prince and Savior. (Acts 2:36, 5:31) He has now regained the glory He had with the Father. (John 17:5)

He is now clothed with an entirely different form of being than on earth. He was among the dead, yet He rose again and is now alive forever holding the keys of death and Hades. (Rev 1:18) He conquered not only death but also the ruler of this world, and He was exalted to be the Lord of the living and the dead. He is the King of life, the fountain of salvation, and God appointed Him as the Judge of the living and the dead.

Moreover, Christ's resurrection was for both His church and the whole world. According to the Larger Catechism, Christ resurrected as a public person, the head of His Church, for their justification. Through His resurrection, He himself was justified, and in Him we were also justified. His resurrection was the public declaration of our innocence. The acquittal of sin, which was embedded in His resurrection, is now applied to us as individuals. For this reason, there is neither wrath nor condemnation for those who are in Christ. God Himself though the death of His Son reconciled with us, and as overlooking His wrath toward us, offered peace and love. Thus, ours is only peace with God and the hope of His glory.

Now by this life Christ took through His resurrection, He will preserve His own in which this Advocate of ours continues to work with His Father. (Rom 6:8-10) Thus, Christ's work of resurrection will continue to eternity, and when the time has fully come, He will bring the resurrection and rebirth of all believers along with the victory in heaven and on earth. (Acts 4:2, 1 Cor 15:12-58)

ASCENDING

Regarding Christ's ascension, the Larger Catechism speaks of His appearance and teaching after His resurrection. Jesus spent 40 days on the earth after His resurrection, and this period was in preparation for His ascension. Everything from that moment on undoubtedly demonstrates that He does not belong to this earth.

Also He visibly went up into the highest heavens. Through such an ascension, He proved that He is worthy of all glory over the entire earth, all natural laws, and even gravity. Moreover, He was not in the form of a Spirit invisible to human eyes; rather, He was taken in the same form we see regular people. This proves that He is now in heaven maintaining His human nature with both Spirit and body. Being our head, He now triumphs over the enemy and prepares a place for us.

Also in His exalted estate, He executed His offices of prophet, priest, and king. He continued to preach to His disciples until He was taken into heaven. We can easily assume that His 40-day-after-resurrection conversations with His apostles pertaining to the kingdom of God probably offered a completely different light to the character and ministry of these apostles. (See the Larger Catechism Q53) After the years of companionship with Jesus, followed by His death, they were probably devastated, yet through these unexpected days with Jesus after His death, they became completely different men and also came to understand Him and His work better than before.

Through such an appearance and the commission to preach the gospel to all nations, Christ offered a good description of their future mission. His teaching, given over these 40 days, is well summarized in His last words for His disciples. (Matt 28:18-20) Before anything else He gave them all authority in heaven and on earth. And with such complete authority, they were commanded to make disciples of all nations, baptizing them in the name of the Father and of the Son and of the Holy Spirit and teaching them to obey everything He has commanded. Encouragement was also given that He will be with them always to the very end of the age. As far as the body goes, He now is apart from us, yet in Spirit He is with us to the end of the age. For this reason, we can be assured it is He, not us, who gathers, reigns over, and preserves His Church. The Lord instructs.

SITTING AT THE RIGHT HAND

What does sitting at the right hand of the Father mean? This means that He is now advanced to the highest favor with God the Father, the right side of God's throne, and the highest of all seats next to God's. Then what is He doing on that seat?

The concept of exaltation reminds us of a king and helps us imagine Christ in heaven still executing the office of king. Christ now evidently reveals all fullness of joy, glory, and power over all things in heaven and on earth. On the one hand, He subdues our enemies, and on the other hand furnishes His ministers and people with gifts and grace. The former is His kingship over all of his enemies (Matt 28:18, 1 Cor 15:25-27, Rev 1:5, 17:14), and the latter is His kingship over Zion, His people, and Church (Ps 2:6, 72:2-7, Isa 9:5, 11:1-5, Luke 1:33, John 18:33). The former is the kingship of power, and the latter is of grace.

In the meantime, this exaltation teaches us that Christ is still executing the office of priest. This office was not a temporary position, but Christ will continue to execute it to eternity. He has been a priest on earth and is now the High Priest in the sanctuary of heaven. How does that make you feel? Probably relieved, for it assures us that we have Christ still praying for us.

Christ's work of intercession in heaven

Christ makes intercession by his appearing in our nature continually before the Father in heaven. Some may take their salvation as if it were the end of their journey telling themselves, "Now that I am saved, everything must be okay." However, such a belief is misleading and brings only more troubles. What makes us blameless and able to be confident before God is Christ's ongoing work of intercession for our sins before God. Thus, what can we do apart from Jesus Christ even now and forever?

Keep this in mind: One of the important confessions of Christians is that we have this High Priest who is sitting on the right side of the heavenly throne.

COMING AGAIN

His exaltation will be revealed in a perfect and clear way when He comes again. On the day of the Lord, that great and dreadful day, He will grant His mercy on His people and judge His enemies.

As prophesied, the Messiah came with the purpose to redeem and judge. However, the prophesies in the Old Testament failed to make enough distinction between the estates of humiliation and exaltation while describing the life of the Messiah. They were, in a way, painted as a single picture, which was somewhat baffling and made His disciples confused. Will this One take over Rome? Then, why does He keep saying that He has to die? On top of everything, what does He mean that He will come again? Why does He say that He has to go up to heaven and come again?

It is the New Testament that more evidently testifies Christ has to come again in order to fulfill each of the yet-to-be fulfilled prophesies of the Old Testament in a specific way. (John 5:22, 27-29) When He came 2,000 years ago, He came in the weakness of a body and in the form of a servant, yet when He comes again, He will reveal Himself to be the conquering King with great power and glory to everyone in this world. (Matt 24:30, Rev 6:2, 19:11)

What will He do when He comes again? He will judge this world with righteousness. Besides God's work of creation, all of God's other work carries the meaning of judgment, but it will be especially so on the last Day of Judgment. On that day, Christ will attain great victory judging both the living and the dead, fulfill His kingdom, and vanquish His enemies for good. His judgment and declaration will be made according to the absolute good. This execution will be brought about in a way that no one and no one's conscience will be able to defend themselves. Coming to light, everything which was hidden before will be revealed, and the sinner himself will come to acknowledge that he deserves only eternal punishment.

Come Lord Jesus, Amen!

Many expressions from this part are borrowed from Our Reasonable Faith by Herman Bavinck and the Westminster Larger Catechism Q55.

RECAP OF CHRIST'S EXALTATION

1. RESURRECTION

Physical resurrection is not enough. Why is that? Because we have bodies.
Through His resurrection, Jesus not only proved His righteousness but also nullified the condemnation He had unfairly received before Pilate.

2. ASCENSION

Through Christ's ascension, both the center of our hearts and the direction of our lives must go upwards--towards the things of heaven. Through His ascension, Christ has taken all our desires to heaven.

3. AT THE RIGHT HAND OF GOD

Keep this in mind: it is not merely a poetic expression. He still continues His work of intercession. At the right hand of God... (Remind yourself of the table regarding Christ's three offices.)

4. COMING AGAIN

There will be no excuses. Everything will be brought into light and altogether revealed.

Where is heaven? Is it out in space?

Heaven is not a particular place, but a kingdom which is under God's reign. God's kingdom has already come among us by the advent of Jesus. The concept of God's kingdom must go beyond merely a place for believers after their death. For those who think of heaven as only a place, God might as well be the same as other gods like Zeus. Also in order to call ourselves the people of God's kingdom, a transformed life worthy of such name is necessary. Being under God's reign means following His law. This is what many great books on God's kingdom concur.

For deeper understandings: The Gospel and Kingdom and According to Plan by Graeme Goldsworthy

---

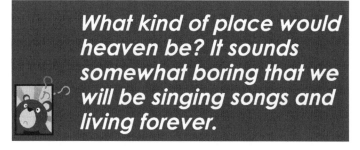

What kind of place would heaven be? It sounds somewhat boring that we will be singing songs and living forever.

We will be living with God in His kingdom full of joy. We must be joyful only because we would be with God. In heaven there will be no disease and pain, and everything will be adorned with gold and silver—yet this is not what would make us full of joy, but God's presence.

While in a nursery, children may appear to be having the best time of their lives with lots of toys. Oh how much they love toys and what they do to prevent others from coming and taking them away. They break a sweat, strive to hold on to them, and even fight. However, what happens when their parents show up? In an instant, they throw the toys aside and run towards their parents. Why? Because parents trumps everything else.

This brings us to the first question of the Shorter Catechism. Heaven is a secondary matter. Do you love God the most? Do you become like a child before Him? Is God the greatest reward and is He alone everything for you? Such a confession is the most pressing at all times. For this is faith.

Discussion Questions

❶ Elaborate the meaning of each office of prophet, priest, and king.

❷ What kind of benefit does it bring to us that Christ executed these three offices in two estates?

❸ Elaborate the meaning of each estate of Christ's humiliation and exaltation.

❹ In what sense does this chapter give us the reason to be grateful?

"IS THE HOLY SPIRIT GOD'S ATTENDANT OR SERVANT?"

"I DON'T SPEAK IN TONGUES. IS IT BECAUSE I AM NOT FULL OF THE HOLY SPIRIT?"

"MY FRIEND HAS A BEAMING FACE AND IS OPTIMISTIC ALL THE TIME.
SHE SEEMS TO BE FULL OF THE HOLY SPIRIT. HOW CAN I BE LIKE HER?"

"I HAVEN'T BEEN DOING DAILY DEVOTIONS AND PRAYERS FOR A WHILE.
I AM WORRIED THAT THE HOLY SPIRIT MIGHT HAVE LEFT ME."

So far we have learned how we can be freed from sin and misery, the result of the fall, and who does this for us; from this chapter on until the end of this Part, we will be learning what kinds of benefits we now can receive through Christ's salvation from sin.

This chapter will cover the means to receive these benefits, the requirements on us and the details. Seen in its entire context, this chapter acts as a hinge between the work of Christ and the benefits of His work of mediation. Given its importance, it would be useful for you to keep the whole mindmap close at hand as you move on with this chapter.

After Q7 we have studied God's work, and especially after Q21 the mediating work of Christ. Q23-28 covered Christ the Mediator, and now through Q29-38 we will be covering what has become available through His mediation.

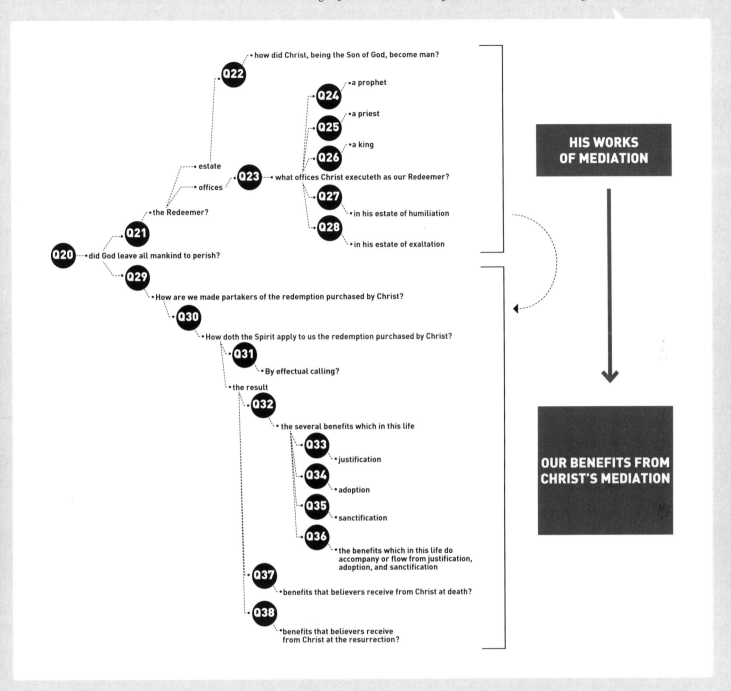

In other words, what Part 1 has been teaching was "how this world and everything in it works"—How God has been working, what happened to us, and what Christ has done for us. Now it is time to see the result of it all. However, the keyword you have to keep in mind from now to Q38 is "benefit."

What is shown in the picture above can make some confused. This picture includes not only the terms like justification, adoption, and sanctification that you have learned in the process of salvation but also death (Q37). How can these be included in the category of benefits? Yet the structure of the Shorter Catechism brings us an important insight: The result of Christ's mediation, the benefits of it, encompasses our entire lives. It is important that we study each question one by one, yet it is

more important that we maintain the macroscopic viewpoint without missing the overall flow of the whole catechism.

Also we have been learning that God does all, and our only responsibility is to have our eyes on Him and Him alone. Is it still so after Q29? Since these are the benefits we have received by His work, then should we bring the focus back on us? The following chapters will prove otherwise.

Now the Bible speaks that even the remainder of our lives is not in our control. That I confess my faith, that I experience some heart changes whether it being abrupt or gradual, that I grow day by day—These are not done by my power but **by his Holy Spirit**, and this is what we will navigate in the following chapters. **The keyword** remains the same, God.

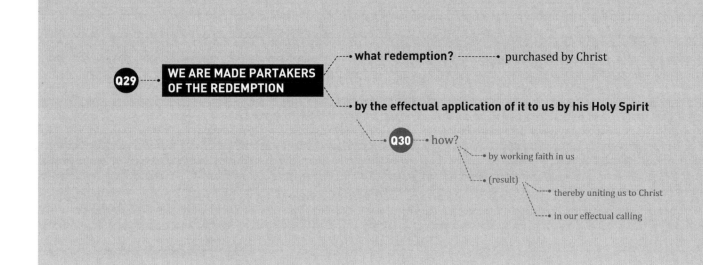

Q29 ---• **what redemption?** --------• purchased by Christ

WE ARE MADE PARTAKERS OF THE REDEMPTION

---• **by the effectual application of it to us by his Holy Spirit**

Q30 ---• how?

• by working faith in us

• (result)

• thereby uniting us to Christ

• in our effectual calling

Q29 How are we made partakers

of the redemption purchased by Christ?

A29 We are made partakers of the redemption

purchased by Christ,

by the effectual application of it to us[1]

by his Holy Spirit.[2]

1.
John 1:11-12

He came unto his own, and his own received him not. But **as many as received him, to them gave he power to become the sons of God,** even to **them that believe on his name.**

2.
Titus 3:5-6

Not by works of righteousness which we have done, but according to **his mercy he saved us, by the washing of regeneration, and renewing of the Holy Ghost;** Which he **shed on us abundantly through Jesus Christ our Saviour.**

THE EXPRESSION OF BEING MADE "PARTAKERS" OF THE REDEMPTION

This is certainly not an everyday expression, and for this reason, some may have a hard time grasping its meaning. If so, I'd recommend you to imagine being invited to a ready-to-go feast. This question could be in other forms: "What do we have to do if we'd like to receive the benefit of Christ's redemption?" Or "What does this work of mediation—the forgiveness of sins and reconciliation with God—have to do with me?" "How can Christ whom I never laid my eyes on redeem me?" "If Christ fulfilled this redemption, then it should be His, not mine."

How would you answer this question? "Is it a good thing now that we can be partakers of the benefit of Christ's redemption? Do we have to be partakers or do we not?"

It is a no-brainer that it is a good thing and we have to. Yet the intention of this question is to give ourselves the opportunity to ascertain that it is truly a benefit that we are made the partakers of the redemption. It may seem needless for some, but this could be easily overlooked.

The Heidelberg Catechism speaks to the first question stating, "That I am not my own, but belong—body and soul, in life and death—to my faithful Savior, Jesus Christ." Can this be your confession? Even if being left with nothing of my own, I can still find comfort and a benefit for this life in the fact that I am a partaker of His redemption and thus belong to Him.

THE EFFECTUAL APPLICATION

This answer uses the preposition "by" twice at the end of it.

1. BY THE EFFECTUAL APPLICATION OF IT TO US

In order for us to partake in Christ's redemption, it must be effectually applied. What made us able to partake in this benefit of redemption? Its effectual application. This will be more deeply dealt with in Q30. Suffice it to say that Christ's redemption is now well applied irresistibly and also regardless of man's states, attitudes, and ranks.

2. BY HIS HOLY SPIRIT

What follows the second "by" introduces who effectually applies Christ's redemption to us. It is the Holy Spirit and His work. Through every moment of our life, death, and resurrection, the Holy Spirit continues to offer the benefit of Christ to us. Q29-38 covers the benefit of Christ's mediation which is, in other words, the work of the Holy Spirit. The lives of believers and everything in them come through the Holy Spirit. Thus it is reasonable to say that the greatest difference between the children of God and those who are not is in His presence or absence among them. It is a wholly different kind of life. This is also the difference between the Church and the world.

It may strike some as strange that the Holy Spirit now reappears long after Q6. Where has He been?

We are now studying God's decrees, and providence in particular has brought us here. God allowed our sin, yet without leaving us gave Christ. Up to this point, the explanation has revolved around Christ, but from this chapter on, the Holy Spirit will be more evidently revealed. However, this does not mean in any way that the Holy Spirit has been idle. The work of the Triune God is done all the time together. Among three persons there is a distinction for sure, but they do not work separately. They work together, yet from our perspective, here the work of the Holy Spirit will appear more evidently. It is the Holy Spirit whose work makes us partakers of Christ's redemption.

Sure enough God elected, offered the solution, and applies it to us. Thus, it is not wrong to say God did it all in a lump sum. Rather the knowledge of the Triune God we have gained so far could enable us to give a more satisfactory description— God the Father elected, God the Son makes the intercession, and God the Spirit applies the benefit of such mediation to us.

The Holy Spirit stays with us throughout everything in our life and death on this earth. Knowing this is the distinction from nonbelievers, the benefit, and the blessing for us.

Q30 will describe more comprehensively what this effectual calling means in detail.

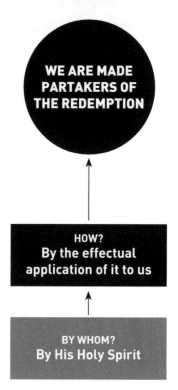

WE ARE MADE PARTAKERS OF THE REDEMPTION

HOW?
By the effectual application of it to us

BY WHOM?
By His Holy Spirit

WHO IS THE HOLY SPIRIT?

Why don't you take a look at the following while examining yourself?

"I don't speak in tongues.
Is it because I am not full of the Holy Spirit?"

"My friend has a beaming face
and is optimistic all the time.
She seems to be full of the Holy Spirit. How can I be like her?"

"I haven't been doing daily devotions and prayers for a while.
I am worried that the Holy Spirit might have left me."

"Someone, a self-proclaimed prophet, prophesied that my sister would go to one of the ivy league schools. Yet this didn't happen. Can almighty God make a mistake?"

"My mom has been sick for a while. She refuses to go to see a doctor believing that the Holy Spirit will heal her. I am really worried."

What is easily overlooked is that the Holy Spirit is a person and God, who works for our ultimate good. Being occupied with the manifestation of our faith, we take only the form of our godliness--how many times we pray, whether we read the Bible first thing in the morning or have any lust in mind--and use it to evaluate whether we are full of the Holy Spirit or not.

The Holy Spirit is neither a mysterious energy nor the source of power. Of course we may understand the Holy Spirit as the power and force in us. Yet the Holy Spirit is not a resource for us to utilize to satisfy ourselves. Of course, the Holy Spirit does give various kinds of gifts. Particular gifts and its demonstration in individuals should not be taken as their capability, but only as the gifts given them with divine purpose. What counts is not the gift, but the giver.

What the Heidelberg Catechism says regarding the Holy Spirit would be beneficial. It is worth multiple readings and meditation on.

First, that the Spirit, with the Father and the Son, is eternal God. Second, that the Spirit is given also to me, so that, through true faith, he makes me share in Christ and all his benefits, comforts me, and will remain with me forever.

The following books would be helpful as well: Q53 of The Commentary on the Heidelberg Catechism by Dr. Zacharias Ursinus and The Holy Spirit by Sinclair Ferguson.

I am not sure if the Holy Spirit is with me.

Such doubt comes when the Holy Spirit is misunderstood only as energy, miraculous signs, or power. Rather, He is a personal God who shares intimate fellowship with us. This kind of misunderstanding is worsened when we become occupied only with the demonstrations of godliness worthy of believers. If you skip church many weeks in a row and rarely read the Bible, and avoid coming across your pastor and other members of your church, you may not be sure whether the Holy Spirit is with you. Had the case been reversed—if you like to come to church, enjoy the company of other believers, are deeply touched when you sing praises—you would probably think that you are full of the Holy Spirit.

Misinterpretation of the Pentecost in Acts 2 may make matters worse. The Holy Spirit indeed made an impressive entrance in Acts 2. Believers witnessed what seemed to be tongues of fire that split apart, and people came to speak in tongues and even prophesied. It left such a strong impression that it still leads people imagine such a scene when they think about the presence of the Holy Spirit. However, the Holy Spirit is now with us without such a dramatic comings and goings.

Then, what would be the right interpretation of the Pentecost in Acts 2? Christ has sent us the Holy Spirit, and it is true that we now have power. Yet this power is not of individuals but of the Church. In such a sense, the Pentecost can be compared to a demonstration, which was given only temporarily to demonstrate the kind of work we have to do as a church. It was an appropriate way to teach the newly-born Church. Yet it need not be so with today's Church. Today the Holy Spirit does not work in such a way, but rather mostly through the Word.

Here is what Paul said in 1 Corinthians 13, "Some of you are occupied with the signs and miracles which is reminiscent of the Pentecost, consider speaking in tongues better than other gifts looking down on those who do not speak in tongues, and continue to speak in tongues in public even though no one understands you. Stop doing that!" If it were the gift from God, it must have been a good one. Then, why does he have to give such a stern warning to them? It was partly for the order of the Church, yet more importantly it was because these gifts are not the heart of our faith.

What Q29 of the Shorter Catechism teaches is that the most important work of the Holy Spirit is **to apply Christ's redemption to us**. This is His primary work. Let me say this again. What is the primary gift the Holy Spirit gives? It is to apply the redemption to us!

We come across people with the power of healing, and they say this is a kind of spiritual gift. There are also those who predict the future, and this is called the gift of prophecy. Are these really God-given?

How can we know that we received the Holy Spirit? How can we discern His work in us? As mentioned before, the Pentecost left us with such a strong impression that we expect to see something similar in order to declare that the Holy Spirit indwells in us. Of course it was the Holy Spirit who gave all the gifts of the Pentecost. Yet the most important work of the Holy Spirit remains to apply Christ's redemption to us. For such a work, He had to allow the Pentecost, various gifts, miracles, and speaking in tongues, but these were only temporary.

Some may resist complaining, "You should not hinder the free work of the Holy Spirit." If such a complaint is justified, then we should continue to ask to rewrite the Bible. Yet God's way is clear that He had the writers write the Bible with His inspiration, and after completing the book, He did not change even a letter from it. It is the same with the Pentecost. For a particular purpose, God allowed it, and it was to fulfill the need of the just-born church. Continually growing, our focus now should go beyond mere gifts.

So-called signs of these days may be from God or may not be. Thus, we have to be very cautious to call them gifts, let alone boasting about what is given. The Word must be first. We will be learning about sacraments and prayer later, but it is the same with them. The Word must be put first. Paul in 1 Corinthians introduced love as what we have to give our full attention to. If you had the gifts and used them, without love, they are nothing. Love, nothing else, is the miracle. Being sinners, we were incapable of loving anyone else but ourselves, yet now being transformed by the Holy Spirit, we have become capable of loving our neighbors. This is the greatest miracle.

All gifts are from the Holy Spirit, the benefits of Christ, the whole process of salvation, and sanctification. This amazing gift, by which the change of our character, to love, to have willingness to serve our neighbors, and the change of our whole person occurs, is given by the Holy Spirit. Forgetting all of this, if one values and seeks after only the temporary event of the Pentecost, which was allowed only for some particular gifts with a special purpose, this would be the sign of immaturity.

OUTPOURING OF THE HOLY SPIRIT ON THE DAY OF PENTECOST

Herman Barvinck, a renowned Dutch theologian, interpreted the outpouring of the Holy Spirit on the day of Pentecost as the Church itself singing the wonderful works of God in myriad languages. The Church, being filled with the Holy Spirit in its early days, came to experience extraordinary powers and various gifts, yet its focus remained none other than praising God's works in general. What could these works be?

Through Christ's work of mediation, we have become reconciled with God, and at this pinnacle of history, God from His side sent us the Comforter, the Holy Spirit through Jesus, and poured His love and grace down on us. Also the Holy Spirit unites us with Christ in a mysterious way, and through this fellowship with Christ, every believer comes to enjoy all the blessings and benefits of Christ.

Moreover, Barvinck points out that the recipients of such gifts are **His church** rather than individual believers. He offers his explanations on "How these gifts came to the Church" and "How the Old Testaments prophecies were fulfilled" in the following sections and maintains his focus on the role of the Holy Spirit and how He unites us with Christ. Q58 of the Larger Catechism also offers its explanation on "those who can partake in the benefits of Christ" more in detail. (See Chapter 19 of Our Reasonable Faith by Herman Bavinck.)

By the benefit given us by our Lord, we are now able to see the kingdom of God, which existed before eternity yet was hidden from us. **The way we see the Church in this sense must also be broadened**.

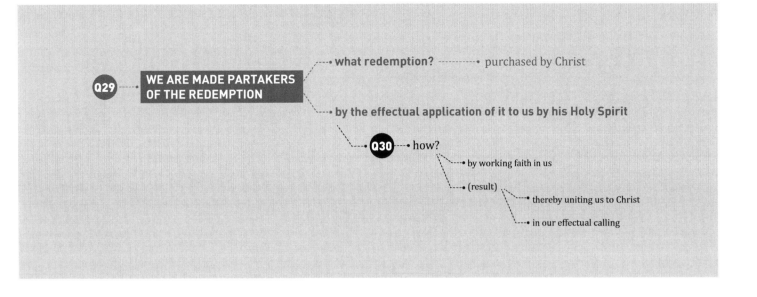

Q29 WE ARE MADE PARTAKERS OF THE REDEMPTION
- what redemption? ----- purchased by Christ
- by the effectual application of it to us by his Holy Spirit
  - **Q30** how?
    - by working faith in us
    - (result)
      - thereby uniting us to Christ
      - in our effectual calling

Q30 How doth the Spirit apply to us the redemption purchased by Christ?

A30 The Spirit applieth to us the redemption purchased by Christ,
by working faith in us,[1,2,3]
and thereby uniting us to Christ
in our effectual calling.[4,5]

1.
Ephesians 1:13-14

In whom ye also trusted, after that ye heard the word of truth, the gospel of your salvation: in whom also after that **ye believed, ye were sealed with that holy Spirit of promise,** Which is the earnest of our inheritance until the redemption of **the purchased possession,** unto the praise of his glory.

2.
John 6:37, 39

All that the Father giveth me shall come to me; and him that cometh to me I will in no wise cast out......And this is the Father's will which hath sent me, that of **all which he hath given me I should lose nothing,** but should **raise it up again at the last day.**

3.
Ephesians 2:8

For **by grace are ye saved through faith;** and that not of yourselves: **it is the gift of God.**

4.
Ephesians 3:17

That **Christ may dwell in your hearts by faith; that ye, being rooted and grounded in love.**

5.
1 Corinthians 1:9

God is faithful, by whom ye were called unto **the fellowship of his Son Jesus Christ our Lord.**

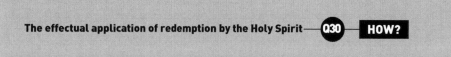

This question is an extension of Q29, which was about the key work of the Holy Spirit, the application of redemption to us. How does He apply redemption in detail?

ON WHICH GROUND? THAT CHRIST HAS PAID IT ALL

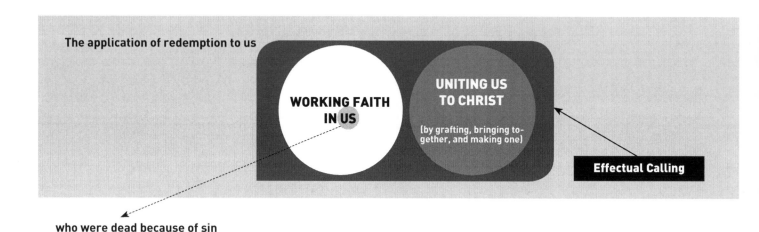

The application of redemption to us

WORKING FAITH IN US

UNITING US TO CHRIST
(by grafting, bringing together, and making one)

Effectual Calling

who were dead because of sin

We have heard numerous times that it is through faith we are united with God, and by faith we are saved. Does this sound so familiar that you feel like skipping to the next part? Yet, do not be so sure. For it is very likely you do not know what it means let alone how to articulate its meaning yourself. Let us give our focus point by point.

1. THIS FAITH COMES IN OUR EFFECTUAL CALLING. WHY IS THAT?

This is the way God grants faith. No one can resist His calling. According to His attributes, this cannot be otherwise. If He calls, no one can be either in death or in sin any longer. This is not a matter of our unwillingness (We do not want to) but

inability (We cannot not do). God calls! How can this not work? If He calls, everyone has to come. There is no way that we could not come. God's calling would surely awake even a decomposing corpse.

Recall what you have learned about God in Q4.

2. WE BECOME UNITED TO CHRIST IN OUR EFFECTUAL CALLING. WHY IS THAT?

Our union with Christ is as certain as our faith. This is more than holding hands with Christ as if after a while we could go our separate way from Jesus. If so, He would not have called this effectual. This union with Christ is to be united as one. Inseparable!

He has purchased us. It is a done deal. God the Father elected, Christ paid the price by His death, and now God the Spirit effectually calls the elected without losing even one. Christ's blood, even a drop of it, should not be wasted. What confirms this calling is not just Christ's blood, but more importantly God's attributes. Now neither height nor depth can separate us from God. This is the way that we have come to have faith and become a Christian. "I believe" not because "I" believed but because the Holy Spirit has given me the faith itself. Because the Holy Spirit effectually called us, faith has come to work in us, and we have become united to Christ. What an effectual calling it is!

How would you answer to the question, "How did you become a Christian?" Does your answer sound like the following? "I spent many years trying to find the answer only to fail. Christ was the answer all along, and I finally came to find Him at the end of a stormy life." Such an answer may sound charming. Yet this is not an appropriate one. For this is only how we see it. It is not I but the Holy Spirit who directed us to this destination, God Himself. He is the initiator, and thus the owner of our faith and life.

You may answer now, "In the Holy Spirit's effectual calling." This may sound awkward at first, yet it is more appropriate implying "God called me" or "The Holy Spirit picked me up and placed me here."

Just recall what you have learned about God. God works all the time in an effectual and perfect way. He saves those He had in His mind to save. For example, if He had number 1, 4, 5, 6, 9, 12, and 18 in His mind to save, it should be exactly those who are saved. God elected them, Jesus paid the price by His death, and now the Holy Spirit calls them without losing even one. No one can alter the names recorded in the book of life. Neither height nor depth, no one in this world can.

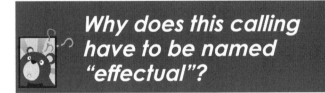

Why does this calling have to be named "effectual"?

Do you picture God make an announcement to unspecified individuals, that is, to all humankind informing them of the way to salvation and waiting for anyone to respond? If God does so, this would not match the God we have learned about in Q5.

Many people tend to think that Jesus opened the door to salvation for unspecified individuals and is calling, and we have to respond to that calling. In this logic, what makes God's calling effectual or not depends on me. If I responded and came, then it would make it an effectual calling. If I did not respond and resisted, then this would not be an effectual calling. It did not work out after all.

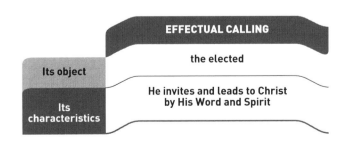

The expression of being partakers of the redemption?

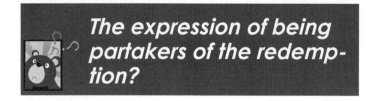

We have repeated that God's calling is effectual and no one can resist His calling. In other words, God is so powerful that His mere calling not only works faith in us but unites us to Christ.

In terms of the structure of the entire Catechism, we are now in one of God's executions, providence. He called and brought us into the place of life through the Mediator, so what other choice do we have than to come to the place He prepared?

These days I am not sure if I am even a Christian let alone if God really exists.

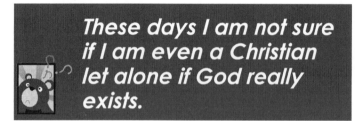

Some may identify with the above saying, "Just like God is unchanging, God-given faith is unchanging—I get it. Yet what bothers me is the remnant of sin in my body and my feelings left for the things of this world. It is indeed tough to overcome. Please pray for me!"

Any believer can relate to this, having experienced his own weakening faith and doubt. However, studying the Shorter Catechism, we have come to find one thing that never changes. On our end, things may appear to change all the time. Yet this faith has been originated by the Holy Spirit. Regardless of our condition, we belong to Christ.

Thus, the best advice for those who may be feeling the above is this: **Place your confidence not on yourself but God**. Imagine two people holding hands together. It takes only one to keep those hands together. For even though one person lets his hand go while the other does not, those hands cannot go separate ways.

What if Jesus stayed? Why did Jesus have to be replaced by the Holy Spirit?

It is not right to make a division between the age of Jesus and the age of the Holy Spirit. As we have learned about the Trinity, the three persons in God always work together. Jesus worked also in the days of Old Testament. Yet it was only when He came to the earth in the form of a human, it appeared so. It is the same with the Holy Spirit, and He is the Spirit of Christ.

Are you disappointed that Jesus went up to the heaven? You should not be. **The Holy Spirit, who is the Spirit of Christ**, is now with all churches and saints at the same time. As long as the Holy Spirit is with us, we are with Christ. As long as the Holy Spirit is with us, the redemption of Christ is effectually applied, our faith cannot be shifted, the mysterious union with Christ cannot be broken, and we continue to be with Christ.

For deeper understanding, refer to: Baptism and Fullness by John Stott, The Person and Ministry of the Holy Spirit by Edwin Palmer, The Holy Spirit by Sinclair Ferguson, and Keep in Step with the Spirit by James Packer.

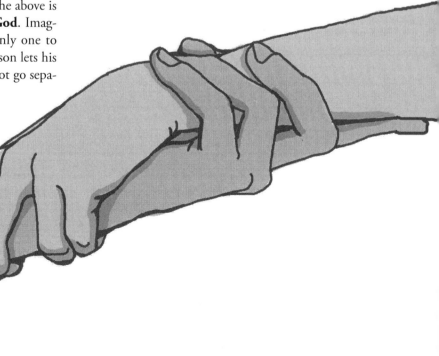

IN-DEPTH STUDY : CHURCH AS A UNITED BODY

The gathering of the elected, who have been mysteriously united with Christ, is called the Church. Q59-66 of the Larger Catechism, while explaining being united with the body of Christ, introduces the Church.

VISIBLE CHURCH	INVISIBLE CHURCH
A society made up of all such as in all ages and places of the world who profess the true religion (Including their children) Under God's special care and government	The whole number of the elect That number has not changed even by one

Among the elect, there could be one who has not gone to a visible church while he was on this earth. In the same way, among the members of a visible church, there could be one who is not a member of the invisible church.

If your understanding of the Church has been merely the gathering of the believers in God, then it needs to go deeper. The Shorter Catechism does not deal with the invisible Church, yet an understanding of this Church is required. For this will clarify that the church of the Old Testament and that of the New Testament is one, and there is only one Church through all ages, from the creation to the end of this world. Being sinners, we are nothing without Christ. Only Christ is the Truth and the Way and the Life. The gathering of those who are elected and united to this Christ is the invisible Church.

WHY IS IT IMPORTANT THAT WE MAKE A DISTINCTION BETWEEN THE VISIBLE CHURCH AND THE INVISIBLE ONE?

Because this is good for us. The picture we have about the Church is the body whose head is Christ. However, what we see and experience in reality is quite far from this picture, being immature, wounded, and lacking in every way. How are we supposed explain such a gap between the ideal and reality? Some leave church altogether carrying their wounds. Others complain that the church is full of lies and is like a whitewashed tomb. Yet our Lord offers **comfort** in that He is preserving this invisible Church pure and blameless while He reaches out to the visible church having its own flaws and shame with His hands of grace and protection.

According to Q65 of the Larger Catechism, the special benefits the invisible Church enjoys by Christ are the union and communion. The union is that the elected become joined to Christ, and this Christ as our Advocate not only becomes our head and commander, but takes all. Who could be better or more beneficial than Christ Himself? Jesus Christ alone is the greatest gift of all for us.

Are you heading in the right direction?

The barometer you could use to examine yourself as you study is your gratitude for everything you come to understand. Do you become more grateful the more you study this Catechism? If so, then you are heading in the right direction. Be encouraged and continue your journey!

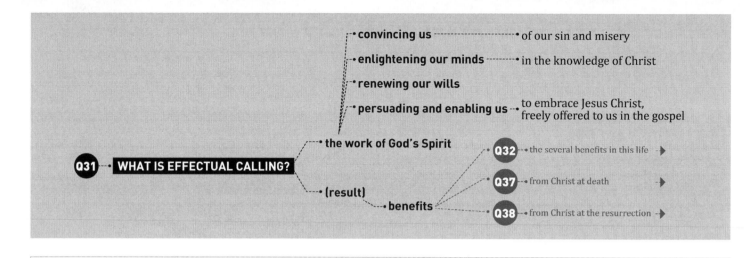

Q31 What is effectual calling?

A31 Effectual calling is the work of God's Spirit,[1,2]

whereby, convincing us of our sin and misery,[3]

enlightening our minds in the knowledge of Christ,[4]

and renewing our wills,[5]

he doth persuade and enable us

to embrace Jesus Christ,

freely offered to us in the gospel.[6,7]

1.
2 Timothy 1:9

Who hath saved us, and called us with an holy calling, not according to our works, but **according to his own purpose and grace, which was given us** in Christ Jesus before the world began.

2.
2 Thessalonians 2:13-14

But we are bound to give thanks always to God for you, brethren beloved of the Lord, because God hath from the beginning chosen you to salvation **through sanctification of the Spirit** and belief of the truth: Whereunto **he called you** by our gospel, to the obtaining of the glory of our Lord Jesus Christ.

3.
Acts 2:37

Now when they heard this, **they were pricked in their heart,** and said unto Peter and to the rest of the apostles, Men and brethren, **what shall we do?**

4.
Acts 26:18

To open their eyes, and to turn them from darkness to light, and from the power of Satan unto God, that they may receive forgiveness of sins, and inheritance among them which are sanctified by faith that is in me.

5.
Ezekiel 36:26-27

A new heart also will I give you, and a new spirit will I put within you: and I will take away the stony heart out of your flesh, and I will give you an heart of flesh. And I will put my spirit within you, and **cause you to walk in my statutes,** and ye shall keep my judgments, and do them.

6.
John 6:44-45

No man **can come to me,** except the Father which hath sent me draw him: and I will raise him up at the last day. It is written in the prophets, And they shall be all taught of God. Every man therefore that hath heard, and hath learned of the Father, **cometh unto me.**

7.
Philippians 2:13

For it is **God which worketh in you both to will and to do** of his good pleasure.

Q30 covered the way the effectual calling is applied, and Q31 now covers the details of this.

Following the question, "What is effectual calling?", the answer clarifies that this has been the work of God's Spirit from the beginning. Before elaborating on the details, this premise should be made certain.

Examine yourself. Regarding your faith, what is the thing that you have done yourself? What did you know about God, and what have you come to take away? You may have thought that you did it all, but it was the Holy Spirit.

Four details follow. There should be, of course, more, but these are offered as the key works of the Holy Spirit. This question can be rephrased: "How can we describe more in detail that we have now placed our faith in Jesus Christ and belong to Him?"

- He convinces us of our sin and misery.
- He enlightens our minds in the knowledge of Christ.
- He renews our wills.
- He persuades and enables us to embrace Jesus Christ.

All these four come to us by surprise. They are indeed the miracle of miracles. Let us take a look one by one.

HE CONVINCES US OF OUR SIN AND MISERY

Because of man's fall, we fell into the state of sin and misery. Now the Holy Spirit convinces us of such a state. This sounds somewhat comical. For this means without His convincing, we remain unconvinced of our own sin and misery. Why is that? It is our state after all and how can we now know it? And this answer asserts that we are simply unable to acknowledge even our own state unless the Holy Spirit calls. This is the state in which so many people in this world are. How miserable this is! And we were just like that. Without knowing the miserable state they are in, they continue to deny their need of salvation. I live a morally good life, thus there should be no problem. If one mentions that salvation comes only through Christ, then they would accuse him of being a religious fanatic and Christianity of being too exclusive. It is because they remain unconvinced of their sin and misery.

HE ENLIGHTENS OUR MINDS IN THE KNOWLEDGE OF CHRIST

The Holy Spirit enlightens the minds of those who are convinced of their sin and misery and are surprised at the state in which they exist with the knowledge of Jesus Christ. Without His work, there is no use continually explaining the Bible, for no one would come to understand it. And no one can say, "It was the Holy Spirit who convinced me of sin and misery, but now I have to utilize my intelligence to learn further." First and foremost, the Holy Spirit convinces us of the sin and misery in us. And He leads us to acknowledge that we absolutely cannot save ourselves, but there is One who can save us from this sin and misery. Also He helps us understand the precious blood of Jesus of 2,000 years ago, helps us desire to get to know Him more, and in the end helps us develop the heart to be more like Him. In every way, this is a gift.

HE RENEWS OUR WILLS

The Holy Spirit teaches us and makes us understand. Then, some may ask, "Isn't at least my will mine?" However, even our will must be renewed by the Holy Spirit. No one could say, "Christ made himself known to me, and now I respond to Him." Apart from the work of the Holy Spirit, nothing can renew our will. You may come up with slogans to live by like "Get out, sin!" "Keep the Law!" or "Cheers, everybody!" but all of these are destined to fail. Even our will is what He renews.

HE PERSUADES AND ENABLES US TO EMBRACE JESUS CHRIST

In the end it is a question of who accepts Christ. It is the Holy Spirit. We do not come to accept Christ by our own power or will, but the Holy Spirit enables us to. He persuades our minds, which used to go other directions, changes them, prepares them suitably for Christ, and makes us desire Him. Here, the word persuade was used in order to describe the process.

In all matters, God never forces. He does not hijack and crazy-glue us to anything. He does not treat us as if we were robots. He makes us do everything out of our desire and in fact offers the power for us to do so. This is a wholly different level of gift and also the reason to be ever more grateful.

WHAT CHRIST? THE ONE FREELY OFFERED TO US IN THE GOSPEL

Another significant fact is mentioned in the last line: All these things were freely given. There were no strings attached for any of these benefits. From the first question of the Shorter Catechism up to this point of Q31, nothing was offered in return of our payment. From the moment of creation up until now, all of these have been offered to us without any condition demanded on us. "All will be given to you only if you do such and such." No, nothing happened in such a way.

EVEN FAITH IS THE WORK OF THE HOLY SPIRIT

Why does God give faith as a gift? It is, by imputing Christ's righteousness, to make us righteous, which is for God to have a fellowship with us. In other words, faith is the tool and instrument for us to fellowship with God. It is neither a reward nor a condition. When misunderstood, this surely brings trouble. Religion keeps on saying that we have to do something to have fellowship with God. Yet this is not true, for we are now having fellowship with God just as we are. Some may still insist, "Among everything else, at least faith should be mine."
[partial mindmap]

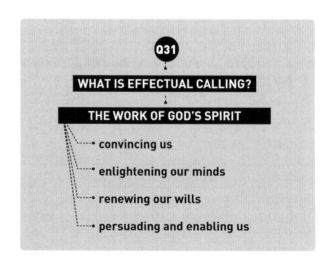

WHY DO WE KEEP ON FALLING INTO THIS ERROR?

Why do we easily fall into this kind of thought that we have to do something for our salvation?

1. "God has given, and now I want to do something for Him." This is because we do not understand what "freely" means. If we only came to realize how broke we are, it would become as clear as it can be that there is no other way to receive anything than for free.

Yet this kind of thought may be taken as a good and innocent one. The fallen nature of man is better revealed in what comes next.

2. "It is all give and take. I have to offer something in order to get something greater in return." What underlies this kind of thought is calculation and the desire for rewards. The Bible surely speaks of rewards, yet this must be understood with cau-

tion. Rewards of the Bible ultimately refer to God and more specifically to the benefits of mediation we are now learning. These benefits are entirely different from such a scheming and secular concept of rewards.

So many Christians are falling into such an error. What is worse is that this does not stop at being just an error or a mistake, but will eventually usher them into idolatry. When God is misunderstood, anything that we do for God will turn out to be resistance against Him. We may think we are now serving God with great zeal, but in reality we could be serving only an idol of our creation. How preposterous this would be! That is why we should constantly examine ourselves with the holy Words of God. (Heb 4:12)

For deeper understanding, refer to: God is the Gospel by John Piper

BE SPIRITUAL VS. BE GODLY

Spirituality is one of the terms about which today's Christians not only feel comfortable but have come to use in the place of other traditional Christian terms. The problem is that being an ambiguous term itself, this replacement has made countless conversations also ambiguous. What it has come to replace for example are terms like training in godliness, the fullness of the Holy Spirit, faith, love, fellowship among believers, the life after Christ, and living according to the Word, to name a few.

Our worldview should revolve around God and Him alone. **What makes Christians anxious is only the thought that we have to earn or work for something**. It may be a little step, but I'd like to suggest bringing the traditional Christian terms of the Bible back into our conversations. What if we replace the term spirituality with godliness?

> Lord, let me live a godly life before you.

Discussion Questions

❶ By the work of the Holy Spirit, what key benefits have we come to receive?

❷ Read Eph 2:1 and Col 2:13. Elaborate their meaning relating them to Q13-19 we have previously studied.

❸ Elaborate how the effectual calling should be effectual relating it to Q4-6 we have previously studied.

❹ In what sense does this chapter give us the reason to be grateful?

THE BENEFITS OF MEDIATION: THE COMMUNION IN GRACE

"CHRISTIANS CALL THEMSELVES THE CHILDREN OF GOD, YET THEY APPEAR TO BE WORSE. THE FATHER DOES NOT DISCIPLINE HIS OWN CHILDREN. SUCH A GOD IS UNTRUSTWORTHY."

"I HAVE GONE TO CHURCH FOR A LONG TIME, YET I DON'T SEE ANY CHANGES IN ME. EVERY TIME I SIT AND LISTEN TO SERMONS, I CANNOT HELP BUT QUESTION, 'WHAT AM I DOING HERE?' I FEEL SORRY AND ASHAMED! I MAY NEED A BREAK."

We are now studying the benefits that come with the effectual calling. Here it is also important to understand the matter at hand in the context of whole the catechism. This chapter will present the benefits of mediation in three categories: in this life, at death, and at resurrection.

The general way to explain salvation is a process through which the steps of salvation are listed one by one such as calling, conversion, justification, adoption, and so on. Instead of such a process and result, the Shorter Catechism offers the benefits of redemption in a rather larger frame. According to the Shorter Catechism, this whole process including our life, death, and resurrection, is the result of Christ's mediation and the benefits we receive thereby.

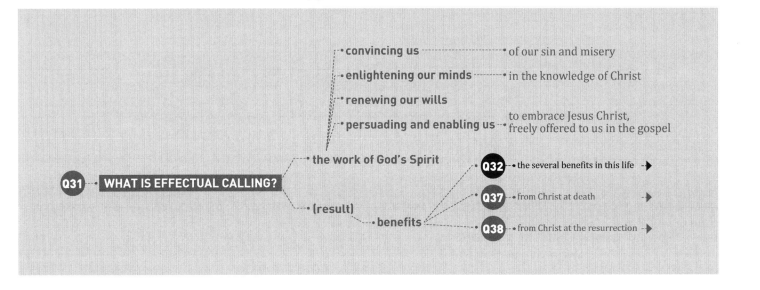

- convincing us .... of our sin and misery
- enlightening our minds .... in the knowledge of Christ
- renewing our wills
- persuading and enabling us ... to embrace Jesus Christ, freely offered to us in the gospel
- the work of God's Spirit

Q31 • **WHAT IS EFFECTUAL CALLING?**

- (result)
- benefits
  - **Q32** • the several benefits in this life →
  - **Q37** • from Christ at death →
  - **Q38** • from Christ at the resurrection →

Q32 What benefits do they that are effectually called partake of in this life?

A32 They that are effectually called do in this life partake
of justification,[1] adoption,[2] and sanctification,
and the several benefits which in this life
do either accompany or flow from them.[3]

1.
Romans 8:30

Moreover whom he did predestinate, them he also called: and **whom he called, them he also justified:** and whom he justified, them he also glorified.

2.
Ephesians 1:5

Having predestinated us unto **the adoption of children** by Jesus Christ to himself, according to the good pleasure of his will.

3.
1 Corinthians 1:26, 30

For ye see your calling, brethren, how that not many wise men after the flesh, not many mighty, not many noble, are called… But of him are ye in Christ Jesus, who of God is made **unto us wisdom, and righteousness, and sanctification, and redemption.**

Here comes the word **benefit**. What a significant term, for it communicates well what the effectually called partake of. Instead of penance, labor, training, incentive, or competition, we now get to partake of "benefit." Salvation is freely given, which makes it impossible for us to say to ourselves, "Now let's earn our keep" or "We still need some training to make ourselves worthy of the Kingdom."

At the same time, it communicates that what we are partaking of is indeed good for us. What would these benefits be and how good?

In answering this question, we encounter a prerequisite that these benefits are for those who are effectually called. This means the union with Christ is necessary to partake of these benefits. God calls the elected for this union with Christ, and this effectual calling is also known as an inner call. These precious benefits are only for those who are effectually called. Having this in mind, now let us begin to explore what these benefits are one by one.

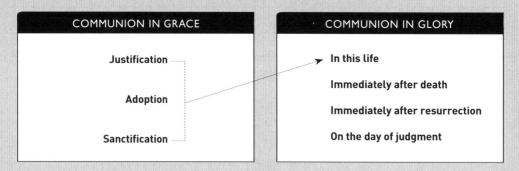

**OUR BENEFITS BROUGHT BY GOD'S EFFECTUAL CALLING
(Q69, Q82 IN THE LARGER CATECHISM)**

COMMUNION IN GRACE	COMMUNION IN GLORY
Justification	In this life
Adoption	Immediately after death
Sanctification	Immediately after resurrection
	On the day of judgment

The Larger Catechism explains this under two categories--communion in grace and communion in glory. Our life is now in personal fellowship and companionship with God. It is His grace that has brought us up to this point, and it should only be His glory that the remainder of ours lives must focus on. Both communions are made available by the Holy Spirit, and it is a blessed and glorious communion with Christ along with the whole Church.

We are almost there!

THE BENEFITS BROUGHT BY THE UNION WITH CHRIST

It begins by explaining the benefits brought by the union with Christ in three categories. Broadly, they could be divided into in this life, at death, and at resurrection, and Q32 opens the door with the benefits in this life. Three benefits are included in those that believers partake of in this life: justification, adoption, and sanctification. These are the most significant and fundamental benefits given for believers on this earth. Several other benefits also accompany these three. This discussion will continue in Q36.

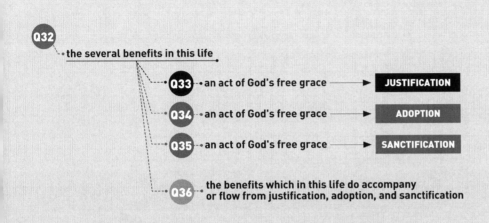

Justification is to account a person righteous; adoption is to receive him as God's children; sanctification is to make him holy. Detailed descriptions for each will be provided with the respective answers for Q33, 34, and 35. In addition, Q36 will explain several other benefits.

Yet these answers can make some shrug their shoulders for their unexpectedness. If rephrased, the question becomes, "What is the good of becoming a Christian and going to church?" The Shorter Catechism offers its answer that God makes us righteous, His children, and holy. How does that sound to you? Are these what you have expected? Probably not.

Justification, adoption, and sanctification… These are the blessings prepared for Christians on this earth. Do they fit into your definition of blessing? And what did you expect to enjoy when you became a Christian and went to church? Probably health, a peaceful mind, money, and less trouble for your family to name a few. Also what would you answer to the question, "What kind of good have you enjoyed since you became a Christian?" What would generally follow are: fellowship with other believers, encouraging sermons, a peaceful and pure mind, opportunities to serve the church and neighbors, and personal growth. Yet what are the benefits of Q32? Instead of the above, it offers justification, adoption, and sanctification. What are these? Are they really blessing?

Some may flip the pages saying, "It must be wrong. There should be more." We are now dealing with the benefits on this earth, yet the above appears to be only the benefits of heaven. This reflects that what we have been desiring may not be the key benefits from Christ. The key benefits are justification, adoption, and sanctification. However, part of us keeps saying, "Now, on the top of such things, there must be other blessings. Some immediate good!"

This is worth pondering. Being accounted not a sinner but righteous, becoming a child of God, and in reality becoming holy—are they not the key blessings man has been pursuing? People of this world may understand for example winning the lottery or seeing the investment in our house price rise as a blessing, but this is not how the true Christian faith understands the blessing.

From Q33, we will be taking a close look at true blessings.

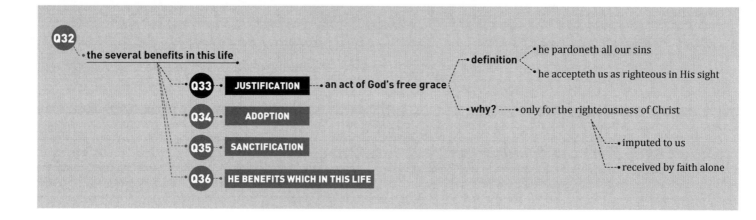

Q32 • the several benefits in this life

Q33 • JUSTIFICATION • an act of God's free grace

• definition
- he pardoneth all our sins
- he accepteth us as righteous in His sight

• why? • only for the righteousness of Christ
- imputed to us
- received by faith alone

Q34 • ADOPTION

Q35 • SANCTIFICATION

Q36 • HE BENEFITS WHICH IN THIS LIFE

Q33   What is justification?

A33   Justification is an act of God's free grace,

wherein he pardoneth all our sins,[1, 2]

and accepteth us as righteous in his sight,[3]

only for the righteousness of Christ

imputed to us,[4]

and received by faith alone.[5, 6]

1.
Romans 3:24-25

Being justified freely by his grace through the redemption that is in Christ Jesus: Whom God hath set forth to be a propitiation through faith in his blood, to declare his righteousness **for the remission of sins** that are past, through the forbearance of God.

2.
Romans 4:6-8

Even as David also describeth the blessedness of the man, unto whom God imputeth righteousness without works, Saying, Blessed are they **whose iniquities are forgiven, and whose sins are covered.** Blessed is the man to **whom the Lord will not impute sin.**

3.
2 Corinthians 5:19, 21

To wit, that God was in Christ, reconciling the world unto himself, **not imputing their trespasses unto them;** and hath committed unto us the word of reconciliation......For he hath made him to be sin for us, who knew no sin; **that we might be made the righteousness of God in him.**

4.
Romans 5:17-19

For if by one man's offence death reigned by one; much more they which receive abundance of grace and **of the gift of righteousness** shall reign in life by one, Jesus Christ. Therefore as by the offence of one judgment came upon all men to condemnation; even so **by the righteousness of one the free gift came upon all men unto justification of life.** For as by one man's disobedience many were made sinners, so **by the obedience of one shall many be made righteous.**

5.
Galatians 2:16

Knowing that a man is not justified **by the works of the law, but by the faith of Jesus Christ,** even we have believed in Jesus Christ, that we might be justified by the faith of Christ, and not by the works of the law: for by the works of the law shall no flesh be justified.

6.
Philippians 3:9

And be found in him, not having mine own righteousness, which is of the law, but **that which is through the faith of Christ,** the righteousness which is **of God by faith.**

The definition of justification is offered with the prerequisite that it is an act of God's free grace. Interestingly this will be repeated in the following, adoption in Q34 and sanctification in Q35. Justification is one of the benefits for those united with Christ in this life and is also an act of God's free grace. That is what this prerequisite makes sure to communicate, and this shows that all questions in the Shorter Catechism are meticulously designed.

The answer continues:
1) He pardons all our sins.
2) He accepts us as righteous in His sight.

And this is not the righteousness of ours but of Christ's, which is imputed to us. This also is not received with any kind of payments or good works but by faith alone. Every line of this question is essentially worthy of some thought and consideration.

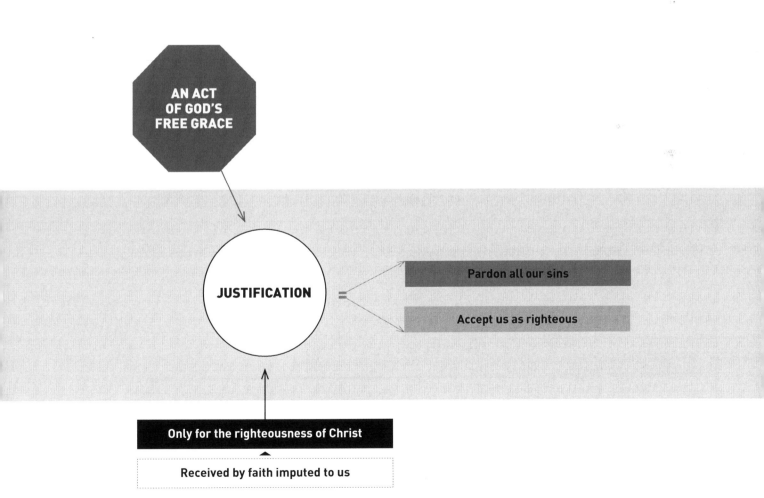

WHAT IS JUSTIFICATION?

Let us take a look of a detailed description of this. What is justification? It is **to pardon our sins** and **to accept us as righteous**. This means despite our true identity—not righteous—that He account us so. The reason is as follows: the righteousness of Christ has been imputed to us that we are accounted as righteous. By faith alone.

Justification, which is to call someone righteous, is a legal term. Regardless of one's sin, the court declares him innocent, and such a verdict removes all the responsibilities of his sin. In other words, it is **to pretend that we have righteousness**, which in reality we do not have at all. Let me reiterate. It is "not" that God sees the tiny bit of righteousness in us and magnifies it. As we have learned, we do not have any righteousness in us. Despite Jesus' completed work, we still struggle with sin, yet now we are declared righteous. This is justification.

Imagine a person who was just floundering in sin. God picked him up from such a state and brought him into the light. Standing in his filth, he must feel mortified. What if this is the state in which he must remain for good? His only name is a sinner, and there is nothing he can do about his guilt? No one in history regardless of his greatness was able to shake the title of sinner off himself. There was no way to solve this problem on our end, yet God changed our names into the righteous ones. And He clothed us with Christ's righteousness and through His righteousness accepted us as so. He called us so knowing how terrible we have been. What could make us more grateful or more joyful? It is indeed the greatest—truly deep but quiet—love, and it should overwhelm us. This is the privilege and benefit for those who are united with Christ.

However, being freely given, we tend to take this benefit for granted. Yet, this is only free in a sense that we did not pay for it, but its cost was extremely high. How much should we have paid to the court for this justification? If converted to numbers, it would be infinite, for it required the blood of Jesus Christ the only Son. Christ, who is God, laid Himself down to save us, and **the value of this is surely supreme**. That is why the topic of Christ's perfect obedience and His sufficient work of redemption cannot be overlooked in the discussion of justification.

There is one phrase remaining, and this may appear to contradict the above. The phrase "by faith alone" was the slogan of the Reformation and is still an important concept. This expression, by faith, must not excuse us to change our focus and say that our faith has worked as an instrument, for this is not the point. Certainly, salvation by faith does not mean that it was not free or we had to do something for it. What have we learned about the One who works this faith in us? This was the gift from the Holy Spirit. The focus of this expression, by faith alone, should be on the fact that we did not pay anything worth being accounted righteous. Even this faith was a gift.

"For it is by grace you have been saved, through faith-and this not from yourselves, it is the gift of God not by works, so that no one can boast." (Eph 2:8-9)

We have this incredible guarantee, Jesus Christ, and He makes us sinners as righteous as He is before the Father. We are, in legal terms, the righteous. J That can bring us mixed feelings, gladness/thankfulness along with shame/embarrassment. Yet God's final say regarding our legal status is "Righteous." How great is that!

Now the catechism introduces us to the greatest and most central benefit of all, of which "Justification" comes as its first part. We have to take this simple yet profound proclamation into our hearts and be eternally grateful, giving the answer of "Justification" to the question, "What would be the most fundamental benefit given to our lives?", "Oh, I'd rather win the lottery jackpot! That would be THE benefit of my life." Frankly speaking that is where some of us are in terms of understanding the benefit we can receive from God. However, God's final way over us is, "You are righteous. Yours is eternal life!" How can anything of this world compare with that? Indeed, nothing can!

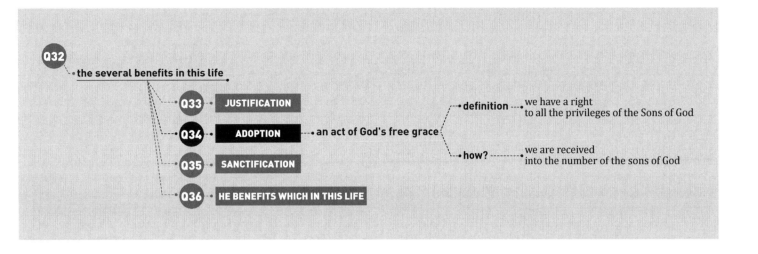

Q34 What is adoption?

A34 Adoption is an act of God's free grace,[1]
        whereby we are received into the number,
        and have a right to all the privileges of the sons of God.[2,3]

1.
1 John 3:1

Behold, **what manner of love the Father hath bestowed upon us, that we should be called the sons of God:** therefore the world knoweth us not, because it knew him not.

2.
John 1:12

But as many as received him, **to them gave he power to become the sons of God,** even to them that believe on his name.

3.
Romans 8:17

And **if children, then heirs; heirs of God, and joint-heirs with Christ;** if so be that we suffer with him, that we may be also glorified together.

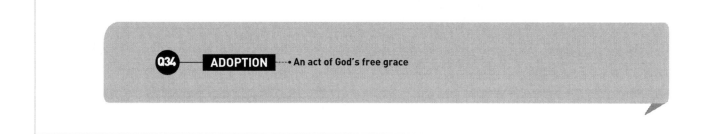

The definition of adoption is also offered with the prerequisite that it is an act of God's free grace. Both justification and adoption, and even sanctification, are acts of God's free grace. This is only being repeated because it has been misconstrued many times in the history.

As its definition describes, through this adoption, we come **to enjoy all the privileges as the sons of God**. It should not come as a surprise that the privileges of the son come along with sonship.

While describing adoption, a unique expression "being received into the number" has been put to use. This implies that there is a set number of God's children, and this is the same as the number of the elect. In other words, this is the number of the invisible church and God's chosen ones (children). As God is unchanging, this number is also unchanging. And we are received into this number. How certain God's reserved seats are! We should find the confidence of our faith and hope of comfort in this truth.

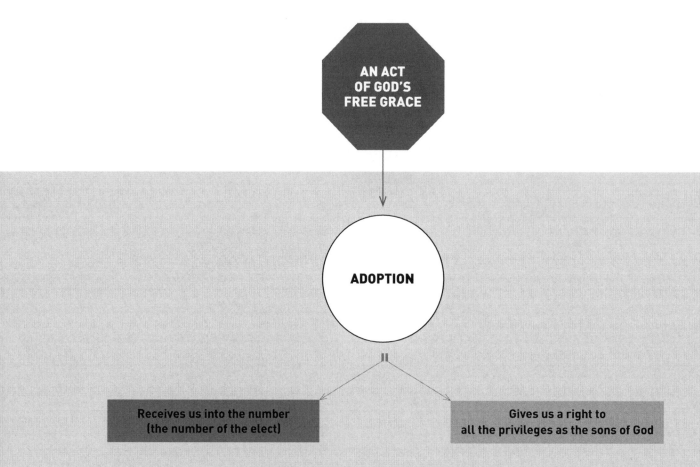

WHAT IS ADOPTION?

Through justification, we were made righteous. Taking a step further, God now makes us His children. Adoption may appear to be the result of calling and justification, and its description merely repeats what we have seen before. Yet one thing that draws our attention is the phrase "God receives us into the number of the elect." This eliminates any room for argument or negotiation. God has set the number of the elect, which makes it unchangeable. It is not that we were not on the roll at first, and God is now writing our names down on it; rather, we were on the roll from the beginning, but only at a certain point of our lives, it appears so to us.

Now we are the children of God. It is sealed. Yay for us! We are now under the care and the rule of our heavenly Father. We now can enjoy all the freedom and privileges of His son. We are also the heirs. How great is this!

GIVES US PRIVILEGES AS THE SONS OF GOD

If you reserved a hotel room, the room should be made available upon your arrival. If breakfast was included, you should not worry about going into the restaurant the next morning. For these privileges would be your right. It is the same with the privileges made yours through adoption. No one could ask you now, "Who are you?" or "What allows you to…?" You now have this privilege, and no one should come in the way.

Yet you should know that this privilege includes that of begin scolded when you do wrong. This is how the parent-child relationship works. If you are not the child, you will not be scolded but just thrown out. Parents may scold their child, but never abandon them. Thus, being the children of God, we are secure at all times. So are our souls. Thus, take heart!

Westminster **LARGER CATECHISM Q74**

Q. 74   What is adoption?
A. 74   Adoption is an act of the free grace of God,
        in and for his only Son Jesus Christ,
          whereby all those
              that are justified
              are received into the number of his children,
              have his name put upon them,
              the Spirit of his Son given to them,
              are under his fatherly care and dispensations,
              admitted to all the liberties and privileges of the sons of God,
              made heirs of all the promises,
              and fellow-heirs with Christ in glory.

WHAT IS PRIVILEGE?

The Larger Catechism explains that we are "made heirs of all the promises, and fellow-heirs with Christ in glory." (Larger Catechism Q74)

Here the heir refers to the successor or beneficiary, by which a son secures the legal entitlement to the property of the Father. All the blessings a son has from his Father—both in this world (all His promises) and in the world to come (eternal life) —are included in this privilege. However, it is worth noting the privilege of a son should extend to discipline as well. Bad things can and do happen to believers just as they can and do happen to non-believers. Yet the believers take such things like sons of the Father as part of such a privilege, thus with gratitude.

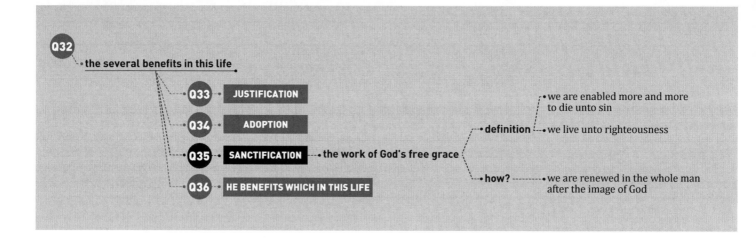

Q35 What is sanctification?

A35 Sanctification is the work of God's free grace,[1]
   whereby we are renewed in the whole man
     after the image of God,[2]
  and are enabled more and more
    to die unto sin,
    and live unto righteousness.[3, 4]

1.
2 Thessalonians 2:13

But we are bound to give thanks always to God for you, brethren beloved of the Lord, because God hath from the beginning chosen you to salvation **through sanctification of the Spirit** and belief of the truth.

2.
Ephesians 4:23-24

And be **renewed in the spirit of your mind**; And that ye put on the new man, **which after God is created in righteousness and true holiness.**

3.
Romans 6:4, 6

Therefore we are buried **with him by baptism into death**: that like as Christ was raised up from the dead by the glory of the Father, even so we also should walk in newness of life.....Knowing this, that our old man is crucified with him, that the body of sin might be destroyed, **that henceforth we should not serve sin.**

3.
Romans 8:1

There is therefore now no condemnation to them which are in Christ Jesus, **who walk not after the flesh, but after the Spirit.**

The third key benefit, sanctification, is about to be explored. Here, its context should be taken with caution. I'd like to bring your attention to three things.

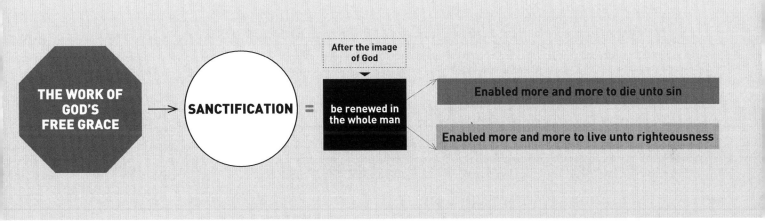

1. WORK: REGARDING JUSTIFICATION AND ADOPTION, THE PHRASE "AN ACT OF GOD'S FREE GRACE" WAS PUT TO USE.

Here, with sanctification, "The work of God's free grace" is being used. There is a distinction between these two. "An act" refers to the job done in a short period of time, and "the work" refers to the job being done over a long period of time. In other words, sanctification takes time and requires constant change, which makes it a process. Meanwhile the previously discussed were rather instantaneous and conceptual. However, God works sanctification over one's entire life.

At first, no one is holy. Even after becoming a Christian, one could still put his trust in the number of zeros in his bank account. But such trust should fade away. There may be ups and downs, but in a broader view, the graph should only go upwards. The trend of sin should make a downward curve while the trend of righteousness should make a rising one. Not everyone will make the same progress as far as its degree and rate go. But in the end God should complete the sanctification to His desire.

2. GOD: NOW, LET US BRING OUR FOCUS ON GOD.

Sanctification is God's work. Its process, way, and result are all God's work and God-given. It is easy to fall into the error that everything up to this point has been done <u>by God</u>, but not from this point on. Yet this is not true. Even this, sanctification, is the work of God.

3. GRACE: SANCTIFICATION ITSELF IS A BENEFIT, FOR IT IS THE WORK OF GOD'S "GRACE."

In time and through the powerful work of the Holy Spirit, the death and resurrection of Christ is being applied to those God elected. And it is <u>by this grace</u>, that we are enabled more and more to die unto sin and live unto righteousness. What else is grace and benefit than this to us? :)

IS IT NECESSARY THAT WE ARE MADE HOLY?

Some may say, "We are saved not by our righteousness, but by being clothed with Christ's righteousness. Doesn't this make sanctification unnecessary? We are already saved and upon death we will go to heaven. Then what is the use of it?"

Here, we need to go back to the creation of man. In the beginning when God created man, He did so in His own image. But being corrupted by sin, we are now far from the state in which we were created. Christ, being our Mediator, restored our relationship with God, and the Holy Spirit now brings us to the place we were destined to be, the holy state worthy of the people of the holy kingdom. This is sanctification. In this sense, it seems quite necessary.

THE POSITION OF "REPENTANCE" IN THE CATECHISM

1. IT IS WORTH REPEATING

Part 1 of the Shorter Catechism is about "What man is to believe concerning God," and Part 2 is about "What duty God requires of man." Repentance does not appear until Part 2. (Q 87) Also in the Larger Catechism repentance is not covered along with justification but with sanctification. This implies that we should not emphasize "the act of repentance" as if it earned us justification. Rather, repentance is essential for maintaining our relationship with God, which is closely related to sanctification. In other words, our repentance is not the means we utilize to earn our salvation but the practice we execute due to already-given salvation. It is the same with faith. (Q31)

2. SANCTIFICATION IS THE WORK OF GOD.

Then, in which ways does He work? It is through sanctification that we are enabled more and more to die unto sin. Q75 of the Larger Catechism defines sanctification as "having the seeds of repentance unto life, and all other saving graces, put into their hearts, and those graces so stirred up, increased, and strengthened, (as that) they more and more die unto sin, and rise unto newness of life." And the description of repentance follows in Q76 that "he so grieves for and hates his sins, as that he turns from them all to God, purposing and endeavoring constantly to walk with him in all the ways of new obedience." Thus, repentance is not a one-time resolution but a struggle with the remnant of sin in our lives. "Spiritual Warfare," what a fitting name, and what makes this warfare still a benefit for us is that this is already won.

Repentance as a saving grace enables us to see and sense the horror of our sin, take hold of God's mercy in Christ, which should make us deeply grieve for and belligerently hate our sin, turn from our sins with specific actions, have a purpose to walk with God and new obedience, and also constantly endeavor to do all of the above. Repentance should include all of the above, which are gifts from God. (Refer to Q76 in the Larger Catechism)

Without the light of the Holy Spirit and the Bible, we could not have repented. Unable to know our sin, even the first step of the above could not have been made. God not only gives us all but lead us. Whatever labor we are putting into our sanctifi- cation, it is only so because this labor itself is the work of God in us.

THE DIFFERENCE BETWEEN JUSTIFICATION AND SANCTIFICATION

For the in-depth study, the following tables are designed incorporating Q77 of the Larger Catechism and chapter 22 of Our Reasonable Faith by Herman Bavinck. Yet their key distinction lies in justification being the legal declaration of holiness and sanctification being the process towards actual holiness.

JUSTIFICATION	SANCTIFICATION
God imputes the righteousness of Christ	God imputes the righteousness of Christ
Sin is pardoned	Sin is pardoned
It equally frees all believers from the revenging wrath of God Perfectly in this life, they never fall into condemnation	It equally frees all believers from the revenging wrath of God Perfectly in this life, they never fall into condemnation

Q77 of the Larger Catechism

JUSTIFICATION	SANCTIFICATION
It delivers man from his guilt	It delivers him from the pollution of sin
Man's consciousness is changed	His being is changed
By means of it, man comes to stand in a right relationship again	By means of it, man become good again and able to do good

Chapter 22 of *Our Reasonable Faith* by Herman Bavinck

THE IMPERFECTION OF SANCTIFICATION

The imperfection of sanctification arises "from the remnants of sin abiding in every part of [believers], and the perpetual lustings of the flesh against the spirit; whereby they are often foiled with temptations, and fall into many sins, are hindered in all their spiritual services, and their best works are imperfect and defiled in the sight of God." (Q78 of the Larger Catechism)

Because of the remnant of sin, we cannot attain perfect sanctification in this life. Our fight against sin is without end. We will conquer our sin eventually, but being strangers on this earth, we have to fight with this and often fail. We understand this not only through the Bible but through life experience. When we set our minds to live according to God's will, things easily become rough and come to entangle us.

What underlies the process of sanctification is the principle of God's amazing love. God lets His children grow not through a mechanical way but a personal fellowship. We may not have anything to boast about, even the strength to stand, or our own merits, yet God requires of us something unimaginable, "Be perfect as your heavenly Father is perfect." Who can dare to achieve such a demand of God? Yet God does not stop picking us up when we fall and continues to lead us with His staff and rod. This is the way He loves us. In this way, He continues to have fellowship with us.

> *If He did save and justify us, He could have made us strong enough to conquer all sins. Why did He have to make us to struggle? Is our salvation only partial, not a perfect one?*

God intended to work this way, and His work is always perfect. God's way is above ours both in its quality and size.

> *If sanctification is not the work of ourselves, then we can just sit around doing nothing. God will work it out, so why bother?*

We are not robots. God loves us in a personal way. Moreover, God works in us to have the will and to act accordingly. Because this is none other than God, it would be really difficult for you just to sit around doing nothing.

> *Why didn't God make all people reach maturity at once, instead of placing them in various levels? I get that this is His discipline, but He seems so demanding.*

It is probably because He wanted us to look after one another acknowledging that we all are members in Christ. Mature ones can give their hands to rather immature and young believers, and share their own life experiences of sanctification as a comfort to them. Through this kind of serving, we can truly be members in Christ, and this kind of community can be a great benefit to us.

> *Does sanctification work in a gradual way? Is our growth supposed to be steady? Yet I feel like I am moving backwards these days?*

Yes, sanctification is gradual, but we cannot judge our growth by its appearance. Because sanctification is God's work, it must be evaluated in God's perspective. Sanctification is not equal in all of us. Anyone can have a zeal for God's grace, but this may not always be dramatic.

The question at hand may carry a hidden intention to judge and condemn another believer. "If one is a believer in the process of sanctification, he should grow as time passes." Be always ready to offer an answer to such a statement. There is just an inch gap between knowing sanctification as God's gift and benefit and judging others.

We cannot make a good judgment regarding the process of others' sanctification let alone our own. What is more appropriate than repeating such a comment above like a Pharisee is to pray for mercy beating our own chest like a tax collector. If admonition is in need, then more wisdom should be prayed for and included in the process.

I DON'T HAVE THE ASSURANCE OF SALVATION. HOW CAN I HAVE THIS ASSURANCE OF SALVATION?

Being one of the most famous questions in church, the above may sound familiar to you. This has been so for such a long time that even the Larger Catechism has come to include it.

"May not true believers, by reason of their imperfections, and the many temptations and sins they are overtaken with, fall away from the state of grace?" (Q79)

The above question encompasses everything we have been learning. And this is, theologically speaking, the doctrine of perseverance.

A: *"True believers, by reason of the unchangeable love of God, and His decree and covenant to give them perseverance, their inseparable union with Christ, His continual intercession for them, and the Spirit and seed of God abiding in them, can neither totally nor finally fall away from the state of grace, but are kept by the power of God through faith unto salvation."* (For God has elected them, and they are the chosen elect!)

The answer is crystal clear: "No, true believers cannot fall away from the state of grace, but are kept through faith unto salvation." But what if we can agree to this only with our head, but not with our hearts? And this is what Q80 asks.

"Can true believers be infallibly assured that they are in the estate of grace, and that they shall persevere therein unto salvation?"

So far we have come to know not only the imperfection of our sanctification but also God's eventual protection of us in the process of it. Yet, from our perspective, can true believers have an infallible assurance of his salvation? What would those who may be stuck in the process of sanctification or have fallen away form the protection of the Church say? Their response is likely to be doubtful. Yet let us take a look at the answer of the Larger Catechism.

A: *"Such as truly believe in Christ, and endeavor to walk in all good conscience before Him, may, without extraordinary revelation, by faith grounded upon the truth of God's promises, and by* the Spirit (enabling them to discern in themselves those graces to which the promises of life are made, and bearing witness with their spirits that they are the children of God,) *be infallibly assured that they are in the estate of grace, and shall persevere therein unto salvation."*

Yes, the answer is a thousand times yes. "Yes, they can be infallibly assured that they are in the estate of grace, and shall persevere therein unto salvation." Yet what deserves a second look is the basis of such an assurance. The reason we can have this assurance of grace and salvation is on God's work and protection for us, never on us.

"Then, are all true believers at all times assured of their present existence in the estate of grace, and that they shall be saved?"

Regarding the question of the assurance of salvation, the answer was "Yes." But here the question gets even tougher. "Then, all believers at all times have this assurance?" For the one who cannot be sure of his salvation, this question could be terrifying. Let's take a look at its answer.

A: *"Assurance of grace and salvation not being of the essence of faith, true believers may wait long before they obtain it; and, after the enjoyment thereof, may have it weakened and intermitted, through manifold distempers, sins, temptations, and desertions; yet are they never left without such a presence and support of the Spirit of God as keeps them from sinking into utter despair."*

The answer is "No, not all believers have this assurance at all times." As it has been clarified in the beginning, *the assurance of salvation is not the essence of faith.* What a wise answer! We may not have the assurance, yet this has nothing to do with our salvation.

Taking all of the above, we may conclude, "Yes, we can have the assurance of salvation, yet oftentimes it may get weakened. However, because it is not the essence of our faith, we do not have to be anxious." What a relief!

"But whoever blasphemes against the Holy Spirit will never be forgiven; he is guilty of an eternal sin." (Mark 3:29)

Concerning what we have just learned about the assurance of salvation, another question may arise. "Then, now being saved, can we not have any thought or action that resists God?" Yes, we can, for our faith can surely be weakened. However, this must not be confused with the blasphemy against the Holy Spirit, in which one falls away from God for good even though he once received the objective revelation and subjective enlightenment, and further realized and tasted the truth. How can anyone leave God for good while being given God's revelation and enlightenment? Then, by any chance, can I?

Regarding salvation, the key point is that salvation belongs to God's predestination and was given to the elect before the creation of the world. Yet there are things made available also to nonbelievers; for example, they may also pursue morality, goodness, and truth, be given a stable environment on this earth, have joyful emotions, and so on. Thus, it should not be strange that the light of the Word itself and the precious enlightenment of the Holy Spirit could be given them as well. God is not only the God of the elect, but of all creatures, being the creator and ruler of all.

Then, who commits this unpardonable sin, the blasphemy against the Holy Spirit? Only the non-elect can. They also can have the thirst for the truth, which will bring them to the Word, and with the enlightenment of the Holy Spirit to some degree, they can come to realize and taste it. They also can taste God's holiness, wisdom, and goodness. However, they eventually come to hate and refuse it, and resist God even disrupting the faith of others without any pangs on their conscious. When such a hardness of conscious reaches its peak, they may come to commit the sin of blasphemy against the Holy Spirit. To sum up, with a certain purpose, God reveals His goodness and holiness to the non-elect only for a while, and they could come to know what it is, yet according to their corrupt nature, they end up actively resisting God.

Thus, this terrifying statement, regarding the blasphemy against the Holy Spirit, is an ultimatum and last warning given to the non-elect, yet even this God uses as a means to reprimand His own children. Here the Father's grace and love for His own children are demonstrated through a rebuke toward the children of others.

Discussion Questions

❶ Were you saved because you believed, or did you come to believe because you were saved? Explain this in your own words.

❷ What makes us come to worship every Sunday despite of our sins in the past week?

❸ Share whether you are currently enjoying the privileges given to and worthy of the children of God?

❹ How would you explain the relationship between our faith and actions relating to Q33-35?

❺ In what sense does this chapter give us the reason to be grateful?

Jan Hus Memorial, Prague in the Czech Republic

The Jan Hus Memorial stands at one end of Old Town Square, Prague, where he lived. He not only repudiated the moral decay of Roman Catholics but also translated the Latin Bible into the local language, which in the end brought him to martyrdom—he was burned at the stake in 1415. He was inspired by the teachings of John Wycliffe and became an inspiration for many other Reformers in the centuries that followed like Martin Luther of Germany, Ulrich Zwingli of Switzerland, and John Calvin also to name a few.

Q36~38 THE BENEFITS OF MEDIATION: THE COMMUNION IN GLORY

"WOULD FAITH IN JESUS AND MEMBERSHIP IN THE CHURCH BRING US A PROMOTION
OR SALARY INCREASE AT WORK AND GREATER INFLUENCE WITH OTHERS?"
"I HAVE GONE TO CHURCH FOR TEN YEARS, YET MY LIFE IS STILL IN MISERY.
IS IT BECAUSE GOD LEFT ME? AM I NOT SAVED?"
"DEATH IS THE WAGES OF SIN. THEN, WHY SHOULD THE FORGIVEN STILL DIE?"
"HOW LONG SHOULD WE WAIT UNTIL RESURRECTION AFTER WE DIE?
IF IT TAKES A LONG TIME, IT MUST BE QUITE BORING."

At last, we are now at the final chapter of Part 1. Here we will be taking a look at the second aspect of the benefits of mediation, the communion in glory.

Our life is now a glorious one, and this can be discussed in three parts: in the remaining life on earth, at death, and at the resurrection. Why don't you take a minute and think about what glory is? Would it be appropriate for us to speak of glory about man's life? Our life is, in general, disorderly and rugged. This is experientially true, which makes the title, the communion in glory, bizarre. Also what about death being the communion in glory? All people die, for the wages of sin is death. Being the punishment, death is what everyone fears. Yet this also is included in the communion in glory.

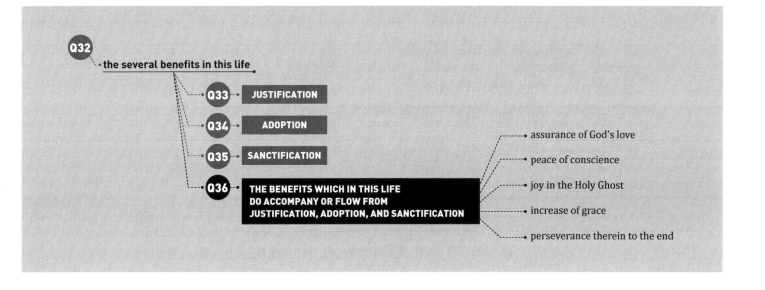

Q36 What are the benefits which in this life do accompany or flow
from justification, adoption, and sanctification?

A36 The benefits which in this life do accompany or flow
from justification, adoption, and sanctification, are,
assurance of God's love,
peace of conscience,[1]
joy in the Holy Ghost,[2]
increase of grace,[3]
and perseverance therein to the end.[4,5]

1.
Romans 5:1-2, 5

Therefore **being justified by faith, we have peace with God through our Lord Jesus Christ:** By whom also we have access by faith into this grace wherein we stand, and rejoice in hope of the glory of God...... And **hope maketh not ashamed; because the love of God is shed abroad in our hearts** by the Holy Ghost which is given unto us.

2.
Romans 14:17

For **the kingdom of God** is not meat and drink; but righteousness, and peace, and **joy in the Holy Ghost.**

3.
Proverbs 4:18

But **the path of the just is as the shining light, that shineth more and more unto the perfect day.**

4.
1 John 5:13

These things have I written unto you that believe on the name of the Son of God; that **ye may know that ye have eternal life,** and that ye may believe on the name of the Son of God.

5.
1 Peter 1:5

Who **are kept** by the power of God through faith unto salvation ready to be revealed in the last time.

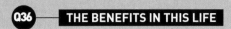

THE BENEFITS IN THIS LIFE:
those accompany or flow from justification, adoption, and sanctification

We are now studying effectual calling and the benefits brought by this calling in doctrinal terms of justification, adoption, and sanctification, one by one. Let us recap. How was the work of Jesus' mediation applied to our church and us? It was due to the Holy Spirit's effectual calling. In order to take a good look, we divided those benefits into three: in this life, at death, and at the resurrection. Among these, we just finished studying the benefits in this life, which are justification, adoption, and sanctification.

Through the above, we have come to realize once again that everything is the work of God in us. We have done nothing. It was by faith alone, and even this faith was the gift from God. Everything is given to us.

Here we will be studying the benefits that accompany or flow from justification, adoption, and sanctification. These will be more evident as the product of justification, adoption, and sanctification. In other words, these should be changes and benefits found in born-again believers. What a life and joy these are for every believer! While studying this chapter, examine your life, and I pray that you would come to the end of it with nothing but gratitude.

THE RESULT OF EFFECTUAL CALLING

The glimpse of the benefits mentioned in the answer to Q36 makes us realize the expectation of this world for us. They would like to see the state of heaven, which does not have any want in it. They would like to see the assurance of God's love abounding among believers. And is this not what the life of the Church and believers must demonstrate if everything were going well? Through these ways, our justification, adoption, and sanctification can be communicated and experienced in our everyday life.

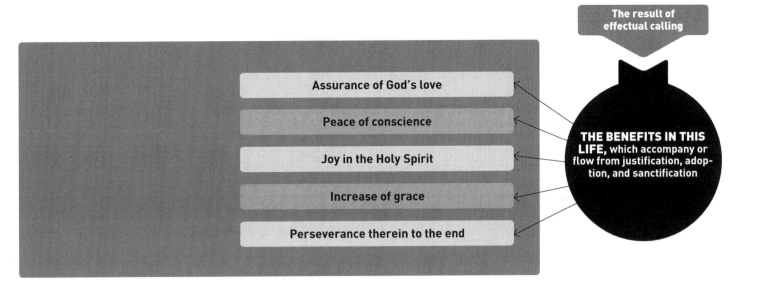

Assurance of God's love

Peace of conscience

Joy in the Holy Spirit

Increase of grace

Perseverance therein to the end

THE BENEFITS IN THIS LIFE, which accompany or flow from justification, adoption, and sanctification

HOWEVER, YOU MUST BE WARY OF THE FOLLOWING

1. EVERYTHING IS NOT WHAT IT SEEMS.

One may appear that he has a clear conscience and great joy in the Spirit, yet this may be so only in his appearance while his inner being is quite far from it. What appears on the surface can be deceptive, being corrupt with lies. A Peaceful appearance, joy, and even a high level of perseverance can be also found in other religions. Even non-believers can appear to have something similar as well. At the same time, what is contrary is also true. Not all good things within can be seen on the outside. Churches may not appear to possess any of these benefits, yet this may be so only on the outside. For this reason, discerning wisdom is necessary. We should not judge by appearances.

2. THIS IS ALSO A PROCESS. GRACE INCREASES!

To increase is to become greater in its amount and degree, from a zero to more. And this may bring disappointment given the progress one has made so far. What one may feel as progress reaches 80% should be different from that at 10%. The latter would feel overwhelmed by the future and can grow weary more easily. However, what should comfort us is that our hearts cannot be pure all the time, grief can oftentimes overwhelm us, and unbearable pain can visit us along the way. However, being a process, these will not stay with us forever, and believers are those who persevere through it all.

What differentiates believers from others is found in what they consider as their benefits. Believers should take what God has given in their life as their benefits and reasons to boast. Remember that this life is a benefit. The remaining life of ours belongs to the work of the Holy Spirit. God's love is unchanging and is assured to us. Our conscience may rebuke us making us uncomfortable, but the peace of tomorrow is promised. This process can be painful and we may hate it, yet despite that, all of it is benefit to us.

Why does God make us go through this process? Because it is beneficial for us. The relationship between a man and a woman provides a good example. They may fall in love at first sight, yet in the process of getting to know each other, they can go through painful quarrels and arguments. However, this process will be worth it in the end, for this will make their relationship healthier and more mature.

Now we have covered what constitutes our lives and learned everything in our lives is **indeed the benefits from God**. Well, it is time to turn to death. :) And for believers, death comes with the news of resurrection. Let's turn to Q37-38.

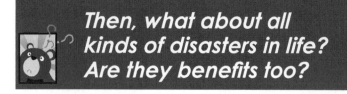

Then, what about all kinds of disasters in life? Are they benefits too?

Yes, they are to believers, for they are God's instruments of training and reprimand. It may appear that both believers and non-believers are under the same influence of the disasters in this life, yet they carry wholly different meanings and intention. For non-believers, they are the wrath of God and the punishment of curse. Yet for believers, they are the means of parental training, the rod of love, and this makes even disasters blessings for them.

Job's three friends rebuked Job as if he had earned God's punishment with his unknown sin. They were more inclined to the thought "What goes around comes around" than to the ways of God's providence. God's providence does not work in a way of mechanical accounting through which He collects the exact amount we owe Him, rather in the process through which He offers as much as His children need in both form of blessings and disasters. This is how He raises and educates His children. This way of His education for the elect is to be understood as the process of the loving care of a Parent, yet for the non-elect this is understood as the punishment and wrath of God. It may look like the same rod, but it is completely different depending on whom it is used upon.

If pain and disasters in this life came both on believers and non-believers, then I'd prefer to be a Christian only after I get to enjoy this world more.

You may choose that, but you have to be aware that you are missing the point. God Himself is the greatest blessing, and coming to serve Him as early as you can will offer you the greatest happiness. This is what the Shorter Catechism constantly testifies, while calling for our value system to change. If you insist on continuing to live your life without knowing God and neglecting Him, then you have to understand that you are wasting your life in just as many days of misery as you do so.

Q37

- THE BENEFITS BELIEVERS RECEIVE FROM CHRIST AT DEATH
  - the souls
    - are made perfect in holiness
    - do immediately pass into glory
  - their bodies
    - being still united to Christ
    - do rest in their graves till the resurrection

Q38

- THE BENEFITS BELIEVERS RECEIVE FROM CHRIST AT THE RESURRECTION
  - being raised up in glory
  - shall be openly acknowledged and acquitted · · in the day of judgement
  - shall be made perfectly blessed · · in the full enjoying of God to all eternity

---

Q37 What benefits do believers receive from Christ at death?

A37 The souls of believers are at their death
made perfect in holiness,[1]
and do immediately pass into glory;[2, 3, 4]
and their bodies, being still united to Christ,[5]
do rest in their graves[6]
till the resurrection.[7]

1.
Hebrews 12:23

To the general assembly and church of the firstborn, which are written in heaven, and to God the Judge of all, and **to the spirits of just men made perfect.**

6.
Isaiah 57:2

He shall enter into peace: **they shall rest in their beds,** each one walking in his uprightness.

2.
2 Corinthians 5:1, 6, 8

For we know that if our earthly house of this tabernacle **were dissolved, we have a building of God,** an house not made with hands, eternal in the heavens......
Therefore we are always confident, knowing that, whilst we are at **home in the body, we are absent from the Lord.**......We are confident, I say, and willing rather to be **absent from the body, and to be present with the Lord.**

3.
Philippians 1:23

For I am in a strait betwixt two, having a desire **to depart, and to be with Christ;** which is far better.

7.
Job 19:26-27

And though after my skin worms destroy this body, yet **in my flesh shall I see God: Whom I shall see for myself,** and mine eyes shall

4.
Luke 23:43

And Jesus said unto him, Verily I say unto thee, **To-day shalt thou be with me in paradise.**

behold, and not another; though my reins be consumed within me.

5.
1 Thessalonians 4:14

For if we believe that Jesus died and rose again, even so them also **which sleep in Jesus** will God bring with him.

Some may find this question outrageous: "What kind of benefits are there now being dead? You'd better not mention it at my funeral." However, what is implied in this question is the confidence that for believers even death is a benefit. What are your thoughts on this? Do you agree that even death is a ben-efit for believers? Yes, it is. There is no greater misfortune than death, yet even this death is a benefit. This only reflects what a great benefit we have been given from Christ.

FROM CHRIST

The phrase in the question, from Christ, highlights that even this benefit comes from the redemption of Christ and belongs to the communion of glory with Him. Even at the moment of death, we remain in union with Christ, and this phrase "from Christ" confirms this truth. We do not stand as individuals but as those united with Christ. Either in life and death, we cannot be separated from Christ. Now let us take a look at the answer point by point.

SOULS AND BODIES

The answer is given in two ways, souls and bodies. This is because we are made of both. This answer reassures us while expelling any fear, for this guarantees the perfect resurrection of both our souls and bodies. If resurrected only with souls, then we will be ghosts; if only with bodies, then zombies. :(Who would like to be either of these?

Regarding when we enter into heaven, there exist many misunderstandings. However, we certainly will not wander through this world undertaking unresolved business or wait to see some lights, but we will immediately pass into glory.

Also regarding our souls being made perfect, this is worth comparison with the sanctification we have previously learned (Q35). No matter how one has lived, in the end, everyone will be made equally perfect. After being made so, in the highest place, we will meet God and see Him face to face while our bodies wait for the full redemption.

1. OUR SOULS, MADE PERFECT IN HOLINESS, IM-MEDIATELY PASS INTO GLORY.

The death of a believer is a final stop at which he finishes the process of his sanctification and is made perfect in the holiness God desires. Then he immediately passes into glory. After the whole process of sanctification, his soul comes to its perfection. This is 100% in its degree. Then he enters into where he can see God face to face and be near to Him.

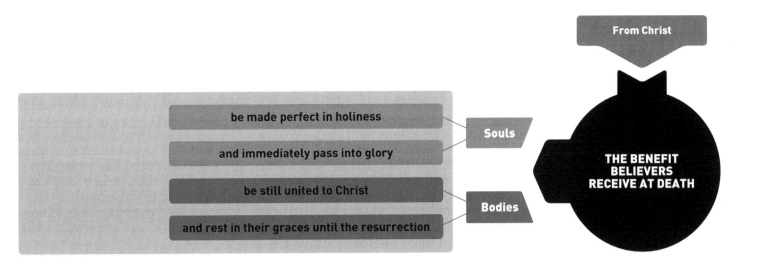

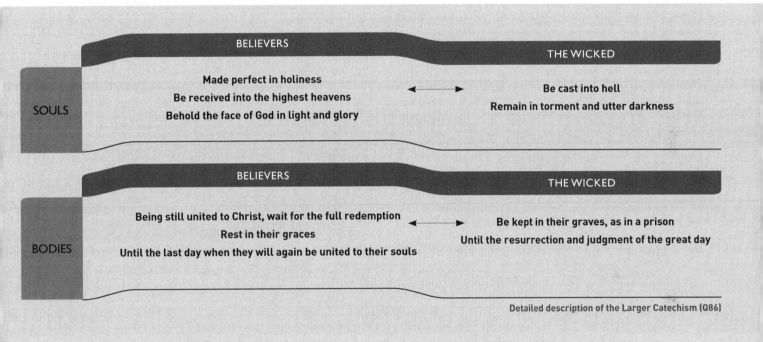

Detailed description of the Larger Catechism (Q86)

2. BEING STILL UNITED TO CHRIST, THEIR BODIES REST

Even if the above is so with our souls, we scientifically know that our bodies must die and then decompose. Yet the Shorter Catechism says that our bodies "do rest." Imagining our bodies decomposing or resting causes completely different reactions in us. The bodies in this answer are the ones of those still united to Christ. (Union with Christ has been explained on in the part of Q30.)

Pause a minute and try to imagine yourself stepping into the coffin prepared for you. Utter darkness stifles you; your body

that betrays you decomposes, and maggots become your sole company; everything makes you petrified, wanting to be out of this nightmare instantly. Who would ever want to die? No one!

Believers should not worry what happens to their bodies after they die. Our bodies will rest. For this reason, death should not be a reason for us to fear. Moreover, this rest is only temporary. If we had to stay in the grave forever, then it would not be called rest, but imprisonment. Yet our rest in the grave is only until the resurrection.

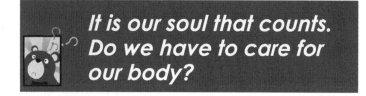

It is our soul that counts. Do we have to care for our body?

God created our precious bodies. Among all creatures, man is God's masterpiece, and being created in soul and body, both are equally precious. It is not that our souls carry more significance than our bodies.

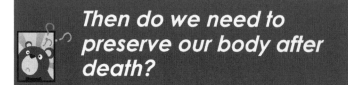

Then do we need to preserve our body after death?

Taking the above in a literal way, some have mistaken the importance of our body even to the point of superstition. In the Middle Ages, people used to understand damage to the body as equal to breaking the union with Christ. Burning at the stake would be a good example. This method of execution was cruel enough to let a living person die in a flames, yet more so when he was affected by the fear and concern that his body might be destroyed and later unable to be united with Christ.

When not burned at the stake, some bodies were even taken out from their graves and then beheaded. This was to damage the body, which would linger in pain even after the resurrection. However, such efforts are in vain, because the body of a believer cannot be harmed after resurrection. Regardless of what happens, his body will remain united with Christ. Thus, there are no worries. The believers of the early churches were put to death thrown in with beasts and torn into pieces in the Coliseum of Rome, yet even in such a situation, they did not lose their hope of resurrection. Those with a right and systematic faith can be fearless even at the moment of death.

at death

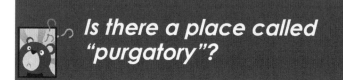

What about prayer for the dead?

We do not need to pray for the dead. The story of David in 2 Sam 12:21-23 might be helpful. "His servants asked him, 'Why are you acting this way? While the child was alive, you fasted and wept, but now that the child is dead, you get up and eat!' He answered, 'While the child was still alive, I fasted and wept. I thought, 'Who knows? The LORD may be gracious to me and let the child live.' But now that he is dead, why should I fast? Can I bring him back again? I will go to him, but he will not return to me.'"

It is rather us that need prayer. The dead are already in their glory having fellowship with God; thus, it is not only unnecessary but also wrong that we pray for their well-being or expect any blessings from them.

Is there a place called "purgatory"?

According to Catholics, this is a place inhabited by the souls of sinners who are expiating their sins before going into heaven. However, there are no biblical grounds for this. Being stuck with the problem of sin lingering even after justification and the misunderstanding of sanctification, people came to doubt whether they could get into heaven in such a sinful state, and in the end were prompted to come up with this seemingly logical doctrine of an in-between place. For them it was just unimaginable that they immediately pass into heaven. However, believers will immediately pass into the glory and be with God.

The doctrine of purgatory in a way was an effort to resolve the problem of lingering sin in believers when not being properly equipped with knowledge, and later it came to provide the grounds for one of the key issues, which attributed to the fall of Catholicism, indulgences. The message that the living can reduce the pain of the deceased, their beloved ones, by making an offering eventually deceived so many ignorant people. The ripple effect of the wrongful doctrine is indeed great. The Reformer Luther revealed what was behind the facade in the following, which triggered the great movement of the Reformation.

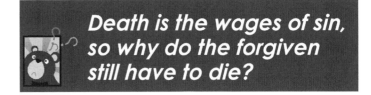

Death is the wages of sin, so why do the forgiven still have to die?

If bodies resurrect as well, then what will happen to the decomposed or the cremated? Also will the disabled continue to live so in heaven?

This question is also included in the Larger Catechism.

"Q85: Death being the wages of sin, why are not the righteous delivered from death, seeing all their sins are forgiven in Christ?"

Death is the wages of sin. This means that we die because of sin, which may lead us to another assumption that those who are saved from sin in Christ should not die. Some may presume as follows: To have to die means to have sin, and to die as the elect means that the redemption in Christ is not complete. Now let us take a look at the answer.

"A : The righteous shall be delivered from death itself on the last day and even in death are delivered from the sting and curse of it although they die, yet it is out of God's love
1) to free them perfectly from sin and misery
2) to make them capable of further communion with Christ in glory, which they then enter upon."

The answer is "they shall be delivered." Even though Christ forgave all their sins, this only means that He removed the penalty of their sins, not that He made them unable to sin. Thus, even the elect may remain in their sin and die. Yet the nature of this death is different from others, not having fear or dread. On the last day, they shall be delivered from death itself and even from its sting and curse.

The environment keeps its balance as our decomposed bodies go back to the soil, the soil provides nutrients to other plants, and the plants provide nutrients to other animals. With the knowledge of such a scientific truth, how are we supposed to understand the resurrection of our bodies? Recall what we have learned in creation. The key teaching in creation was that God created everything from nothing. If God could have created us from nothing, then it should not be any problem for Him to resurrect us from any of the states above.

"As he was praying, the appearance of his face changed, and his clothes became as bright as a flash of lightning." (Luke 9:29)
When Jesus was changed, people could still recognize Him. We will be likewise.

"For the trumpet will sound, the dead will be raised imperishable, and we will be changed." (1 Cor 15:52)
We will be changed into the imperishable. This will be an entirely different body from the current one.

All of the above helps us have an entirely different perspective on death. Death is neither the termination nor the transition to an inferior state. And this is because of God's love. His love completely frees us from sin and misery, enables us to have fellowship with Christ and take part in His glory. Thus, death for believers is only a transition to the resurrection and greater glory.

The church father, Polycarp, a disciple of Apostle Paul and the leader of the church in Smyrna, was burned at the stake, for he refused to worship the Roman emperor. (ca. 155)

Q37 → THE BENEFITS BELIEVERS RECEIVE FROM CHRIST AT DEATH

• the souls ⋯• are made perfect in holiness
• do immediately pass into glory
• their bodies ⋯• being still united to Christ
• do rest in their graves till the resurrection

Q38 → THE BENEFITS BELIEVERS RECEIVE FROM CHRIST AT THE RESURRECTION

• being raised up in glory
• shall be openly acknowledged and acquitted ⋯• in the day of judgement
• shall be made perfectly blessed ⋯• in the full enjoying of God to all eternity

Q38   What benefits do believers receive from Christ at the resurrection?

A38   At the resurrection,
believers being raised up in glory,[1]
shall be openly acknowledged and acquitted
in the day of judgement,[2,3]
and made perfectly blessed
in the full enjoying of God[4,5] to all eternity.[5,6]

1.
1 Corinthians 15:43

It is sown in dishonour; **it is raised in glory:** it is sown in weakness; it is raised in power.

2.
Matthew 25:23

His lord said unto him, **Well done, good and faithful servant;** thou hast been faithful over a few things, I will make thee ruler over many things: enter thou into the joy of thy lord.

3.
Matthew 10:32

Whosoever therefore shall confess me before men, **him will I confess also before my Father which is in heaven.**

4.
1 John 3:2

Beloved, now are we the sons of God, and it doth not yet appear what we shall be: but we know that, when he shall appear, we shall be like him; **for we shall see him as he is.**

5.
1 Corinthians 13:12

For now we see through a glass, darkly; but **then face to face:** now I know in part; but **then shall I know even as also I am known.**

6.
1 Thessalonians 4:17-18

Then we which are alive and remain shall be caught up together with them in the clouds, to meet the Lord in the air: and **so shall we ever be with the Lord.** Wherefore comfort one another with these words.

Here is the very last question of Part 1 in the Shorter Catechism. This will be about resurrection. We may take the resurrection as given, but the world around us denies it. The Bible teaches that we will also resurrect in the future. Importantly just like the death of believers, which has just been covered, the resurrection is also being covered pertaining to the benefits coming from the union with Christ. Q38 explains the resurrection in three parts. Let us take a look point by point.

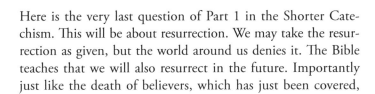

1. WHAT WILL HAPPEN AT THE RESURRECTION?

We will be raised up in glory. This is written in a passive sense in order to highlight that it is God who raises us up. The Larger Catechism expands this idea to "being then again united to their souls forever." Our appearance after the resurrection will be the same while at the same time different just like that of Jesus after His resurrection. We can only imagine whether our appearance will be shining, look handsome or beautiful, have the ability to walk through walls, or be able to be at multiple places at the same time. These are merely imaginings, yet we will surely change into a better and perfect appearance. After the resurrection of Jesus, His disciples did not recognize Him at first, but He still carried the marks of the nails and the spear on His body. Like the appearance of Jesus after His resurrection, we will not be given an entirely different body than now.

2. TWO THINGS WILL HAPPEN ON THE DAY OF JUDGMENT: we will be openly acknowledged and acquitted

Life according to God's will oftentimes results in conflict with the people of this world. Unwilling to compromise, we have to suffer the ridicule from others and sometimes disappointment with ourselves. If this world were all there is, then we would surely be the foremost of fools. However, despite all the ridicule of this world, on the day of resurrection and judgment, we will be openly acknowledged while the wicked will be ashamed.

For now, people may be able to pretend to be good, yet on that day, the wicked, whose wickedness being plainly revealed, will be at a loss, but we will be approved good before God, who knows everything. Of course it is neither by our righteousness nor merit. Then, how can we be approved? Because we will be clothed with the perfect righteousness of Christ, which was the teaching of justification. We will abound with Christ's righteousness. Every remaining sin and weakness of ours will be removed on that day. Q37 has taught us that when a believer dies, his holiness will come to its perfection. On that day, we will stand before God as perfectly holy ones and be approved.

3. AND WHAT DOES THIS MEAN TO US?

Q38 describes this as a perfect blessing. It is the utmost one. This goes beyond our experience and imagination. For this reason, Q90 of the Larger Catechism offers an account of being "filled with inconceivable joys." Due to the limit of our experience and understanding, no one in this life is able to come to grasp its meaning.

We may wonder what we will do in heaven or how to amuse ourselves with eternity on our hands. But what is important regarding life in heaven is that it is life of the utmost blessing, which is glorious communion with God. It is life with God. Recall the attributes of God you have learned in Q4 and the decrees of His which have followed up to Q38. This is it. This is the God whom we have been thankful for and overwhelmed with. We will never be bored. How can we?

Here comes the last line of Q38, and the opening line of the whole catechism reappears—to enjoy God. On that day, we will be in the full enjoyment of God for all eternity. Place your hope on that day. Your earnest hope.

THE CONTRAST BETWEEN THE RIGHTEOUS AND THE WICKED ON THE DAY OF JUDGMENT (FROM THE LARGER CATECHISM Q89-90)

Q89 WHAT SHALL BE DONE TO THE WICKED AT THE DAY OF JUDGMENT?	Q90 WHAT SHALL BE DONE TO THE RIGHTEOUS AT THE DAY OF JUDGMENT?
At the day of judgment, the wicked Shall be set on Christ's left hand	At the day of judgment, the righteous, being caught up to Christ in the clouds, shall be set on his right hand
Upon clear evidence, and full conviction of their own consciences, Shall have the fearful	openly acknowledged and acquitted, shall join with him in the judging of reprobate angels and men
just sentence of condemnation pronounced against them	shall be received into heaven where they shall be fully and forever freed from all sin and misery filled with inconceivable joys
shall be cast out from the favorable presence of God, and the glorious fellowship with Christ, his saints, and all his holy angels	made perfectly holy and happy both in body and soul in the company of innumerable saints and holy angels but especially in the immediate vision and fruition of God the Father, of our Lord Jesus Christ, and of the Holy Spirit, to all eternity
[to where?] into hell, be punished with unspeakable torments, both of body and soul, with the devil and his angels forever	this is the perfect and full communion which the members of the invisible church shall enjoy with Christ in glory at the resurrection and day of judgment.

They make an extreme contrast, don't they?

AUTHOR'S NOTE

Numerous heresies of this world have something in common as far as their eschatology goes in that they encourage on one hand fear and on the other self-indulgence. When compared to the eschatology introduced in the Shorter Catechism, this only highlights what a great blessing, beauty, and fulfillment Christ has prepared for His followers on that day. Yes, the end of this world can make some fearful and others self indulgent, yet for the believers in Christ, it should no more. Rather, it should make us expectant and hopeful, for this day will be the day we finally reach the summit that we have been striving for.

The entire study of the Shorter Catechism led us to understand with "inexpressible" joy and honor that we are among the elect of the Lord. Christ, the Alpha and Omega, will hold us in His arms from the beginning to the end, crown us with the crown of honor, and exalt us even to the place to judge the fallen angels and men.

Yet what excites us the most is the hope that one day we will see His face in person. There, in the holy city of the Father, will be nothing lacking, no one who is not another brother or sister. We wait for the day so eagerly!

Discussion Questions

❶ Despite of the rugged reality of this world, we can be assured of God's love and salvation. What could be the primary reason for this?

❷ Even at the moment of death, what would make us fearless and even see death as a benefit?

❸ What makes the last Day of Judgment our hope and comfort?

❹ Read Matt 12:28, Rom 8:32, 14:8. Then summarize what you have learned in this chapter.

❺ In what sense does this chapter give us the reason to be grateful?

....

....

....

....

....

....

....

SHORTER CATECHISM
PART 2

Now we begin the second part of what the Bible principally teaches. While studying,
let's refer to the whole map provided in this book or the app-WSC MAP.

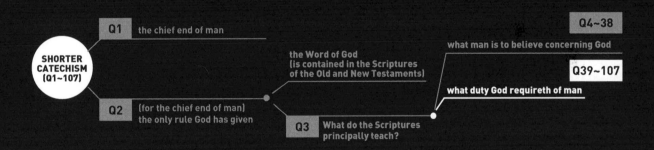

Q1 the chief end of man

SHORTER CATECHISM (Q1~107)

Q2 (for the chief end of man)
the only rule God has given

the Word of God
(is contained in the Scriptures
of the Old and New Testaments)

Q3 What do the Scriptures
principally teach?

Q4~38
what man is to believe concerning God

Q39~107
what duty God requireth of man

It is always important to visually see your current location in
the whole catechism. If not, it will be quite impossible for one
to come to acknowledge and truly appreciate the meaning and
the weight of "What duty God requireth of man."

REVIEWING UP TO WHERE WE HAVE COME

It is always important to visually see your current location within the whole catechism. If you are leading a study group, you have to make sure before proceeding that every group member understands where they are in the entire structure of this catechism. This will benefit the group members to understand and appreciate why Ten Commandments had to appear where it does and what implications it should bring to themselves. This will surely give them another reason to diligently continue the study and keep their interest unfaltering even after the Ten Commandments.

Having the entire structure of the catechism drawn on a wall-size piece of construction paper and hung on a wall could be a way to do this. Or a patchwork of smaller-sized papers could also work. You are welcome to refer to the map of this book(p.16-17) or the app of WSC MAP for the Entire Mindmap of the Shorter Catechism.

"Make sure about the entire structure and flow by drawing map!"

God demands our obedience. How does that sound to you? Does that make you instantly feel repulsed and dog-tired as if it ties you to something you shouldn't be responsible for? It could. However, the Shorter Catechism Part 2 will teach you that it takes obedience for you to know and experience "genuine freedom" and "greater joy."

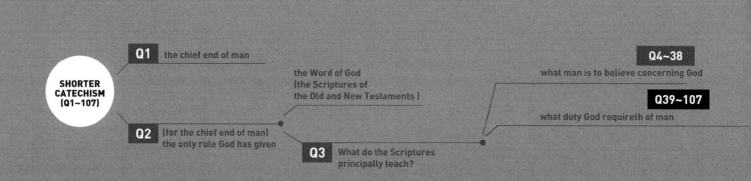

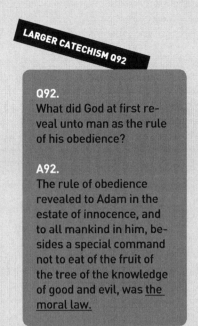

Q92.
What did God at first reveal unto man as the rule of his obedience?

A92.
The rule of obedience revealed to Adam in the estate of innocence, and to all mankind in him, besides a special command not to eat of the fruit of the tree of the knowledge of good and evil, was <u>the moral law.</u>

Then how can we obey? What would be the criteria for this? The Shorter Catechism Q40 teaches us that God gave us Moral Law, which holds us to a higher level of accountability. We should neither see this Law like other trivial laws of this world nor comply with it just in form's sake. This Moral Law separates itself from other ethics, norms or laws made by man for their convenience. Rather, it is God's eternal Law that goes beyond all of the above, and God Himself demands that we obey it. (Refer to the Larger Catechism Q92 and compare with it.)

The map below presents the introduction of Part 2, connecting it to the Ten Commandments in more detail. Just as there was a rule regarding the purpose of our life (Shorter Catechism Q2), there should be a rule regarding our "obedience." Moral Law is that rule, and the Ten Commandments is the summarized form of this Law. Before moving on to the next page, take a moment to consider the map and try to become familiar with the logical flow of the entire catechism.

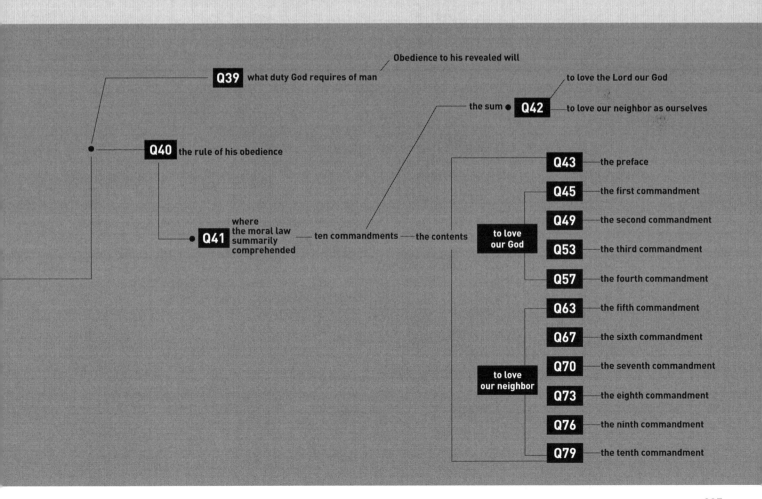

Q39~44 | MORAL LAW

"THE TEN COMMANDMENTS WERE FOR THE PEOPLE IN THE OLD TESTAMENTS.
SINCE THEN, A LONG TIME HAS PASSED.
I DON'T THINK IT IS RELEVANT TO OUR LIVES ANY MORE."
"DIDN'T JESUS COMPLETE THE LAW?
THIS MEANS WE NEED NOT KEEP THE LAW ANY MORE."
"I KNOW MANY NON-CHRISTIANS WHO LIVE MORALLY GOOD LIVES.
HOW AM I SUPPOSED TO UNDERSTAND THAT?"

The chief end of man is to glorify God and enjoy Him forever. (The first question of the Shorter Catechism) For this end, God has revealed His will to man and demands man to obey it. This, what man is demanded to obey, is the theme of Part 2. Then, what is this revealed-will and where can we find it? As seen in the second question, it is found solely in the Bible. Thus, it is not strange to imagine the theme of Part 2, what is required of man, is also about getting to know God—not about what we are to do but who He is.

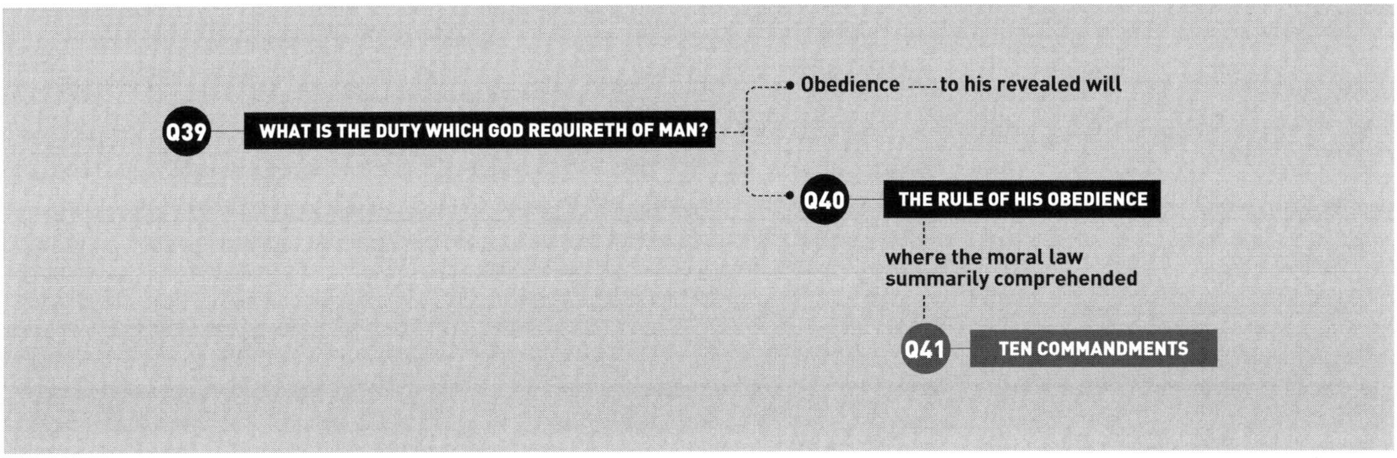

WHAT IS THE DUTY WHICH GOD REQUIRETH OF MAN? — Q39

Obedience ---- to his revealed will

Q40 — **THE RULE OF HIS OBEDIENCE**

where the moral law summarily comprehended

Q41 — **TEN COMMANDMENTS**

Q39 What is the duty which God requireth of man?

A39 The duty which God requireth of man,
is obedience to his revealed will.[1,2]

Q40 What did God at first reveal to man for the rule of his obedience?

A40 The rule which God at first revealed to man
for his obedience,
was the moral law.[3,4]

1.
Micah 6:8

He hath shewed thee, O man, what is good; and **what doth the Lord require of thee, but to do justly, and to love mercy, and to walk humbly with thy God?**

2.
1 Samuel 15:22

And Samuel said, Hath the Lord as great delight in burnt offerings and sacrifices, as in obeying the voice of the Lord? Behold, **to obey is better than sacrifice,** and to hearken than the fat of rams.

3.
Romans 2:14-15

For when the Gentiles, which have not the law, do by nature the things contained in the law, these, having not the law, **are a law unto themselves:** Which shew **the work of the law written** in their hearts, their conscience also bearing witness, and their thoughts the mean while accusing or else excusing one another.

4.
Romans 10:5

For Moses describeth the righteousness which is **of the law, That the man which doeth those things shall live by them.**

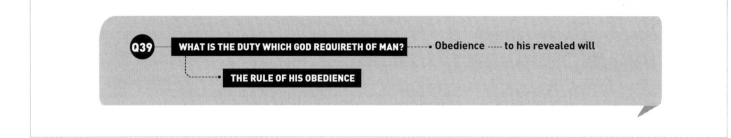

1. HIS REVEALED WILL

Here this question makes clear that God revealed His will to man (us). Why is this important? This proves that God is neither irrelevant to us nor an abstract being as many assume. Rather He comes to us and whispers in our ears, demanding our obedience to Him. His manner makes us look like His equals, more than creatures or mindless robots. The Most High One comes and speaks into our ears. Doesn't this make us grateful?

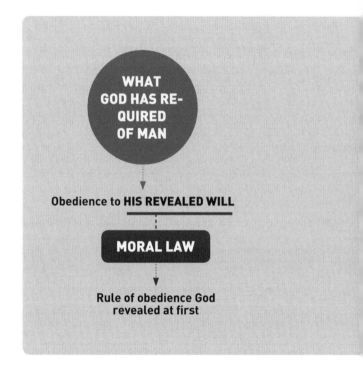

2. RULE OF OBEDIENCE—MORAL LAW

Now it is time to think about what this moral law, the rule of obedience, means. Moral law is God's will proclaimed. (Q39) This law commands that our soul and body, our whole person, obey the entire law, and this demonstrates that our whole person is closely tied to this law. In simpler terms, we are not created to live as we see fit, but to live in obedience to God's will; and the moral law is given to let us know what this will is. Otherwise we would be left powerless to know how to live our lives. The rule of obedience is really the most fitting name for this moral law.

The biblical meaning of obedience can be gleaned from the One who lived His entire life in perfect obedience. As studied in Part 1, this One is Christ, and the greatest motivation of His obedience was love. Thus, we wouldn't be wrong to conclude: by revealing His own will to us and demanding our obedience to Him, God is calling us into a loving relationship with Him.

As we will learn from Q41, this moral law has been revealed in various references throughout the Bible under the name of the Law, yet among all of these references, the Ten Commandments successfully summarize it. Thus, it is not strange to conclude the main theme of the Ten Commandments we are about to see is to love our God and neighbor. And this matches to the answer Jesus Himself gave to a religious leader in Matt 22:37-40.

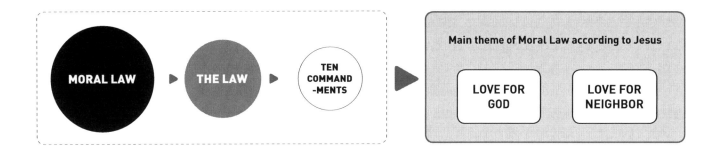

WHAT DOES THIS TEACHING LEAVE US WITH?

Now can you say that your obedience to Him is your blessing? And can you really mean it as you say it? It does not mean your knowledge of His will should be perfect and so should be your obedience. A thousand times, no. Rather, now, knowing where to head (obedience) and having a willing heart (out of love) is enough. And this is the perfect place for us to begin this new journey to the second part of the Shorter Catechism. It is no other place than the place of gratitude and joy.

3. THE OBJECT OF MORAL LAW—ALL MAN

Now let us take a look on the word "man" in Q39. This refers neither male nor "those who choose to follow God's will." This literally means "all" man, human kind.

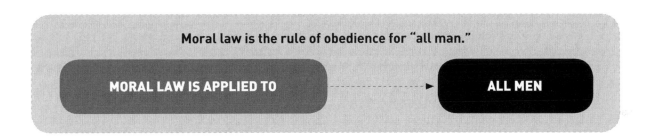

You may have heard some say: "If someone is destined to go to hell, it should not matter how he lives his life." Or "If someone is not a believer, how easy her life must be."

Yet the nature of moral law forbids such a thought. Moral law is 1) given to all human kind, 2) comprehensive and absolute in its concept and 3) unchangeable. For this law perfectly reflects who God is—eternal, unchangeable, and the Lord of all (Q4). These attributes demand His will, which is revealed in moral law, to be the same—eternal, unchangeable, and governing all men on this earth. Coming back to the question above, despite one's eternal home being either heaven or hell, everyone is required to live according to God's will. One may resist, or even try to ignore it all together; however, nothing is able to altar this Truth.

Besides the general application for all man, this law has some special applications for believers who are united with Christ. These are significant privileges which, when acknowledged, should bring distinct differences in the life of believers.

Moral law (1) shows believers how much they are bound to Christ for His fulfilling, (2) provokes believers to more thankfulness, and (3) encourages believers to conform themselves to this rule of obedience.

WHAT IS THE USE OF MORAL LAW TO THE UNBELIEVERS?
After all, they have nothing to do with God, being unwilling to listen to any of God's words. Why is moral law given to all man?

What is the use of moral law to the unbelievers? After all, they have nothing to do with God, being unwilling to listen to any of God's words. Why is moral law given to all man?

After the fall, every one was made unable to earn righteousness and eternal life through the moral law. Yet this moral law still carries a significant role for "all" men, which can be outlined in the following three points.

A. TO ALL MAN

Moral law informs them of the holy nature and will of God, and of their duty, as binding them to walk accordingly. And it convinces them of their disability to keep it, and of the sinful pollution of their nature, hearts, and lives. It also humbles them in the sense of their sin and misery, and thereby helps them to have a clearer understanding of the need they have of Christ, and of the perfection of his obedience.

What moderates the effects of man's deep-seated sinfulness is the above use of moral law. It suppresses sin; morality and conscience exist and find their places even in unbelievers; society runs without moving beyond atrocity. This is to protect the people of God from utmost hate, revenge, and hostility.

B. TO THE UNREGENERATE (*WHICH INCLUDES BOTH THE NON-ELECT AND IN THE PASSAGE OF TIME THE NOT-YET-REGENERATED)

Moral law leaves them inexcusable and under the curse thereof, upon the continuance in the estate and way of sin. Also it awakens their consciences to flee from the wrath to come, and drives them to Christ.

C. TO THE REGENERATE

Moral law does not condemn them any longer. Rather it makes them more grateful, as leading them to watchful obedience to this law. It may still convict their hearts, yet it cannot bring any changes in their assured salvation in the Lord. Rather it shows, provokes, and is used in greater effect. The Bible presents Christ as the One who obeyed this law in the perfect way, and through this example helps us be full of gratitude and praises and even encourages us to follow this law of God gladly in every aspect of our lives.

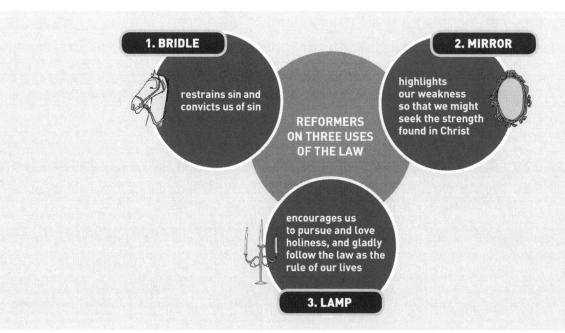

1. BRIDLE — restrains sin and convicts us of sin

2. MIRROR — highlights our weakness so that we might seek the strength found in Christ

REFORMERS ON THREE USES OF THE LAW

3. LAMP — encourages us to pursue and love holiness, and gladly follow the law as the rule of our lives

WHAT SHOULD I DO WITH THE GUILT THAT MORAL LAW BRINGS?

THE LAW CONDEMNS	THE GOSPEL FREES
man feels guilty and hopeless.	man feels joyful and delighted.

(ACTUAL) GUILT VS. FEELING GUILTY

We may assume, if indeed saved, we should not feel guilty any longer. Yet, in reality, it does not work that way. Despite the assurance of salvation in Jesus, because of our own weakness and the residue of sin, we still live with guilty-feelings. However, is this normal? Does this mean that I still have guilt to deal with? The answer to this question is, you should not worry. For this guilty-feeling over our sins is none other than the evidence that Holy Spirit is doing His good work in us. That you came to acknowledge your sin and are now willing to repent of it is another gift of the Holy Spirit. In that sense, your guilty-feelings are as normal as can be; however, it does not mean that we don't need to repent of our sins any more.

Moral law always condemns man. Yet as the elect we are freed from such condemnation and made righteous. We may carry guilty-feelings about our sins, yet God through the complete work of Christ's redemption carried all of our guilt away, which is the sure reason to be joyful and delighted.

Yes, moral law will constantly accuse us. Yet it is not to condemn us any longer; rather, it is to saturate us with joy for being freed. How does accusation bring joy? The more we become enlightened of the law, the more we come to understand our need of the gospel, which will lead us in the end to acknowledge faith in Jesus Christ, who is in the process making us as perfect as the law demands. What a joy and gratitude belongs to us! We don't need to live in guilt any longer, for the heavy burden is being taken away and the perfection of the beautiful law will be ours soon.

"Therefore, since we are surrounded by such a great cloud of witnesses, let us throw off everything that hinders and the sin that so easily entangles, and let us run with perseverance the race marked out for us. Let us fix our eyes on Jesus, the author and perfecter of our faith, who for the joy set before him endured the cross, scorning its shame, and sat down at the right hand of the throne of God." (Hebrews 12:1-2)

Then why do Christians even with assurance of salvation still serve the law of sin?

As was discussed in Q35 of Shorter Catechism Part 1, this arises from the remnants of sins abiding in every part of them.

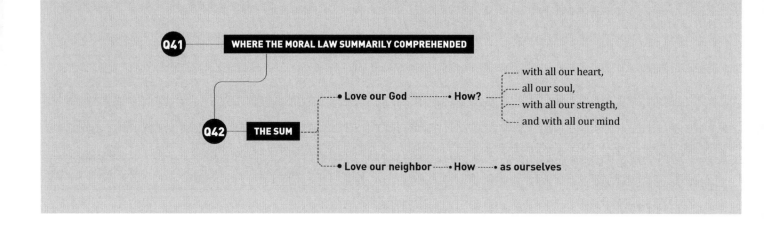

Q41 Where is the moral Law summarily comprehended?

A41 The moral Law is summarily comprehended in the ten commandments.[1,2]

Q42 What is the sum of the ten commandments?

A42 The sum of the ten commandments is,

      To love the Lord our God

            with all our heart,

            with all our soul,

            with all our strength,

         and with all our mind;

    and our neighbor as ourselves.[3]

1.
Deuteronomy 10:4

And he wrote on the tables, according to the **first writing, the ten commandments,** which the Lord spake unto you in the mount out of the midst of the fire in the day of the assembly: and the Lord gave them unto me.

2.
Matthew 19:17

And he said unto him, Why callest thou me good? there is none good but one, that is, God: but if thou wilt enter into life, **keep the commandments.**

3.
Matthew 22:37-40

Jesus said unto him, **Thou shalt love the Lord thy God with all thy heart, and with all thy soul, and with all thy mind.** This is the first and great commandment. And the second is like unto it, **Thou shalt love thy neighbour as thyself. On these two commandments hang all the law and the prophets.**

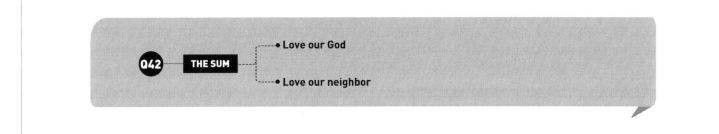

Q42 — THE SUM
- Love our God
- Love our neighbor

Have this engraved on your mind and heart!
Memorize the summary of the Ten Commandments.

THE LOCATION OF THE TEN COMMANDMENTS

"God required?" obedience to His revealed will
"Rule of obedience?" moral law
"Moral law?" Proclaimed the will of God to all mankind
"Summarized in?" the Ten Commandments

THE SUMMARY OF THE TEN COMMANDMENTS

To love the Lord our God
To love our neighbor as ourselves

"WITH HEART, SOUL, STRENGTH AND MIND"

Mull over these words as if chewing on them.
Digest them and make them truly yours.

The Ten Commandments is the pinnacle of moral law, and it is interpreted and elaborated throughout the 66 books in the Bible, sometimes explicitly, other times implicitly, and in various forms of analogy and historical account. Jesus in the book of Matthew reiterated this truth. If condensed in the briefest form, moral law is love.

Reference Material: Luther's Shorter Catechism

Elaborating the Ten Commandments, Luther also points out such a meaning of the Ten Commandments, to fear and love God. At the end of every commandment, he added a clause, "We should fear and love God."

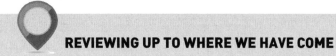

REVIEWING UP TO WHERE WE HAVE COME

The Ten Commandments takes a huge portion in the Shorter Catechism. (Q43-81) Embarking on such a time- and energy-consuming journey, there are two things I want readers to be informed about.

1. ITS STRUCTURE

Before all, please take a look at the Ten Commandments your-self.

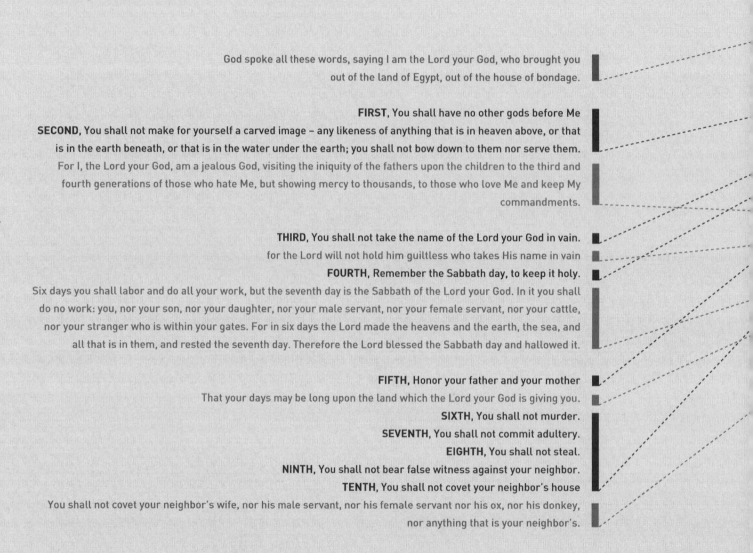

God spoke all these words, saying I am the Lord your God, who brought you out of the land of Egypt, out of the house of bondage.

FIRST, You shall have no other gods before Me

SECOND, You shall not make for yourself a carved image – any likeness of anything that is in heaven above, or that is in the earth beneath, or that is in the water under the earth; you shall not bow down to them nor serve them. For I, the Lord your God, am a jealous God, visiting the iniquity of the fathers upon the children to the third and fourth generations of those who hate Me, but showing mercy to thousands, to those who love Me and keep My commandments.

THIRD, You shall not take the name of the Lord your God in vain. for the Lord will not hold him guiltless who takes His name in vain

FOURTH, Remember the Sabbath day, to keep it holy. Six days you shall labor and do all your work, but the seventh day is the Sabbath of the Lord your God. In it you shall do no work: you, nor your son, nor your daughter, nor your male servant, nor your female servant, nor your cattle, nor your stranger who is within your gates. For in six days the Lord made the heavens and the earth, the sea, and all that is in them, and rested the seventh day. Therefore the Lord blessed the Sabbath day and hallowed it.

FIFTH, Honor your father and your mother That your days may be long upon the land which the Lord your God is giving you.

SIXTH, You shall not murder.

SEVENTH, You shall not commit adultery.

EIGHTH, You shall not steal.

NINTH, You shall not bear false witness against your neighbor.

TENTH, You shall not covet your neighbor's house You shall not covet your neighbor's wife, nor his male servant, nor his female servant nor his ox, nor his donkey, nor anything that is your neighbor's.

What is unique is that prior to offering the commandments themselves, there comes an opening line, the preface. This comes with an explicit purpose to emphasize the One who provides these commandments through revealing His position, experience, and credentials. This will be dealt with more in detail later. For now it suffices to say the Ten Commandments consists of three parts: the preface, the commandments themselves, and additional reasons.

The structure of the Ten Commandments is (Refer to Q100 of the Larger Catechism.):

THE PREFACE

THE SUBSTANCE
(the commandments themselves)

SEVERAL REASONS ARE ANNEXED TO SOME OF THEM,
THE MORE TO ENFORCE THEM.

2. RULES TO BE KNOWN FOR THE RIGHT UNDERSTANDING OF THE TEN COMMANDMENTS

God requires all men to obey His eternal moral law, and this law is summarized in the Ten Commandments. God's infinite will, being delivered to finite man, a summarization should have been necessary. And the Larger Catechism suggests several rules to be observed for its right understanding. (Larger Catechism Q99)

To name a few: Because the law is perfect, it binds everyone unto entire and thorough obedience; for the law is spiritual, it reaches the understanding, will, affections, and soul. For instance, because covetousness is idol worship, there should be a connection between the eighth and first commandments, and in the same way because Christian ethics itself finds its foundation in the love for God, without obedience to the first through third commandments, we may keep the others in vain. Also rather than being bound in Thou shall or Thou shall not, we should pay attention to the commandments' original intentions. Not only the direct and indirect causes of sin and provocation but sins unknowingly committed should also be guarded against.

We should not attempt to bring this law down to the level of other ancient laws. Rather, we should take the Ten Commandments and let it rule over our entire life with its passion and richness.

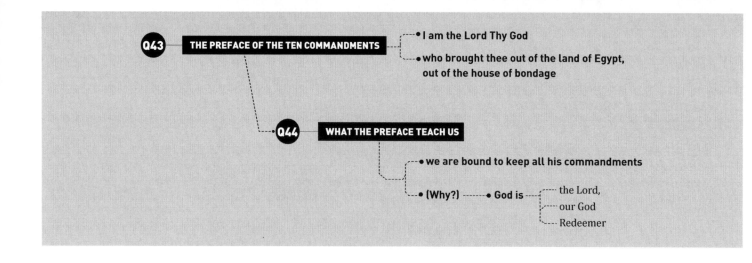

Q43 What is the preface to the ten commandments?

A43 The preface to the ten commandments is in these words,

I am the Lord Thy God,

which have brought thee out of the land of Egypt,

out of the house of bondage.[1]

Q44 What doth the preface to the ten commandments teach us?

A44 The preface to the ten commandments teacheth us,

That because God is The Lord, and our God, and Redeemer

therefore we are bound

to keep all his commandments.[2,3]

1.
Exodus 20:2

I am the Lord thy God, which have brought thee out of the land of Egypt, out of the house of bondage.

2.
Luke 1:74-75

That he would grant unto us, that **we, being delivered out of the hand of our enemies, might serve him** without fear, In holiness and righteousness before him, all the days of our life.

3.
1 Peter 1:15-19

But as he which hath called you is holy, **so be ye holy** in all manner of conversation; Because it is written, **Be ye holy; for I am holy.** And if ye call on the Father, who without respect of persons judgeth according to every man's work, pass the time of your sojourning here in fear: **Forasmuch as ye know that ye were not redeemed** with corruptible things, as silver and gold, from your vain conversation received by tradition from your fathers; **But with the precious blood of Christ,** as of a lamb without blemish and without spot.

THE PREFACE OF THE TEN COMMANDMENTS

"I am the Lord Thy God, who brought thee out of the land of Egypt, out of the house of bondage."

In the preface, God, who gives these very commandments, is introduced. And this is how He is introduced "[the One] who brought you out of the land of Egypt, out of the house of bondage."

What does this mean to you? What would "being brought out of Egypt" have meant to the Israelites? This is a great opportunity to recall what you have learned in the sections about sin and misery (Q13-19) and the covenant of grace (Q20-).

God, whom we come to encounter in part 2, is the same God who made the covenant with us in part 1. In other words, it is through the Ten Commandments God guarantees His covenant with us. Grace and the law never contradict each other. The preface states that the law that we are about to receive should be understood in God's covenant; it should not appear as the means of oppression or duty. Because the giver is God, whatever is given should be deemed as grace and blessing.

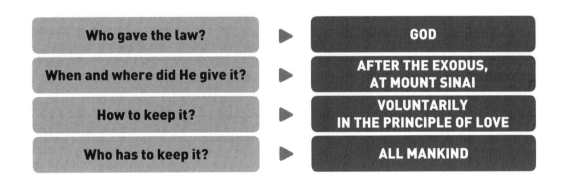

Who gave the law?	▶	GOD
When and where did He give it?	▶	AFTER THE EXODUS, AT MOUNT SINAI
How to keep it?	▶	VOLUNTARILY IN THE PRINCIPLE OF LOVE
Who has to keep it?	▶	ALL MANKIND

WHO GAVE THE LAW?

"I am the Lord, thy God." Here it is implied that God is sovereign, independent, and unable to be limited and influenced by others at all. God, out of His absolute sovereignty and pleasing will, offered the mercy of covenant to His people.

WHEN DID GOD GIVE THE LAW?

It was given after the exodus at Mount Sinai. It is chronolo-gically important that God gave the law after freeing the Israelites from Egypt, for it teaches us that the law is not the condition of salvation, but the result of it.

HOW SHOULD WE KEEP THE LAW?

As the preface of the Ten Commandments clarifies, God's salvation comes as the result of His love for His people. And this love requires His people to love Him back. In other words, this law should be kept in the principle of love. Could it appear as a mere set of rules of conduct to conform to? Probably. But this will lead us only to legalism.

WHO SHOULD KEEP THE LAW?

All mankind, from the old to the young, should obey God's will. In the house, the role of parents cannot be overemphasized. Parents should talk about God's love day and night, and teach the law as the principle of love while keeping its focus in love.

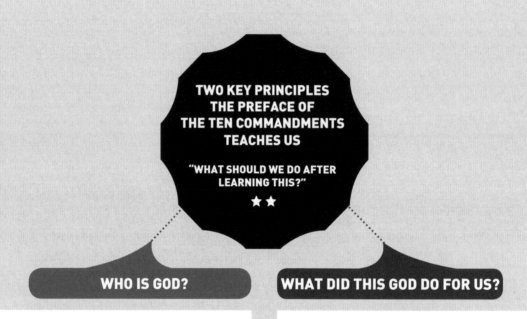

TWO KEY PRINCIPLES THE PREFACE OF THE TEN COMMANDMENTS TEACHES US

"WHAT SHOULD WE DO AFTER LEARNING THIS?"

★ ★

WHO IS GOD?

WHAT DID THIS GOD DO FOR US?

"The Lord thy God"

The Bible describes God as eternal, unchanging and all-mighty Lord, and at the same time, as the One who establishes a covenant with the Israelites and with us. Who is this God? He is the holy One. *"I the LORD your God, am holy."* (Lev 19:2) Because the Giver of this law is holy, this law also demands holiness of us, and God by having us keep this law makes us His own people and children.

"Brought us out of the land of Egypt, out of the house of bondage"

Just as He brought the Israelites out of the bondage of Egypt, He surely brought us out of spiritual bondage. Here Egypt means our sinful state where we have befallen. What this preface teaches us is that the Commandments are given by our Redeemer God. Thus, it is only right that we exalt Him as our God and keep His Commandments in love and gratitude.

God not only makes but also keeps His covenant. As this preface reveals God's promise to Abraham, the father of Israel, the salvation of Israel, and how He saw it through. The same God promised us salvation in Jesus Christ. And He will surely see it through.

Discussion Questions

❶ God required obedience of us. Why is that a gift to us?

❷ God's eternal moral law is applied to all mankind. Why is that important to us?

❸ Explain the difference between *guilty-feelings* we have before the law and our *actual guilt* which is enough to condemn us in the end.

❹ Read Ps 89:26-32 and summarize this chapter.

❺ In what sense does this chapter give us the reason to be grateful?

John Knox House, Edinburgh in Scotland

John knox is a presbyterian leader of the Scottish Reformation during the 16th century. Below the coat of arms of this house, you can see the sentence, 'Love God above all and your neighbor as yourself' written in Scottish archaic words. John knox is a presbyterian leader of the Scottish Reformation during the 16th century.

"WHAT IS THE POINT OF GIVING IMPOSSIBLE-TO-KEEP COMMANDMENTS?"
"IT IS SUCH A CHALLENGE TO BELIEVE IN GOD WHO IS INVISIBLE.
CAN'T HE GIVE US SOMETHING VISIBLE TO HELP US OUT?"
"WHAT DOES KEEPING-SUNDAY-HOLY MEAN?
IT SEEMS EVERY CHURCH UNDERSTANDS IT DIFFERENTLY?"

Now we enter into the Ten Commandments, the pinnacle of God's eternal law. Every Christians must have heard the phrase, the Ten Commandments, yet not many of them have actually taken a close look at them. Use this opportunity to enlighten yourself with the "values" God requires of us.

The Ten Commandments take up a huge portion in the Shorter Catechism, a quarter of it. Continue to check your current location in the whole structure of the catechism, and also constantly encourage yourself, for this will be a time- and energy-consuming process. While exposing yourself to the Ten Commandments, never stop asking yourself how each commandment could be applied to your life in practical ways. It is important that you become enlightened about something previously unknown to you, yet what is more important is that you let God's commandments actually transform your life even if it is just bit by bit. As stated before, the Ten Commandments can be divided into two commands, to love God (Commandments 1-4) and to love neighbors (Commandments 5-10).

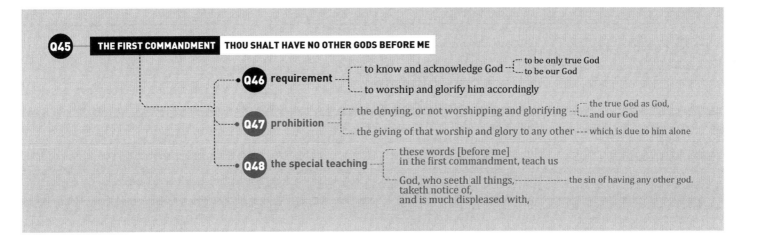

The 1st Commandment

Q45 Which is the first commandment?

A45 The first commandment is, Thou shalt have no other gods before me.[1]

Q46 What is required in the first commandment?

A46 The first commandment requireth us

to know and acknowledge God

to be the only true God,

and our God;[2, 3]

and to worship and glorify him accordingly.[4, 5]

1.
Exodus 20:3

Thou shalt have no other gods before me.

2.
1 Chronicles 28:9

And thou, Solomon my son, **know thou the God of thy father,** and serve him with a perfect heart, and with a willing mind; for the Lord searcheth all hearts, and understandeth all the imaginations of the thoughts: if thou seek him, he will be found of thee; but if thou forsake him, he will cast thee off for ever.

3.
Deuteronomy 26:17

Thou hast avouched the Lord this day to be thy God, and to walk in his ways, and to keep his statutes, and his commandments, and his judgments, and to hearken unto his voice.

4.
Matthew 4:10

Then saith Jesus unto him, Get thee hence, Satan: for it is written, **Thou shalt worship the Lord thy God,** and him only shalt thou serve.

5.
Psalm 29:2

Give unto the Lord the glory due unto his name; worship the Lord in the beauty of holiness.

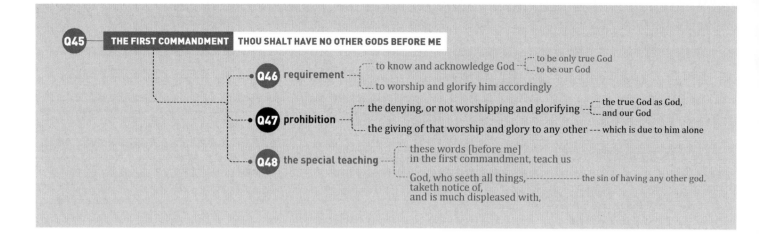

Q45 THE FIRST COMMANDMENT THOU SHALT HAVE NO OTHER GODS BEFORE ME

Q46 requirement --- to know and acknowledge God --- to be only true God
                                                 --- to be our God
         --- to worship and glorify him accordingly

Q47 prohibition --- the denying, or not worshipping and glorifying --- the true God as God,
                                                                        and our God
         --- the giving of that worship and glory to any other --- which is due to him alone

Q48 the special teaching --- these words [before me]
                             in the first commandment, teach us
         --- God, who seeth all things, --- the sin of having any other god.
             taketh notice of,
             and is much displeased with,

The 1st Commandment

Q47 What is forbidden in the first commandment?

Q47 The first commandment forbiddeth
the denying,[1] or not worshipping and glorifying
the true God as God,[2] and our God;[3]
and the giving of that worship and glory to any other,
which is due to him alone.[4]

1.
Psalm 14:1

The fool hath said in his heart, **There is no God.** They are corrupt; they have done abominable works; there is none that doeth good.

2.
Romans 1:21

Because that, when they knew God, **they glorified him not as God,** neither were thankful; but became vain in their imaginations, and their foolish heart was darkened.

3.
Psalm 81:10-11

I am the Lord thy God, which brought thee out of the land of Egypt: open thy mouth wide, and I will fill it. But **my people would not hearken to my voice;** and Israel would none of me.

4.
Romans 1:25-26

Who changed the truth of God into a lie, and **worshipped and served the creature more than the Creator,** who is blessed for ever. Amen. For this cause God gave them up unto vile affections: for even their women did change the natural use into that which is against nature.

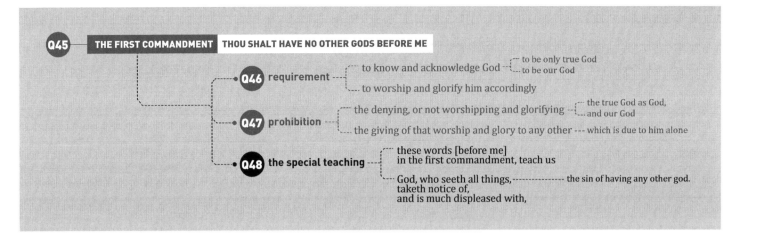

Q46 requirement — to know and acknowledge God — to be only true God / to be our God

— to worship and glorify him accordingly

Q47 prohibition — the denying, or not worshipping and glorifying — the true God as God, and our God

— the giving of that worship and glory to any other --- which is due to him alone

Q48 the special teaching — these words [before me] in the first commandment, teach us

— God, who seeth all things, taketh notice of, and is much displeased with, -------------- the sin of having any other god.

The 1st Commandment

Q48 What are we specially taught by these words, [before me] in the first commandment?

A48 These words [before me] in the first commandment, teach us,

That God, who seeth all things,

taketh notice of, and is much displeased with,

the sin of having any other god.[1,2]

1.
Ezekiel 8:5-6

Then said he unto me, Son of man, lift up thine eyes now the way toward the north. So I lifted up mine eyes the way toward the north, and behold northward at the gate of the altar this image of jealousy in the entry. He said furthermore unto me, Son of man, seest thou what they do? even **the great abominations** that the house of Israel committeth here, that I should go far off from my sanctuary? but turn thee yet again, and thou shalt see greater abominations, etc, to the end of the Chapter.

2.
Psalm 44:20-21

If we have forgotten the name of our God, **or stretched out our hands to a strange god; Shall not God search this out?** for he knoweth the secrets of the heart.

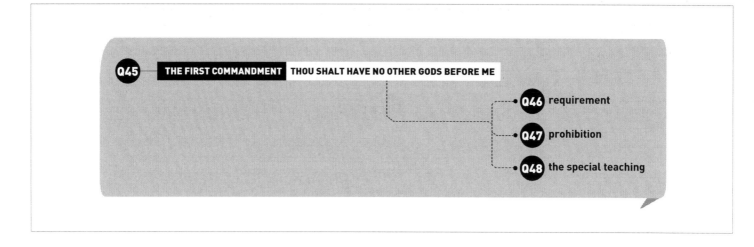

Commandment 1	the object of love
Commandment 2	the way to love
Commandment 3	the attitude of love
Commandment 4	the symbol (example, sample) of love

THE MEANING OF THE FIRST COMMANDMENT: THE OBJECT OF LOVE

Q46:

Duty, required of man in the first commandment, is to know and acknowledge God, and furthermore to worship and glorify Him. At its heart, this overlaps with the chief purpose of man, proclaimed in Q1 of the Shorter Catechism. In other words, to love God is both our duty and blessing. Thus, this commandment encourages us to continuously pursue Him, the object of our love.

Q47:

Read the list of things God forbade. (next page) What do you see? Most likely yourself. Only with the lips have you been speaking of your love for God, yet in your mind you have borne a number of idols and with your hands violated the commandment countless times.

It is also helpful to consider human relationships as an example. How would you feel if the one you love loves another or something more than you? It must be hard to bear even such a thought if you indeed love that person. That is what love is. In the same way, what God requires and forbids perfectly cross.

There is no rooms for compromise, for this would make a perfect contradiction. Thus, our choice should be clear to do as required and avoid things forbidden.

Q48:

Yet there is a problem. Despite the obviousness of the command and our effort, we end up either constantly or intermittently doing things God has forbidden. What a perverse and arrogant attempt it is to serve God and idols together!

It seems the word "before me" has been placed especially for those who daily experience the above. That God takes special notice of and is much displeased with having other gods before Him provides us more reasons to be watchful of this particular sin. Not only should we guard against other idols in our lives, but we should also be startled and quickly come to the place of repentance whenever recognizing we are serving God and other idols together.

DETAILED DESCRIPTION ON THE FIRST COMMANDMENT
from the Larger Catechism (Q104-105)

The duties required	The sins forbidden
the knowing and acknowledging of God to be the only true God, and our God; • to worship and glorify him accordingly; • by thinking, meditating, remembering, highly esteeming, honoring, adoring, choosing, loving, desiring, fearing of him • believing him; trusting, hoping, delighting, rejoicing in him; being zealous for him; calling upon him, giving all praise and thanks, and yielding all obedience and submission to him with the whole man • being careful in all things to please him, and sorrowful when in anything he is offended, and walking humbly with him.	• atheism, in denying or not having a God; • idolatry, in having or worshiping more gods than one, or any with or instead of the true God; • the not having and avouching him for God, and our God • the omission or neglect of anything due to him, required in this commandment; • ignorance, forgetfulness, misapprehensions, false opinions, unworthy and wicked thoughts of him; • bold and curious searching into his secrets; • all profaneness, hatred of God, self-love, self-seeking, and all other inordinate and immoderate setting of our mind, will, or affections upon other things, and taking them off from him in whole or in part; • vain credulity, unbelief, heresy, misbelief, distrust, despair, incorrigibleness, and insensibleness under judgments, hardness of heart, pride, presumption, carnal security, tempting of God; • using unlawful means, trusting in unlawful means; • carnal delights and joys; • corrupt, blind, and indiscreet zeal; • lukewarmness, and deadness in the things of God; • estranging ourselves, and apostatizing from God • praying, or giving any religious worship, to saints, angels, or any other creatures; • all compacts and consulting with the devil, and hearkening to his suggestions; • making men the lords of our faith and conscience; • slighting and despising God and his commands; • resisting and grieving of his Spirit, discontent and impatience at his dispensations, charging him foolishly for the evils he inflicts on us; • ascribing the praise of any good we either are, have, or can do, to fortune, idols, ourselves, or any other creature.

The first commandment teaches us 1) to love God alone, 2) not to have any other in our heart, and 3) to give Him the highest seat in our life. Also this commandment provides us warnings and fear. Yet this word of warning helps us live an obedient life and in Him be reassured and grateful. Indeed, the original intent of the Ten Commandments is to give us rest and blessing, never to oppress us with fear.

Whatever you trust something more than God, that is your "other god." To trust man more than God is also to serve some "other god." That you don't give thanks to God and that you grumble against Him out of discontentment regarding your own life is also a violation of the first commandment.

In light of today's study on the first commandment, what did you come to see in yourself and how do you plan to practice this commandment in your life?

	What I shouldn't be doing	What I should be doing
IN CHURCH		
IN MY FAMILY		
IN SCHOOL/ MY WORK-PLACE		

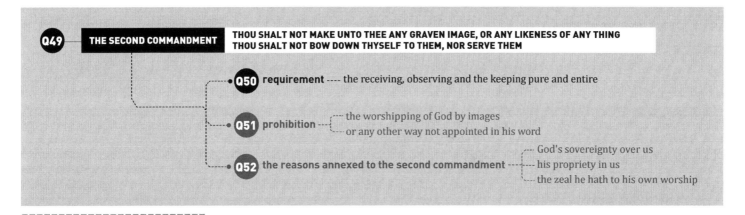

The 2nd Commandment

Q49 Which is the second commandment?

A49 The second commandment is,

Thou shalt not make unto thee

    any graven image,

    or any likeness of any thing that is in heaven above,

    or that is in the earth beneath,

    or that is in the water under the earth:

Thou shalt not bow down thyself to them, nor serve them:

for I the Lord thy God am a jealous God,

visiting the iniquity of the fathers upon the children

    unto the third and fourth generation of them that hate me,

and shewing mercy unto thousands of them that love me, and keep my commandments.[1]

Q50 What is required in the second commandment?

A50 The second commandment requireth

    the receiving, observing,

    and keeping pure and entire,

        all such religious worship and ordinances

            as God hath appointed in his word.[2,3,4]

1.
Exodus 20:4-6

Thou shalt not make unto thee any graven image, or any likeness of any thing that is in heaven above, or that is in the earth beneath, or that is in the water under the earth: Thou shalt not bow down thyself to them, nor serve them: for I the Lord thy God am a jealous God, visiting the iniquity of the fathers upon the children unto the third and fourth generation of them that hate me; And shewing mercy unto thousands of them that love me, and keep my commandments.

2.
Deuteronomy 32:46

And he said unto them, Set your hearts unto all the words which I testify among you this day, which ye shall command your children **to observe to do, all the words of this law.**

3.
Matthew 28:20

Teaching them to observe all things whatsoever I have commanded you: and, lo, I am with you alway, even unto the end of the world. Amen.

4.
Acts 2:42

And **they continued stedfastly in the apostles' doctrine** and fellowship, and in breaking of bread, and in prayers.

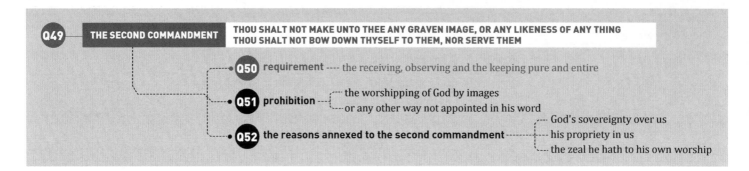

Q49 — **THE SECOND COMMANDMENT** — THOU SHALT NOT MAKE UNTO THEE ANY GRAVEN IMAGE, OR ANY LIKENESS OF ANY THING THOU SHALT NOT BOW DOWN THYSELF TO THEM, NOR SERVE THEM

Q50 requirement ---- the receiving, observing and the keeping pure and entire

Q51 prohibition — the worshipping of God by images / or any other way not appointed in his word

Q52 the reasons annexed to the second commandment ------- God's sovereignty over us / his propriety in us / the zeal he hath to his own worship

The 2nd Commandment

Q51 What is forbidden in the second commandment?

A51 The second commandment forbiddeth the worshipping of God

by images,[1,2]

or any other way not appointed in his word.[3]

Q52 What are the reasons annexed to the second commandment?

A52 The reasons annexed to the second commandment are,

God's sovereignty over us,[4]

his propriety in us,[5]

and the zeal he hath to his own worship.[6]

1.
Deuteronomy 4:15-19

Take ye therefore good heed unto yourselves, (for ye saw no manner of similitude on the day that the Lord spake unto you in Horeb out of the midst of the fire,) Lest ye corrupt yourselves, and **make you a graven image, the similitude of any figure, the likeness of male or female; The likeness of any beast that is on the earth, the likeness of any winged fowl that flieth in the air; The likeness of any thing that creepeth on the ground, the likeness of any**

fish that is in the waters beneath the earth: And lest thou lift up thine eyes unto heaven, and when thou seest the sun, and the moon, and the stars, even all the host of heaven, **shouldest be driven to worship them, and serve them,** which the Lord thy God hath divided unto all nations under the whole heaven.

5.
Psalm 45:11

So shall the king greatly desire thy beauty: for **he is thy Lord; and worship thou him.**

2.
Exodus 32:5, 8

And when Aaron saw it, he built an altar before it; and Aaron made proclamation, and said, To-morrow is a feast to the Lord. ......They have turned aside quickly out of the way which I commanded them: **they have made them a molten calf, and have worshipped it,** and have sacrificed thereunto, and said, These be thy gods, O Israel, which have brought thee up out of the land of Egypt.

3.
Deuteronomy 12:31-32

Thou shalt not do so unto the Lord thy God: for every **abomination to the Lord, which he hateth,** have they done unto their gods; for even **their sons and their daughters they have burnt in the fire to their gods.** What thing soever I command you, observe to do it: thou shalt not add thereto, nor diminish from it.

4.
Psalm 95:2-3, 6

Let us come before his presence with thanksgiving, and make a joyful noise unto him with psalms. **For the Lord is a great God, and a great King above all gods......O come, let us worship** and bow down; let us kneel before **the Lord our maker.**

6.
Exodus 34:13-14

But ye shall destroy their altars, break their images, and cut down their groves. For **thou shalt worship no other god: for the Lord,** whose name is Jealous, is **a jealous God.**

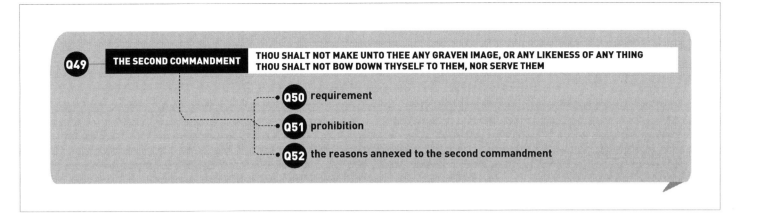

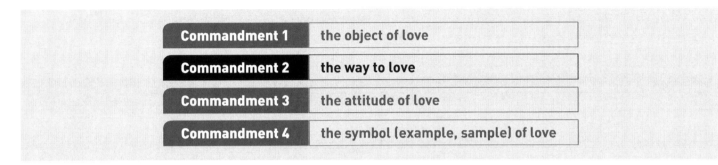

THE MEANING OF THE SECOND COMMANDMENT: THE WAY TO LOVE

Q49:

Through the first commandment we have learned the object of our love. And we were encouraged to actually obey this commandment. Now through the second commandment, we will be learning the proper way to love God.

Ask yourself: How should we love? Despite being frequently asked, this question's answer remains unknown to most people. Yet this commandment offers us a clue: We should **love in the way that the one we love demands**. If we force the way as we see fit, he/she would not feel loved, but rather challenged.

We may begin by examining the way we worship. Is our worship designed to please God or to please ourselves? How have you been in your corporate worship on the Lord's Day and in your personal worship in life in general, for the Bible commands us to offer our bodies as living sacrifices?

Some may ask: "Didn't God say that He loves me? Then, can't He allow us to love Him in a way I want?" This is the way fallen human beings see love, which falls very short of God's perfect and blameless love. Remember it is good, a blessing in fact, for us to follow the way God requires. And doesn't this

way of love, that we abandon our own ways and love and obey God only as He demands, communicate the same message as Jesus? "Deny yourself and take up your cross and follow me."

Q50-52:

Things required and forbidden in this commandment successfully communicate the weight God has assigned to His worship and ordinances. Also things connected to them greatly emphasize how God hates false worship and loves true worship.

If so, we should pay great attention not to turn Sunday worship merely into a ritual by participating without knowing the meaning of each component. What does it mean that we pray in Christ's name, that we give thanks to God, that we read, preach, and hear the Word, that we perform sacraments, to name a few? Also what are the various meetings in church for? What are the roles of elders, deacons, and pastors? The presbytery and general assembly? Discipline, fasting, swearing, and vowing—When should these be done and for what reason? For us to love God as required in the second commandment, we need to know the above.

Also we should resist and be watchful of false worship, which lurks in our way at all times. Yet at the same time, we should be careful to use our alertness not to judge others, especially those who long to worship God but lack in the knowledge of doing it correctly.

DETAILED DESCRIPTION ON THE SECONDCOMMANDMENT
from the Larger Catechism (Q108-109)

God uses all things in the world (both life and prosperity, death and destruction) as His means and demands for us to serve Him rightly. (Deut 30:11-15)

The duties required	The sins forbidden
• the receiving, observing, and keeping pure and entire, all such religious worship and ordinances as God hath instituted in his word; • particularly prayer and thanksgiving in the name of Christ; • the reading, preaching, and hearing of the word; • the administration and receiving of the sacraments; • church government and discipline; • the ministry and maintenance thereof; • religious fasting; • swearing by the name of God; • vowing unto him; • as also the disapproving, detesting, opposing, all false worship; • according to each one's place and calling, removing it(=false worship), and all monuments of idolatry.	• all devising, counseling, commanding, using, and any wise approving, any religious worship not instituted by God himself; • tolerating a false religion; • the making any representation of God, of all or of any of the three persons, either inwardly in our mind, or outwardly in any kind of image or likeness of any creature whatsoever; • all worshiping of it, or God in it or by it; • the making of any representation of feigned deities, and all worship of them, or service belonging to them; • all superstitious devices, corrupting the worship of God, adding to it, or taking from it, whether invented and taken up of ourselves, or received by tradition from others, though under the title of antiquity, custom, devotion, good intent, or any other pretense whatsoever; • simony; • sacrilege; • all neglect, contempt, hindering, and opposing the worship and ordinances which God hath appointed.

1. THE MATTER OF IMAGES

As revealed in the first commandment, God wants us to worship Him alone, and here in the second commandment, He forbids any kind of worship offered in the form of an idol. Yet we seem to never give up wanting to see an object even if it requires a creative imagination or even crafting one ourselves. We continuously attempt to see what is made invisible to us.

Yet such an attempt to make an idol is entirely forbidden, for this is destined to fail and without an exception brings misunderstanding and wrongful concepts of God. (Part 1, Q4-6) That is why God has always revealed Himself through the Word.

To make invisible God visible is to put the infinite One into a finite box. This will only bring belittlement and dishonor to Him.

2. THE MATTER OF WORSHIP

The second commandment requires us to worship God in His way. Here are two principles:

The most fundamental principle concerning the way of worship is found in John 4:24. "God is spirit, and his worshipers must worship in the Spirit and in truth," and God is looking for such worshippers. Also Rom 12:1 teaches us that our life is worship. At the same time, it teaches us that God prefers obedience to sacrifice (1 Sam 15:22). Thus, every moment of our lives, we have to offer worship by obedience as the Word demands.

This leads us to the order of our weekly service. Each and every component of service requires its own meaning and the proper attitude of the attendee. Congregational service on Sunday should focus on God's glory and honor instead of our emotion, and lead us into repentance and remind us of the assurance of forgiveness and give us confidence. Everything in the worship service should revolve around God, for He is the center of everything we offer to Him. For this, every component and the order of the service should be considered and prayed for in advance, so it can lead the congregation only to God Himself. Also the one who attends the service should apply his or her efforts to grasp the meaning of each and every component and order of service.

A JEALOUS GOD?

According to this commandment, we should not make any idols and bow down to them, for God is a jealous God. This confusing-sounding expression about God carries the following five meanings.

1. **Our God.** His is our creator and preserver—the giver of all the good things which we have been enjoying. And it is such a base ingratitude not to render obedience to Him.

2. **Mighty God.** He is able to punish the wicked, as well as reward the obedient. He is, therefore, to be feared and worshiped above all others.

3. **Jealous God.** This signifies how ardently He loves those that are his.

4. **God that visits our iniquity.** In these words, He reveals the greatness of His wrath and punishment on sin, in that He threatens that we must not imitate and approve of this sin.

5. **God who shows mercy.** By this promise, He magnifies His mercy.

Zacharias Ursinus on the Second Commandment from The commentary of Dr. Zacharias Ursinus on the Heidelberg catechism

In the light of today's study on the second commandment, what did you come to see in yourself and how do you plan to practice this commandment in your life?

	What I should be doing	What I shouldn't be doing
IN CHURCH		
IN MY FAMILY		
IN SCHOOL/ MY WORK-PLACE		

14

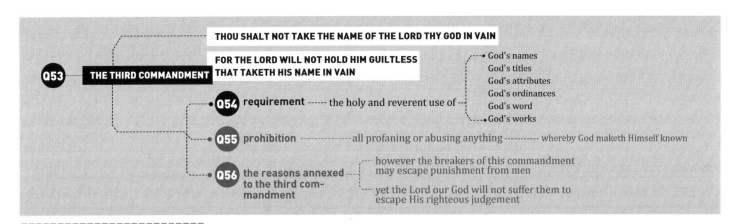

THOU SHALT NOT TAKE THE NAME OF THE LORD THY GOD IN VAIN

Q53   THE THIRD COMMANDMENT   FOR THE LORD WILL NOT HOLD HIM GUILTLESS THAT TAKETH HIS NAME IN VAIN

Q54 requirement ----- the holy and reverent use of
- God's names
- God's titles
- God's attributes
- God's ordinances
- God's word
- God's works

Q55 prohibition ------------- all profaning or abusing anything ---------- whereby God maketh Himself known

Q56 the reasons annexed to the third commandment
- however the breakers of this commandment may escape punishment from men
- yet the Lord our God will not suffer them to escape His righteous judgement

The 3rd Commandment

Q53   Which is the third commandment?

A53   The third commandment is,

Thou shalt not take the name of the Lord thy God in vain:

for the Lord will not hold him guiltless that taketh his name in vain.[1]

Q54   What is required in the third commandment?

A54   The third commandment requireth

the holy and reverent use

of God's names,[2,3] titles,[4] attributes,[5] ordinances,[6] word,[7] and works.[8]

1.
Exodus 20:7

Thou shalt not take the name of the Lord thy God in vain; for the Lord will not hold him guiltless that taketh his name in vain.

2.
Matthew 6:9

After this manner therefore pray ye: Our Father which art in heaven, **Hallowed be thy name.**

3.
Deuteronomy 28:58

If thou wilt not observe to do all the words of this law that are written in this book, that **thou mayest fear this glorious and fearful name, THE LORD THY GOD.**

4.
Psalm 68:4

Sing unto God, sing praises to his name: **extol him** that rideth upon the heavens **by his name JAH,** and rejoice before him.

5.
Revelation 15:3-4

And they sing the song of Moses the servant of God, and the song of the Lamb, saying, Great and marvellous are thy works, **Lord God Almighty; just and true** are thy ways, **thou King of saints.** Who shall not fear thee, O Lord, and glorify thy name? for **thou only art holy:** for all nations shall come and worship before thee; for thy judgments are made manifest.

6.
Malachi 1:11,14

For from the rising of the sun even unto the going down of the same my name shall be great among the Gentiles; and in every place **incense shall be offered** unto my name, and a pure offering: for my name shall be great among the heathen, saith the Lord of hosts...... But **cursed be the deceiver, which hath in his flock a male,** and voweth, and **sacrificeth unto the Lord a corrupt thing:** for I am a great King, saith the Lord of hosts, and my name is dreadful among the heathen.

7.
Psalm 138:1-2

I will praise thee with my whole heart: before the gods will I sing praise unto thee. **I will worship** toward thy holy temple, and praise thy name for thy lovingkindness and **for thy truth: for thou hast magnified thy word above all thy name.**

8.
Job 36:24

Remember **that thou magnify his work,** which men behold.

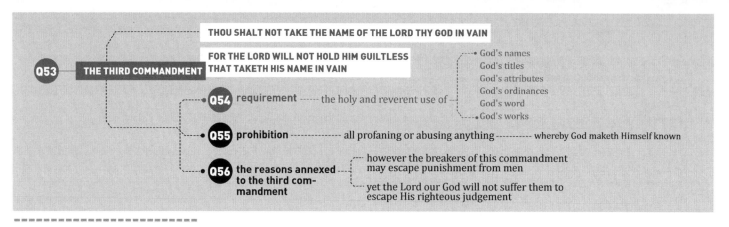

The 3rd Commandment

Q55 What is forbidden in the third commandment?

A55 The third commandment forbiddeth

all profaning or abusing of any thing

whereby God maketh himself known.[1,2,3]

Q56 What is the reason annexed to the third commandment?

A56 The reason annexed to the third commandment is,

That however the breakers of this commandment may escape punishment from men,

yet the Lord our God will not suffer them to escape his righteous judgement.[4,5,6]

1.
Malachi 1:6-7, 12

A son honoureth his father, and a servant his master: if then I be a father, **where is mine honour? and if I be a master, where is my fear?** saith the Lord of hosts **unto you**, O priests, **that despise my name.** And ye say, Wherein have we despised thy name? **Ye offer polluted bread upon mine altar;** and ye say, Wherein have we polluted thee? In that ye say, The table of the Lord is contemptible......But **ye have profaned it**, in that ye say, The table of the Lord is polluted; and the fruit thereof, even his meat, is contemptible.

2.
Malachi 2:2

If ye will not hear, and if ye will not lay it to heart, **to give glory unto my name**, saith the Lord of hosts, **I will even send a curse** upon you, and I will curse your blessings; yea, I have cursed them already, because ye do not lay it to heart.

5.
1 Samuel 3:13

For I have told him that **I will judge his house for ever** for the iniquity which he knoweth; **because his sons made themselves vile, and he restrained them not.**

3.
Malachi 3:14

Ye have said, It is vain to serve God: and **what profit is it that we have kept his ordinance,** and that we have walked mournfully before the Lord of hosts?

6.
Deuteronomy 28:58-59

If thou wilt not observe to do all the words of this law that are written in this book, that thou mayest fear this glorious and fearful name, THE LORD THY GOD;

4.
1 Samuel 2:12, 17, 22, 29

Now the sons of Eli were sons of Belial; they knew not the Lord...... Wherefore **the sin of the young men was very great before the Lord:** for men abhorred the offering of the Lord......Now Eli was very old, and heard

all that his sons did unto all Israel; and how they lay with the women that assembled at the door of the tabernacle of the congregation...... Wherefore kick ye at my sacrifice and at mine offering, which I have commanded in my habitation; and honourest thy sons above me, to make yourselves fat with the chiefest of all the offerings of Israel my people?

Then the Lord will make thy plagues wonderful, and the plagues of thy seed, even great plagues, and of long continuance, and sore sicknesses, and of long continuance.

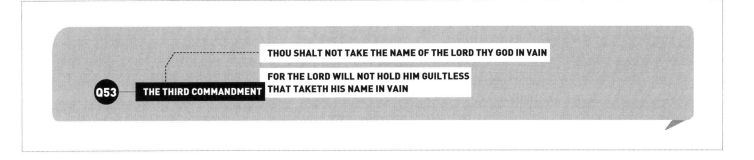

THOU SHALT NOT TAKE THE NAME OF THE LORD THY GOD IN VAIN

FOR THE LORD WILL NOT HOLD HIM GUILTLESS THAT TAKETH HIS NAME IN VAIN

Q53 — THE THIRD COMMANDMENT

Commandment 1	the object of love
Commandment 2	the way to love
Commandment 3	the attitude of love
Commandment 4	the symbol (example, sample) of love

ATTITUDE OF LOVE

Q53:

The third commandment is about the attitude of love. Attitude is a reflection of the heart, and for this reason it is impossible to pretend to have a sincere attitude when there is no heart at all. Where your heart is, there your attitude follows.

Literally interpreted, the third commandment is only about what is being said with our lips. Being raised in a Christian family, I always thought at least this commandment has nothing to do with me. However, reflecting on the teaching of this catechism, I see how untrue that was.

You may go ahead and read a description of early church Christians made by an unknown observer. (Reading Material, p. 237) What if another observation is made of today's Christians? I feel greatly anxious about it, for the world seems to be tired of us and even to scoff and ridicule us. It is probably due to the great difference between the label on us, God's people, and the attitude we have toward God.

If someone calls your mother names (or anyone you love dearly), this would surely upset you. Boys break into fights over this kind of mischief all the time. Yet due to the easy access to Internet (the open platform of self expression and discussion) God's name is being profaned in more ways today than at any time before in history.

Yet instead of blaming others and fighting against the world,

we should deem the world's voice as a prophet's and **examine our lives and churches up close**. The light, now being hidden under our weaknesses and sins, is still there and can shine bright once again into the world. What is required of God's people is to seek after God's grace, and take the moral law of God as the rule of our lives and actually practice it.

"My heart, O God, is steadfast; I will sing and make music with all my soul." (Ps 108:1)

Q54-56:

The Larger Catechism(Q112, 113) expands the description on this commandment even to little and insignificant things, which reveals how dull our hearts have become toward God's word.

The Reformers, the writers of this catechism, have taken this explicit and severe commandment of God seriously, and applied it to themselves as to repent of every bit of their sins where they fall short of God's standard. Then why are today's Christians different? It is probably either that we have forgotten how high our God is and how lowly we are or that we misunderstand the two natures of believers—already justified but still remaining in the corruption of sin—we have been pretending that we are already glorified, mature, blameless, and we have become complacent.

IN PARTICULAR: "WILL NOT HOLD HIM GUILTLESS"

This is for emphasis. God gave His people the permission to call Him as intimately as their "daddy." God surely is that intimate—He is our Abba Father, —yet at the same time very special. We should not take this kindness of God as the license to call His name in vain and treat Him profanely. To those He gives out this warning: "I will not hold him guiltless."

DETAILED DESCRIPTION OF THE THIRD COMMANDMENT
from the Larger Catechism (Q112-113)

The duties required	The sins forbidden
• be holily and reverently used in thought, meditation, word, and writing **(What?)** • the name of God, his titles, attributes, ordinances, the word, sacraments, prayer, oaths, vows, lots, his works, and whatsoever else there is whereby he makes himself known, **(How?)** • by an holy profession, and answerable conversation, **(Purpose?)** • to the glory of God, and the good of ourselves, and others.	• the not using of God's name as is required; • the abuse of it in an ignorant, vain, irreverent, profane, superstitious, or wicked mentioning or otherwise using his titles, attributes, ordinances, or works, by blasphemy, perjury; • all sinful cursings, oaths, vows, and lots; • violating of our oaths and vows, if lawful; and fulfilling them, if of things unlawful • murmuring and quarreling at, curious prying into, and misapplying of God's decrees and providences; • misinterpreting, misapplying, or any way perverting the word, or any part of it, to profane jests, curious or unprofitable questions, vain janglings, or the maintaining of false doctrines; • abusing it, the creatures, or anything contained under the name of God, to charms, or sinful lusts and practices; • the maligning, scorning, reviling, or any wise opposing of God's truth, grace, and ways; • making profession of religion in hypocrisy, or for sinister ends; • being ashamed of it, or a shame to it, by unconformable, unwise, unfruitful, and offensive walking, or backsliding from it.

14

"The Christians are not distinguished from other men by country, by language, nor by civil institutions. For they neither dwell in cities by themselves, nor use a peculiar tongue, nor lead a singular mode of life. They dwell in the Grecian or barbarian cities, as the case may be; they follow the usage of the country in dress, food, and the other affairs of life. Yet they preset a wonderful and confessedly paradoxical conduct.

They dwell in their own native lands, but as strangers. They take part in all things, as citizens; and they suffer all things, as foreigners. Every foreign country is a fatherland to them, and every native land is a foreign. They marry, like all others; they have children; but they do not cast away their offspring. They have the table in common, but not wives. They are in the flesh, but do not live after the flesh. They live upon the earth, but are citizens of heaven. They obey the existing laws, and excel the laws by their lives. They love all, and are persecuted by all. They are unknown, and yet they are condemned. They are killed and are made alive. They are poor and make many rich. They lack all things, and in all things abound. They are reproached, and glory in their reproaches. They are calumniated, and are justified. They are cursed, and they bless. They receive scorn, and they give honor. They do good, and are punished as evil-doers. When punished, they rejoice, as being made alive. By the Jews they are attacked as aliens, and by the Greeks persecuted; and the cause of the enmity their enemies cannot tell.

In short, what the soul is in the body, the Christians are in the world. The soul is diffused through all the members of the body, and the Christians are spread through the cities of the world. The soul dwells in the body, but it is not of the body; so the Christians dwell in the world, but are not of the world. The soul, invisible, keeps watch in the visible body; so also the Christians are seen to live in the world, but their piety is invisible. The flesh hates and wars against the soul, suffering no wrong from it, but because it resists fleshly pleasures; and the world hates the Christians with no reason, but that they resist its pleasures. The soul loves the flesh and members, by which it is hated; so the Christians love their haters. The soul is enclosed in the body, but holds the body together; so the Christians are detained in the world as in a prison but they contain the world. Immortal, the soul dwells in the mortal body; so the Christians dwell in the corruptible, but look for incorruption in heaven. The soul is the better for restriction in food and drink; and the Christians increase, though daily punished. This lot God has assigned to the Christians in the world; and it cannot be taken from them."

The community of Christians thus from the first felt itself, in distinction from Judaism and from heathenism, the slat of the earth, the light of the world, the city of God set on a hill, the immortal soul in a dying body; and this its impression respecting itself was no proud conceit, but truth and reality, acting in life and in death, and opening the way through hatred and persecution even to an outward victory over the world.

from the chapter of "General Character of Ante-Nicene Christianity" p. 9-10 in History of the Christian Church by Philip Schaff

The third commandment offers a significant and practical principle about making an oath. A falsely-made oaths profanes God's name, and even though it may be sincere, a practice that is abused for unnecessary reasons is also a vulgar use of God's name. Without the confidence to keep it, we should not make an oath.

However, does this mean that we cannot make any oath at all? (Some insist that is what Christ says in Matt 5:34.) Calling this a reckless conclusion, The French Reformer, John Calvin interprets this verse as saying making an oath "in vain" is forbidden, not all oaths however. This is reasonable, given that making oaths is an essential part of our lives from giving a testimony in courts to drawing a contract. The following is what Calvin said in his Institutes of Christian Religion.

"In the first place, we must consider what an oath is. An oath, then, is calling God to witness that what we say is true.... It is no slight insult to swear by him and do it falsely: hence in the Law this is termed profanation, (Lev. 19: 12.) For if God is robbed of his truth, what is it that remains? Without truth he could not be God." (Institutes of Christian Religion, II. 8. 23-24)

"I hold, therefore, that there is no better rule than so to regulate our oaths that they shall neither be rash, frivolous, promiscuous, nor passionate, but be made to serve a just necessity; in other words, to vindicate the glory of God, or promote the edification of a brother. This is the end of the Commandment." (Institutes of Christian Religion, II. 8. 27)

Also holding to the principle of interpreting scripture by scripture, it is worth noting what other scriptures say about this matter. *"Do not swear falsely by my name and so profane the name of your God. I am the Lord."* *(Lev 19:12)* This verse gives a scriptural basis to Calvin's view that the third commandment forbids an oath made "by God's name" in vain.

	YES	NO
Commandment 1 **OBJECT OF LOVE**	Only God	Yes both to God and others
Commandment 2 **WAY TO LOVE**	As God ordained and wants	If it seems right in my eyes, it should be okay
Commandment 3 **ATTITUDE OF LOVE**	So my loving mind and heart will match with my attitude	Unmatched heart and attitude

When we profess God's name, but do not live answerably to it, we take it in vain. 'They profess that they know God, but in works they deny him.' (Titus 1:16). When men's tongues and lives are contrary to one another, when, under a mask of profession, they lie and cozen, and are unclean, they make use of God's name to abuse him, and take it in vain... When the heathen saw the Jews, who professed to be God's people, to be scandalous, it made them speak evil of God, and hate the true religion for their sakes.

Ten Commandments by Thomas Watson (p. 85)

APPLICATION AND SHARING OF THE THIRD COMMANDMENT

In the light of today's study on the third commandment, what did you come to see in yourself and how do you plan to practice this commandment in your life?

	What I should be doing	What I shouldn't be doing
IN CHURCH		
IN MY FAMILY		
IN SCHOOL/ MY WORK-PLACE		

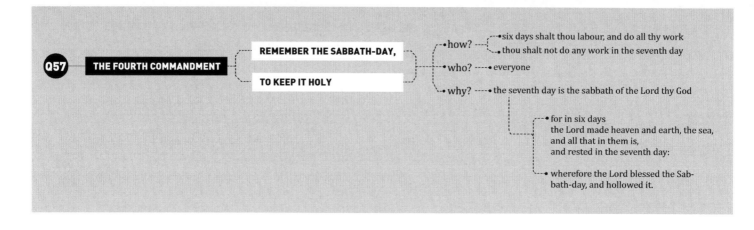

REMEMBER THE SABBATH-DAY,

TO KEEP IT HOLY

- how? — • six days shalt thou labour, and do all thy work
  - • thou shalt not do any work in the seventh day
- who? — • everyone
- why? — • the seventh day is the sabbath of the Lord thy God
  - • for in six days the Lord made heaven and earth, the sea, and all that in them is, and rested in the seventh day:
  - • wherefore the Lord blessed the Sabbath-day, and hallowed it.

The 4th Commandment

Q57 Which is the fourth commandment?

A57 The fourth commandment is,

Remember the Sabbath-day, to keep it holy.

Six days shalt thou labour, and do all thy work:

but the seventh day is the sabbath of the Lord thy God:

in it thou shalt not do any work, thou, nor thy son, nor thy daughter,

thy man-servant, nor thy maid-servant,

nor thy cattle, nor thy stranger that is within thy gates:

For in six days

the Lord made heaven and earth, the sea,

and all that in them is, and rested the seventh day:

wherefore the Lord blessed the Sabbath-day,

and hallowed it.[1]

1.
Exodus 20:8-11

Remember the sabbath day, to keep it holy. Six days shalt thou labour, and do all thy work: But the seventh day is the sabbath of the Lord thy God: in it thou shalt not do any work, thou, nor thy son, nor thy daughter, thy man-servant, nor thy maid-servant, nor thy cattle, nor thy stranger that is within thy gates: For in six days the Lord made heaven and earth, the sea, and all that in them is, and rested the seventh day: wherefore the Lord blessed the sabbath day, and hallowed it.

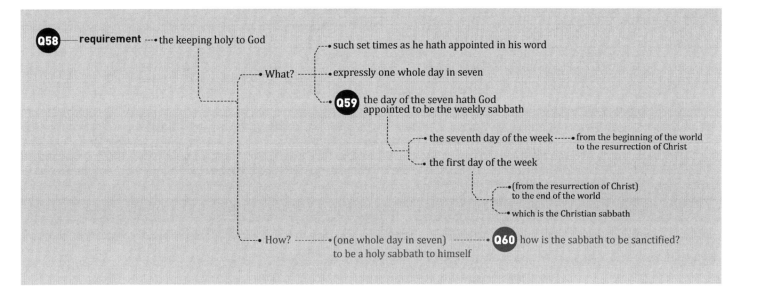

Q58 What is required in the fourth commandment?

A58 The fourth commandment requireth

the keeping holy to God such set times as he hath appointed in his word;

expressly one whole day in seven, to be a holy sabbath to himself.[1]

Q59 Which day of the seven hath God appointed to be the weekly sabbath?

A59 From the beginning of the world to the resurrection of Christ,

God appointed the seventh day of the week to be the weekly sabbath;

and the first day of the week ever since,

to continue to the end of the world,

which is the Christian sabbath.[2, 3, 4]

1.
Deuteronomy 5:12-14

Keep the sabbath day to sanctify it, as the Lord thy God hath commanded thee. Six days thou shalt labour, and do all thy work; But **the seventh day is the sabbath of the Lord thy God: in it thou shalt not do any work,** thou, nor thy son, nor thy daughter, nor thy man-servant, nor thy maid-servant, nor thine ox, nor thine ass, nor any of thy cattle, nor thy stranger that is within thy gates; that thy man-servant and thy maid-servant may rest as well as thou.

2.
Genesis 2:2-3

And on the seventh day God ended his work which he had made; and **he rested on the seventh day from all his work** which he had made. And **God blessed the seventh day, and sanctified it:** because that in it he had rested from all his work which God created and made.

3.
1 Corinthians 16:1-2

Now concerning the collection for the saints, as I have given order to the churches of Galatia, **even so do ye. Upon the first day of the week** let every one of you lay by him in store, as God hath prospered him, that there be no gatherings when I come.

4.
Acts 20:7

And upon the first day of the week, when the disciples came together to break bread, Paul preached unto them, ready to depart on the morrow; and continued his speech until midnight.

Q60 how is the sabbath to be sanctified? ········• by a holy resting all that day

How? ···•spending the whole time
in the public and private exercises of God's worship

resting from such worldly employments and recreations
as are lawful on other days

exception ····•the works of necessity
•the works of mercy

The 4th Commandment

Q60 How is the sabbath to be sanctified?

A60 The sabbath is to be sanctified

by a holy resting all that day,[1,2]

even from such worldly employments and recreations

as are lawful on other days;[3]

and spending the whole time

in the public and private exercises of God's worship,[4,5,6,7]

except so much as is to be taken up in the works of necessity and mercy.[8]

1.
Exodus 20:8-10

Remember the sabbath-day, to keep it holy. But the seventh day is **the sabbath of the Lord thy God: in it thou shalt not do any wor**k, thou, nor thy son, etc.

7.
Isaiah 66:23

And it shall come to pass, that from one new-moon to another, and **from one sabbath to another, shall all flesh come to worship before me,** saith the Lord.

8.
Matthew 12:1-31

[the entire chapter] At that time Jesus went on the sabbath-day through the corn; and his disciples were an hungred, and began to pluck

2.
Exodus 16:25-28

And Moses said, Eat that to day; for to-day is a sabbath unto the Lord: to-day ye shall not find it in the field. Six days ye shall gather it; but on the seventh day, which is the sabbath, in it there shall be none. And it came to pass, that there went out some of the people on the seventh day for to gather, and they found none. And the Lord said unto Moses, How long refuse ye to keep my commandments and my laws?

the ears of corn, and to eat. But when the Pharisees, etc. **It is lawful to do well on the sabbath-days.**

3.
Nehemiah 13:15-19,21-22

In those days saw I in Judah some **treading wine-presses on the sabbath, and bringing in sheaves, and lading asses; as also wine, grapes, and figs, and all manner of burdens,** which they brought into Jerusalem on the sabbath-day: **and I testified against them in the day wherein they sold victuals.** There dwelt men of Tyre also therein, **which brought fish, and all manner of ware, and sold on the sabbath** unto the children of Judah, and in Jerusalem. Then **I contended with the nobles of Judah,** and said unto them, **What evil thing is this that ye do, and profane the sabbath-day?** Did

not your fathers thus, and did not our God bring all this evil upon us, and upon this city? yet ye bring more wrath upon Israel by profaning the sabbath. And it came to pass, that when the gates of Jerusalem began to be dark before the sabbath, I commanded that the gates should be shut, and charged that they should not be opened till after the sabbath: and some of my servants set I at the gates, that there should no burden be brought in on the sabbath-day......Then I testified against them, and said unto them, **Why lodge ye about the wall?** if ye do so again, I will lay hands on you. From that time forth **came they no more on the sabbath.** And I commanded the Levites that they should cleanse themselves, and

that they should come and keep the gates, to sanctify the sabbath-day. Remember me, O my God, concerning this also, and spare me according to the greatness of thy mercy.

4.
Luke 4:16

And he came to Nazareth, where he had been brought up: and, as his custom was, he went into the synagogue **on the sabbath-day,** and **stood up for to read.**

5.
Acts 20:7

And upon the **first day of the week,** etc. [See Genesis 2:2]

6.
Psalm 92

[title, A psalm or song for the sabbath-day.]

Q61 — prohibition
- the omission or careless performance of the duties required
- the profaning the day by idleness
- doing that which is in itself sinful
- doing by unnecessary thoughts, words, or works, ·········• about our worldly employments or recreations

Q61 What is forbidden in the fourth commandment?

A61 The fourth commandment forbiddeth

the omission or careless performance of the duties required,[1, 2, 3]

and the profaning the day by idleness,[4]

or doing that which is in itself sinful,[5]

or by unnecessary thoughts, words, or works,

about our worldly employments or recreations.[6, 7]

1.
Ezekiel 22:26

Her priests have violated my law, and have profaned mine holy things: they have put no difference between the holy and profane, neither have they shewed difference between the unclean and the clean, and **have hid their eyes from my sabbaths,** and I am profaned among them.

2.
Amos 8:5S

Saying, When will the new-moon be gone, that we may sell corn? and **the sabbath, that we may set forth wheat,** making the ephah small, and the shekel great, and falsifying the balances by deceit?

3.
Malachi 1:13

Ye said also, Behold, **what a weariness is it!** and ye have snuffed at it, saith the Lord of hosts; and ye brought that which was torn, and the lame, and the sick; thus ye brought an offering: should I accept this of your hand? saith the Lord.

4.
Acts 20:7,9

And upon the first day of the week, when the disciples came together to break bread, Paul preached unto them, ready to depart on the morrow; and continued his speech until midnight......And there sat in a window a certain young man named Eutychus, being **fallen into a deep sleep:** and as Paul was long preaching, he sunk down with sleep, and fell down from the third loft, and was taken up dead.

5.
Ezekiel 23:38

Moreover this they have done unto me: they have defiled my sanctuary in the same day, and **have profaned my sabbaths.**

6.
Jeremiah 17:24-26

And it shall come to pass, if ye diligently hearken unto me, saith the Lord, **to bring in no burden** through the gates of this city on the sabbath-day, but hallow the sabbath day, to **do no work therein;** Then shall there enter into the gates of this city kings and princes sitting upon the throne of David, riding in chariots and on horses, they, and their princes, the men of Judah, and the inhabitants of Jerusalem; and this city shall remain for ever. And they shall come from the cities of Judah, and from the places about Jerusalem, and from the land of Benjamin, and from the plain, and from the mountains, and from the south, bringing burnt offerings, and sacrifices, and meat offerings, and incense, and bringing sacrifices of praise, unto the house of the Lord.

7.
Isaiah 58:13

If thou turn away thy foot from the sabbath, **from doing thy pleasure on my holy day,** and call the sabbath a delight, the holy of the Lord, honourable; and shalt honour him, **not doing thine own ways, nor finding thine own pleasure, nor speaking thine own words:**

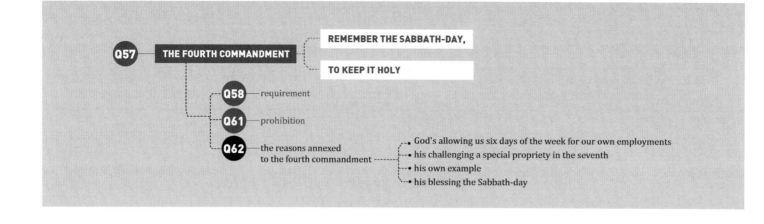

Q62 What are the reasons annexed to the fourth commandment?

A62 The reasons annexed to the fourth commandment are,

God's allowing us six days of the week for our own employments,[1]

his challenging a special propriety in the seventh,

his own example,

and his blessing the sabbath-day.[2]

1.
Exodus 20:9

Six days shalt thou labour, and do all thy work.

2.
Exodus 20:1

For in six days the Lord made heaven and earth, the sea, and all that in them is, and rested the seventh day: wherefore the Lord **blessed the sabbath-day,** and hallowed it.

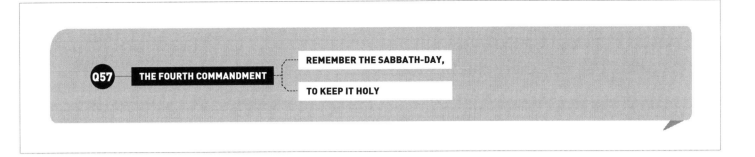

Commandment 1	the object of love
Commandment 2	the way to love
Commandment 3	the attitude of love
Commandment 4	the symbol (example, sample) of love

MEANING OF THE FOURTH COMMANDMENT: SYMBOL (EXAMPLE, SAMPLE) OF LOVE

The first commandment teaches whom we love (God alone), the second in which way we should love (by ordained ordinances), and the third in which attitude we should love (holily). Then what does the next commandment teach? Our discussion has been revolving around what genuine love looks like. Where can we find such a love? Of course, in heaven, some might answer. Then, can we never find it, even the glimpse of it, on this earth?

It is through this commandment we come across the example (sample or symbol) of this love. In keeping the Lord's day holy, we get to see this love in the most vivid form, and this is why the Lord's day should be called the example of this love. If we love God, we should love Him in the same way we keep this day holy, and the blessings we receive through this love shares the nature of the blessings we receive through the Lord's day.

The literal requirement of this commandment is to take a full day of rest, which may sound like one among many other Dos and Don'ts. Yet its purpose along with those of other commandments is not to bind us; rather, it is to benefit us. By giving ourselves an entire day to think about God and worship Him, we can be filled with joy in Him and rejuvenated to live another six days holily. Thus this day should not be kept out of duty and against our will, but acknowledging God's love and grace, kept out of willingness and a heart of obedience.

"REMEMBER"

A word is added to the commandment—"Remember." Even though God's way is always good for us, we are forgetful and slow to remember His commandments. His voice over this word, remember, is sweet rather than fearful.

MATTER OF FOCUS

By keeping the Lord's Day holy, we practice our faith in an actual way and also confess it both to ourselves and others. That I come to church, that I take a full of rest, these speaks none other than my life is not revolving around this earth but is heading towards the eternal rest in a new heaven and earth. As we keep this commandment, in other words, acknowledging God as our focus and continuously practicing it in our lives, the Lord's Day becomes an example and sample of this eternal rest that believers earnestly long for.

Keeping the Lord's Day holy has also been dealt with in Part 1, p. 117. I pray that our discussion has changed your Lord's Day experience to become more grateful and joyous.

DETAILED DESCRIPTION ON THE FOURTH COMMANDMENT
from the Larger Catechism (Q117, 119)

The duties required	The sins forbidden
• a holy resting all the day, • not only from such works as are at all times sinful, but even from such worldly employments and recreations as are on other days lawful; • making it our delight to spend the whole time (except so much of it as is to be taken up in works of necessity and mercy) in the public and private exercises of God's worship: • to that end, we are to prepare our hearts, and with such foresight, diligence, and moderation, to dispose and seasonably dispatch our worldly business, that we may be the more free and fit for the duties of that day.	• all omissions of the duties required, • all careless, negligent, and unprofitable performing of them, and being weary of them • all profaning the day by idleness, and doing that which is in itself sinful; and by all needless works, words, and thoughts, about our worldly employments and recreations.

HOW WE CAN KEEP THIS DAY HOLY

Keeping the day holy does not mean that we sit idle doing nothing. Rather we need to take initiative to keep this day as is commanded.

HOME:

Preparation on the prior day is necessary. Without preparation, it is highly likely that the Lord's day will pass just like any other. It would be helpful to have more conversations among family members and remind each other of the true meaning of rest.

CHURCH:

It will be a neglect of duty if the church does not diligently teach its members the meaning of the moral law and Ten Commandments to help them come to cherish the Lord's day through public worship. Also, for those who have to miss the service due to some compelling circumstances, the church should offer other forms of worship and teaching.

SOCIETY:

We have to divert our interest all together from worldly businesses and entertainments, so that our rest may find its way into the society where we belong. Remember this commandment is not only for us, but for all mankind.

We may come up with many excuses, and some of them are certainly reasonable. Yet it comes down to a matter of desire: Do I want to keep this day holy as God commanded? Asking this question to ourselves will be a wonderful starting point for us.

APPLICATION AND SHARING OF THE FOURTH COMMANDMENT

In the light of today's study on the fourth commandment, what did you come to see in yourself and how do you plan to practice this commandment in your life?

	What I should be doing	What I shouldn't be doing
IN CHURCH		
IN MY FAMILY		
IN SCHOOL/ MY WORK- PLACE		

"DOS AND DON'TS WON'T WORK! IT IS SO OLD-FASHIONED!"
"YOU DON'T KNOW THE WORLD AT ALL.
IT IS SO COMPETITIVE NOW THAT BY LOVING AND CARING WE CANNOT SURVIVE."
"CHRISTIANS SEEM TO EXCEL ONLY IN CHURCH.
AT THEIR HOMES AND WORKPLACES, MANY OF THEM FALL SO BEHIND."
"LOVE YOUR GOD AND LOVE YOUR NEIGHBOR!
GRANTED THAT I HAVE TO LOVE GOD, BUT WHO IS MY NEIGHBOR? IT IS HARD TO DEFINE."

The Good Samaritan

From the fifth commandment, the second part begins. As has been mentioned (p. 213), from the first to the fourth, the Ten Commandments deals with loving God, and from the fifth to the tenth, it deals with loving neighbors. However, these two sections are so closely related that the latter brings our attention to honoring and loving God. It is nearly impossible to set a clear distinction between these two.

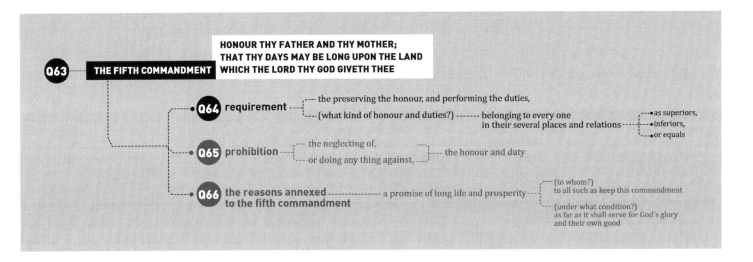

Q63 Which is the fifth commandment?

A63 The fifth commandment is, Honour

thy father and thy mother; that thy days may be long upon the land which the Lord thy God giveth thee.[1]

Q64 What is required in the fifth commandment?

A64 The fifth commandment requireth

the preserving the honour,

and performing the duties,

belonging to every one in their several places and relations,

as superiors,[2] inferiors,[3] or equals.[4]

1.
Exodus 20:12

Honour thy father and thy mother: that thy days may be long upon the land which the Lord thy God giveth thee.

2.
Ephesians 5:21

Submitting yourselves one to another in the fear of God.

3.
1 Peter 2:17

Honour all men. Love the brotherhood. Fear God. **Honour the king.**

4.
Romans 12:10

Be kindly affectioned one to another with brotherly love; **in honour preferring one another.**

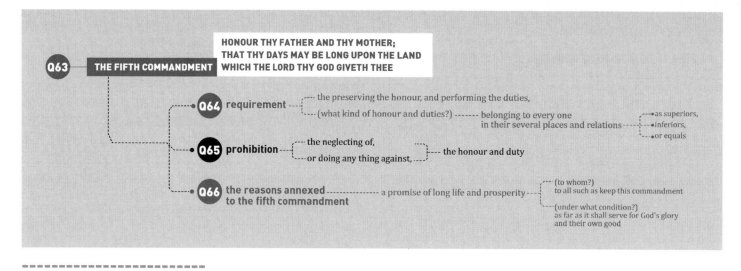

Q63 THE FIFTH COMMANDMENT — HONOUR THY FATHER AND THY MOTHER; THAT THY DAYS MAY BE LONG UPON THE LAND WHICH THE LORD THY GOD GIVETH THEE

Q64 requirement — the preserving the honour, and performing the duties, — (what kind of honour and duties?) — belonging to every one in their several places and relations — as superiors, inferiors, or equals

Q65 prohibition — the neglecting of, or doing any thing against, — the honour and duty

Q66 the reasons annexed to the fifth commandment — a promise of long life and prosperity — (to whom?) to all such as keep this commandment — (under what condition?) as far as it shall serve for God's glory and their own good

The 5th Commandment

Q65 What is the forbidden in the fifth commandment?

A65 The fifth commandment forbiddeth

the neglecting of, or doing any thing against,

the honour and duty

which belongeth to every one in their several places and relations.[1,2,3]

1.
Matthew 15:4-6

For God commanded, saying, Honour thy father and mother: and, **He that curseth father or mother, let him die the death.** But ye say, **Whosoever shall say to his father** or his mother, It is a gift, by whatsoever thou mightest be profited by me, And honour not his father or his mother, he shall be free. **Thus have ye made the commandment of God of none effect** by your tradition.

2.
Ezekiel 34:2-4

Son of man, prophesy against the shepherds of Israel, prophesy, and say unto them, Thus saith the Lord GOD unto the shepherds, **Woe be to the shepherds of Israel that do feed themselves!** should not the shepherds feed the flocks? Ye eat the fat, and ye clothe you with the wool, ye kill them that are fed: but **ye feed not the flock. The diseased have ye not strengthened, neither have ye healed that which was sick, neither have ye bound up that which was broken, neither have ye brought again that which was driven away, neither have ye sought that which was lost;** but with force and with cruelty have ye ruled them.

3.
Romans 13:8

Owe no man any thing, but to love one another: for he that loveth another hath fulfilled the law.

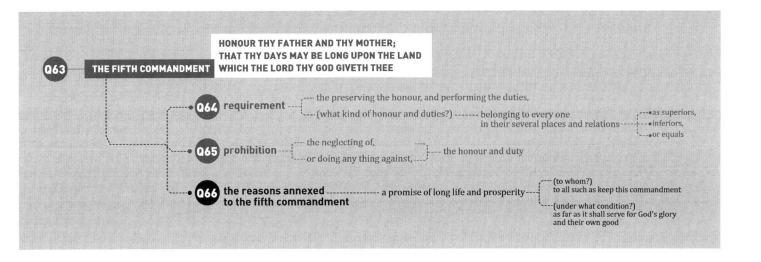

Q63 THE FIFTH COMMANDMENT | HONOUR THY FATHER AND THY MOTHER; THAT THY DAYS MAY BE LONG UPON THE LAND WHICH THE LORD THY GOD GIVETH THEE

Q64 requirement --- the preserving the honour, and performing the duties, --- (what kind of honour and duties?) ------- belonging to every one in their several places and relations --- as superiors, inferiors, or equals

Q65 prohibition --- the neglecting of, or doing any thing against, --- the honour and duty

Q66 the reasons annexed to the fifth commandment ------ a promise of long life and prosperity --- (to whom?) to all such as keep this commandment --- (under what condition?) as far as it shall serve for God's glory and their own good

---

Q66 What is the reason annexed to the fifth commandment?

A66 The reason annexed to the fifth commandment,

is a promise of long life and prosperity

(as far as it shall serve for God's glory and their own good)

to all such as keep this commandment.[1,2]

1.
Deuteronomy 5:16

Honour thy father and thy mother, as the Lord thy God hath commanded thee; **that thy days may be prolonged, and that it may go well with thee, in the land** which the Lord thy God giveth thee.

2.
Ephesians 6:2-3

Honour thy father and mother, (which is the first commandment with promise,) **That it may be well with thee, and thou mayest live long on the earth.**

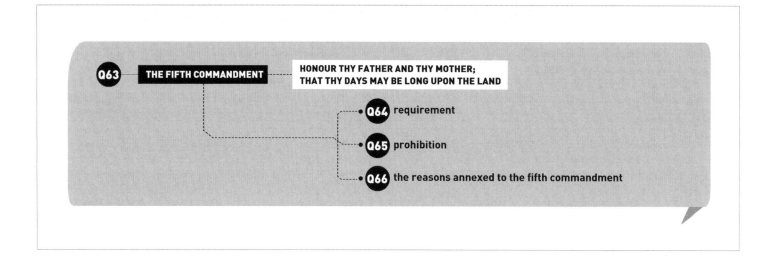

Q63 — THE FIFTH COMMANDMENT — HONOUR THY FATHER AND THY MOTHER; THAT THY DAYS MAY BE LONG UPON THE LAND

Q64 requirement

Q65 prohibition

Q66 the reasons annexed to the fifth commandment

MEANING OF THE FIFTH COMMANDMENT:
Preserving the honor and performing the duties

God must have created man to love each other. And such an intention of the Creator and His principle in the creation highlight all the more the misery of man, for it comes as an enormous challenge to love our neighbor let alone an invisible God, our Creator.

Here we are commanded to love our parents, which is in most cases understood as our earthly parents on this earth. Yet this commandment includes all created man—from superiors to equals to inferiors—and it reveals the wretched state of man (being unable to love) and the most high and good will of the Creator for man (to love neighbors).

Then what does it include in detail? Please refer to the list from the Larger Catechism.(Q127-132).

The requirements on superiors remind us of both our earthly parents and our heavenly Father. Sometimes it is a simple reminder like the above that successfully awakens gratitude in us for the things God is doing for us, His children. At the same time it make us reflect on our shortcomings in the way we treat our inferiors. Reflect on yourself, your body and soul, in the light of the law and offer your life in worship. For that is the proper use of the law. (p. 210)

Things forbidden begin with a question, which greatly embarrasses most of us. Ask yourself: "What percentage of my life is now being used for my own glory?" In other words, what percentage of your life is now being used to make yourself look good to other people and seek after ease, profit and pleasure for yourself?

What is worse than the fact that we are inclined to this "inordinate seeking" is that this seeking is being deemed as both natural and right in this world. This is encouraged rather than denied or resisted.

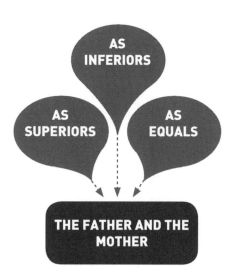

Let us

Regard the dignity and worth of each other and pay respect to each other, and also rejoice in each others' gifts and advancement as our own. What is important above all is to practice—to accept this commandment of God as the one we should obey and practice accordingly.

DETAILED DESCRIPTION ON THE FIFTH COMMANDMENT
from the Larger Catechism (Q127-132)

	The duties required	The sins forbidden
inferiors to their superiors	• all due reverence in heart, word, and behavior; • prayer and thanksgiving for them; • imitation of their virtues and graces; • willing obedience to their lawful commands and counsels; • due submission to their corrections; • fidelity to, defense, and maintenance of their persons and authority, according to their several ranks, and the nature of their places; • bearing with their infirmities, and covering them in love, that so they may be an honor to them and to their government.	• all neglect of the duties required toward them; • envying at, contempt of, and rebellion against their persons and places, in their lawful counsels, commands, and corrections; • cursing, mocking, and all such refractory and scandalous carriage, as proves a shame and dishonor to them and their government.
superiors to their inferiors	**according to that power they receive from God, and that relation wherein they stand,** • to love, pray for, and bless their inferiors; • to instruct, counsel, and admonish them; • countenancing, commending, and rewarding such as do well; • discountenancing, reproving, and chastising such as do ill; • protecting, and providing for them all things necessary for soul and body: • by grave, wise, holy, and exemplary carriage, to procure glory to God, honor to themselves, and so to preserve that authority which God hath put upon them.	• besides the neglect of the duties required of them, an inordinate seeking of themselves, their own glory, ease, profit, or pleasure; • commanding things unlawful, or not in the power of inferiors to perform; • counseling, encouraging, or favoring them in that which is evil; • dissuading, discouraging, or discountenancing them in that which is good; • correcting them unduly; • careless exposing, or leaving them to wrong, temptation, and danger; • provoking them to wrath; • or any way dishonoring themselves, or lessening their authority, by an unjust, indiscreet, rigorous, or remiss behavior.
equals	• to regard the dignity and worth of each other, in giving honor to go one before another; • to rejoice in each others' gifts and advancement, as their own.	• besides the neglect of the duties required, the undervaluing of the worth, envying the gifts, grieving at the advancement or prosperity one of another; • usurping pre-eminence one over another.

The commandments between equals follows and should extend to all—from superiors to inferiors. They appear only to repeat what other religions and ethics of this world and society say. Should this be a reason to be a snob and try to invent something better and new?

In my humble opinion, the problem is that we don't see the urgent need to practice this commandment. These things are neither too hard for us nor far off (Deut 30:11-14), and are given for us to practice as a rule of life.

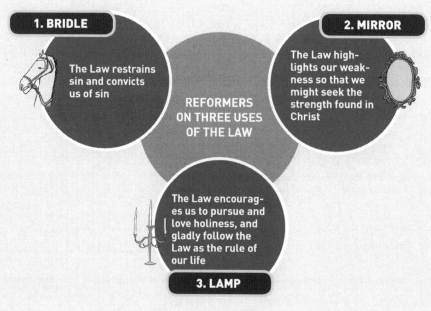

USE THE TIPS BELOW FOR GROUP DISCUSSIONS
(Prepare: blank paper, newspapers or magazines, scissors, glue, and colored pens)

You may apply these directions to the Fifth to Tenth Commandments

1. Write down on a blank paper the topics related with the fifth commandment

2. From newspapers or magazines, cut out some images that are related to the topics and glue them on the paper. You may draw some images yourself.

3. Share your thought while paying attention to the different/common perspectives among your members.

FREELY SHARE ABOUT THE FOLLOWING TOPICS REGARDING THE FIFTH COMMANDMENT

Social welfare for the elderly

cold relationships

racism

competition/selfishness

child bearing

talking behind the backs of others

bullying

coups

FREELY NAVIGATE OTHER TOPICS AMONG YOUR GATHERING

Excessive competition and a performance-oriented culture, providing for family members, social welfare, public and private facilities for care and happiness of the elderly, human relationships, leadership, self-esteem, counseling, emotional coaching, punishment, government authority, dictatorships, public service ethics, protest, civil disobedience, tax, work ethics, union-management relations, fellow feelings, praise, talk behind someone's back, jealousy, competition, badmouthing others (especially parents with one's spouse or one's spouse with someone else), good communication skills like sympathy and attentive listening, public order and sense of order, people who appear different or weaker than me, race, an intolerable and neglectful attitude toward one's nation, tax evasion, low voting turnout, governments established by ill means like coups, etc.

In the light of today's study on the fifth commandment, what did you come to see in yourself and how do you plan to practice this commandment in your life?

	What I should be doing	What I shouldn't be doing
IN CHURCH		
IN MY FAMILY		
IN SCHOOL/ MY WORK-PLACE		

15

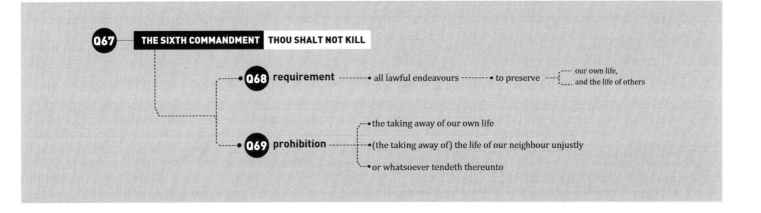

The 6th Commandment

Q67 Which is the sixth commandment?

A67 The sixth commandment is, Thou shalt not kill.[1]

Q68 What is required in the sixth commandment?

A68 The sixth commandment requireth

all lawful endeavours

to preserve our own life,[2] and the life of others.[3]

Q69 What is forbidden in the sixth commandment?

A69 The sixth commandment forbiddenth

the taking away of our own life, or the life of our neighbour unjustly,

or whatsoever tendeth thereunto.[4, 5]

1.
Exodus 20:13

Thou shalt not kill.

2.
Ephesians 5:28-29

So ought men to love their wives **as their own bodies:** he that loveth his wife loveth himself. For **no man ever yet hated his own flesh;** but nourisheth and cherisheth it, even as the Lord the church.

3.
1 Kings 18:4

For it was so, when Jezebel cut off the prophets of the Lord, that **Obadiah took an hundred prophets, and hid them by fifty in a cave, and fed them with bread and water.**

4.
Acts 16:28

But **Paul cried** with a loud voice, saying, **Do thyself no harm;** for we are all here.

5.
Genesis 9:6

Whoso sheddeth man's blood, by man shall his blood be shed: for in the image of God made he man.

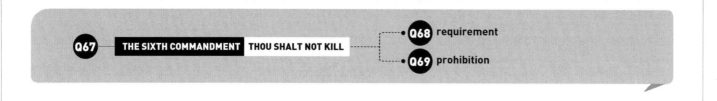
MEANING OF SIXTH COMMANDMENT: SANCTITY OF LIFE

The heart of the sixth commandment is to teach the fear for the life of man. God treasures our lives. As we love God, we should love the life of man He created.

The proper understanding of this commandment not to murder goes hand in hand with the proper understanding of human life that is created in God's own image. Who has the right to harm a creature made after-God's-own-image? And does this gives us the foundation to preserve both our own life and other's?

From a wider perspective, this commandment is not only "not to" murder but "to" treat our neighbor with the right attitude of gentleness, peace, mercy and kindness. Once again the Ten Commandments is not a mere set of dos and don'ts. We have to humbly listen to the hidden intention of God, which always includes active practice of good and righteous deeds.

The list from the Larger Catechism follows:

DETAILED DESCRIPTION ON THE SIXTH COMMANDMENT
from the Larger Catechism (Q135-136)

The duties required	The sins forbidden
• all careful studies, and lawful endeavors, to preserve the life of ourselves and others	• all taking away the life of ourselves, or of others, except in case of public justice, lawful war, or necessary defense;
(How?)	• the neglecting or withdrawing the lawful and necessary means of preservation of life;
• by resisting all thoughts and purposes, subduing all passions, avoiding all occasions, temptations, and practices which tend to the unjust taking away the life of any;	• sinful anger, hatred, envy, desire of revenge;
	• all excessive passions, distracting cares
• by just defense thereof against violence, patient bearing of the hand of God, quietness of mind, cheerfulness of spirit; a sober use of meat, drink, physic, sleep, labor and recreations;	• immoderate use of meat, drink, labor, and recreations
• by charitable thoughts, love, compassion, meekness, gentleness, kindness; peaceable, mild and courteous speeches and behavior; forbearance, readiness to be reconciled, patient bearing and forgiving of injuries, and requiting good for evil; comforting and succoring the distressed, and protecting and defending the innocent.	• provoking words, oppression, quarreling, striking, wounding, and whatsoever else tends to the destruction of the life of any.

The left list reveals the fact we have committed countless murders. We have indeed so carelessly participated in hatred, desire of revenge, anger, worries, immoderation, quarreling, violence, wounding, and provoking words. How often have we tried to retain ourselves from these things? Rather, being hurt, have we not deemed these things only natural and right for us?

Who expected to see the mention of meat, drink, sleep, labor, and physics in the commandment not to murder? Who imagined that overeating and abuse could have anything to do with murder? Given the above detailed description of this commandment, it appears more challenging to keep this commandment in developed countries, for it is the tendency of man to utilize everything he has to make his life more convenient and abundant, not the other way around.

Also from another perspective, this commandment commands us to treat others only with love, meekness, peace, mercy and kindness. God has given us certain people to love, and not to love them is to murder before God. Some may have been confident that they have kept all the laws from their youth, yet it is only so when you don't read between the lines in the Ten Commandment. How patient and gracious our God is!

LIFE-GIVING WORK

As seen in previous commandments, the Ten Commandments is not a mere set of dos and don'ts. Rather, it demands an essential and foundational change in man. In other words, our focus should not be on what I do and don't but into which being I grow and into which direction I am heading.

According to evolutionism and materialism, life is no more than a product of physical chemical reactions of organic matter. However, according to the Bible, it is much more, the product of creation, and this understanding not only justifies but also calls us to the life-giving work.

STRANGERS, NOT PERMANENT RESIDENTS

The life of believers on this earth is compared to that of a stranger, whose ultimate interest is not in this world but in his eternal home of rest. Thus, while both acknowledging and living according to God's reign over every aspect of our lives, we should daily remind ourselves that we are no other than strangers in this world.

This world may constantly tempts us to "settle down" to make a permanent home in this word, and such temptation comes in various ways both in business and in our personal lives. How should we react? The golden rule is to trust God as to obey His rule, determining to be grateful and content with whichever results He may bring in the end. Acknowledging God's absolute sovereignty is the foundation of our faith, the proper way to understand the world and to practice our faith, and the honorable way of life!

FREELY SHARE ABOUT THE FOLLOWING TOPICS
REGARDING THE SIXTH COMMANDMENT

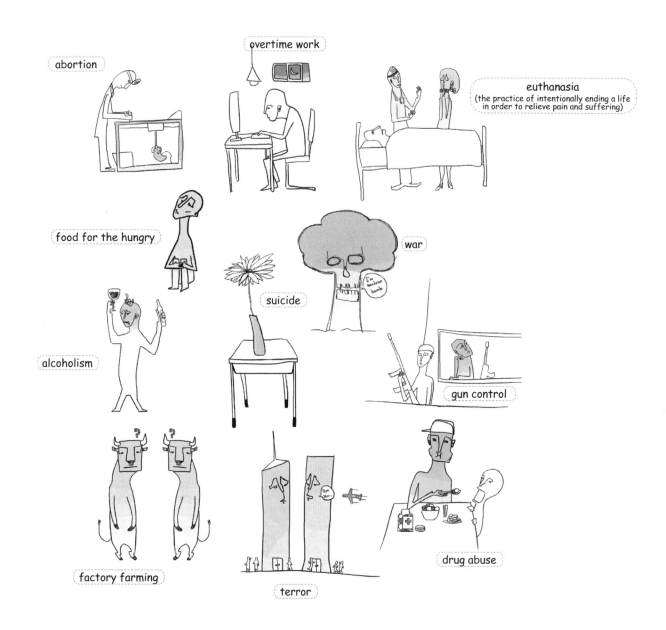

FREELY NAVIGATE OTHER TOPICS AMONG YOUR GATHERING

War, terror, national defense, public order, conscientious objector, violence, self-defense, gun control, racism, AI(Artificial Intelligence), genome editing, human rights, the treatment of refugees, overtime work, vacation, labor law, rage and forgiveness, online games (especially RPG games), food for the hungry, relief activities, In Vitro Fertilization, intrauterine insemination (a fertility treatment that involves placing sperm inside a woman's uterus to facilitate fertilization), adoption, abortion, biotechnology, gene therapy, stem cell research, cremation and burial, death sentences, suicide, euthanasia, health management, alcoholism, drug abuse, factory farming, culling populations for health concerns, etc.

APPLICATION AND SHARING OF THE SIXTH COMMANDMENT

In the light of today's study on the sixth commandment, what did you come to see in yourself and how do you plan to practice this commandment in your life?

	What I should be doing	What I shouldn't be doing
IN CHURCH		
IN MY FAMILY		
IN SCHOOL/ MY WORK-PLACE		

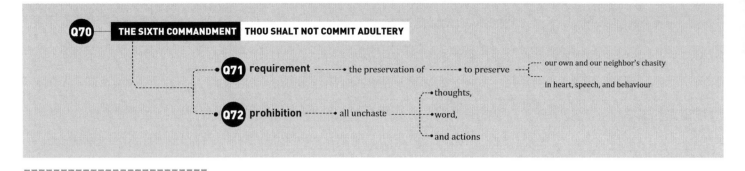

Q70 THE SIXTH COMMANDMENT — THOU SHALT NOT COMMIT ADULTERY

Q71 requirement · the preservation of · to preserve — our own and our neighbor's chasity · in heart, speech, and behaviour

Q72 prohibition · all unchaste — thoughts, word, and actions

The 7th Commandment

Q70 Which is the seventh commandment?

A70 The seventh commandment is, Thou shalt not commit adultery.[1]

Q71 What is required in the seventh commandment?

A71 The seventh commandment requireth
the preservation of our own and our neighbor's chasity,
in heart, speech, and behaviour.[2, 3, 4]

Q72 What is forbidden in the seventh commandment?

A72 The seventh commandment forbiddeth
all unchaste thoughts, words and actions.[5, 6, 7]

1.
Exodus 20:14

Thou shalt not commit adultery.

2.
1 Corinthians 7:2-3, 5, 34, 36

Nevertheless, **to avoid fornication,** let every man have his own wife, and let every woman have her own husband. **Let the husband render unto the wife due benevolence: and likewise also the wife unto the husband......Defraud ye not one the other,** except it be with consent for a time, that ye may give yourselves to fasting and prayer; and come together again, that Satan tempt you not for your incontinency...... There is difference also between a wife and a virgin. The unmarried woman careth for the things of the Lord, **that she may be holy both in body and in spirit:** but she that is married careth for the things of the world, how she may please her husband......But if any man think that he behaveth himself uncomely toward his virgin, if she pass the flower of her age, and need so require, let him do what he will, he sinneth not; **let them marry.**

3.
Colossians 4:6

Let your speech be alway with grace, seasoned with salt, that ye may know how ye ought to answer every man.

4.
1 Peter 3:2

While they behold **your chaste conversation** coupled with fear.

5.
Matthew 15:19

For **out of the heart proceed** evil thoughts, murders, **adulteries, fornications,** thefts, false witness, blasphemies.

6.
Matthew 5:28

But I say unto you, That whosoever looketh on a woman **to lust after her hath committed adultery** with her already in his heart.

7.
Ephesians 5:3-4

But **fornication, and all uncleanness,** or covetousness, **let it not be once named among you,** as becometh saints; **Neither filthiness, nor foolish talking,** nor jesting, which are not convenient; but rather giving of thanks.

SEVENTH COMMANDMENT: SACRED MARRIAGE AND FAMILY

"Infidelity" is an item that the media is eager to include, which not only reflects on our condition but also (worse yet) re-defines such words as affection, love, sympathy and happiness, and in the end brings a negative effect on our judgment.

God forbids any sexual relationships outside marriage. This gift of God remains as a gift only in the boundary of marriage. This means out of seven billion people in this world, we are allowed to have sexual relationship only with our spouse.

It seems that the world is against the idea of sexual sins when it is discussed in terms of sex trafficking, rape, and having an affair. However, the only reason is the worry that these sins may cause social disorder, which is why everything else is permitted outside the law. However, the seventh commandment of God extends to man-made law and demands that we take sexual fidelity as the goal of our holiness and the rule of life.

God desires that we preserve the institution of family through sex. And it is through this means man and woman come to make "one body." Thus, "Thou shall not commit adultery" is not merely "not to" but rather "to" use sex between man and woman as the means of blessing. To better understand this, let us take a look at the Larger Catechism (Q138-139).

This list in the next page, which forbids not only the sin of adultery but also its causes and opportunities, makes it clearly evident that this commandment above does not make any harmony at all with this world. Our society is now so pervaded with this particular sin that adultery seems to fail to bring any shame on our conscience and also to be easily justified for various reasons.

The greatest blessing for man comes from our obedience to God's words. The Bible encourages us to resist sin even to the point of shedding blood. No matter what this world says (or permits), the only rule given us as the goal, example, and the rule of our lives is God's commandments.

Living in such a permissive world, we can be easily tossed back and forth and carried about. What we need is a clear standard and the courage to stand firm. Yet even so, we are not free of the danger to fall into temptation. Many of today's young people suffer greatly due to the condemnation of this commandment. Unfortunately, some choose to leave church seeking after the freedom of this world. Yet apart from God, our only Refugee, no one finds real freedom.

Regarding this commandment, the best resort is to admit that we are weak and sinful. Avoid this sin at all cost—not only the sin itself but all the causes and opportunities as mentioned in the Larger Catechism. Examine your life in the light of the Word, offer fervent prayer to God, and hide yourself under His protective wings.

Keep me as the apple of your eye; hide me in the shadow of your wings. (Ps 17:8)

The family is not merely the result of a social contract as evolutionism and materialism insist. It is rather the symbol of heaven. Use your marriage and family to restore such a purpose. That is another (more active) aspect of keeping this seventh commandment.

What if someone outside your marriage comes at you for real, flirting with you and wanting you? If any part of you sees that as a pleasant opportunity and desires to take advantage of it even out of curiosity, I can tell you that you have already violated this commandment. However, this kind of temptation usually comes in such a subtle way, it is hard even to recognize what it is and where it leads you. Yet at the end of the day, the one who will be accountable for your life is you, not the one who tempted you! However, it is easy to overlook this simple fact, while making efforts to justify ourselves. "I am not saying I am proud of myself, but I am just trying to help out. Look how poor he/she is!" "My case is totally different. There was no choice." "This is not about lust. I have reasons for this. And they are good ones!" These self-justifying excuses can easily take over our mind and heart.

What should we do then? The story of Joseph speaks volume to those who are in the same situation. We should run away, and this simple action can protect and preserve three things--1) the other family, 2) our family and the covenant between me and my spouse, and most importantly 3) the pure and blameless relationship with God which the above earthly relationship represents. Yet there might be some costs. It may cause unexpected trouble in your relationship and undeserving ridicule from the world, and even revenge and unfair treatment can follow. Just remember how spiteful Potiphar's wife was and what kind of trouble she brought on Joseph! Yet all the cost combined should not be compared to remaining in sin, which makes us unworthy of our loving Husband!

DETAILED DESCRIPTION ON THE SEVENTH COMMANDMENT
from the Larger Catechism (Q138-139)

The duties required	The sins forbidden
• chastity in body, mind, affections, words, and behavior;	• besides the neglect of the duties required, are, adultery, fornication, rape, incest, sodomy, and all unnatural lusts;
• and the preservation of it in ourselves and others;	• all unclean imaginations, thoughts, purposes, and affections;
• watchfulness over the eyes and all the senses;	• all corrupt or filthy communications, or listening thereunto;
• temperance,	• wanton looks, impudent or light behavior, immodest apparel;
• keeping of chaste company, modesty in apparel;	• prohibiting of lawful, and dispensing with unlawful marriages;
• marriage by those that have not the gift of continency, conjugal love, and cohabitation;	• allowing, tolerating, keeping of stews (or brothel, whorehouse) and resorting to them;
• diligent labor in our callings;	• entangling vows of single life, undue delay of marriage; having more wives or husbands than one at the same time;
• shunning all occasions of uncleanness, and resisting temptations thereunto.	• unjust divorce, or desertion;
	• idleness, gluttony, drunkenness, unchaste company;
	• lascivious songs, books, pictures, dancings, stage plays;
	• all other provocations to, or acts of uncleanness, either in ourselves or others.

* Why are the items like idleness, gluttony and drunkenness forbidden in this commandment? Because as in David's adultery with Bathsheba, these behaviors can lead us to commit adultery.

FREELY SHARE ABOUT THE FOLLOWING TOPICS REGARDING THE SEVENTH COMMANDMENT

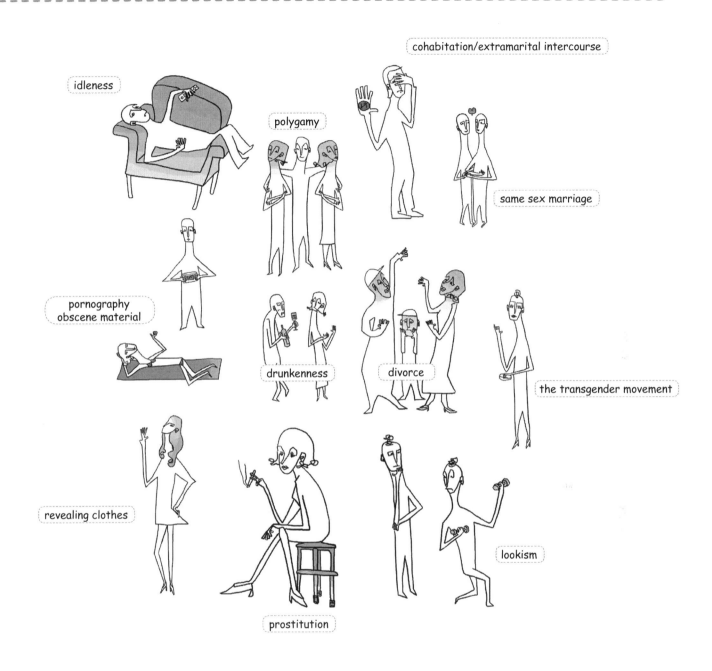

idleness

cohabitation/extramarital intercourse

polygamy

same sex marriage

pornography obscene material

drunkenness

divorce

the transgender movement

revealing clothes

prostitution

lookism

FREELY NAVIGATE OTHER TOPICS AMONG YOUR GATHERING

Marriage, cosmetic surgery, waiting until marriage, petting, premarital sex, divorce, celibacy, cohabitation, having an affair, dirty jokes, sexual harassment, sexism, Me too campaign, extramarital intercourse, masturbation, pornography, prostitution, sex trafficking, misogyny, incest, the transgender movement, homosexuality, idleness, gluttony, drunkenness, fashion trends, etc.

APPLICATION AND SHARING OF THE SEVENTH COMMANDMENT

 In the light of today's study on the seventh commandment, what did you come to see in yourself and how do you plan to practice this commandment in your life?

	What I should be doing	What I shouldn't be doing
IN CHURCH		
IN MY FAMILY		
IN SCHOOL/ MY WORK-PLACE		

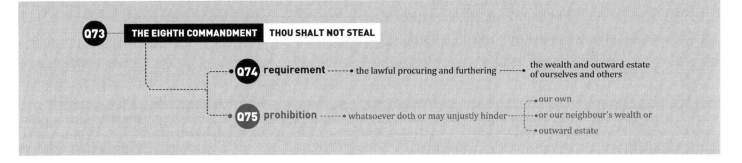

Q73 THE EIGHTH COMMANDMENT THOU SHALT NOT STEAL

Q74 requirement ------ the lawful procuring and furthering ------ the wealth and outward estate of ourselves and others

Q75 prohibition ------ whatsoever doth or may unjustly hinder ------ our own
or our neighbour's wealth or
outward estate

The 8th Commandment

Q73 Which is the eighth commandment?

A73 The eighth commandment is, Thou shalt not steal.[1]

Q74 What is required in the eighth commandment?

A74 The eighth commandment requireth

the lawful procuring and furthering

the wealth and outward estate of ourselves and others.[2, 3, 4, 5, 6, 7]

1.
Exodus 20:15

Thou shalt not steal.

2.
Genesis 30:30

For it was little which thou hadst before I came, and it is now increased unto a multitude; and the Lord hath blessed thee since my coming: and now **when shall I provide for mine own house also?**

3.
1 Timothy 5:8

But **if any provide not for his own, and specially for those of his own house, he hath denied the faith,** and is worse than an infidel.

4.
Leviticus 25:35

And if thy brother be waxen poor, and fallen in decay with thee; then **thou shalt relieve him; yea, though he be a stranger,** or a sojourner: that he may live with thee.

5.
Deuteronomy 22:1-5

Thou shalt not see thy brother's ox or his sheep go astray, and **hide thyself from them: thou shalt in any case bring them again unto thy brother.** And if thy brother be not nigh unto thee, or if thou know him not; then **thou shalt bring it unto thine own house,** and it shall be with thee until thy brother seek after it, and **thou shalt restore it to him again. In like manner shalt thou do with his ass,** and so shalt thou do with his raiment; and with all lost thing of thy brother's, which he hath lost, and thou hast found, shalt thou do likewise: thou mayest not hide thyself. Thou shalt not see thy brother's ass or his ox fall down by the way, and hide thyself from them; **thou shalt surely help him to lift them up again.** The woman shall not wear that which pertaineth unto a man, neither shall a man put on a woman's garment: for all that do so are abomination unto the Lord thy God.

6.
Exodus 23:4-5

If thou meet thine enemy's ox or his ass going astray, **thou shalt surely bring it back to him again.** If thou see the ass of him that hateth thee lying under his burden, and wouldest forbear to help him; **thou shalt surely help with him.**

7.
Genesis 47:14, 20

And Joseph gathered up all the money that was found in the land of Egypt, and in the land of Canaan, **for the corn which they bought:** and Joseph brought the money into Pharaoh's house......**And Joseph bought all the land of Egypt** for Pharaoh; for the Egyptians sold every man his field, because the famine prevailed over them: so the land became Pharaoh's.

Q74 requirement ----- the lawful procuring and furthering ----- the wealth and outward estate of ourselves and others

Q75 prohibition ----- whatsoever doth or may unjustly hinder ----- our own
----- or our neighbour's wealth or
----- outward estate

Q75 What is forbidden in the eighth commandment?

A75 The eighth commandment forbiddeth

whatsoever doth or may unjustly hinder

our own or our neighbour's wealth or outward estate.[1, 2, 3, 4]

1.
Proverbs 21:17

He that loveth pleasure shall be a poor man; he that loveth wine and oil shall not be rich.

2.
Proverbs 23:20-21

Be not among winebibbers; among riotous eaters of flesh: For the drunkard and the glutton shall come to poverty; and drowsiness shall clothe a man with rags.

3.
Proverbs 28:19

He that tilleth his land shall have plenty of bread: but he that followeth after vain persons shall have poverty enough.

4.
Ephesians 4:28

Let him that stole **steal no more:** but rather let him labour, working with his hands the thing which is good, that he may have to give to him that needeth.

EIGHTH COMMANDMENT: LIFE OF A STEWARD

If it were before learning about the sixth commandment, most of us would have felt confidence regarding the eighth commandment. Yet now we all wonder what God's true intention with this commandment not to steal would be.

The eighth commandment is related to private property protection. It is not strange that we have to keep the use and disposal of the estate and wealth that God has entrusted to us as also sacred.

As you may assume, this commandment goes beyond merely not to bring any harm on the property of other. Neither is this about keeping our own property without actively exercising our stewardship. This is rather a comprehensive matter: we have to obtain, maintain, utilize and dispose of our property as stewards for God. Refer to the Larger Catechism for detailed information.

DETAILED DESCRIPTION ON THE EIGHTH COMMANDMENT
from the Larger Catechism (Q141-142)

The duties required	The sins forbidden
• truth, faithfulness, and justice in contracts and commerce between man and man;	• besides the neglect of the duties required
• rendering to everyone his due;	• theft, robbery, man-stealing, and receiving anything that is stolen;
• restitution of goods unlawfully detained from the right owners thereof;	• fraudulent dealing, false weights and measures, removing land-marks, injustice and unfaithfulness in contracts between man and man, or in matters of trust;
• giving and lending freely, according to our abilities, and the necessities of others;	• oppression, extortion, usury, bribery, vexatious lawsuits, unjust enclosures and depopulations;
• moderation of our judgments, wills, and affections concerning worldly goods;	• engrossing commodities to enhance the price;
• a provident care and study to get, keep, use, and dispose these things which are necessary and convenient for the sustentation of our nature, and suitable to our condition;	• unlawful callings, and all other unjust or sinful ways of taking or withholding from our neighbor what belongs to him, or of enriching ourselves;
• a lawful calling, and diligence in it;	• covetousness;
• frugality;	• inordinate prizing and affecting worldly goods;
• avoiding unnecessary lawsuits, and suretyship, or other like engagements;	• distrustful and distracting cares and studies in getting, keeping, and using them(=worldly goods);
• an endeavor, by all just and lawful means, to procure, preserve, and further the wealth and outward estate of others, as well as our own.	• envying at the prosperity of others;
	• as likewise idleness, prodigality, wasteful gaming;
	• and all other ways whereby we do unduly prejudice our own outward estate[wealth], and defrauding ourselves of the due use and comfort of that estate[wealth] which God hath given us.

The eight commandment includes somewhat unexpected requirements, for instance that we have to pursue diligence and make endeavors for the wealth and outward estate of others. It may appear irrelevant to this particular commandment—not to steal, but when its cause-and-effect relationship is considered—that idleness leads to poverty and poverty to stealing—it sounds more convincing. Also, in poverty, it is more likely that we end up exhausting the share of others.

In another (more active) perspective, this commandment could be understood as saying that we have to make endeavors to help those in need make their lives better, in the end helping them to live as we live. This goes right against today's culture, which is all about "me"—how I can have more and live better.

The list of forbidden things does not take much time to con-

vict us of our sin. If you work for a company, especially a marketing one, then both knowingly and unknowingly you face temptations to "steal" and many times actually fall. Today's culture not only encourages but also justifies exaggerated advertisement and packaging, and even to hide the problems of products. This world is so pervaded with this sin that it is indeed hard to distinguish what is sin from what is not. Thus, constantly ask God to keep you out of this sin and give you discernment. If you are caught in the middle, remind yourself that it is always better to suffer financial loss than to sin against God.

The Larger Catechism does not restrict this commandment to private matters but as applies it to collective social matters as well. The following are examples.

At this point we have to ask ourselves, in the midst of pervasive evil in our society, what it means to remain holy apart from evil. How are we supposed to understand Jean Valjean's stealing bread not out of greed but hunger? His action should be understood in a social perspective, through distributive justice, for example.

Relating to the eighth commandment, the following topics should be considered: Collectivism/NIMBY, unfair trade, illegal accumulation of wealth of religious leaders, moral character of politicians, resource/food power, global warming and the Kyoto protocol, etc.

FREELY SHARE THE FOLLOWING TOPICS REGARDING THE EIGHTH COMMANDMENT

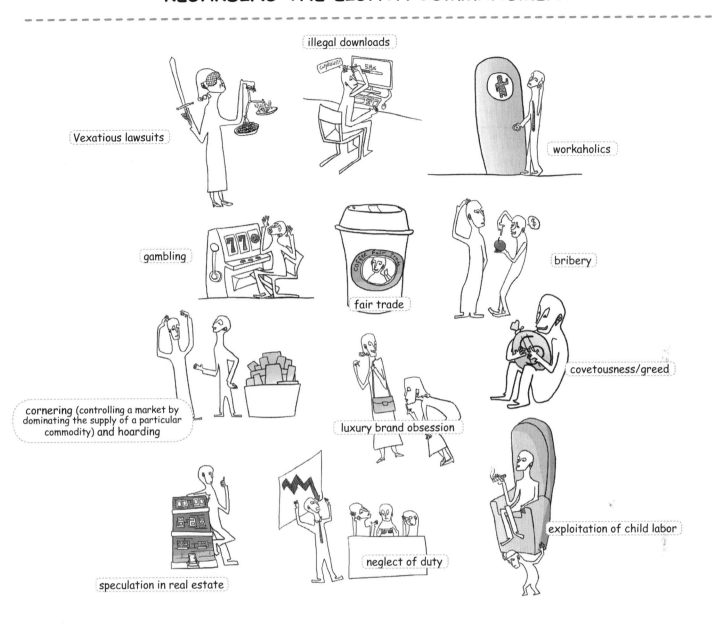

FREELY NAVIGATE OTHER TOPICS AMONG YOUR GATHERING

Moderation and frugality, environmental protection, occupation, consumption activity, guarantee, extortion, usury, robbery, theft, abduction, handling stolen goods, fraud, agreement violation, forgery of documents, speculation in the area of development, engrossing/cornering, redevelopment, expropriation, , gambling, lotteries, cyber money, distributive justice, collectivism/ NIMBY, unfair trade, resource/food power, the Kyoto protocol, electric cars, ecofriendly energy, public welfare budgeting, recycling secondhand goods, aid for the poor and homeless, speculation, insurance, saving, retirement, inheritance, financial management principles for home/company/ church, fair trade, donation, time killing in work place, illegal internet downloads, Virtual Currency, etc

In the light of today's study on the eighth commandment, what did you come to see in yourself and how do you plan to practice this commandment in your life?

	What I should be doing	What I shouldn't be doing
IN CHURCH		
IN MY FAMILY		
IN SCHOOL/ MY WORK- PLACE		

Q76 | **THE NINTH COMMANDMENT** | **THOU SHALT NOT BEAR FALSE WITNESS AGAINST THY NEIGHBOUR**

Q77 requirement ----- • the maintaining and promoting --------- • what? ---- • of truth between man and man
            • of our own and our neighbour's good name

            • When? --- • (basically all the time)
                        • especially in witness-bearing

Q78 prohibition ----- • whatsoever is prejudical to truth, or injurious ----- • to our own or our neighbour's good name

The 9th Commandment

Q76 Which is the ninth commandment?

A76 The ninth commandment is, Thou shalt not bear false witness against thy neighbour.[1]

Q77 What is required in the ninth commandment?

A77 The ninth commandment requireth

the maintaining and promoting

of truth between man and man,[2]

and of our own and our neighbour's good name,[3]

especially in witness-bearing.[4]

Q78 What is forbidden in the ninth commandment?

A78 The ninth commandment forbiddeth

whatsoever is prejudical to truth, or injurious

to our own or our neighbour's good name.[5, 6, 7]

1.
Exodus 20:16

Thou shalt not bear false witness against thy neighbour.

2.
Zechariah 8:16

These are the things that ye shall do, **Speak ye every man the truth to his neighbour; execute the judgment of truth** and peace in your gates.

3.
3 John 12

Demetrius hath good report of all men, and of the truth itself: yea, and **we also bear record;** and ye know that our record is true.

4.
Proverbs 14:5, 25

A faithful witness will not lie: but a false witness will utter lies......**A true witness delivereth souls:** but a deceitful witness speaketh lies.

5.
1 Samuel 17:28

And Eliab his eldest brother heard when he spake unto the men: and Eliab's anger was kindled against David, and he said, Why camest thou down hither? and with whom hast thou left those few sheep in the wilderness? **I know thy pride, and the naughtiness of thine heart;** for thou art come down that thou mightest see the battle.

6.
Leviticus 19:16

Thou shalt not go up and down as a tale-bearer among thy people; **neither shalt thou stand against the blood of thy neighbour:** I am the Lord.

7.
Psalm 15:3

He that backbiteth not with his tongue, nor doeth evil to his neighbour, **nor taketh up a reproach against his neighbour.**

MEANING OF NINTH THE COMMANDMENT: TRUTHFUL LIFE

The list of forbidden things in this commandment (Q144~155 of the Larger catechism) appears to describe the daily lives of any human being. Lying is easily justified, and also widely encouraged as the art of living in this world. We lie for various reasons such as to gain profits and to escape a crisis. This is the natural tendency of weak and sinful human beings. Who among man can be truthful at all moments?

Yet given this moral law, which transcends all ages and places, God demands our obedience. This is the reason why we should speak the truth, only the truth, in our relationships with our neighbors at all times. God knows that we are weak yet still demands truthfulness. His help is promised. Thus…

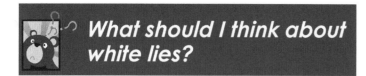

What should I think about white lies?

God's commandment is "not to lie" and this is "regardless of any conditions and reasons." Yet we dare to make a special category of "white lies" and even call them good and necessary. For instance, the Egyptian midwives lied, and because of their lies, Hebrew babies were able to survive.

Some may continue, "There are more examples in the Bible of people who lied yet were blessed in the end?" However, the Bible never justifies the means (in this case, lies) in the light of the good of the end. We'd better see such examples in a way that, despite their floundering in sin and weaknesses, God still remembered and redeemed His elect in the end.

White lies go unnoticed under the name of flexibility and even praised due to the good it brings to others. This is pure pragmatism, of course, for pragmatism does not have any interest in what is true or not, but only in its practical consequences. If its practical consequences are great, then even lies could be deemed right and wise. Should we judge God's eternal and absolute law according to worldly standards? No, it should be the other way around. God commanded us not to lie, and this refers to all lies.

"What modern system of philosophy violates the sacredness of truth? The philosophy called 'pragmatism,' which teaches that the important question is not whether something is true, but whether it works. According to pragmatism, success is the test of truth. Something is to be accepted if it 'works'; we are not to measure things by an absolute standard of truth such as the Bible." Vos, J. G., & Williamson, G. I. (2002). *The Westminster larger catechism: a commentary*. Phillipsburg, NJ: P&R Pub., 387.

Pray

That God would give wisdom to discern (eyes and ears)
That God would give power to speak the truth (mouth)
That God would give heart to acknowledge the truth (heart)

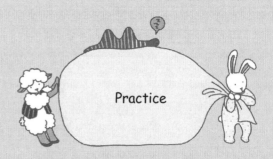

Practice

• Make an effort to find worth and strength in your family and friends. And pray for yourself so that you may acknowledge them without jealousy and envy. This prayer is necessary, for it will be more challenging than you think.

• Give thanks to God who has given such worth and strength to them and try to imitate them. And here is a heads-up: this will also be challenging.

• Avoid meetings where people speak ill of somebody, especially while that person is not present. If you can't, gently direct the conversation to other topics. Otherwise, your presence will be understood as condoning such talk and end up encouraging their behavior.

DETAILED DESCRIPTION ON THE NINTH COMMANDMENT
from the Larger Catechism (Q144-145)

The duties required

- the preserving and promoting of truth between man and man, and the good name of our neighbor, as well as our own;

- appearing and standing for the truth;

- from the heart, sincerely, freely, clearly, and fully, speaking the truth, and only the truth, in matters of judgment and justice, and in all other things whatsoever;

- a charitable esteem of our neighbors;

- loving, desiring, and rejoicing in their good name;

- sorrowing for and covering of their infirmities;

- freely acknowledging of their gifts and graces, defending their innocence;

- a ready receiving of a good report, and unwillingness to admit of an evil report, concerning them;

- discouraging talebearers, flatterers, and slanderers;

- love and care of our own good name, and defending it when need requireth

- keeping of lawful promises;

- studying and practicing of whatsoever things are true, honest, lovely, and of good report.

The sins forbidden

- all prejudicing the truth, and the good name of our neighbors, as well as our own, especially in public judicature;

- giving false evidence, suborning false witnesses, wittingly appearing and pleading for an evil cause, outfacing and overbearing the truth;

- passing unjust sentence, calling evil good, and good evil;

- rewarding the wicked according to the work of the righteous, and the righteous according to the work of the wicked;

- forgery, concealing the truth, undue silence in a just cause, and holding our peace when iniquity calleth for either a reproof from ourselves, or complaint to others;

- speaking the truth unseasonably, or maliciously to a wrong end, or perverting it to a wrong meaning, or in doubtful or equivocal expressions, to the prejudice of the truth or justice;

- speaking untruth, lying, slandering, backbiting, detracting, talebearing, whispering, scoffing, reviling, rash, harsh, and partial censuring;

- misconstructing intentions, words, and actions;

- flattering, vainglorious boasting, thinking or speaking too highly or too meanly of ourselves or others;

- denying the gifts and graces of God;

- aggravating smaller faults;

- hiding, excusing, or extenuating of sins, when called to a free confession;

- unnecessary discovering of infirmities;

- raising false rumors, receiving and countenancing evil reports, and stopping our ears against just defense;

- evil suspicion;

- envying or grieving at the deserved credit of any;

- endeavoring or desiring to impair it, rejoicing in their disgrace and infamy;

- scornful contempt, fond admiration;

- breach of lawful promises;

- neglecting such things as are of good report, and practicing, or not avoiding ourselves, or not hindering what we can in others, such things as procure an ill name.

FREELY SHARE THE FOLLOWING TOPICS REGARDING THE NINTH COMMANDMENT

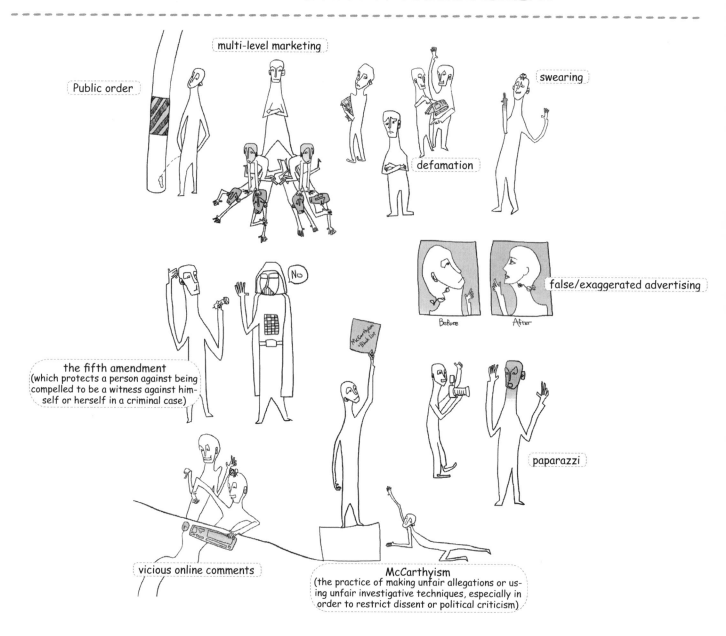

FREELY NAVIGATE OTHER TOPICS AMONG YOUR GATHERING

Law-abidingness, citizenship, public order, paparazzi, defamation (exposing false truth or truth), false/exaggerated advertising, multi-level marketing, conversational method, improving one's logic and its demonstration, talk behind another's back, swearing, white lies, confirmation hearings, false/exaggerated information on resumes/self-introductions, distorted reports, propaganda and McCarthyism, dealings on credit, whistleblower protection (which protects federal whistleblowers who work for the government and report agency conduct), tax saving and tax evasion, the concept and criteria of sovereign rating (which give investors insight into the level of risk associated with investing in a particular country and also includes political risks), recall systems, freedom of speech/press/assembly/association, freedom of expression and pre-censorship, the right to an attorney, the fifth amendment, presumption of innocence, online comments, messenger chatting, SNS, compliments, emotion coaching, etc.

APPLICATION AND SHARING OF THE NINTH COMMANDMENT

 In the light of today's study on the ninth commandment, what did you come to see in yourself and how do you plan to practice this commandment in your life?

	What I should be doing	What I shouldn't be doing
IN CHURCH		
IN MY FAMILY		
IN SCHOOL/ MY WORK-PLACE		

Q79 THE TENTH COMMANDMENT · · · THOU SHALT NOT COVET THY NEIGHBOUR'S HOUSE...

Q80 requirement ----- full contentment --
- •with a right and charitable frame of spirit --•toward our neighbour, and all this is his
- •with our own condition

Q81 prohibition
- •all discontentment --------------------•with our own estate
- •envying or grieving --------------------•at the good of our neighbour
- •all inordinate motions and affections ------•to any thing that is his

---

The 10th Commandment

Q79 Which is the tenth commandment?

A79 The tenth commandment is, Thou shalt not covet thy neighbour's house, thou shalt not covet thy neighbour's wife, nor his man-servant, nor his maid-servant, nor his ox, nor his ass, nor any thing that is thy neighbour's.[1]

Q80 What is required in the tenth commandment?

A80 The tenth commandment requireth

full contentment with our own condition,[2,3]

with a right and charitable frame of spirit

toward our neighbour, and all that is his.[4,5,6,7]

1.
Exodus 20:17

Thou shalt not covet thy neighbour's house, thou shalt not covet thy neighbour's wife, nor his manservant, nor his maidservant, nor his ox, nor his ass, nor any thing that is thy neighbour's.

2.
Hebrews 13:5

Let your conversation be without covetousness; and **be content with such things as ye have:** for he hath said, I will never leave thee, nor forsake thee.

3.
1 Timothy 6:6

But godliness **with contentment** is great gain.

4.
Job 31:29

If I rejoiced at the destruction of him that hated me, or **lifted up myself when evil found him.**

5.
Romans 12:15

Rejoice with them that do rejoice, and weep with them that weep.

6.
1 Timothy 1:5

Now the end of the commandment is charity out of a pure heart, and of a good conscience, and of faith unfeigned.

7.
1 Corinthians 13:4-7

Charity suffereth long, and is kind; **charity envieth not; charity vaunteth not itself,** is not puffed up, **Doth not behave itself unseemly,** seeketh not her own, is not easily provoked, thinketh no evil; Rejoiceth not in iniquity, but rejoiceth in the truth; **Beareth all things,** believeth all things, hopeth all things, **endureth all things.**

Q80 requirement ----- full contentment ---- •with a right and charitable frame of spirit --•toward our neighbour, and all this is his
•with our own condition

Q81 prohibition ---- •all discontentment -------------------•with our own estate
•envying or grieving -----------------•at the good of our neighbour
•all inordinate motions and affections -----•to any thing that is his

---

Q81 What is forbidden in the tenth commandment?

A81 The tenth commandment forbiddeth

all discontentment with our own estate,[1,2,3]

envying or grieving at the good of our neighbour,[4,5]

and all inordinate motions and affections to any thing that is his.[6,7,8]

1.
1 Kings 21:4

And Ahab came into his house **heavy and displeased** because of the word which Naboth the Jezreelite had spoken to him: for he had said, I will not give thee the inheritance of my fathers: And **he laid him down upon his bed, and turned away his face, and would eat no bread.**

2.
Esther 5:13

Yet all this availeth me nothing, so long as I see Mordecai the Jew sitting at the king's gate.

3.
1 Corinthians 10:10

Neither murmur ye, as some of them also murmured, and were destroyed of the destroyer.

4.
Galatians 5:26

Let us not be desirous of vain-glory, provoking one another, **envying one another.**

5.
James 3:14, 16

But **if ye have bitter envying** and strife in your hearts, glory not, and lie not against the truth......For **where envying and strife is,** there is confusion and every evil work.

6.
Romans 7:7-8

What shall we say then? Is the law sin? God forbid. Nay, I had not known sin, but by the law: for **I had not known lust, except the law had said, Thou shalt not covet.** But sin, taking occasion by the commandment, **wrought in me all manner of concupiscence.** For without the law sin was dead.

7.
Romans 13:9

For this, Thou shalt not commit adultery, Thou shalt not kill, Thou shalt not steal, Thou shalt not bear false witness, **Thou shalt not covet;** and if there be any other commandment, it is briefly comprehended in this saying, namely, Thou shalt love thy neighbour as thyself.

8.
Deuteronomy 5:21

Neither shalt thou desire thy neighbour's wife, neither shalt thou covet thy neighbour's house, his field, or his man-servant, or his maid-servant, his ox, or his ass, or any thing that is thy neighbour's.

Q79 | THE TENTH COMMANDMENT | THOU SHALT NOT COVET THY NEIGHBOUR'S HOUSE...

Q80 requirement

Q81 prohibition

MEANING OF THE TENTH COMMANDMENT: SELF-CONTENTMENT

This commandment is the last straw that breaks the camel's back. Who can stand before God's uncomprimising commandments?

"Do not covet your neighbor's house, wife, nor any thing of your neighbor's." This draws a clear line between greed and contentment in man's heart. We have seen all kinds of miseries and tragedies caused by man's greed throughout history, literature, and arts. Here the Shorter Catechism offers a very straightforward and obvious solution. "Keep yourself from greed and be content!"

THE SURE WAY TO AVOID GREED, BE CONTENT!

God wants us to love our neighbor, which should include turning our backs from loving ourselves—being greedy—and running towards the opposite direction. How can this be done? By being content! For only the content are generous to others. Contentment is, in a nutshell, to acknowledge that my current state is the best. And this comes only when we have faith in God that He brings the best for us as He foreordained in His decrees.

Not being content, we will try to fill our lack by the means of other things, which will cause a vicious cycle. Contentment has little to do with the amount of one's possessions especially compared to that of others, but everything to do with the willingness and ability to be aware and to acknowledge that God alone gives worth and happiness to your life. Once you begin to measure the worth of your life by your wealth and possessions, this will drive contentment out of your heart and leave only covetousness in it.

THE FINALE OF LOVING YOUR NEIGHBOR

The Shorter Catechism furthers its horizon as encouraging us to pursue a more active way to love our neighbor. "Look to the interests of your neighbor." (Phil 2:4) This commandment is to be applied to all neighbors regardless of their merit and attitude.

Even if a neighbor seems only to waste God's gifts and makes you think that he no longer deserves your love, you should not judge. We are commanded not to judge but help our neighbor so that he may live in a way to glorify God and enjoy Him forever. Remember, loving our neighbor is the same as loving our God.

DETAILED DESCRIPTION ON THE TENTH COMMANDMENT
from the Larger Catechism (Q147-148)

The duties required	The sins forbidden
• such a full contentment with our own condition, • such a charitable frame of the whole soul toward our neighbor, • that all our inward motions and affections touching him, tend unto, and further all the good which is his.	• discontentment with our own estate; • envying and grieving at the good of our neighbor, together with all inordinate motions and affections to anything that is his.

FREELY SHARE THE FOLLOWING TOPICS REGARDING THE TENTH COMMANDMENT

lotteries

Staying open 24/7

carbon emission/ecosystem damage

exploitation

the rich and poor

shopping addiction

exhaustion of resources

the super-rich

binge eating

the accumulation of wealth

the arms industry

FREELY NAVIGATE OTHER TOPICS AMONG YOUR GATHERING

The accumulation of wealth, capitalism, investment in stocks, speculation in lands, staying open 24/7, exploitation of wages, employees abusing overtime pay, employers cheating employees out of overtime, the super-rich passing their power to their descendants, prosperity gospel, excessive spending and squandering, shopping addiction, luxury items, brand name products, gluttony, workaholics, exhaustion of resources, ecosystem damage, gold/gem mining, forest destruction, aid and donations, reclamation and cultivation, certified emission reductions, private use of work's property, simple but not shabby, downshifting, slow living, eco life, funds, church offering, lotteries, pure wealth and pure poverty, etc.

In the light of today's study on the tenth commandment, what did you come to see in yourself and how do you plan to practice this commandment in your life?

	What I should be doing	What I shouldn't be doing
IN CHURCH		
IN MY FAMILY		
IN SCHOOL/ MY WORK- PLACE		

15

CONCLUSION

> In light of the fifth to ninth commandments, the list below appears only to repeat itself. This is because the tenth commandment is more to expose the problem underlying all of them. Include in your discussion the way this commandment should affect your value system and your daily life. *"Everyone who hears these words of mine and puts them into practice is like a wise man."* (Matt 7:24)

Here comes the end of the Ten Commandments.

The Ten commandments are
the knowledge of the Lord and the guidelines of a covenant life.

The Pharisees were excellent in keeping the law,
yet their efforts were only for rewards and self-exaltation.
We are not to repeat their mistakes,
but willingly keep this law,
the knowledge of the Lord and the guidelines of a covenant life.

"ANYWAY, WE CANNOT KEEP ALL THE LAWS. HOW MEANINGLESS THEN! BELIEVE AND REPENT, THAT IS THE BEST WE CAN DO."

"AM I NOT BETTER THAN THE PEOPLE WHOSE SINS ARE HEINOUS? I MUST LOOK BETTER THAN THEM BEFORE GOD."

Thus far the second part of the Shorter Catechism, we have learned that the duty God requires of man is "the moral law." Since this law is "summarized" in the Ten Commandments, we have carefully studied each and every one of them and even considered applications for our daily lives. Then, is this all? If we try to practice one commandment after another, then our problems disappear? Not necessarily. The most common response after learning the Ten Commandments is either becoming legalistic or falling into despair because of their challenging requirements. For this reason, it is equally important for us to know and utilize God-given means of grace, which will be navigated in this chapter.

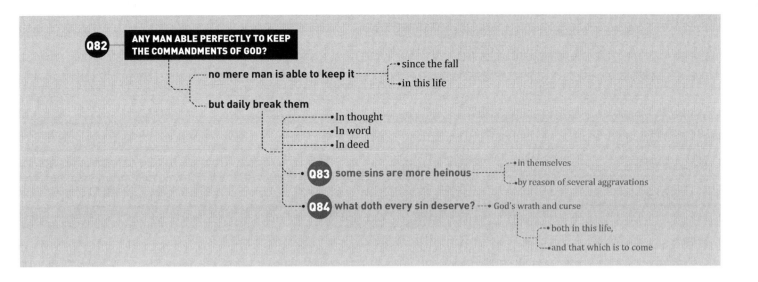

Q82 Is any man able perfectly to keep the commandments of God?

A82 No mere man since the fall
is able in this life perfectly
to keep the commandments of God,[1,2,3]
but doth daily break them
in thought, word, and deed.[4,5,6,7]

1.
Ecclesiastes 7:20

For there is not a just man upon earth, **that doeth good, and sinneth not.**

2.
1 John 1:8, 10

If we say that we have no sin, we deceive ourselves, and the truth is not in us......**If we say that we have not sinned,** we make him a liar, and his word is not in us.

3.
Galatians 5:17

For **the flesh lusteth against the Spirit,** and the Spirit against the flesh: and these are contrary the one to the other; so that **ye cannot do the things that ye would.**

4.
Genesis 6:5

And God saw that the wickedness of man was great in the earth, and **that every imagination of the thoughts of his heart was only evil continually.**

5.
Genesis 8:21

And the Lord smelled a sweet savour; and the Lord said in his heart, I will not again curse the ground any more for man's sake; for **the imagination of man's heart is evil from his youth;** neither will I again smite any more every thing living, as I have done.

6.
Romans 3:9-21

What then? are we better than they? No, in no wise: for we have before proved both Jews and Gentiles, **that they are all under sin.**—And so on to Verse 21.

7.
James 3:2-13

For **in many things we offend all. If any man offend not in word, the same is a perfect man,** and able also to bridle the whole body.—And so on to Verse 13.

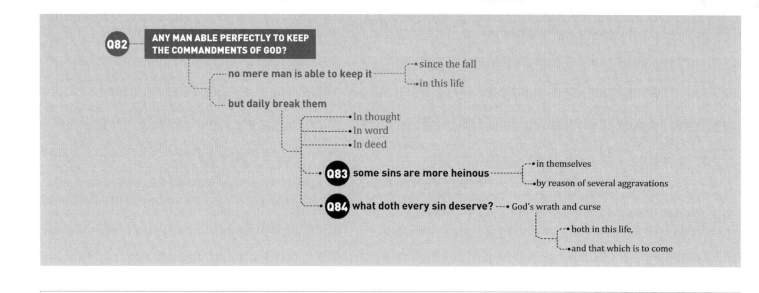

Q82 **ANY MAN ABLE PERFECTLY TO KEEP THE COMMANDMENTS OF GOD?**

- no mere man is able to keep it
  - since the fall
  - in this life
- but daily break them
  - In thought
  - In word
  - In deed

Q83 **some sins are more heinous**
  - in themselves
  - by reason of several aggravations

Q84 **what doth every sin deserve?** — God's wrath and curse
  - both in this life,
  - and that which is to come

Q83 Are all transgression of the law equally heinous?

A83 Some sins in themselves,

and by reason of several aggravations,

are more heinous in the sight of God than others.[1, 2, 3]

Q84 What doth every sin deserve?

A84 Every sin deserveth God's wrath and curse,

both in this life, and that which is to come.[4, 5, 6, 7]

1.
Ezekiel 8:6, 13, 15

He said furthermore unto me, Son of man, seest thou what they do? even the great abominations that the house of Israel committeth here, that I should go far off from my sanctuary? but turn thee yet again, and **thou shalt see greater abominations**......He said also unto me, Turn thee yet again, and **thou shalt see greater abominations that they do**......Then said he unto me, Hast thou seen this, O son of man? turn thee yet again, and **thou shalt see greater abominations than these.**

2.
1 John 5:16

If any man see his brother sin a sin which is not unto death, he shall ask, and he shall give him life for them that sin not unto death. **There is a sin unto death:** I do not say that he shall pray for it.

3.
Psalm 78:17, 32, 56

And they sinned yet more against him by provoking the most High in the wilderness...... **For all this they sinned still, and believed not for his wondrous works......Yet they tempted and provoked the most high God,** and kept not his testimonies.

4.
Ephesians 5:6

Let no man deceive you with vain words: for **because of these things cometh the wrath of God upon the children of disobedience.**

6.
Lamentations 3:39

Wherefore doth a living man complain, **a man for the punishment of his sins?**

5.
Galatians 3:10

For as many as are of the works of the law are under the curse: for it is written, **Cursed is every one that continueth not in all things which are written in the book of the law to do them.**

7.
Matthew 25:41

Then shall he say also unto them on the left hand, **Depart from me, ye cursed,** into everlasting fire, prepared for the devil and his angels.

16

OVERCOME DESPAIR AND SEEK AFTER GRACE

If you are a true believer, then you know that your redemption is not brought by your own obedience but only by God's grace. And this knowledge should make believers desire God Himself more than before. After learning about His expectations of man, we believers now come to desire "Ah that's the way of life I want; I don't need anything else now." As we learned in the first part of the Shorter Catechism, the only reason that we are made "willing" to obey God's commandments is because we love Him who loves us.

I have seen many churches and Christian homes faithfully teach the first part of the Shorter Catechism but not so much the second. I have to tell you the second part of the catechism is equally important as the first. This is because the second part is closely related to our daily lives. The following chapter is the backbone of the second part of the Shorter Catechism. Check as often as possible where the particular question and answer of your study is located within the whole context.

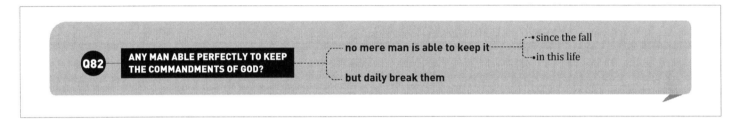

Q82 ANY MAN ABLE PERFECTLY TO KEEP THE COMMANDMENTS OF GOD?

no mere man is able to keep it
• since the fall
• in this life

but daily break them

THE POINT OF Q82

"We are not able to keep the commandments of God, but daily break them." Then are these commandments, which we cannot keep, nominal, all flash, and meaningless? Of course not. The following explanation can be of help.

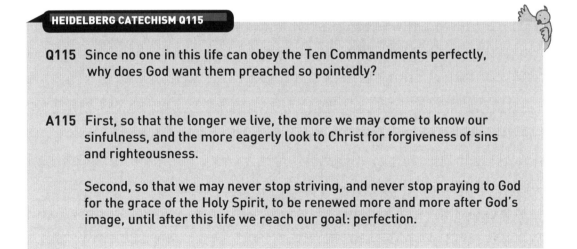

HEIDELBERG CATECHISM Q115

Q115 Since no one in this life can obey the Ten Commandments perfectly, why does God want them preached so pointedly?

A115 First, so that the longer we live, the more we may come to know our sinfulness, and the more eagerly look to Christ for forgiveness of sins and righteousness.

Second, so that we may never stop striving, and never stop praying to God for the grace of the Holy Spirit, to be renewed more and more after God's image, until after this life we reach our goal: perfection.

What a proper way to answer! Let us imagine for a minute that God has given us able-to-keep commandments and we actually succeeded to keep them to their perfection; then we would have fallen into self-righteousness—which is the most dangerous place where anyone can fall. **Instead, because we cannot keep them**, we end up looking to Christ all the more eagerly and continue to endeavor and depend on God.

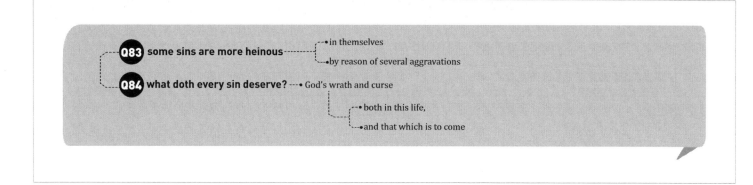

Q83 some sins are more heinous
- in themselves
- by reason of several aggravations

Q84 what doth every sin deserve? • God's wrath and curse
- both in this life,
- and that which is to come

IS THIS THE PROPER PLACE TO DISCUSS SIN?

Now the question of sin re-appears. Why is this? The second part of the Shorter Catechism presents the Ten Commandments and the Lord's Prayer, and in between is located the Means of Grace. And the matter of sin appears right before the discussion of the Means of Grace. We have learned that due to the mediation of Christ, we are now without guilt but still struggling with the residue of sin. (Refer to Q35)

God hates sin and His hate reaches even the residue of it. For this reason, what usually comes after the study of the Ten Commandments is our great despair. For we find that we are far from keeping them perfectly but we daily break them in our thoughts, words, and deeds. And here the Shorter Catechism refreshes the air and offers a solution to our dilemma—warning us to keep the law even when daily failing—through the discussion of the Means of Grace.

When creating man, God gave him the power to obey him, yet man willfully disobeyed and fell. In his fall, we are now made unable to keep God's commandments. God's law stands strong regardless of our ability. All sins, even insignificant ones, are heinous in the sight of God. For God's law directly reflects God's attributes (His holiness, righteousness, goodness, and so on), and these attributes are the expression of God Himself. Thus, if we disobey (resist) God's law, no matter how little and insignificant our sins are, we resist God Himself, which will result in great consequences, God's wrath and curse.

THROUGH THE BIBLE, GOD'S COMMANDMENTS

The commandments require of us perfection in our thoughts, words, and deeds, yet we actively violate them.

WE COME TO REALIZE THAT WE CANNOT KEEP THEM PERFECTLY

This is the purpose of giving the commandments, to reveal our utter inability. It kills us, completely so, to bring us to life. For this reason, the commandments are not a curse anymore, but the invitation and guidance to glory.

WHICH LEADS TO REALIZING OUR SIN AND MISERY

We should not see the commandments as an object of fear. We should see above and beyond—our holy, faithful, and righteous God. Christ, who satisfied God's wrath for my sake, is my only hope.

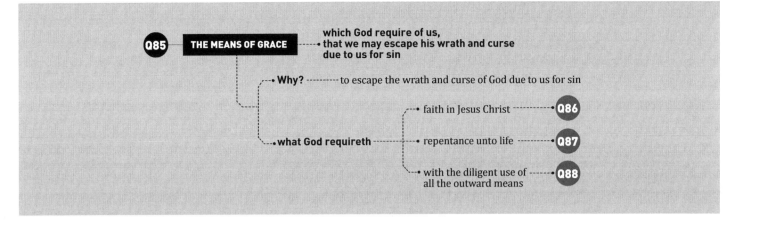

Q85 What doth God require of us, that we may escape his wrath and curse due to us for sin?

A85 To escape the wrath and curse of God due to us for sin,
God requireth of us
faith in Jesus Christ,
repentance unto life,[1]
with the diligent use of all the outward means
whereby Christ communicateth to us the benefits of redemption.[2, 3, 4]

1.
Acts 20:21

Testifying both to the Jews, and also to the Greeks, **repentance toward God, and faith toward our Lord Jesus Christ.**

2.
Proverbs 2:1-5

My son, if thou wilt receive my words, and hide my commandments with thee; So that thou incline thine ear unto wisdom, and apply thine heart to understanding; Yea, if thou criest after knowledge, and liftest up thy voice for understanding; If thou seekest her as silver, and searchest for her as for hid treasures; **Then shalt thou understand the fear of the Lord, and find the knowledge of God.**

3.
Proverbs 8:33-36

Hear instruction, and be wise, and refuse it not. Blessed is the man that heareth me, watching daily at my gates, waiting at the posts of my doors. For **whoso findeth me findeth life, and shall obtain favour of the Lord.** But he that sinneth against me wrongeth his own soul: all they that hate me love death.

4.
Isaiah 55:3

Incline your ear, and come unto me: hear, and **your soul shall live;** and I will make an everlasting covenant with you, even the sure mercies of David.

Q85 **THE MEANS OF GRACE** ········• which God require of us,
that we may escape his wrath and curse
due to us for sin

FAITH AND REPENTANCE

First and foremost, these two are gifts. Despite the wording God "requires" of us these two, faith and repentance are none other than the gifts that God Himself prepared for the elect in His great knowledge of our needs. These are God's gifts in disguise! Indeed what, among the things we have learned so far, was not a gift from God? Not a single thing.

Faith and repentance were briefly mentioned in the chapter Communion of Grace, in Part 1, but now, after the Ten Com-

mandments, they are given our full attention. There is a reason for this. It is not to present them as what we have to do to earn our redemption. But it is given in poignant pain, which comes with the acknowledgement that we have disobeyed and resisted God. What is the role of our faith and repentance? We are redeemed not because of our faith and repentance, but because of the mediation of Christ and the work of the Holy Spirit. Our faith and repentance only follow the complete change God bring on us.

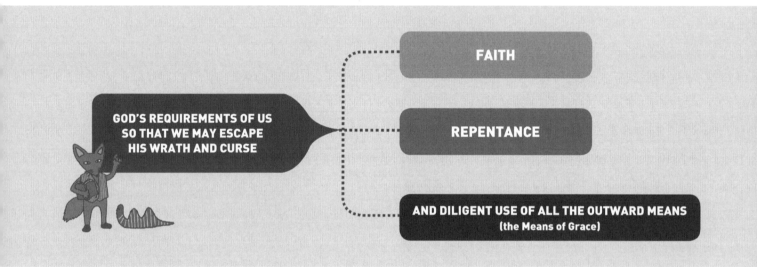

What is also important here is to know how faith and repentance are related to the following, the Means of Grace.

What is this Means of Grace? As mentioned before, it is "whereby God communicates to us the benefits of redemp-

tion." Recalling Q29, we have already received the benefits of redemption in Christ through the Spirit. However, what this particular question teaches us is that grace's means are given to us to effectively deliver what is ours already.

....

....

....

....

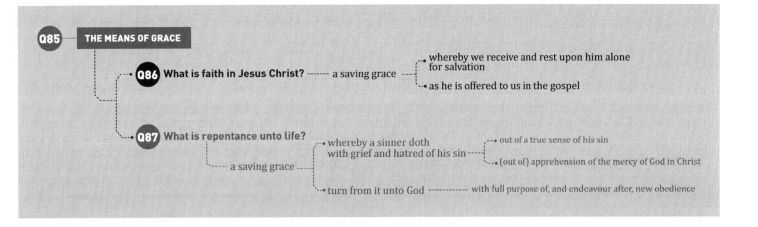

Q86 What is faith in Jesus Christ?

A86 Faith in Jesus Christ is a saving grace,[1]

whereby we receive

and rest upon him alone for salvation,

as he is offered to us in the gospel.[2, 3, 4, 5]

1.
Hebrews 10:39

But we are not of them who draw back unto perdition; but of them that **believe to the saving of the soul.**

2.
John 1:12

But **as many as received him,** to them gave he power to become the sons of God, even to them that believe on his name.

3.
Isaiah 26:3-4

Thou wilt keep him in perfect peace, whose **mind is stayed on thee; because he trusteth in thee.** Trust ye in the Lord for ever: for in the Lord JEHOVAH is everlasting strength.

4.
Philippians 3:9

And be found in him, not having mine own righteousness, which is of the law, but **that which is through the faith of Christ,** the righteousness which is of God by faith.

5.
Galatians 2:16

Knowing that a man is not justified by the works of the law, but **by the faith of Jesus Christ, even we have believed in Jesus Christ, that we might be justified** by the faith of Christ, and not by the works of the law: for by the works of the law shall no flesh be justified.

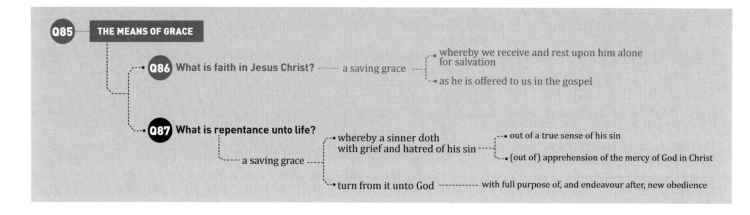

Q86 What is faith in Jesus Christ? ------ a saving grace ---- whereby we receive and rest upon him alone for salvation

as he is offered to us in the gospel

Q87 What is repentance unto life?

a saving grace ---- whereby a sinner doth with grief and hatred of his sin ---- out of a true sense of his sin

(out of) apprehension of the mercy of God in Christ

turn from it unto God ---------- with full purpose of, and endeavour after, new obedience

---

Q87 What is repentance unto life?

Q87 Repentance unto life is a saving grace,[1]

whereby a sinner,

out of a true sense of his sin,[2]

and apprehension of the mercy of God in Christ,[3, 4]

doth, with grief and hatred of his sin,

turn from it unto God,[5, 6]

with full purpose of, and endeavour after, new obedience.[7, 8]

1.
Acts 11:18

When they heard these things, they held their peace, and glorified God, saying, Then hath God also to the Gentiles granted **repentance unto life.**

6.
Ezekiel 36:31

Then shall ye remember your own evil ways, and your doings that were not good, and **shall lothe yourselves in your own sight for your iniquities** and for your abominations.

2.
Acts 2:37-38

Now when they heard this, **they were pricked in their heart,** and said unto Peter and to the rest of the apostles, Men and brethren, what shall we do? Then Peter said unto them, **Repent,** and be baptized every one of you in the name of Jesus Christ for the remission of sins, and ye shall receive the gift of the Holy Ghost.

3.
Joel 2:12

Therefore also now, saith the Lord, **Turn ye even to me** with all your heart, and with fasting, and with weeping, and with mourning.

7.
2 Corinthians 7:11

For, behold, this selfsame thing, that ye sorrowed after a godly sort, what carefulness it wrought in you, yea, what clearing of yourselves, yea, what indignation, yea, what fear, yea, **what vehement desire, yea, what zeal,** yea, what revenge! In all things ye have approved yourselves to be clear in this matter.

4.
Jeremiah 3:22

Return, ye backsliding children, and I will heal your backslidings. Behold, **we come unto thee; for thou art the Lord our God.**

8.
Isaiah 1:16-17

Wash you, make you clean; put away the evil of your doings from before mine eyes; cease to do evil; **Learn to do well;** seek judgment; relieve the oppressed; judge the fatherless; plead for the widow.

5.
Jeremiah 31:18-19

I have surely heard **Ephraim bemoaning himself** thus; Thou hast chastised me, and I was chastised, as a bullock unaccustomed to the yoke: turn thou me, and I shall be turned; for thou art the Lord my God. Surely after that I was turned, **I repented;** and after that I was instructed, **I smote upon my thigh: I was ashamed,** yea, even confounded, because I did bear the reproach of my youth.

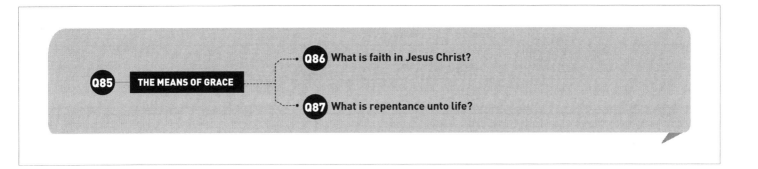

Here it is critical to learn the definition of faith and repentance. Refer to the below diagram.

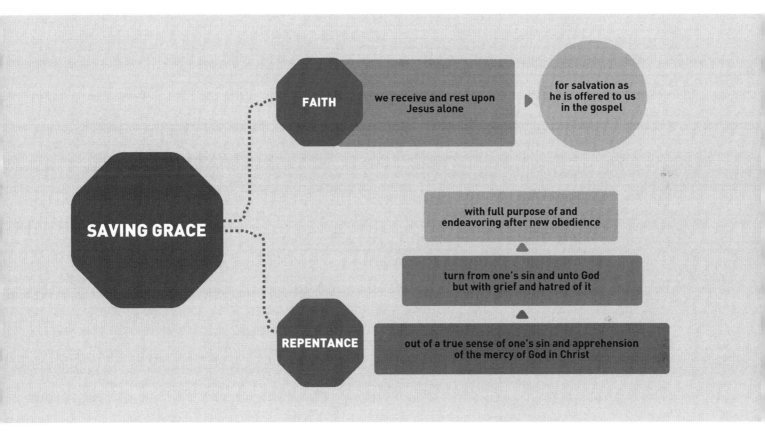

For both faith and repentance, the expression "saving grace" is used. Yet the following definitions are different. Compare and contrast these two, and own them in your heart. Your effort to move beyond intellectual understanding will be worthwhile, for these are the blessed means to get closer to God.

As mentioned, all sins, even the little and insignificant ones, deserve God's wrath and curse. Yet out of His mercy God gave us a way to escape. Also remember that despite being called requirements, this is not our work but that of the Holy Spirit.

Review

What was one of the primary works of the Holy Spirit? It is to give (gift) us the benefit of mediation. What would be the greatest benefit for man? As we have learned it is "to participate in the redemption of Christ." If we trace it back, it all started from the Covenant of Grace. Once again it is quite crucial you proceed with Part 2 holding the map (the entire structure) in your hands! (Refer to Part 1 p. 155)

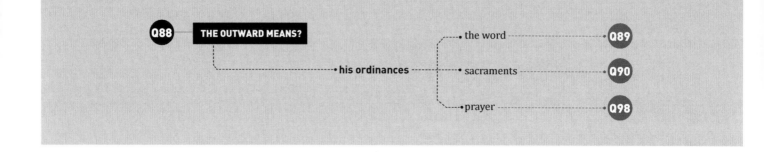
Q88 What are the outward means
whereby Christ communicateth to us the benefits of redemption?

A88 The outward and ordinary means
whereby Christ communicateth to us the benefits of redemption,
are his ordinances,
especially the word, sacraments, and prayer;
all which are made effectual to the elect for salvation.[1,2]

1.
Matthew 28:19-20

Go ye therefore, and **teach all nations, baptizing them** in the name of the Father, and of the Son, and of the Holy Ghost; **Teaching them to observe all things** whatsoever I have commanded you: and, lo, I am with you alway, even unto the end of the world. Amen.

2.
Acts 2:42, 46-47

And they continued stedfastly **in the apostles' doctrine and fellowship, and in breaking of bread, and in prayers**......And they, continuing daily with one accord **in the temple, and breaking bread from house to house,** did eat their meat with gladness and singleness of heart. Praising God, and having favour with all the people. And **the Lord added to the church daily such as should be saved.**

1. Q 88: INTRODUCTION (OR OUTLINE)

Q 88 introduces the upcoming topics. Following this question, a detailed explanation of the word sacrament (Baptism and the Lord's Supper) and prayer (the Lord's prayer) will be presented.

2. WHAT ARE THE OUTWARD MEANS?

For us to escape God's wrath and curse, besides through faith and repentance, outward (visible) ordinances are given. However, it takes more than our desire to follow these ordinances, for we do not know how. That is why God has offered us this means. This giving-certain-means to us implies the existence of other neither fundamental nor appropriate means. For example, asceticism through a monastic life, self-torture, meditation, and pilgrimage to sacred places should not have the same places as God-given ordinances.

What did God require of us to escape His wrath and curse? It is "faith and repentance with the diligent use of all the outward means!" And what do these outward means include? "The word, sacrament, and prayer!" What vast grace and benefits these three means especially can bring us! We are never to stop utilizing them throughout our lives.

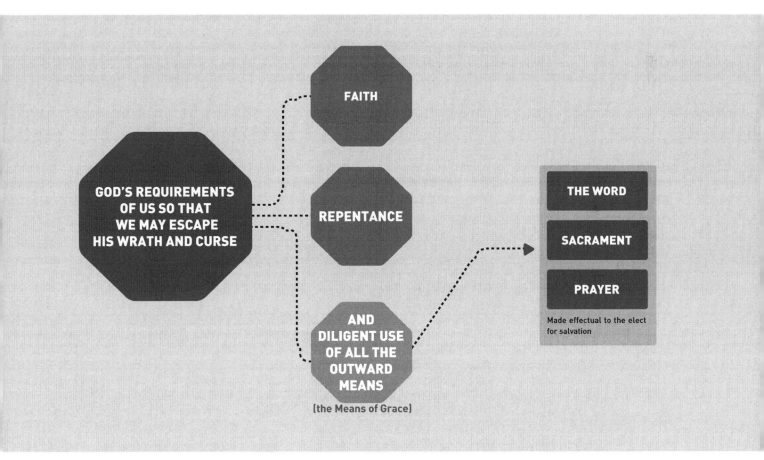

SUMMARY OF Q85-88

Outward means include the word, sacrament, and prayer, and their purpose is to communicate the benefits of Christ's media-

tion. Recall the previous study to discover its meaning.

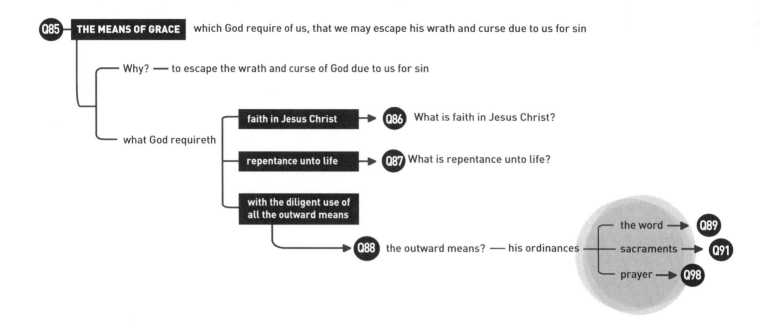

Q85 **THE MEANS OF GRACE** which God require of us, that we may escape his wrath and curse due to us for sin

Why? — to escape the wrath and curse of God due to us for sin

what God requireth

- faith in Jesus Christ → **Q86** What is faith in Jesus Christ?
- repentance unto life → **Q87** What is repentance unto life?
- with the diligent use of all the outward means → **Q88** the outward means? — his ordinances
  - the word → **Q89**
  - sacraments → **Q91**
  - prayer → **Q98**

Its meaning is: Everything we have learned, the union with Christ and the communion of grace which includes justification, adoption, sanctification, and glorious fellowship with Christ in this life, right after death, at resurrection and at judgment, is to be delivered by these means: the word, sacraments, and prayer.

God is the author of our faith, which means that our faith works according to His purpose and plan. We will never find ourselves being made perfect overnight. God is as orderly as He is personal. And the way He works is the same. He uses ordained-ordinances to bring all church members into oneness in Him. This is what makes our faith different from other superstitious religions and personal preferences.

And these ordinances are "for certain" effectual to the elect for their salvation. Because the work of the triune God is the same as He is and perfect (without error), and because this is the same One who chose the elect and He is calling His people according to His ordinances, His people cannot help but respond. The word, sacrament, and prayer—among all of grace's means, they are the most significant and they are for certain effectual to the elect.

Ordinances

Ordinances are in other words prescribed forms in our religious practice. You may think of Sunday worship as an example, which includes the word, sacrament, and prayer as its fundamental elements. For this reason, in this chapter Means of Grace and ordinances are used interchangeable. Now having learned that these ordinances are effectual for our salvation, we should be grateful for them, diligently getting to know and participate in them with the right attitude.

Given the term outward, may we assume that there are other inward ordinances?

Probably. Because faith and repentance are gifts given to our heart by the Holy Spirit, there may exist other inward means as well. The word, sacrament, and prayer are visible ones, and for that reason, they could be called outward means.

The Larger Catechism Q154 adds another expression, ordinary, to its answer making "the outward and ordinary means." Is it because there exists other extra-ordinary means?

God is of course not limited by particular ordinances, which means He can work through any extra-ordinary means as He wishes. However, God has chosen certain ones—the word, sacrament, and prayer—as the most ordinary ones, and these are guaranteed in the Bible. For that reason we should no longer seek any other extra-ordinary works of God.

THE MEANS OF GRACE VS. THE CONDITION OF GRACE

Be aware there is not another set of conditions which you need to fulfill to "earn" His grace; rather, it is purely by the means of grace that Christ uses to communicate His grace to you.

Discussion Questions

❶ Why is it a grace that God requires of us that which cannot be fulfilled?

❷ We repeat the fall before God's commandments. What do we need because of this?

❸ Christ has taken care of our sin once and for all. Then what is the reason that we still have to be watchful of our sin?

❹ In what ways are faith and repentance the same and different?

❺ Why do you think God has offered us the means of grace?

❻ In what sense does this chapter give us the reason to be grateful?

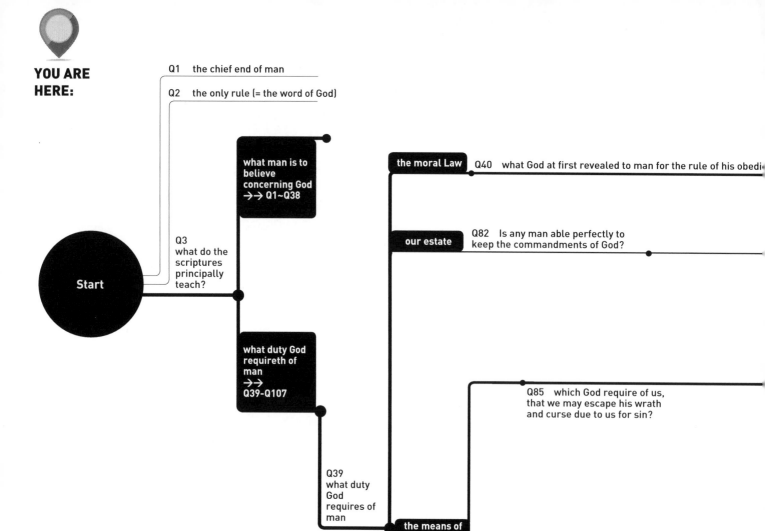

YOU ARE HERE:

Q1   the chief end of man

Q2   the only rule (= the word of God)

Start

Q3
what do the
scriptures
principally
teach?

what man is to believe concerning God →→ Q1~Q38

what duty God requireth of man →→ Q39-Q107

the moral Law   Q40   what God at first revealed to man for the rule of his obedie

our estate   Q82   Is any man able perfectly to keep the commandments of God?

Q85   which God require of us, that we may escape his wrath and curse due to us for sin?

Q39
what duty
God
requires of
man

the means of grace

Right after the teaching of the Ten Commandments, the Shorter Catechism made it clear that no man is able to keep the law to its perfection, and all sins are heinous enough to bring God's wrath and curse. It has been by nothing other than His grace that made us His church, and now the catechism makes it once again clear for this life we need His grace continuously.

Now the Shorter Catechism offers the reason why we as the members of His church ought to live with nothing but diligence. We have this duty of repentance and faith, and for these we need to diligently use the outward means, the word, sacraments, and prayer. Other means are only secondary.

The Shorter Catechism Part 1 was all about the foundation of our faith. Now through the first half of Part 2 (the Ten Commandments) we have covered the life of believers and the means of that life will follow.

Before getting into the discussion,

1. Make sure not to take any of those means, the word, sacraments, and prayer as a certain work we do. Yes, these are God's requirements, yet these are God's gift and blessings in disguise. Receive them with gratitude!

2. Commit yourself to getting to know them. It is easy to assume that we know them already—the word, sacraments, and prayer, because being in church we have not only heard about them but put them into practice countless times in the past. However, do you know them enough to give the exact definition of each of them? If not, take this study as a blessed opportunity!

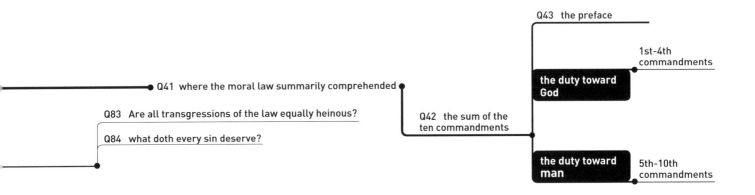

Q43 the preface

the duty toward God — 1st-4th commandments

Q42 the sum of the ten commandments

the duty toward man — 5th-10th commandments

Q41 where the moral law summarily comprehended

Q83 Are all transgressions of the law equally heinous?

Q84 what doth every sin deserve?

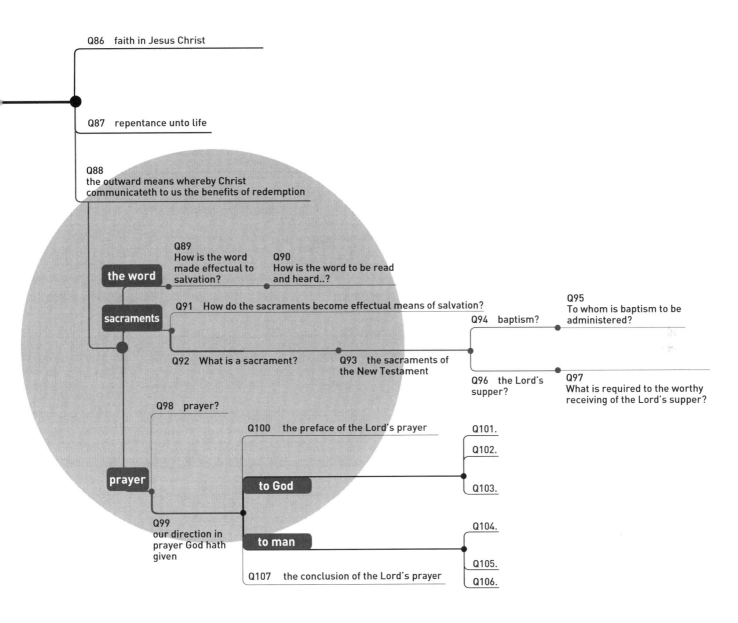

Q86 faith in Jesus Christ

Q87 repentance unto life

Q88
the outward means whereby Christ communicateth to us the benefits of redemption

the word

Q89
How is the word made effectual to salvation?

Q90
How is the word to be read and heard..?

sacraments

Q91 How do the sacraments become effectual means of salvation?

Q92 What is a sacrament?

Q93 the sacraments of the New Testament

Q94 baptism?

Q95
To whom is baptism to be administered?

Q96 the Lord's supper?

Q97
What is required to the worthy receiving of the Lord's supper?

prayer

Q98 prayer?

Q100 the preface of the Lord's prayer

to God

Q101.
Q102.
Q103.

Q99
our direction in prayer God hath given

to man

Q104.
Q105.
Q106.

Q107 the conclusion of the Lord's prayer

"I READ NOT ONLY THE BIBLE BUT MANY OTHER CHRISTIAN BOOKS. ALSO I PRAY. THE ONLY THING IS THAT I DON'T GO TO CHURCH. IS THAT A PROBLEM?"

"FOR ME, IT IS WAY BETTER TO PARTICIPATE IN A SMALL GROUP THAN JUST SIT AND LISTEN TO A SERMON. WHAT IF I SKIP CHURCH ALTOGETHER AND JUST ATTEND A SMALL GROUP?"

"POWER TO THE WORD? ISN'T IT RATHER TO THE PERSON WHO LISTENS TO THE WORD AND PUTS IT INTO ACTION?"

Violating God's law, we now deserve His wrath and curse. Yet for us to escape these dire consequences, God requires of us "Repentance" to God, "faith" in the Lord Jesus Christ, and the diligent use of all the "outward means" whereby Christ communicates to us the benefits of redemption. The outward means include the word, sacraments, and prayer, and these ordinances are made effectual to the elect for salvation. In the following chapters, these will be discussed in detail.

▲ The background illustration is Geumsan Church, located in Gimje, South Korea was built in the early days of Korean missions. What is interesting about this church is that it modeled its shape on one of the Korean letters, ㄱ, to separate women from men as they sit for service.

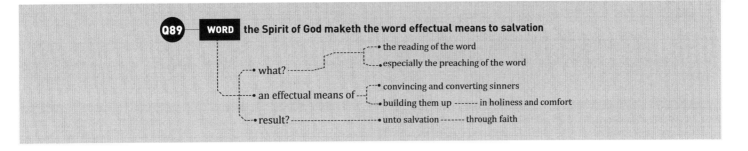

Q89 → WORD the Spirit of God maketh the word effectual means to salvation

what? ---• the reading of the word
---• especially the preaching of the word

an effectual means of --• convincing and converting sinners
--• building them up ------- in holiness and comfort

result? --------------------• unto salvation ------- through faith

Q89 How is the word made effectual to salvation?

A89 The Spirit of God maketh
the reading, but especially the preaching of the word,
an effectual means
of convincing and converting sinners,
and of building them up in holiness and comfort,
through faith, unto salvation.[1, 2, 3, 4, 5, 6, 7, 8, 9]

1.
Nehemiah 8:8

So they **read in the book in the law of God distinctly,** and gave the sense, and caused them to understand the reading.

7.
2 Timothy 3:15-17

And that from a child thou hast known **the holy scriptures, which are able to make thee wise unto salvation** through faith which is in Christ Jesus. All scripture is given by inspiration of God, and **is profitable for doctrine, for reproof, for correction, for instruction in righteousness; That the man of God may be perfect,** throughly furnished unto all good works.

2.
1 Corinthians 14:24-25

But if all prophesy, and there come in one that believeth not, or one unlearned, **he is convinced of all, he is judged of all:** And thus are the secrets of his heart made manifest; and so falling down on his face, **he will worship God,** and report that God is in you of a truth.

8.
Romans 10:13-17

For whosoever shall call upon the name of the Lord shall be saved. How then shall they call on him in whom they have not believed? and **how shall they believe in him of whom they have not heard? and how shall they hear without a preacher?** And how shall they preach, except they be sent? as it is written, How beautiful are the feet of them that preach the gospel of peace, and bring glad tidings of good things! But they have not all obeyed the gospel. For Esaias saith, Lord, who hath believed our report? So then faith cometh by hearing, and hearing by the word of God.

3.
Acts 26:18

To open their eyes, and to turn them from darkness to light, and from the power of Satan unto God, that they may receive forgiveness of sins, and inheritance among them which are sanctified by faith that is in me.

4.
Psalm 19:8

The statutes of the Lord are right, rejoicing the heart: the commandment of the Lord is pure, **enlightening the eyes.**

9.
Romans 1:16

For I am not ashamed of the gospel of Christ: for **it is the power of God unto salvation** to every one that believeth; to the Jew first, and also to the Greek.

5.
Acts 20:32

And now, brethren, I commend you to God, and **to the word of his grace, which is able to build you up, and to give you an inheritance among all them which are sanctified.**

6.
Romans 15:4

For whatsoever things were written aforetime were **written for our learning;** that we through patience and **comfort of the scriptures might have hope.**

We must
- attend thereunto ---- with diligence, preparation, and prayer
- receive it with faith and love
- lay it up in our hearts
- practise it in our lives

Q90 How is the word to be read and heard,
that it may become effectual to salvation?

A90 That the word may become effectual to salvation,
we must attend thereunto thereto
with diligence,[1] preparation,[2] and prayer;[3]
receive it with faith and love,[4, 5]
lay it up in our hearts,[6]
and practise it in our lives.[7, 8]

1.
Proverbs 8:34

Blessed is the man that heareth me, watching daily at my gates, **waiting at the posts of my doors.**

2.
1 Peter 2:1-2

Wherefore **laying aside all malice, and all guile, and hypocrisies, and envies, and all evil speakings,** As new-born babes, **desire the sincere milk of the word,** that ye may grow thereby.

3.
Psalm 119:18

Open thou mine eyes, that I may behold wondrous things out of thy law.

4.
Hebrews 4:2

For unto us was the gospel preached, as well as unto them: but the word preached did not profit them, **not being mixed with faith in them that heard it.**

5.
2 Thessalonians 2:10

And with all deceivableness of unrighteousness in them that perish; **because they received not the love of the truth,** that they might be saved.

6.
Psalm 119:11

Thy word have I hid in mine heart, that I might not sin against thee.

7.
Luke 8:15

But that on the good ground are they, which **in an honest and good heart, having heard the word, keep it,** and bring forth fruit with patience.

8.
James 1:25

But whoso looketh into the perfect law of liberty, and **continueth therein,** he being not a forgetful hearer, but a doer of the work, this man shall be blessed in his deed.

Q89:

The catechism teaches that the Holy Spirit makes not only the "reading of the word" but especially the "preaching of it" an effectual means. This statement—that the "word" actually convinces and converts sinners and builds them up through faith unto salvation—should sound absurd.

How can the word—written-down on mere paper and preached by a mere man (no matter how eloquent he is)—possses this much power, even enough to save a sinner?

The answer to this question is found in the Holy Spirit. He does that; He makes the word an effectual means. Such power of the word makes us examine the way we treat it, especially the preaching of it, for we are indeed quick to forget what was preached to us. Then, what would be the proper way to read and listen to the word? Let us take a look at the following question and answer.

Q90:

Q90 presents the proper attitude toward the word. Given this standard, the following applications seem applicable:

1. We should read the word *with conviction* that what we read is the Word of God and it is God Himself who enlightens us to understand what we read. When we read the word with this conviction, our attitude will surely change.

2. We should examine *our diligence* in reading His words. It is not enough that we use our leftover time to read God's word. Instead, we should set up a block of time out of the day and come up with a detailed reading plan.

For more applications, you may refer to the Larger Catechism Q157, 159-160.

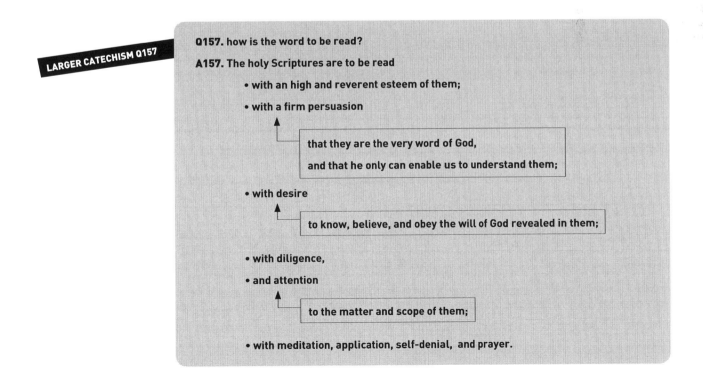

LARGER CATECHISM Q157

Q157. how is the word to be read?

A157. The holy Scriptures are to be read

- with an high and reverent esteem of them;
- with a firm persuasion

  that they are the very word of God,

  and that he only can enable us to understand them;

- with desire

  to know, believe, and obey the will of God revealed in them;

- with diligence,
- and attention

  to the matter and scope of them;

- with meditation, application, self-denial, and prayer.

HOW IS THE WORD OF GOD TO BE PREACHED BY THOSE THAT ARE CALLED THEREUNTO?

They that are called to labour in the ministry of the word, are
to preach sound doctrine,

DILIGENTLY,

in season and out of season;

PLAINLY,

not in the enticing words of man's wisdom,

but in demonstration of the Spirit, and of power;

FAITHFULLY,

making known the whole counsel of God;

WISELY,

applying themselves to the necessities and capacities of the
hearers;

ZEALOUSLY,

with fervent love to God and the souls of his people;

SINCERELY,

aiming at his glory, and their conversion, edification, and
salvation.

WHAT IS REQUIRED OF THOSE THAT HEAR THE WORD PREACHED?

It is required of those that hear the word preached,

THAT THEY ATTEND UPON IT

with diligence, preparation, and prayer;

EXAMINE

what they hear by the Scriptures;

RECEIVE

the truth with faith, love, meekness, and readiness of mind,

as the word of God;

MEDITATE, AND CONFER OF IT;

HIDE IT IN THEIR HEARTS,

AND BRING FORTH THE FRUIT OF IT IN THEIR LIVES.

Larger Catechism
Q159 ~ Q160

MATTERS TO PONDER WHILE READING THE WORD

While the word is given for our benefit, it is not right for us to use it as we wish. Keep in mind the following two suggestions as you read the word.

1. Remain in the context: Do not take a verse or two out of context to force it to fit your particular needs. Instead read the word in its context.

2. Be aware of the intention of the author: This is closely related to the above. The word is of course relevant to our daily lives, but that does not mean that we can read things into the word bending its meaning as we wish.

It is also important that

3. We do not take the word as our work to earn God's grace. The word is the means of grace, not the condition of it. There is no magical power in and of the word itself. We cannot make God love us more or less by reading the word or not reading it.

However, the most important matter regarding the reading of the word is to actually **4. Read.** The Bible is not an object for you to protect and cherish. (You cherish it so much you do not even open it.) Read it. Open it. If it helps, underline it and highlight it. Why don't we make it our goal to wear it out after years of really reading it?

Discussion Questions

❶ How does the word become the effectual means of grace to us?

❷ How are we supposed to hear messages? Share your thoughts based on what you have learned throughout this chapter.

❸ In what sense does this chapter give us the reason to be grateful?

YOU ARE HERE:

Commit yourself to getting to know them. As the title suggests, this section is about outward means, visible to our eyes. Thus it is easy to assume that we know them already—the word, sacraments, and prayer, because being in church we have not only heard about them but have put them into practice countless times in the past.

However, how many of us would be able to articulate an explanation about what each one of these means? Some may give shallow definitions, but in general the correct and extensive definitions are not known to Christians. But if it was really important for us to utilize these means for our salvations, then we should know them well enough to give clear definitions in our own words!

In addition, where this section is located within the entire Shorter Catechism is worth noting. It will benefit you if you can memorize the entire teachings of Q89-107. This is not unusual. Readers come up with various questions while studying this section, so please use the reference material of this book to help you.

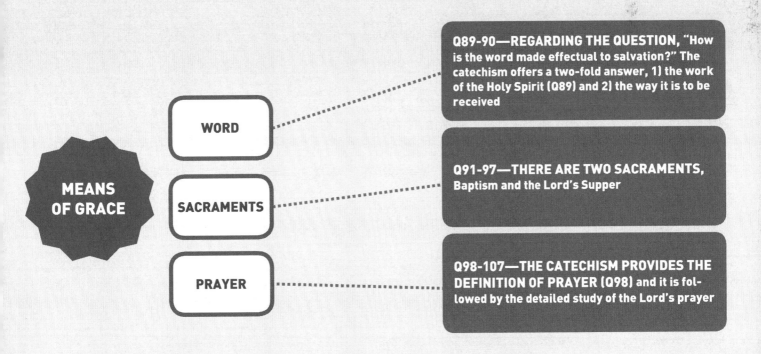

MEANS OF GRACE

WORD — **Q89-90—REGARDING THE QUESTION, "How is the word made effectual to salvation?"** The catechism offers a two-fold answer, 1) the work of the Holy Spirit (Q89) and 2) the way it is to be received

SACRAMENTS — **Q91-97—THERE ARE TWO SACRAMENTS,** Baptism and the Lord's Supper

PRAYER — **Q98-107—THE CATECHISM PROVIDES THE DEFINITION OF PRAYER (Q98)** and it is followed by the detailed study of the Lord's prayer

Q91~97 MEANS OF GRACE: WORD, SACRAMENTS, AND PRAYER

"I GOT BAPTIZED WHEN I WAS IN MIDDLE SCHOOL.
I DIDN'T HAVE ANY THOUGHTS BACK THEN.
NOW THAT I HAVE THIS PASTOR I REALLY RESPECT, CAN I BE RE-BAPTIZED?"
"SOME CHURCHES LET ANYONE SHARE THE BREAD AND WINE
BUT OTHER CHURCHES LET ONLY THE BAPTIZED. WHICH IS RIGHT?"
"I FEEL SO SINFUL THAT I DON'T WANT TO TAKE THE BREAD AND WINE."

Now we get into the second means of grace, sacraments (Baptism and the Lord's Supper), and this will be covered from here to Q97. It is quite a lot to digest. In the previous chapter we learned that the word builds us up in faith through its power to convince. It is the same with sacraments; It builds us up through its power to represent, confirm, and apply the benefit we received in Christ. This is the fundamental concept of sacraments.

The following questions and answers deal with (1) the definition of sacraments, (2) the kinds of sacraments, and (3) the proper attitude in participation.

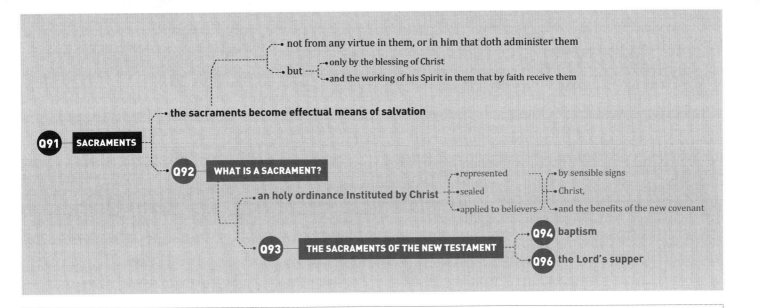

Q91 How do the sacraments become effectual means of salvation?

A91 The sacraments become effectual means of salvation,

not from any virtue in them,

or in him that doth administer them;

but only by the blessing of Christ,[1,2,3]

and the working of his Spirit

in them that by faith receive them.[4]

1. 1 Peter 3:21	**2.** Matthew 3:11	**3.** 1 Corinthians 3:6-7	**4.** 1 Corinthians 12:13
The like figure whereunto even baptism doth also now save us, **(not the putting away of the filth of the flesh, but the answer of a good conscience toward God,)** by the resurrection of Jesus Christ.	I indeed baptize you with water unto repentance: but he that cometh after me is mightier than I, whose shoes I am not worthy to bear: **he shall baptize you with the Holy Ghost,** and with fire.	I have planted, Apollos watered; but **God gave the increase.** So then neither is he that planteth any thing, neither he that watereth; but God that giveth the increase.	For **by one Spirit are we all baptized into one body,** whether we be Jews or Gentiles, whether we be bond or free; and **have been all made to drink into one Spirit.**

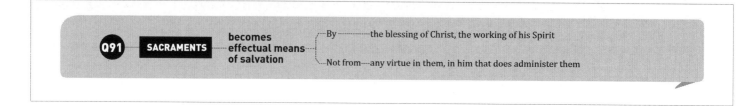

Regarding the way the sacraments become effectual means of grace, a two-fold answer is given:

From which it is not:
Any virtue in sacraments
The person that does administer sacraments

By which it is:
The Blessing of Christ
The working of His Spirit

Through the first part of the Shorter Catechism, we have learned that it is the Holy Spirit who works the faith in us. Here it is the same. Yet it sounds exactly opposite, for it appears now a lot of work is being dumped on us that we should read/hear the word and even participate sacraments. Yet is this not our work but the work of the Holy Spirit? It is quite confusing. However, yes, it is still the work of the Holy Spirit. Sacraments are the means, not the condition.

Ursinus

Why are these two sacraments, Baptism and the Lord's Supper, holy in a way that others are not?

Because Christ has instituted them. These are the only two ordinances that Christ Himself instituted. For this reason we need to distinguish these two from others.

This can also be applied to the church calendar—the special seasons and days we celebrate such as Thanksgiving, Christmas, and Easter. Many mistake these days as holier than other Sundays, and surely more so than other days of the week. However, this is completely wrong. There should be meanings to these seasons and days, but we should not put more emphasis on them than other days. For these are made by man.

What about marriage and memorial services? These are very meaningful occasions to those who are involved to the events. Yet churches should not place as much importance on them as on the sacraments Christ Himself instituted. It suffices to say here that Christ instituted only two sacraments—Baptism and the Lord's Supper. There is none other than these two in the entire Bible. And the principle that sets something as a sacrament and another not is whether its holy authority came from Christ and Him alone.

The Middle Age Church and Roman Catholic Church misunderstood this and observed seven sacraments in total. They included the most important milestones of our lives into the extent of sacraments, for example birth and marriage! All these life stages are meaningful, but by labeling them sacraments, Christ's authority and man's tradition became mixed. Why these should not be included in the extent of sacraments will be discussed in the following chapters.

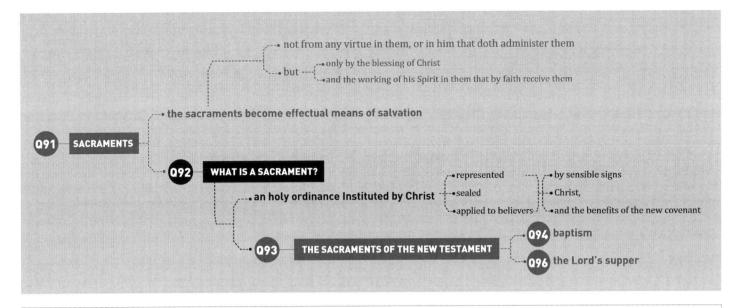

Q92 What is a sacrament?

A92 A sacrament is an holy ordinance instituted by Christ;
wherein, by sensible signs, Christ, and the benefits of the new covenant,
are represented, sealed, and applied
to believers.[1, 2, 3]

1.
Genesis 17:7, 10

And I will establish my covenant between me and thee, and thy seed after thee, in their generations, for an everlasting covenant, to be a God unto thee, and to thy seed after thee......**This is my covenant,** which ye shall keep, between me and you, and thy seed after thee; **Every man-child among you shall be circumcised.**

2.
Exodus 12. through out

3.
1 Corinthians 11:23, 26

For I have received of the Lord that which also I delivered unto you, That **the Lord Jesus** the same night in which he was betrayed **took bread**......For as often **as ye eat this bread, and drink this cup,** ye do shew the Lord's death till he come.

1. "CHRIST, AND THE BENEFITS OF THE NEW COVENANT"

Recall the "benefit" you have learned in Chapter 11 and 12.

2. WHAT DOES "SENSIBLE SIGNS" MEAN?

On a bended knee a man proposes, "Will you marry me?" Between his right thumb and index finger there is a ring. This ring is to make their relationship known to both themselves and others; in other words, to make what is invisible by its nature now visible. Sacraments are the same. We may sometimes wonder if our salvation is true asking ourselves "Am I really saved?" At these moments, God uses the sacraments to confirm our salvation. That is what this sensible sign does for us.

Because this part is very important, let us refer to the Larger Catechism to enrich our studies.

THE PURPOSE OF SACRAMENTS:

According to the Larger Catechism, its purpose is five-fold.

A162 A sacrament is a holy ordinance instituted by Christ in his church,

LARGER CATECHISM Q162

1. to signify, seal, and exhibit unto those that are within the covenant of grace, the benefits of his mediation;

2. to strengthen and increase their faith, and all other graces;

3. to oblige them to obedience;

4. to testify and cherish their love and communion one with another;

5. to distinguish them from those that are without.

All of the above are FOR us! How great His kindness is that He helps us to see and sense (even eat) this invisible and spiritual grace of His! The best example of this making-invisible-grace-visible in the Bible would be manna, with which God fed the Israelites in the wilderness. God could have filled them without raining manna from heaven, yet He chose this way to bless them every day for forty years. The Israelites not only gleaned the visible sign of grace with their own hands but also chewed and swallowed. What a privilege this must have been, and equally it is so with the sacraments given to us today!

Ursinus said,

The best book that I read on the topic of sacraments was The Commentary of Zacharias Ursinus on the Heidelberg Catechism. The expression "a visible sign of an invisible grace" is from his book.

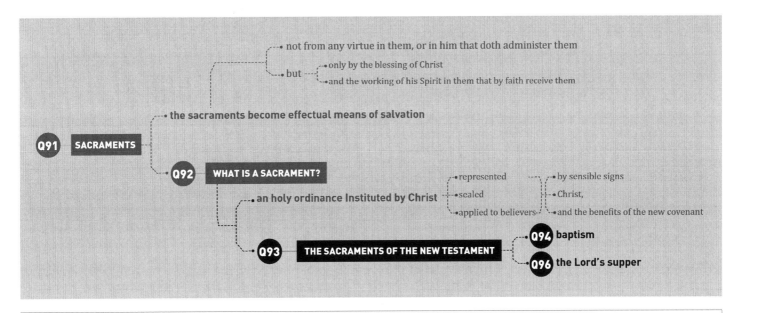

- not from any virtue in them, or in him that doth administer them
- but
  - only by the blessing of Christ
  - and the working of his Spirit in them that by faith receive them

- the sacraments become effectual means of salvation

Q91 SACRAMENTS

Q92 WHAT IS A SACRAMENT?

an holy ordinance Instituted by Christ
- represented
- sealed
- applied to believers
  - by sensible signs
  - Christ,
  - and the benefits of the new covenant

Q93 THE SACRAMENTS OF THE NEW TESTAMENT
- **Q94** baptism
- **Q96** the Lord's supper

Q93 Which are the sacraments of the New Testament?

A93 The sacraments of the New Testament are,
Baptism,[1] and the Lord's supper.[2]

1.
Matthew 28:19

Go ye therefore, and teach all nations, **baptizing them** in the name of the Father, and of the Son, and of the Holy Ghost.

2.
Matthew 26:26-28

And as they were eating, **Jesus took bread,** and blessed it, and brake it, and gave it to the disciples, and said, Take, eat; this is my body. And **he took the cup,** and gave thanks, and gave it to them, saying, Drink ye all of it: For this is my blood of the new testament, which is shed for many for the remission of sins.

Christ in the New Testament instituted only two sacraments, Baptism and the Lord's Supper. This stands in stark distinction from Roman Catholic tradition, for they have added five more to the above and call them sacraments. The additional five rites are Confirmation or Chrismation, Penance, Anointing of the Sick, Holy Orders, and Matrimony. However, there is no biblical ground in calling them sacraments, for Christ did not institute them.

Not to make the same mistake, not to use God and His name for our own needs and purposes, we need to pay close attention. This concept is closely related to the second commandment not to have any graven image unto ourselves.

SACRAMENTS

Q91 of the Shorter Catechism was "How do the sacraments become effectual means of salvation?" The answer that follows is "not from any virtue in them, or in him that does administer them; but only by the blessing of Christ, and the working of his Spirit in them."

From its two-fold answer—*from which it is not and by which it is*—we may infer that when this answer was given, the errors and exploitation among those who ministered the sacraments might have been quite prevalent. This inference becomes more convincing when the number of questions both the Westminster Larger Catechism and the Heidelberg Catechism dedicated for this particular matter is counted. (Refer to the graph below.)

It is equally important for us to correct what is wrong and to acknowledge the significance of sacraments as the means of God's grace. Once again both the knowledge and the practice are equally important, and neither of them should be neglected.

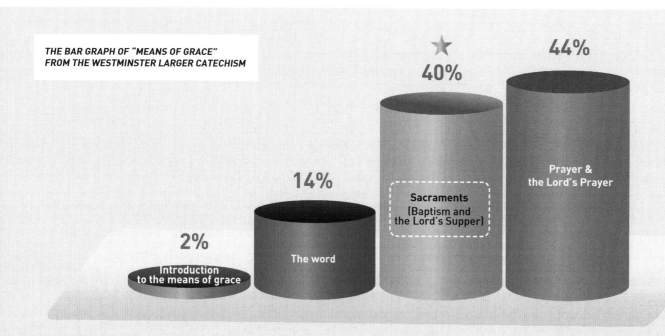

THE BAR GRAPH OF "MEANS OF GRACE" FROM THE WESTMINSTER LARGER CATECHISM

2% — Introduction to the means of grace

14% — The word

★ 40% — Sacraments (Baptism and the Lord's Supper)

44% — Prayer & the Lord's Prayer

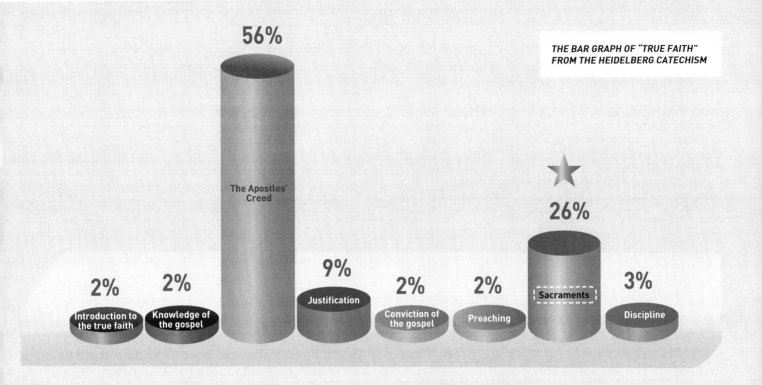

56%

The Apostles' Creed

2%
Introduction to the true faith

2%
Knowledge of the gospel

9%
Justification

2%
Conviction of the gospel

2%
Preaching

26%
Sacraments

3%
Discipline

"A VISIBLE SIGN OF AN INVISIBLE GRACE"

The Sacraments that Christ instituted Himself in the New Testament include two elements, the (visible) sign and (invisible) grace. It is so with both Baptism and the Lord's Supper. Keeping a good balance between the two, we should not make a mistake either by assigning a magical power to the rite itself or by going another direction.

Remember who you are—utterly sinners! But forgiving us, God has given us this title, the baptized member of the church, and even invited us to His Supper! What a grace and what a gift!

Without these thoughts and gifts, we

— would be seeing only the buildings made of bricks and mortar.
— would be merely attending church without being unable to see beyond the disappointing worldly crowd.
— would be seeing only the empty seats in the sanctuary.
— would not miss any opportunity to commit sins and end up being disgusted by our own sinfulness.
— would be gradually getting lost in our faith, overwhelmed by loneliness, isolation, darkness, desperation, injustice, despondency, frustration and despair.
— would be unable to find anything trustworthy in this world.

Still, God made us the baptized members of His church and invited us to His table. How could He see us as those worthy to be His family to share His table? This amazing love and grace gives us assurance.

Then is today's church free of any errors?
Unfortunately, not! It is always possible people come to participate in sacraments with superstitious and enchanted errors and selfish motives. Also due to their lack of knowledge, people could come without proper examination of self and could practice just as a ritual. These are the example of errors in need of fixing.

Even today we have these many possible errors, so how many more errors were there in the days of Calvin and the Reformation. We can only imagine what this day would have become today without their efforts to reform these sacraments. The dreadfulness of this thought makes us give thanks to God for the special grace He bestowed on them! May God bless today's churches that they may execute the sacraments in the right way and mark themselves as the true church of God!

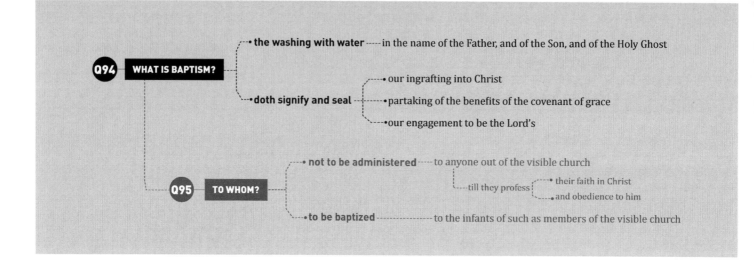

Q94 What is baptism?

A94 Baptism is a sacrament,
      wherein the washing with water
            in the name of the Father, and of the Son, and of the Holy Ghost,[1]
      doth signify and seal
            our ingrafting into Christ,
            and partaking of the benefits of the covenant of grace,
            and our engagement to be the Lord's.[2, 3]

1.
Matthew 28:19

Go ye therefore, and teach all nations, **baptizing them** in the name of the Father, and of the Son, and of the Holy Ghost.

2.
Romans 6:4

Therefore we are **buried with him by baptism into death;** that like as Christ was raised up from the dead by the glory of the Father, even **so we also should walk in newness of life.**

3.
Galatians 3:27

For as many of you **as have been baptized into Christ have put on Christ.**

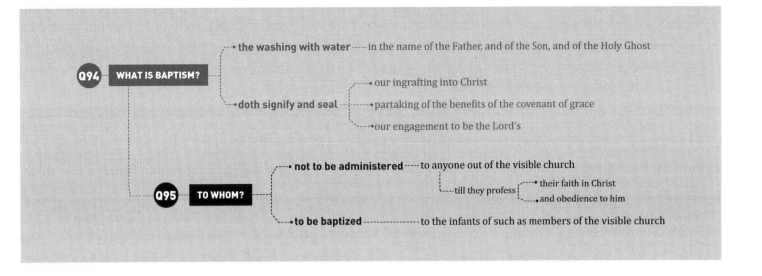

Q94 — WHAT IS BAPTISM?
- **the washing with water** —— in the name of the Father, and of the Son, and of the Holy Ghost
- **doth signify and seal**
  - our ingrafting into Christ
  - partaking of the benefits of the covenant of grace
  - our engagement to be the Lord's

Q95 — TO WHOM?
- **not to be administered** —— to anyone out of the visible church
  - till they profess
    - their faith in Christ
    - and obedience to him
- **to be baptized** —————— to the infants of such as members of the visible church

---

Q95   To whom is baptism to be administered?

A95   Baptism is

not to be administered

to any that are out of the visible church,

till they profess their faith in Christ,

and obedience to him;[1, 2]

but the infants of such as are members of the visible church

are to be baptized.[3, 4, 5, 6]

1.
Acts 8:36-37

And as they went on their way, they came unto a certain water: and the eunuch said, See, here is water; what doth hinder me to be baptized? And Philip said, **If thou believest with all thine heart, thou mayest.** And he answered and said, I believe that Jesus Christ is the Son of God.

2.
Acts 2:38

Then Peter said unto them, **Repent, and be baptized every one of you** in the name of Jesus Christ for the remission of sins, and ye shall receive the gift of the Holy Ghost.

6.
1 Corinthians 7:14

For the unbelieving husband is sanctified by the wife, and the unbelieving wife is sanctified by the husband: else were your children unclean; but **now are they holy.**

3.
Acts 2:38-39

[See before.] **For the promise is unto you, and to your children,** and to all that are afar off, even as many as the Lord our God shall call.

4.
Genesis 17:10

This is my covenant, which ye shall keep, between me and you, and thy seed after thee; **Every man-child among you shall be circumcised. [Compared with Colossians 2:11-12]**

5.
Colossians 2:11-12

In whom also ye are **circumcised with the circumcision** made without hands, in putting off the body of the sins of the flesh by the circumcision of Christ; **Buried with him in baptism,** wherein also ye are risen with him through the faith of the operation of God, who hath raised him from the dead.

Q94:

God gave us the covenant of grace, saying, "I will be your God and you will be my people." In other words, He promised to be with us at all times regardless of our circumstances and conditions. And in the days of the Old Testament, this promise was signified through circumcision. Circumcision was the sign that one belonged to God.

Now Baptism, a sacrament Jesus Himself instituted, plays this outward "sign" that we are the covenant people of God. Just as washing with water cleans away dirt, the blood of Christ cleans away our sins. Once baptized, you may still come to have doubts, but it will be hard to deny the very fact that you have been baptized, and this Baptism symbolizes your death and resurrection in Christ. Baptism is the sign that you belong to God.

Yet there is one thing which should be made clear: It is not through Baptism that salvation comes. Baptism is only the sign of it. If your Baptism didn't accompany your true faith, then it doesn't do anything for you.

Q95:

To the question "to whom is it [Baptism] to be ministered?" the answer opens up with "to whom it is not to be ministered." For this sacrament is that important and should not be rashly ministered. Baptism is not a personal matter—a pledge that you make only to yourself or with the minister—but a public matter in which you become *actually* united with Christ.

In order to be baptized, the following requirements are to be laid out first: that you should be a member of the visible church and are able to publically profess your faith in Christ. Sincere profession is truly necessary. Then how can an infant, who cannot make such a profession, be a possible candidate?

The covenant people of the Old Testament were circumcised only eight days after the birth. In the same way, infants can be baptized. Yet for this, the profession of faith of their parents is required.

We may find grounds for this in that God's grace always comes before our faith. *"You did not choose me, but I chose you."* (John 15:16) Therefore, Christian families can baptize their infants, but this Baptism must be followed with faithful teaching of God's words.

For further understanding: Bringing the Gospel to Covenant Children by Joel Beeke

> My question is about the way to be baptized. Some say the right way to do it is to immerse, and we sprinkle only for the sake of convenience. Is this right?

What is important is the sacrament's "washing" not the sacrament's "way". The literal meaning of Baptism, *baptizo* in Greek, is washing. We cannot infer "immersion" from either Mark 7:4 or Luke 11:38. It will be more than enough if we, through the Baptism, come to acknowledge that our sins are washed away.

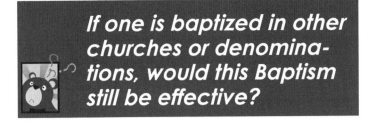

If one is baptized in other churches or denominations, would this Baptism still be effective?

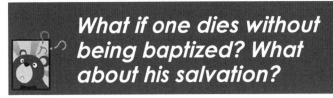

What if one dies without being baptized? What about his salvation?

As we have learned previously, the effect of Baptism is not in any virtue in and of itself. Thus, the Baptism should be accepted even if it was received in other places.

Baptism is a "sign," not a condition. No more or less.

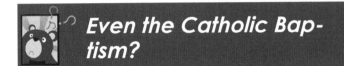

Even the Catholic Baptism?

Yes. Because Baptism is received in the name of the Father, the Son, and the Holy Spirit, if one is baptized in these names then it should be accepted.

Before baptism, the candidate should go through a procedure to ensure his or her faith and its confession. First, the baptism class should be run by their pastor for about two weeks. If necessary, private session between the pastor and candidate should be included. However, it is often seen that this procedure is replaced with a one-time test on sets of questions and answers. (The pastor asks the question and the candidate recites the answers by rote memory.) What would have led to this simplified procedure? There might be two factors, 1) the number of pastors has not increased as much as the believers or 2) the church is no long aware of the importance of the procedure in performing baptism. On top of this, it is not easy to confirm anyone's confession. All the more so when the test session is performed by a pastor that the candidate does not know well.

Three marks of true churches that we should not concede are 1) the preaching of the Word, 2) the administration of the sacraments, and 3) church discipline. It seems like constructive criticism when things go wrong and faithful efforts to make them right are made regarding the first mark, the preaching of the Word. Yet the second mark (sacraments) is more often overlooked. When baptism is given to anyone without confirming their faith, it does disservice to that person because they will mistake baptism as just a church ritual that goes along with church membership. Well-developed education is now in need so baptism can be administered in a way that benefits the believers!

THE PREREQUISITE OF BAPTISM IS TRUE CONFESSION OF FAITH...? WHAT IS THAT?

It is to say, "I profess God to be my Father. I believe His love is demonstrated to me through Christ's birth, death, and resurrection. Now for this love I am eternally grateful, and I take to glorify and enjoy God forever as the end of my life." In other words, if you not only accepted what you have learned so far from the Shorter Catechism but also have the desire to live according to it, then you are ready to make a confession of true faith.

Q167. How is our baptism to be improved by us?

A167. The needful but much neglected duty of improving our baptism,

is to be performed by us all our life long,

especially in the time of temptation,

and when we are present at the administration of it to others;

by serious and thankful consideration

of the nature of it,

and of the ends for which Christ instituted it,

the privileges and benefits conferred and sealed thereby,

and our solemn vow made therein;

by being humbled

for our sinful defilement,

our falling short of,

and <u>walking contrary to,</u>

the grace of baptism, and our engagements;

by growing up <u>to assurance</u>

of pardon of sin,

and of all other blessings sealed to us in that sacrament;

by drawing strength from the death and resurrection of Christ, into whom we are baptized,

for the mortifying of sin,

and quickening of grace;

and by endeavoring to live by faith,

to have our conversation in holiness and righteousness,

as those that have therein given up their names to Christ;

and to walk in brotherly love,

as being baptized by the same Spirit into one body.

IMPROVE BAPTISM?

We are baptized once in our lifetime, yet it should not remain as a onetime event in the past. Rather we are to continuously remember our Baptism and by doing so bring our focus only to Christ. See Q167 of the Larger Catechism for a more detailed description.

"Live a new life." (Rom 6:4)

"How can we live in our sins any longer?" (Rom 6:2)

"Follow in the footsteps of the faithful." (Rom 4:12)

"Have the pledge of a clear conscience toward God." (1 Pet 3:21)

"Be united with him in a resurrection like his." (Rom 6:5)

"Have no division. Instead have equal concern for each other." (1 Cor 12:25)

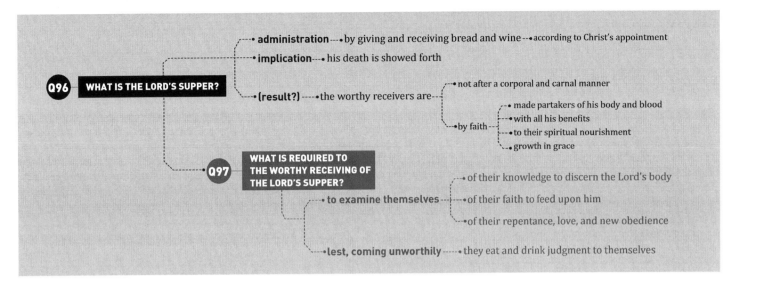

Q96 What is the Lord's supper?

A96 The Lord's Supper is a sacrament,
    wherein, by giving and receiving bread and wine,
      according to Christ's appointment,
  his death is showed forth;
  and the worthy receivers are,
    not after a corporal and carnal manner,
    but by faith, made partakers of his body and blood,
  with all his benefits,
  to their spiritual nourishment, and growth in grace.[1,2]

1.
1 Corinthians 11:23-26

For I have received of the Lord that which also I delivered unto you, That the Lord Jesus the same night in which he was betrayed took bread: And when he had given thanks, he brake it, and said, Take, eat: this is my body, which is broken for you: **this do in remembrance of me.** After the same manner also he took the cup, when he had supped, saying, This cup is the new testament in my blood: this do ye, as oft as ye drink it, in remembrance of me. For as often as ye eat this bread, and drink this cup, **ye do shew the Lord's death till he come.**

2.
1 Corinthians 10:16

The cup of blessing which we bless, is it not the communion of the blood of Christ? The bread which we break, **is it not the communion of the body of Christ?**

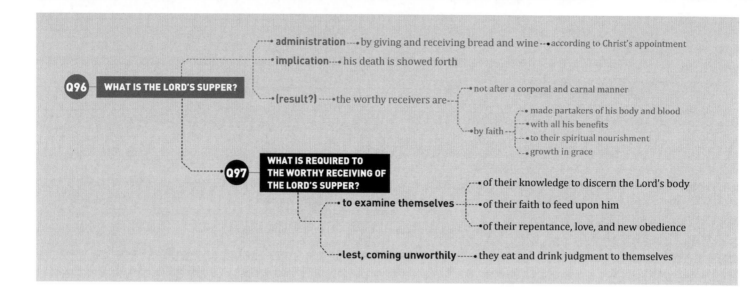

Q97 What is required to the worthy receiving of the Lord's supper?

A97 It is required of them
that would worthily partake of the Lord's supper,
that they examine themselves
of their knowledge to discern the Lord's body,[1]
of their faith to feed upon him,[2]
of their repentance,[3] love,[4] and new obedience;[5]
lest, coming unworthily,
they eat and drink judgement to themselves.[6]

1.
1 Corinthians 11:28-29

But **let a man examine himself, and so let him eat of that bread, and drink of that cup.** For he that eateth and drinketh unworthily, eateth and drinketh damnation to himself, **not discerning the Lord's body.**

2.
2 Corinthians 13:5

Examine yourselves, whether ye be in the faith: prove your own selves: Know ye not your own selves, how that Jesus Christ is in you, except ye be reprobates?

3.
1 Corinthians 11:31

For if **we would judge ourselves,** we should not be judged.

6.
1 Corinthians 11:28-29

But let **a man examine himself, and so let him eat of that bread, and drink of that cup.** For he that eateth and drinketh unworthily, eateth and drinketh damnation to himself, **not discerning the Lord's body.**

4.
1 Corinthians 10:16-17

The cup of blessing which we bless, **is it not the communion** of the blood of Christ? The bread which we break, **is it not the communion** of the body of Christ? **For we, being many, are one bread, and one body: for we are all partakers of that one bread.**

5.
1 Corinthians 5:7-8

Purge out therefore the old leaven, **that ye may be a new lump,** as ye are unleavened. For even Christ our passover is sacrificed for us: Therefore **let us keep the feast,** not with old leaven, neither with the leaven of malice and wickedness; but **with the unleavened bread of sincerity and truth.**

Q96:

Christ Himself appointed the Lord's Supper just like the other sacrament Baptism, and by this giving and receiving bread and wine, Christ's death is showed forth. When we partake in this Supper, we become united with Christ and get to enjoy fellowship with Him. Thus, we should not partake in it after a corporal manner (to satisfy the appetite or fill the stomach) or carnal manner (participating without knowing its spiritual meaning). Then those who receive this Supper, according to the answer, will grow in grace.

This question and answer also teaches the true meaning of the Lord's Supper. Its purpose is to ensure our union and fellowship with Christ. (Regarding communion and fellowship, see p. 165 in Part 1)

The Lord's Supper belongs to the means of grace, which means that it also communicates the benefits of Christ's mediation to us.

What does it mean that it shows forth Christ's death?

Is this Supper merely a symbol or something more? If the latter, how can Christ be in a piece of bread and a cup of wine?

Spiritually Present

Christ is not present in the elements of bread and wine in a physical or material way, rather in the faith of those who receive them Christ is present spiritually. Thus, those who receive these elements should feed on the body and blood of Christ not after a corporal and carnal manner, but in a spiritual manner. Yet truly and really by faith they receive and apply to themselves Christ crucified and all the benefits of his death. (The Larger Catechism Q170) We had better meditate on every word of the above. Wrongful ideas about the Lord's Supper could not only vandalize the true meaning of it but also reduce it to a mere superstitious rite.

Wrongful Ideas about the Lord's Supper
When the elements are distributed...

1. TRANSUBSTANTIATION:

The elements change into the actual body and blood of Christ.

2. CONSUBSTANTIATION:

Christ's body and blood are present "in, with and under" the forms of bread and wine.

3. COMMEMORATION (OR MEMORIALISM):

There is no physical or spiritual presence of Christ in the bread and wine. Rather the Lord's Supper is merely a remembrance of Christ's suffering and death.

TO MAKE IT CLEAR:

We understand Christ is spiritually present in the elements. Those elements do not actually turn into the body and blood of Christ. We do not merely remember His death finding no additional benefits in it. Rather, the Lord's Supper is the actual means of grace and a holy ordinance.

TIP :

During the communion service, people in general close their eyes and meditate on the meaning of the bread and wine. This is good, but why don't we from time to time open our eyes and observe how the service is administered and experience the "Word made visible?"

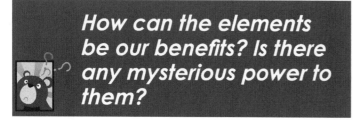

How can the elements be our benefits? Is there any mysterious power to them?

No, the Shorter Catechism makes it clear that there is not any virtue in sacraments or in him that does minister them that make sacraments effectual. Rather, it is by the blessing of Christ and the working of the Holy Spirit. Yet going beyond the idea that these elements are mere symbols of Christ's suffering death, we freely assume that there should be a mysterious power to them. However, this assumption has its foundation in our sinfulness in which we always prefer seeing to believing, and for this reason, it is absolutely false.

Q97:

What the Lord's Supper shows forth is the body of Christ torn for our sake. And this is closely related to what we have learned in the section the Humiliation of Christ in Part 1. (Q/A27)

Here is what the Lord's Supper reminds us of and does for us: First, it reminds us of His death. Through the Lord's Supper we come to once again witness His death. Taking bread, we see His body being torn; Pouring wine, we see His blood being shed. If the image of the Old Testament is to be borrowed, the sacrifice of an animal can be compared to it.

Second, it communicates the benefit of Christ's mediation:

That we feed on Christ's body and blood means that through this Christ-appointed ordinance we become united with Christ, and in this mysterious union both become nourished and grow. The bread is not to fill our stomach and the wine is not to relieve our thirst. Rather, they are to satisfy our spiritual hunger and thirst, and through them we grow.

This is how we "examine" our knowledge; that is, we examine whether we have a solid understanding of what we are told to do. Part 2 of the Shorter Catechism must be understood in the light of Part 1, for to "discern of the Lord's body" is just another way of expressing being able to know and profess faith which has been thoroughly taught in Part 1.

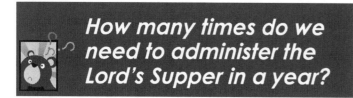

How many times do we need to administer the Lord's Supper in a year?

forced, but all ought to be exhorted and stimulated; the torpor of the sluggish, also ought to be rebuked that all, like persons famishing, should come to the feast. It was not without cause, therefore, I complained, at the outset, that this practice had been introduced by the wile of the devil; a practice which, in prescribing one day in the year, makes the whole year one of sloth."

John Calvin from IV. Sacraments of *Institutes of the Christian Religion*

For its benefits, the more the better! Calvin's words communicate the same idea.

"Each week, at least, the table of the Lord ought to have been spread for the company of Christians, and the promises declared on which we might then spiritually feed. No one, indeed, ought to be

However, given the prevalent ignorance of the true meaning of the sacrament of the Lord's Supper, weekly administration seems quite far-off for now. Repentance of our ignorance and laziness in this matter and the restoration of its meaning and joy must come first.

The Larger Catechism presents us with three things we should be mindful of as we receive the Lord's Supper. Why don't we take a look at them one by one?

1. There is something we should prepare before the Lord's Supper.

Q171. How are they that receive the sacrament of the Lord's supper to prepare themselves before they come unto it?

A171. They that receive the sacrament of the Lord's supper are, before they come, to prepare themselves thereunto,

by examining themselves
> of their being in Christ,
> of their sins and wants;
> of the truth and measure of their knowledge, faith, repentance;
> love to God and the brethren, charity to all men,
> forgiving those that have done them wrong;
> of their desires after Christ,
> and of their new obedience;

and by renewing the exercise of these graces,
by serious meditation,
and fervent prayer.

This is a lot to take in. More detailed explanation follows in Q172.

Q172. May one who doubteth of his being in Christ,
or of his due preparation,
come to the Lord's supper?

A172. One who doubteth of his being in Christ,
or of his due preparation to the sacrament of the Lord's supper,
may have true interest in Christ,
though he be not yet assured thereof;

and in God's account hath it,

if he be duly affected with the apprehension of the want of it,
and unfeignedly desires to be found in Christ,
and to depart from iniquity:

in which case
(because promises are made,
and this sacrament is appointed,
for the relief even of weak and doubting Christians)

he is to bewail his unbelief,
and labor to have his doubts resolved;
and, so doing,
he may and ought to come to the Lord's supper,
that he may be further strengthened.

Another way to put this question is whether anyone who is not perfect can participate in the Lord's Supper. The previous question covered what kind of preparation is required for one to participate in the Lord's Supper. However, we have to admit it is impossible for anyone to make himself or herself perfectly ready as given in its answer. In reality we come to church mostly entangled with the sins of this world. So the question arises: Is it right that I, imperfect and sinful, participate in the Lord's Supper, and by doing so, am I not just adding more sins on myself? This is a legitimate doubt! Yet the answer to this question encourages us that there is all the more reason to participate. If you find yourself weak and sinful, do not hold yourself back. Instead, come to the Table and strengthen yourself. Our first reaction to this call would be taking steps back saying, "How can somebody like me participate in this holy Supper? No way!" Yet this catechism teaches us that for that very reason we have to come to the Supper. Our reaction may appear to be humble and even noble, but in reality it only shows a lack of faith that He prepared all and gave them as gifts for His children. It shows a prideful heart!

LARGER CATECHISM Q174

2. Then what should we be mindful of during the Lord's Supper?

Q174. **What is required of them that receive the sacrament of the Lord's supper in the time of the administration of it?**

A174. It is required of them that receive the sacrament of the Lord's supper, that, during the time of the administration of it,

with all holy reverence and attention
they wait upon God in that ordinance,

diligently observe the sacramental elements and actions,

heedfully discern the Lord's body,

and **affectionately** meditate on his death and sufferings,

and **thereby stir up themselves to a vigorous exercise of their graces;**
　　in judging themselves,
　　and sorrowing for sin;
　　in earnest hungering and thirsting after Christ,
　　feeding on him by faith,
　　receiving of his fullness,
　　trusting in his merits,
　　rejoicing in his love,
　　giving thanks for his grace;
　　in renewing of their covenant with God,
　　and love to all the saints.

Every sentence in this answer speaks volume, but especially the last one. It encourages us to participate in the Lord's Supper in "love for all the saints." It moves our hearts when we see other believers especially the next generation come to faith and share the Table with us. What a joyous moment to see young ones grow to be the members of our body and be on the same journey as us. One of the occasions during which this is seen by all members of the church is through the Lord's Supper. Don't limit the Lord's Supper as the chance for us to come individually in terms of our faith, but be mindful that this is actually the Supper for God's entire family.

3. Lastly, there are duties that follow after the Lord's Supper.

Q175. What is the duty of Christians,

after they have received the sacrament of the Lord's supper?

A175. The duty of Christians,

after they have received the sacrament of the Lord's supper,

is seriously to consider

how they have behaved themselves therein,

and with what success;

if they find quickening and comfort,

to bless God for it,

beg the continuance of it,

watch against relapses,

fulfill their vows,

and encourage themselves

to a frequent attendance on that ordinance:

but if they find no present benefit,

more exactly to review their preparation to,

and carriage at, the sacrament;

in both which,

if they can approve themselves to God and their own consciences,

they are to wait for the fruit of it in due time:

but, if they see they have failed in either,

they are to be humbled,

and to attend upon it afterwards

with more care and diligence.

These should be useful both at times when the Lord's Supper is administered and at every other occasion. We have to keep these things in mind and diligently practice them in our daily lives. Keep these three lessons of the Larger Catechism close to you and utilize them the next time when you participate in the Lord's Supper. It can bring many benefits to you!

It is not only a duty of believers to examine themselves for the Lord's Supper. In addition, the judicatory (the body of a church that disciplines) also holds the responsibility to help its members to participate in the Lord's Supper with proper self-examination. For this, they should pay attention to the hearts and lives of each member, putting their efforts toward education and training. This was a concern also for the reformers.

It takes the whole church to build a congregation that "worthily partakes" in the Lord's Supper. In order to help a congregation to sincerely consider and practice the above and examine themselves accordingly, the disciplining bodies such as the session, presbytery, and synod are needed.

BAPTISM	LORD'S SUPPER
• Number: Once	• Number: Often
• Means: Water	• Means: Bread and wine

• Meaning:
   – To be a sign and seal of our regeneration and ingrafting into Christ
	• Meaning:
	   – to represent and exhibit Christ as spiritual nourishment to the soul, and
	   – to confirm our continuance and growth in him

• Object and Time:
   – Even to infants
	• Object and Time:
	   – only to such as are of years (from teenage years) and ability to examine themselves

WHEREIN DO BAPTISM AND THE LORD'S SUPPER AGREE?

Agreement?

In that the author of both is God.
The spiritual part of both (Baptism and the Lord's Supper) is Christ and His benefits.

Seals of the same covenant

To be dispensed by ministers of the gospel (by none other)

To be continued in the church of Christ (until his second coming)

Discussion Questions

❶ How can sacraments be the effectual means of our salvation?

❷ What kind of benefits can we expect from Baptism?

❸ What kind of benefits can we expect from the Lord's Supper?

❹ What is required of us for Baptism and the Lord's Supper?

❺ In what sense does this chapter give us the reason to be grateful?

Q98 MEANS OF GRACE: WORD, SACRAMENTS, AND "PRAYER"

"DOES GOD LISTEN TO THE PRAYER OF NON-BELIEVERS TOO?"
"PRAY WITHOUT CEASING? THEN, HOW CAN WE DO ANYTHING ELSE OTHER THAN PRAY?"
"I DON'T PRAY BECAUSE I DON'T WANT TO BOTHER GOD."
"100 DAYS OF PRAYER? THAT SOUNDS A BIT RIDICULOUS!"

Now we turn to the third means of grace, prayer. Most Christians regularly pray, probably since the moment of accepting Jesus Christ as their personal Savior. For this reason, many Christians takes this particular means of grace for granted and do not have any second thoughts about it. Through this chapter, we will be able to study the topic of prayer, once again with the Larger Catechism on the side. How well do think you know what prayer is?

On the surface, only Q98 covers this topic of prayer, but the truth is this topic is covered through to the very last question of the Shorter Catechism. (Who would have thought that we have that much to learn about prayer!) What you have to keep in mind is the context, the means of grace, as the Shorter Catechism teaches the most well-known prayer.

Getting into the actual lesson on this topic of prayer, let us take a moment and do a check-up on our knowledge about this very topic. Below are some true or false questions.

TRUE AND FALSE QUIZ ABOUT PRAYER

1. God answers all of our prayers and petitions. --- (   )
2. The sincerity of our prayer expedites the answer from God. -------------------- (   )
3. God knows all our needs, but He waits till we ask. ------------------------------- (   )
4. Prayer is the tool through which we inform God about our needs. ---------- (   )
5. The purpose of prayer is having our way with God. ------------------------------ (   )

The answers to the above questions are all false. Let's try one more. Please fill in the blank.

Phil. 4:6-7
"Do not be anxious about anything, but in every situation, by prayer and petition, with thanksgiving, present your requests to God. [Then] _____ ."

What seems right in the blank, "God will answer your prayer"? As you may know already, what comes in the blank in verse 7 is

"The peace of God, which transcends all understanding, will guard your hearts and your minds in Christ Jesus".

God's will in our prayer?

The success of our prayer should not be determined by the number of answers we get granted but by the amount of change we go through. Our hearts are so arrogant that we do not like the concept of asking somebody's (even God's) help for our needs. However, God's primary will for us is to make us His children, whose hearts desire a close relationship with the Father and blessings from Him.

Upon knowing this will and being grateful for it, the most important lesson we need to learn is to fill our prayer with the same heart and desire as His. The very purpose and highest value of our lives should be that we want God and His presence with a childlike heart throughout the good and bad, throughout the joy and pain, and that we desire His glory and a loving relationship with Him above all.

The greatest answer for our prayer?

The greatest answer for our prayer is then not having our own way with God but coming to understand and love His will for us. For His will done to us is the best gift, the highest goal and the truest blessing we can wish for ourselves.

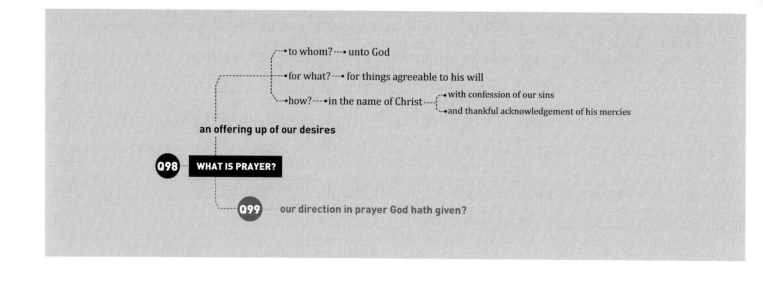

Q98 What is prayer?

A98 Prayer is an offering up of our desires unto God,[1]

for things agreeable to his will,[2]

in the name of Christ,[3]

with confession of our sins,[4, 5]

and thankful acknowledgement of his mercies.[6]

1.
Psalm 62:8

Trust in him at all times; ye people, **pour out your heart before him:** God is a refuge for us. Selah.

2.
1 John 5:14

And this is the confidence that we have in him, that, **if we ask any thing according to his will,** he heareth us.

3.
John 16:23

And in that day ye shall ask me nothing. Verily, verily, I say unto you, **Whatsoever ye shall ask the Father in my name,** he will give it you.

4.
Psalm 32:5-6

I acknowledged my sin unto thee, and mine iniquity have I not hid. **I said, I will confess my transgressions** unto the Lord; and thou forgavest the iniquity of my sin. Selah. **For this shall every one that is godly pray unto thee** in a time when thou mayest be found: surely in the floods of great waters they shall not come nigh unto him.

5.
Daniel 9:4

And **I prayed unto the Lord** my God, and **made my confession,** and said, O Lord, the great and dreadful God, keeping the covenant and mercy to them that love him, and to them that keep his commandments.

6.
Philippians 4:6

Be careful for nothing; but in every thing **by prayer and supplication with thanksgiving** let your requests be made known unto God.

Here we come to learn what prayer is, and the Larger Catechism can be helpful for our understanding of the topic.

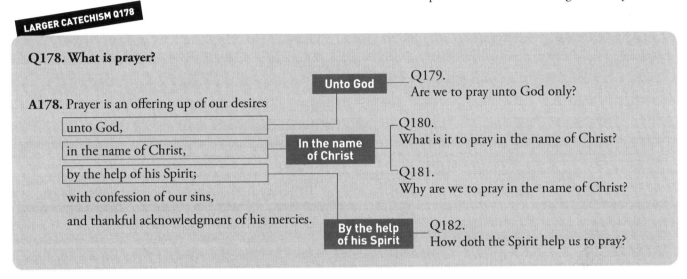

LARGER CATECHISM Q178

Q178. What is prayer?

A178. Prayer is an offering up of our desires

unto God,

in the name of Christ,

by the help of his Spirit;

with confession of our sins,

and thankful acknowledgment of his mercies.

Unto God — Q179. Are we to pray unto God only?

In the name of Christ — Q180. What is it to pray in the name of Christ?

Q181. Why are we to pray in the name of Christ?

By the help of his Spirit — Q182. How doth the Spirit help us to pray?

"I didn't expect to see the triune God in the definition of prayer!"

"Remember: We pray unto God, in the name of Christ and with the help of Holy Spirit."

The Larger catechism Q178 to 185 covers the concept of prayer. As you may be able to see, the simple definition of prayer in Q178 reveals the mysterious work of the triune God in our prayer (First unto God, second in the name of Christ, and lastly by the help of Holy Spirit) and each is extended by the following questions from Q179 to 182. (Q179 Are we to pray unto God only?; Q180 What is it to pray in the name of Christ?; Q181 Why are we to pray in the name of Christ?; Q182 How doth the Spirit help us to pray?) And the following teachings from Q183 to 185 deals with the contents and ways of prayer.

THE DEFINITION OF PRAYER

Simply put, prayer is to offer our desires to God. Come to think of it, this definition of prayer goes against the way we wish to operate our lives. We do not like having to ask anybody for help, seeing it as a sign of weakness. Instead, we long to hear "You can do it all" "Just put your mind to it" or "I believe in you." What's deeply ingrained here is our depraved nature in which we desire to go our own way parting from God. It may appear like humility that we don't want to bother God, but in reality it is arrogance in which we believe in a change for a better life apart from God.

In essence, prayer is to offer our desires to God, and this lead us to the question of how. The latter part of A98 gives us two ways, "confession of our sin" and "thankful acknowledgment of his mercies." For a deeper study of the topic of prayer, the Larger Catechism can be helpful, and we will be utilizing especially what comes after the three prepositions, unto, in and by for such a study.

Q179. Are we to pray **unto God only**?

A179. God only being able

to search the hearts,

hear the requests,

pardon the sins,

and fulfill the desires of all;

and only to be believed in,

and worshipped with religious worship

prayer, which is a special part thereof,

is to be made by all to him alone,

and to none other.

The first matter the Larger Catechism covers is who should be the hearer of our prayer. As the answer clearly states, we are to pray "unto God only." Prayer, being the special part of worship that we should offer only to God, shares the same nature. There would be an object for both, and God alone deserves to be that object.

Roman Catholics taught otherwise, to pray to the Virgin Mary or priests, rather than to God Himself. For example, through the sacrament of penance or confession, a priest offers prayers on behalf of other believers. Though well intentioned (in order to relieve the fear in man), this does not rightly reflect the truth that prayer, being the special part of worship, must have the same object as worship, which God alone deserves.

One reason we should clarify this simple truth that God alone is the proper hearer of our prayer can be found in the attri-butes that belong to Him alone. These attributes are listed in the first part of this answer—that God alone is able to search the hearts, hear the requests, pardon the sins, and fulfill the desires of all. Indeed, who else can do all these things but God? This justifies why we should pray to Him alone!

Let's say there was a father and he told his son to ask him anything. Then, this beloved son went to the man next door and told him to go to his father and ask a favor on behalf of him. What nonsense! That we offer our prayer to God, who is our Father, is a crucial part in our understanding of prayer.

Another encouraging truth this particular answer teaches us is that our God, the sole hearer of our prayer, is indeed "able to fulfill the desires of all." Our God is incomparable. This not only justifies but also qualifies our God to be the sole hearer of our prayer.

Q180. What is it to pray **in the name of Christ**?

A180. To pray in the name of Christ is,

in obedience to his command,

and in confidence on his promises,

to ask mercy for his sake;

not by bare mentioning of his name,

but by drawing

our encouragement to pray,

and our boldness, strength,

and hope of acceptance in prayer,

from Christ and his mediation.

We end our prayer in the name of Christ. This particular question introduces the meaning of such a practice as to "ask mercy for his sake," and given the context we can assume that this refers to the mediating work of Christ. And the way to ask for this mediating work of Christ is to pray "in obedience to his command" and "in confidence on his promise."

Yes, we pray on the basis of the work of Christ, but this question does not stop merely by enlightening us with such a truth, but it gives a list of the concrete blessings we receive by praying in Christ's name: encouragement, boldness, strength and hope. These we can "draw" by praying in His name.

These blessings come as we pray, but at the same time we are able to pray because these blessings come from Christ. If God is really the One we have studied throughout this catechism, holy, utmost and whose glorious light is brighter than all the lights in the universe combined, then there is no way that sinners like us can approach Him on our own, without the mediating work of Christ.

2-2. IM

LARGER CATECHISM Q181

Q181. Why are we to pray **in the name of Christ**?

A181. The sinfulness of man, and his distance from God

by reason thereof, being so great,

as that we can have no access into his presence

without a mediator;

and there being none in heaven or earth

appointed to, or fit for,

that glorious work but Christ alone,

we are to pray in no other name but his only.

We are to pray in no other name but Jesus. Being lowly sinners, we cannot even approach God's throne without the mediator. And it is Christ alone who is both able and qualified to take this position for us. He is officially "appointed to" and "fit for" this ministry. No other one but Christ! Remind yourself of the Larger Catechism Q55 that introduced Christ's mediating work as the very driving force of the grace of redemption. Indeed, everything, even our existence, is meaningless without this mediating work of Christ.

3. BY

LARGER CATECHISM Q182

Q182. How doth **the Spirit help us** to pray?

A182. We not knowing what to pray for as we ought,

the Spirit helpeth our infirmities,

by enabling us

to understand both for whom, and what,

and how prayer is to be made;

and **by** working and quickening in our hearts

(although not in all persons, nor at all times, in the same measure)

those apprehensions, affections, and graces

which are requisite

for the right performance of that duty.

According to the above answer, the Spirit helps our prayer by enabling us to understand and by quickening a few things in our hearts. This enlightening work of Holy Spirit covers from "for whom" we pray to "for what" we pray, even "for how—in what way" we pray. How thorough and practical!

If you recall, the first part of the Shorter Catechism was about "what we need to believe" and this knowledge comes to us mainly through "revelation" in the form of wisdom. However, the second part, "what God requires us," is more about the effects this wisdom brings to our hearts and mobilizes our limbs. For that reason, we can expect more action-oriented answers in the second part of the catechism. The questions below, covering the questions of "for whom" "for what" and "how," can be of help. (Please see the Larger Catechism Q183-85 below.)

In the meantime, it is crucial for us to acknowledge that our prayer has to be offered "by the help of [God the] Spirit" in which He enlightens, convinces and equips us with gratitude and even plants obedient actions into our daily lives. From this, it becomes clear even our prayer is God's grace upon us. Grace comes through God alone, yet He in mysterious ways partners with us helping us draw His grace upon ourselves.

While attempting to fulfill God's requirements of us, we are bound to find ourselves lacking in many different things, to name a few as mentioned in the answer, "apprehensions, affections, and graces" which are required for the right performance of the duty given us. However, this answer assures us that the Spirit surely works and quickens in our hearts all of the above "although not in all persons, not at all times, in the same measure." (Q182) That should embolden and comforts us.

Discussion Questions

❶ What is prayer? Give the definition in your own words utilizing the three prepositions, unto, in and by.

❷ How is the prayer you learned from this chapter different than prayer as you used to think of it?

❸ Why do you think God requires us to pray?

❹ For whom, for what and how do you plan to pray today?

❺ Now take a moment and pray as you planned.

❻ In what sense does this chapter give us the reason to be grateful?

Almost there! Hang in there!

FOR WHOM, FOR WHAT, AND HOW?

LARGER CATECHISM Q183

For Whom?

Q183. **For whom** are we to pray?

A183. We are to pray
for the whole church of Christ upon earth;
for magistrates, and ministers;
for ourselves, our brethren, yea, our enemies;
and for all sorts of men living,
or that shall live hereafter;

but not for the dead,
nor for those that are known to have sinned the sin unto death.

LARGER CATECHISM Q184

For What?

Q184. **For what things** are we to pray?

A184. We are to pray
for all things tending to the glory of God,
the welfare of the church,
our own or others good;

but not for anything that is unlawful.

LARGER CATECHISM Q185

How?

Q185. **How** are we to pray?

A185. We are to pray
with an awful apprehension of the majesty of God,
and deep sense of our own unworthiness,
necessities, and sins;

with penitent, thankful, and enlarged hearts;

with understanding, faith, sincerity, fervency, love,
and perseverance, waiting upon him,

with humble submission to his will.

"DO WE HAVE TO SAY THE LORD'S PRAYER? IT IS NOT MY PRAYER."
"WHEN I HAVE BAD DREAMS AND FEEL OVERSTRESSED,
I FIND SAYING THE LORD'S PRAYER IS HELPFUL."
"I DON'T LIKE THE PART 'AS WE FORGIVE OUR DEBTORS.'
THERE THE PRAYER SOUNDS LIKE BUSINESS."

This chapter will teach us the Lord's prayer and at the same time bring the whole study of the Shorter Catechism to its end.

If the Apostles' Creed was about what we need to believe and the Ten Commandments about what we need to obey, then the Lord's Prayer is about what attitude we as believers need to have in this life.

We should not only pray but live out the Lord's Prayer. Not on our own, but by the power of God who 1) encourages us to pray, 2) listens to our prayer and 3) even empowers us to live as we have prayed. This is to live by faith!

Q99 — **WHAT RULE HATH GOD GIVEN FOR OUR DIRECTION IN PRAYER?**

- the whole word of God is of use to direct us in prayer
- but the special rule of direction is...
  - form of prayer which Christ taught his disciples,
  - commonly called the Lord's prayer

Q99 What rule hath God given for our direction in prayer?

A99 The whole word of God is of use to direct us in prayer;[1]
but the special rule of direction is
that form of prayer which Christ taught his disciples,
commonly called The Lord's prayer.[2,3]

1.
1 John 5:14

And this is the confidence that we have in him, that, if we **ask any thing according to his will,** he heareth us.

2.
Matthew 6:9-18

After this manner therefore pray ye: Our Father which art in heaven, Hallowed be thy name. Thy kingdom come. Thy will be done in earth, as it is in heaven. Give us this day our daily bread. And forgive us our debts, as we forgive our debtors. And lead us not into temptation, but deliver us from evil: For thine is the kingdom, and the power, and the glory, for ever. Amen. For if ye forgive men their trespasses, your heavenly Father will also forgive you: But if ye forgive not men their trespasses, neither will your Father forgive your trespasses. Moreover when ye fast, be not, as the hypocrites, of a sad countenance: for they disfigure their faces, that they may appear unto men to fast. Verily I say unto you, They have their reward. But thou, when thou fastest, anoint thine head, and wash thy face; That thou appear not unto men to fast, but unto thy Father which is in secret: and thy Father, which seeth in secret, shall reward thee openly. **Compared with Luke 11:2-4.**

3.
Luke 11:2-4

And he said unto them, **When ye pray,** say, Our Father which art in heaven, Hallowed be thy name. Thy kingdom come. Thy will be done, as in heaven, so in earth. Give us day by day our daily bread. And forgive us our sins; for we also forgive every one that is indebted to us. And lead us not into temptation; but deliver us from evil.

From Q99 to Q107, we will be learning the detailed rules in prayer. The lessons will be given through line by line analysis of the Lord's Prayer, which is the gift of God for the direction in prayer. The truth is the whole word of God can be of guidance in our prayer, but Christ gave His disciples special guidance in the form of prayer, saying "This is how you should pray". (Matt 6:9-13, Luke 11:2-4) This prayer is usually called "the Lord's Prayer."

This reminds us of God's kindness. By giving us prayer as the means of grace and knowing our infirmities, he provided this guidance for prayer. We should use this generous gift of God with proper understanding, faith and reverence.

Let's look at the structure of the Lord's Prayer first.

As you can see in the table below, the Lord's Prayer can be divided into three parts: preface, petitions, and conclusion. Again the petitions can be divided into two and each petition into three. The possible uses of this prayer is two as shown below. (See the Larger Catechism Q187)

1. As a pattern for other prayers
2. As a prayer itself

MEANS OF GRACE

Word Sacraments Prayer

A PREFACE	●	Our Father, which art in heaven,
PETITIONS — God's glory and His will we should seek	● First	Hallowed be thy Name.
	● Second	Thy Kingdom come.
	● Third	Thy will be done in earth, As it is in heaven.
Things we should seek for our own sake	● Fourth	Give us this day our daily bread.
	● Fifth	And forgive us our trespasses, As we forgive them that trespass against us.
	● Sixth	And lead us not into temptation, But deliver us from evil.
A CONCLUSION	●	For thine is the kingdom, the power, and the glory, For ever and ever. Amen.

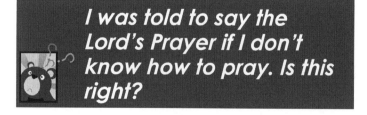

I was told to say the Lord's Prayer if I don't know how to pray. Is this right?

Yes and no. Saying this prayer, we can be surely blessed with God's grace bestowed upon us. And if anyone does not know where to begin regarding his prayer, then the Lord's Prayer can be a great start. However, simply saying the words without any comprehension of their meaning (from rote memory) is useless and a misuse of this great gift.

Q100 THE PREFACE OF THE LORD'S PRAYER

- **to draw near to God**
  - with all holy reverence and confidence
  - as children to a father, able and ready to help us
- **we should pray**
  - with others
  - for others

Q100 What doth the preface of the Lord's prayer teach us?

A100 The preface of the Lord's prayer
(which is, Our Father which art in heaven[1])
teacheth us
to draw near to God
with all holy reverence and confidence,
as children to a father, able and ready to help us;[2, 3]
and that we should pray with and for others.[4, 5]

1.
Matthew 6:9

After this manner therefore pray ye: Our Father which art in heaven, Hallowed be thy name.

2.
Romans 8:15

For ye have not received the spirit of bondage again to fear; but ye have received the Spirit of adoption, whereby **we cry, Abba, Father.**

3.
Luke 11:13

If ye then, being evil, know how to give good gifts unto your children; **how much more shall your heavenly Father** give the Holy Spirit to them that ask him?

4.
Acts 12:5

Peter therefore was kept in prison; but **prayer was made** without ceasing of the church unto God **for him.**

5.
1 Timothy 2:1-2

I exhort therefore, that, first of all, **supplications, prayers, intercessions,** and giving of thanks, be made for all men; **For kings, and for all that are in authority;** that we may lead a quiet and peaceable life in all godliness and honesty.

We have learned in the previous chapter for whom, for what, and how we should pray. The Lord's Prayer, which we are about to delve into, can be the model of such prayer reflecting these principles.

PREFACE OF THE LORD'S PRAYER: OUR FATHER WHICH ART IN HEAVEN

The most important teaching in this preface is: God, being our Father, loves us as a father loves his child. The way He assures us of His fatherly love for us is through enabling us to call Him our Father.

Can our sin ever sever the relationship we have with our heavenly Father? No, even the earthly father-son relationship does not work that way. When we fall or keep on running from and against His will, does His patience ever run out letting us go suffer the consequences of our sins? No, His love and care for us endures till the end. When our rebellions keep on going, what He as our Father does is not to abandon us but to discipline us. This discipline may not appear as something we should be grateful for at the moment, but finding God's love undergirding it, we should be.

Essentially speaking, this gratitude should be our attitude for all things God does for us. The God of Christianity is not a deistic one (who is believed to be merely the Creator without having any personal relationship with His creatures), but the loving Father (who lives with His children and works for their best through everything He does for them in this world.)

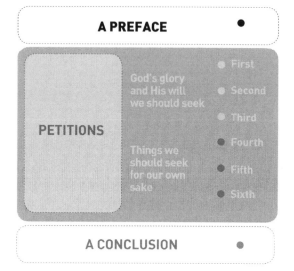

☑ Why does the prayer use the pronouns "Our" and "We"? It is to emphasize that we are to pray with and for others. God wants us to be aware that, having Him as our Father, we have many brothers and sisters in Him and we are to take good care of each other.

☑ The expression of "for others" repeatedly appears from the preface to the second petition. We will be looking at its meaning in more detail in the second petition.

☑ Is God really in heaven? Where is this heaven, in the atmosphere or out in the universe? Because God's presence fills the earth and He is omnipresent, there is no reason to name a particular place of His dwelling. Yet for the expression of His glory and infinite power, heaven is used here for His dwelling place.

☑ Then what can I do in practical terms? Why don't you start by the pledges you made as you studied the first to fourth commandments? Re-writing your pledges can be helpful.

* It may be effective to have the Larger Catechism alongside to read the corresponding questions as you study this portion on the Lord's Prayer through the Shorter Catechism.

LARGER CATECHISM Q189

Q189. What doth the preface of the Lord's Prayer teach us?

A189. The preface of the Lord's Prayer
(contained in these words, *Our Father which art in heaven,*) teacheth us,

when we pray,
to draw near to God

with confidence of his fatherly goodness,
and our interest therein;

with reverence,
and all other childlike dispositions,
heavenly affections,
and due apprehensions

of his sovereign power, majesty,
and gracious condescension:

as also, to pray

with and for others.

CONCLUSION

Key teachings

1. Despite Who He is, the Creator, God allows us to call Him our Father. What undergirds such kindness of His is His love for us.

2. His love is complete and both our body and soul remain in His care.

3. It is through the Lord's Prayer that God teaches us this simple truth, and the prayer also guards us from arrogance as in humility we offer up our desires.

Q101 — **IN THE FIRST PETITION WE PRAY THAT**

- **God would enable us and others to glorify him** ---- God would enable us and others to glorify him
- **he would dispose all things to his own glory**

Q101 What do we pray for in the first petition?

A101 In the first petition (which is, Hallowed be thy name[1]) we pray,
That God would enable us and others to glorify him
in all that whereby he maketh himself known;[2]
and that he would dispose all things to his own glory.[3]

1.
Matthew 6:9

After this manner therefore pray ye: Our Father which art in heaven, Hallowed be thy name.

2.
Psalm 67:2-3

That thy way may be known upon earth, thy saving health among all nations. **Let the people praise thee, O God; let all the people praise thee.**

3.
Psalm 83

Keep not thou silence, O God: hold not thy peace, and be not still, O God. For, lo, thine enemies make a tumult: and they that hate thee have lifted up the head. They have taken crafty counsel against thy people, and consulted against thy hidden ones. They have said, Come, and let us cut them off from being a nation; that the name of Israel may be no more in remembrance. For they have consulted together with one consent: they are confederate against thee: The tabernacles of Edom, and the Ishmaelites; of Moab, and the Hagarenes; Gebal, and Ammon, and Amalek; the Philistines with the inhabitants of Tyre; Assur also is joined with them: they have holpen the children of Lot. Selah. Do unto them as unto the Midianites; as to Sisera, as to Jabin, at the brook of Kison: Which perished at Endor: they became as dung for the earth. Make their nobles like Oreb, and like Zeeb: yea, all their princes as Zebah, and as Zalmunna: Who said, Let us take to ourselves the houses of God in possession. O my God, make them like a wheel; as the stubble before the wind. As the fire burneth a wood, and as the flame setteth the mountains on fire; So persecute them with thy tempest, and make them afraid with thy storm. Fill their faces with shame; that they may seek thy name, O Lord. Let them be confounded and troubled for ever; yea, let them be put to shame, and perish: 18 That men may know that thou, whose name alone is JEHOVAH, art the most high over all the earth.

- Satan's kingdom may be destroyed
- **the kingdom of grace may be advanced** ----ourselves and others brought into it, and kept in it
- **the kingdom of glory may be hastened**

Q102 What do we pray for in the second petition?

A102 In the second petition (which is, Thy kingdom come[1]) we pray,
That Satan's kingdom may be destroyed;[2]
and that the kingdom of grace may be advanced,[3]
ourselves and others brought into it, and kept, in it;[4, 5, 6]
and that the kingdom of glory may be hastened.[7]

1.
Matthew 6:10

Thy kingdom come. Thy will be done in earth, as it is in heaven.

2.
Psalm 68:1, 18

Let God arise, **let his enemies be scattered: let them also that hate him flee before him**......Thou hast ascended on high, **thou hast led captivity captive:** thou hast received gifts for men; yea, for the rebellious also, that the Lord God might dwell among them.

3.
Revelation 12:10-11

And I heard a loud voice saying in heaven, **Now is come** salvation, and strength, and **the kingdom of our God,** and the power of his Christ: for the accuser of our brethren is cast down, which accused them before our God day and night. And they overcame him by the blood of the Lamb, and by the word of their testimony; and they loved not their lives unto the death.

4.
2 Thessalonians 3:1

Finally, brethren, **pray for us, that the word of the Lord may have free course,** and be glorified, even as it is with you.

5.
Romans 10:1

Brethren, my heart's desire and **prayer to God** for Israel is, that **they might be saved.**

6.
John 17: 9, 20

I pray for them: I pray not for the world, but for them which thou hast given me; for they are thine......**Neither pray I for these alone, but for them also which shall believe** on me through their word.

7.
Revelation 22:20

He which testifieth these things saith, Surely I come quickly. Amen. Even so, **come, Lord Jesus.**

- by his grace
- God would make us
  - able
  - willing
    - to know, obey, and submit to his will
    - in all things
    - as the angels do in heaven

Q103 What do we pray for in the third petition?

A103 In the third petition (which is, Thy will be done in earth, as it is in heaven[1]) we pray,

That God, by his grace,

would make us able and willing

to know, obey, and submit to his will

in all things,[2, 3, 4, 5, 6]

as the angels do in heaven.[7]

1.
Matthew 6:10

Thy kingdom come. Thy will be done in earth, as it is in heaven.

2.
Psalm 67

God be merciful unto us, and bless us; and cause his face to shine upon us; Selah. That thy way may be known upon earth, thy saving health among all nations. Let the people praise thee, O God; let all the people praise thee. O let the nations be glad and sing for joy: for thou shalt judge the people righteously, and govern the nations upon earth. Selah. Let the people praise thee, O God; let all the people praise thee. Then shall the earth yield her increase; and God, even our own God, shall bless us. God shall bless us; and all the ends of the earth shall fear him.

3.
Psalm 119:36

Incline my heart unto thy testimonies, and not to covetousness.

4.
Matthew 26:39

And he went a little further, and fell on his face, and prayed, saying, O my Father, if it be possible, let this cup pass from me: **nevertheless, not as I will, but as thou wilt.**

5.
2 Samuel 15:25

And the king said unto Zadok, Carry back the ark of God into the city; **if I shall find favour in the eyes of the Lord,** he will bring me again, and shew me both it, and his habitation.

6.
Job 1:21

And (Job) said, Naked came I out of my mother's womb, and naked shall I return thither: **the Lord gave, and the Lord hath taken away; blessed be the name of the Lord.**

7.
Psalm 103:20-21

Bless the Lord, ye his angels, that excel in strength, that do his commandments, **hearkening unto the voice of his word.** Bless ye the Lord, all ye his hosts; **ye ministers of his, that do his pleasure.**

FIRST HALF: GOD'S GLORY AND WILL

The first three petitions in the Lord's Prayer are about God's glory and will, and we might wonder whether these petitions have anything to do with our daily lives. Isn't prayer for offering up "my" desires?

FIRST PETITION:
the meaning of "Hallowed be thy name"

This petition (Q101) reminds us of the very first question (Q1) of the Shorter Catechism and also the opening question of Part 2 (Q39).

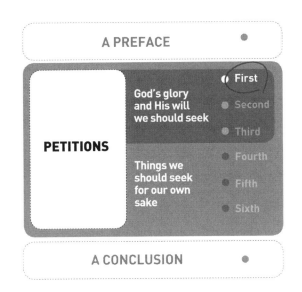

As you remember, the first question of the Shorter Catechism is "what is the chief end of man?" The answer offered to the question is "to glorify God and to enjoy Him forever." There is no way to overemphasize this simple statement, given the weight and scope of its application.

There should only be two answers to this question, no matter how big a population is or how many various expressions may exist: To live for my own happiness (Here God's blessings can be helpful) vs. To glorify God and enjoy Him forever.

Between these two, to which do you feel more inclined? Or are you wondering why it has to be an either-or type of question?

The reality is even many Christians live as if the former was the chief end of their lives, pursuing their own happiness. Yet being so-called Christians, they believe that they need God's blessing for such a life, so they constantly utilize various religious practices to draw God's blessings upon themselves. Living just like pagans, many so-called Christians pursue their own happiness over God's glory justifying themselves saying God wants their happiness too.

Yet the Bible teaches we are to live in the latter way, to glorify God. Such a life is only possible if we come to acknowledge that we are not the center of universe, rather God is, and we are merely the "means" to His glory. The Bible even encourages us to enjoy such a life before God!

The greatest and most important turning point in our lives comes when we become able to (at least willing to) offer the latter as our answer to the question, what is the chief end of our lives? Only then, can we escape the miseries this life is destined to bring upon us.

Let us say that we are lucky enough to accomplish all that we ever desired. How much would that be worth in the end? If we could evaluate our lives in a truly objective way, then we would be able to admit God is leveraging all—both providing the things we desire and trying to avert at all cost even death itself—for a certain purpose, which is to make us believers whose lives glorify God.

This is the core teaching delivered through the first petition of the Lord's Prayer— that we are to pray first and foremost for God's name, not for our needs. *"So whether you eat or drink or whatever you do, do it all for the glory of God." (1 Cor 10:31)*

"Please go ahead and read the first question of the Catechism of the Catholic Church. You may be surprised."

[Review] What does a God-glorifying life look like?

This question was the main subject of Part 1, but now having learned about it even more in Part 2, let us try to turn our thoughts to it once again.

Unlike other gods, being true and living, our God does not require of us mere "practices" but a life lived out for Him. More than any other seemingly holy practices, our life is the worship we offer before God. We go to school, work and make friends. We repeat on a daily basis eating, resting and sleeping. Yet even these seemingly mundane and trivial activities are being used by God to unfold His glorious plan for each and every one of us, which is to make us believers whose lives glorify God alone. Without this plan of God, our lives cannot stand before God, let alone offer the proper worship before Him. It seems that we are merely encouraged to offer this prayer without attaching much meaning to it, but this simple petition reminds us of the purpose of our lives and the ultimate plan of God.

If only we came to see our lives this way, we would be grateful for everything. We would come to offer to live such a life as our prayer, and do so out of sincere love and admiration for such a life. Only then would our obedience naturally follow as well.

Q102 **WHAT WE PRAY FOR IN THE SECOND PETITION**

SECOND PETITION:
the meaning of "Thy kingdom come"

The second petition is also not about "me" but God's kingdom. But what is God's kingdom? Is it someplace that we are currently living in or eagerly waiting to advance to? God's kingdom is not found in any extraordinary phenomenon. Neither does it refer to a place we enter into after death nor to a point in time when the gospel is preached to the end and people in all nations are evangelized. The essence of God's kingdom is found in the presence of His rule. God's kingdom comes when God rules over His people through His spirit, His people obey His words, and His mercy and goodness are revealed in the lives of His people.

A PREFACE

God's glory and His will we should seek — First, Second, Third

PETITIONS

Things we should seek for our own sake — Fourth, Fifth, Sixth

A CONCLUSION

For some Christians, heaven is an escape place to which they expect to flee from all the unfavorable and uncomfortable situations of this world. Metaphors we use to describe heaven encourage such an idea: made of precious jewels, having golden palaces and a sea of glass, and devoid of any pains, tears and death. However, it is God's presence and His rule that makes heaven heaven, not the things mentioned above. What we should look with expectation **to experience in heaven is living in God, following His rules and laws!**

In Luke 15:11-32 we find a well-known story where a wayward son comes back home after squandering all the wealth he inherited from his father, and his father throws a great welcoming party even killing a fattened calf for this son. Feeling unappreciated, the elder son complains to the father, and the father's response is "you are always with me." This response of the father must have been unexpected on the elder son's end, but at the same time, it could have been mind blowing. What is the greatest blessing for us as children? To be with the father. To be with God. As we pray this second petition, "Thy kingdom come," we should examine our hearts so that we may desire God, His presence and rule above all.

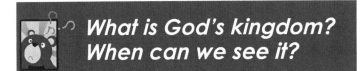

Essentially speaking, God's kingdom is where God's people live in Him. Thus, it can be here with us, and the truth is that it has "already" come among us. At the same time, it has not "yet" come in its fullness, but when it comes in its fullness, God's kingdom will be made clear to all.

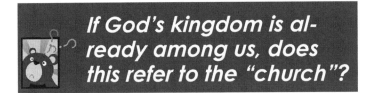

Despite the reality, the church IS where God's kingdom is most effectively revealed. However, the existence of God's Kingdom is just as effective wherever His people submit to His rule as the church.

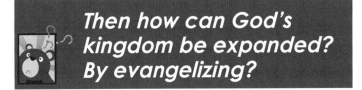

The greater number of believers who follow God's will living as the light and the salt of this world, the further God's kingdom is expanded. However, it must be pointed out that we are not the ones who expand it but God is. We are only to continue to live as the light and salt, share the Word as chances are given, and serve and pray for our neighbor.

On a side note, this question does encourage us to evangelize: "that the kingdom of grace may be advanced, ourselves and others brought into it, and kept, in it." (2 Thess 3:1, Rom 10:1, John 17:9, 20) The doctrine of election and probation does not go against evangelism. Rather, we are told here to pray, to reach out to and to win more souls.

Q103 | **WHAT WE PRAY FOR IN THE THIRD PETITION**

THIRD PETITION: the meaning of "Thy will be done on earth, as it is in heaven"

Does this petition sound like "God, Your will is never done on this earth. Let me pray for THAT now"? Absolutely not. It is true that we are surrounded by many problems of evil in this world and feel for Habakkuk who prayed in great frustration about the success and prosperity of evil people.

However, God's will is being both faithfully and thoroughly accomplished. As mentioned in the Heidelberg Catechism Q1, without the will of God, not even a hair can fall from our heads. Even Satan cannot do anything apart from God's approval. In reality we may be surrounded by those who are openly against God and it seems they are out of God's jurisdiction, but without even knowing it, they are actually contributing to God's work in this world. For God utilizes their (even Satan's) every attempt to impede His will as the means to achieve His will. Thus this petition should focus more on our hearts. "May our hearts be made more like God's and delight in His will so much that we no longer grudgingly submit to Him and His will!"

His will to be done on this earth as is in heaven is **"us" being made "holy and pure."** The object of our love, stated in the Bible, is clear. We are to love God alone (He should be the sole object our love) and He loves us, His chosen people (We are the sole object of His love). God's will is stipulated through the Moral Law, which unfortunately we cannot keep to its perfection, yet God with His good purpose for us will never stop doing His work for us.

Thus, we should pray "Thy will be done on earth" as continuing to conquer our sinful nature with God's Word and make us submit to Him. Indeed, this is the most timely and critical prayer we need to offer!

Object of God's love	→	His chosen people
God's will	→	Us being made holy and pure

Reference Material

It is easily assumed that should we pray the prayer of "Thy kingdom come" we are asking for power and strength enough to advance God's kingdom on His behalf. However, the Larger Catechism puts this idea on hold by offering the following in answer to the second petition. This prayer is rather to "acknowledge ourselves and all mankind to be by nature under the dominion of sin and Satan, [thus] we pray, that the kingdom of sin and Satan may be destroyed...; that the church stands firm in the confidence in God's sovereignty over this world as dispensing God-given ordinances, purging from corruption, and continually desiring Christ's reign over our hearts." The Heidelberg Catechism echoes the same idea as defining this petition as to ask God to "Rule us by your Word and Spirit in such a way that more and more we submit to you!"(Q191)

Also regarding the third petition "Thy will be done" the answer is given as "by nature we and all men are not only utterly un-

able and unwilling to know and do the will of God ... [Thus] we pray, that God would by his Spirit take away from ourselves and others all blindness, weakness...; and by his grace make us able and willing to know, do, and submit to his will in all things." (The Larger Catechism Q192) The Heidelberg Catechism is not far from this idea: "Help us and all people to reject our own wills and to obey your will without any back talk. Your will alone is good." (Q124)

Beauty is in the eyes of beholder, indeed. All catechisms put God at the center, being all about Him—His sovereignty, His power, His grace and His zeal. Depending on the perspective we choose to see the world, everything can and will look as different as day and night. We should be deeply grateful that we are blessed with these historic documents that are surely revolving around God alone, for these offer a great reminder for us who live in a constantly changing world.

- of God's free gift we may receive ----- a competent portion of the good things of this life

- of God's free gift (we may) enjoy ----- his blessing with them

Q104 What do we pray for in the fourth petition?

A104 In the fourth petition (which is, Give us this day our daily bread[1]) we pray,

That of God's free gift

we may receive

a competent portion of the good things of this life,

and enjoy

his blessing with them.[2, 3, 4]

1.
Matthew 6:11

Give us this day our daily bread.

2.
Proverbs 30:8-9

Remove far from me vanity and lies: give me neither poverty nor riches; **feed me with food convenient for me:** Lest I be full, and deny thee, and say, Who is the Lord? or lest I be poor, and steal, and take the name of my God in vain.

3.
Genesis 28:20

And Jacob vowed a vow, saying, If God will be with me, and will keep me in this way that I go, and **will give me bread to eat, and raiment to put on.**

4.
1 Timothy 4:4-5

For every creature of God is good, and nothing to be refused, if it be received with thanksgiving: For **it is sanctified by** the word of God and **prayer.**

Be content!

- God would freely pardon all our sins ----- for Christ's sake
- we are the rather encouraged to ask
  - Because by his grace
  - we are enabled from the heart to forgive others

Q105 What do we pray for in the fifth petition?

A105 In the fifth petition (which is, And forgive us our debts, as we forgive our debtors[1]) we pray,

That God, for Christ's sake,

would freely pardon all our sins;[2, 3]

which we are the rather encouraged to ask,

because by his grace

we are enabled from the heart to forgive others.[4, 5]

1.
Matthew 6:12

And forgive us our debts, as we forgive our debtors.

2.
Psalm 51:1-2, 7, 9

Have mercy upon me, O God, according to thy loving-kindness; according unto the multitude of thy tender mercies **blot out my transgressions. Wash me throughly from mine iniquity, and cleanse me from my sin......Purge me** with hyssop, and I shall be clean; **wash me,** and I shall be whiter than snow......**Hide thy face from my sins, and blot out all mine iniquities.**

3.
Daniel 9:17-19

Now therefore, O our God, hear the prayer of thy servant, and his supplications, and cause thy face to shine upon thy sanctuary that is desolate, for the Lord's sake. O my God, incline thine ear, and hear; open thine eyes, and behold our desolations, and the city which is called by thy name: for we do not present our supplications before thee for our righteousnesses, but for thy great mercies. **O Lord, hear; O Lord, forgive;** O Lord, hearken and do; defer not, **for thine own sake, O my God:** for thy city and thy people are called by thy name.

4.
Luke 11:4

And forgive us our sins; **for we also forgive every one that is indebted to us.** And lead us not into temptation; but deliver us from evil.

5.
Matthew 18:35

So likewise shall my heavenly Father do also unto you, **if ye from your hearts forgive not every one his brother their trespasses.**

God would either — keep us from being tempted to sin
or support and deliver us when we are tempted

Q106 What do we pray for in the sixth petition?

A106 In the sixth petition

(which is, And lead us not into temptation, but deliver us from evil[1]) we pray,

That God would

either keep us from being tempted to sin,[2]

or support and deliver us when we are tempted.[3]

1.
Matthew 6:13

And lead us not into temptation, but deliver us from evil: For thine is the kingdom, and the power, and the glory, for ever. Amen.

2.
Matthew 26:41

Watch and **pray, that ye enter not into temptation:** the spirit indeed is willing, but the flesh is weak.

3.
2 Corinthians 12:7-8

And lest I should be exalted above measure through the abundance of the revelations, there was given to me a thorn in the flesh, the messenger of Satan to buffet me, lest I should be exalted above measure. **For this thing I besought the Lord** thrice, that it might depart from me.

SECOND HALF: A GOD PLEASING LIFE

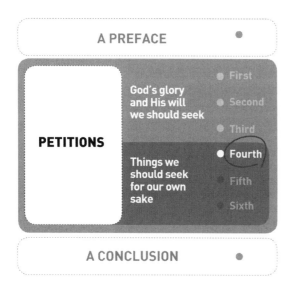

A PREFACE

PETITIONS

God's glory and His will we should seek
- First
- Second
- Third

Things we should seek for our own sake
- Fourth
- Fifth
- Sixth

A CONCLUSION

Moving down to the second half of the Lord's Prayer, we can see the focus is now shifting to ourselves as it teaches the prac-tical ways to please God in our lives. Let us look at the three petitions in the second half of the Lord's Prayer.

Food represents what is needed for—even essential to—both believers and nonbelievers. It is not like only believers need to pray for and receive God's gift. All creatures on this earth, even the underground or undersea animals, live by solar energy. The fact they neither see nor experience the daylight does not change that fact. God is telling us to remember that He is the giver of life itself and encourages us to constantly acknowledge and rely on Him.

Come to think about it, we are in no position for demanding anything from God. God is not obligated to give any blessings to anyone. For this reason, whether His giving appears to us as good or bad, sufficient or lacking, we should be grateful and content. Also rather than being greedy, we should think of those in need as well.

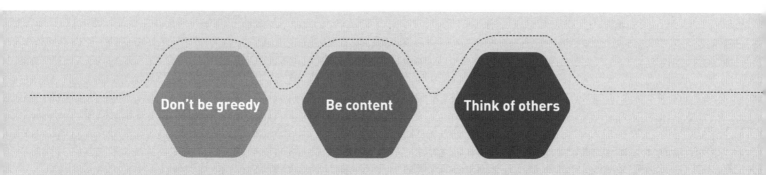

Don't be greedy   Be content   Think of others

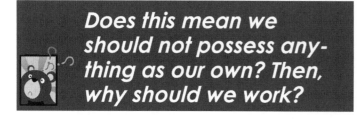

Does this mean we should not possess any-thing as our own? Then, why should we work?

We are to ask for "daily" bread. Then should we not save or invest?

Because we are to ask God to give us our daily bread, what is the point of working? We can just pray. However, God's mes-sage given through the Bible is very clear (see 2 Thess 3:10 and Gen 3:19) that it does not leave any room for such an error.

Yes, we should, for we are to provide help and support to both those in need and society as a whole. Also we are obligated to give our best efforts to holy desires in us to sustain our lives, pursue excellence in service, share with neighbors and glorify God. For these, property management is necessary.

This petition first and foremost calls us to see what we are like—pots with their own blackness yet calling other kettles black—and where we are—deep in our own debts to the Savior of our lives. Out of this candid self-diagnosis, we should be able 1) to come before God only with humility and gratitude for His eternal forgiveness and 2) with willingness to treat others with nothing less than how the Father treated us in His Son.

We don't like to forgive those who have wronged us. Even when we do, we do so only reluctantly. Such disobedience is in many cases rationalized due to our human weakness. Yet believers, who had been forgiven once and for all by the blood of our Savior Jesus, are called to live set apart in a way in which they hate sin and do so aggressively.

Yet it must be noted that this petition does not mean God holds back His forgiveness until we forgive others who wronged us. If so, God's forgiveness becomes a reward that we should earn through the practice of forgiveness. Instead, this petition reminds us of what is only proper for those who have received God's great grace.

When the forgiven debtor of ten thousand bags of gold refused to forgive another debtor merely of a hundred silver coins, those at the scene must have rolled their eyes with unbelief at the mercilessness of this forgiven debtor of ten thousand bags of gold. (Matt 18:21-35) This particular petition must be understood in such a context—that we were forgiven of such a great debt nothing we do for others on this earth is able to be called forgiveness on our end.

"How many times shall I forgive my brother or sister who sins against me? Up to seven times?" At such a question of Peter, Jesus answered "Not seven times, but seventy-seven times." This golden rule has not changed over time; we are to remember the forgiveness offered in grace and do so to others. (Matt 18:21-22)

A PREFACE

PETITIONS

God's glory and His will we should seek

First

Second

Third

Things we should seek for our own sake

Fourth

Fifth

Sixth

A CONCLUSION

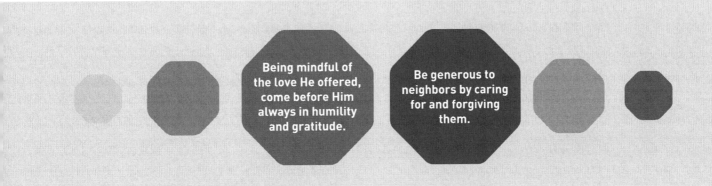

Being mindful of the love He offered, come before Him always in humility and gratitude.

Be generous to neighbors by caring for and forgiving them.

SIXTH PETITION: THE MEANING OF "Lead us not into temptation, but deliver us from evil."

Everyone has had their fair share of falling into temptation, which makes the following a fair question for all of us. Then, at moments like these, what should we do?

God permits temptations only within His love for us. (Part 1, p. 185) In Job's situation (see Job 1:9-11), we can find a couple of parties contributing to the temptations into which Job has been led. The Sabeans might have attacked him only to fatten their bellies, and Satan acted with his own purpose and conviction to have Job eventually betray God. Yet being held in God's loving hands, this temptation was utilized to enable Job to possess an ever greater faith than before. Man may work hard, and so may Satan to bring us trouble. But as far as the purpose and means of those labors go, God's sovereign hand always trumps and remains in charge. This is the first and foremost fact that every believer who might have been led into temptations should acknowledge.

Another question worth pondering pertaining to the matter is that temptation could come in many unexpected ways. Temptations may come both through difficulty/trial and wealth/prosperity. The temptations for Job and Solomon appear just the opposite (for Job difficulties and trials were used but for Solomon it was wealth and prosperity), yet both share the same purpose on Satan's end, to sever our souls from God. Satan never cares about our earthly bodies and lives. When a person suffers in earthly needs greatly enough and long enough, his soul can grow bitter and become alienated from God, but the opposite way (earthly wealth and prosperity) works just as effectively to distract a person from the Provider of all.

However, mere knowledge of Satan's intention does not empower us with the ability to overcome it. No one is equipped to perfectly overcome temptation on his own. Rather, man is prone to love sin, follow Satan's lead to temptation and eventually jeopardize his eternal life. It makes a huge difference to acknowledge our human weakness.

What we must do in the days of trouble is not to find ways to overcome temptation on our own but to "take refuge in God." At the same time, we should ask for His mercy to be with us so as not to make us fall into the same temptation again and to enlighten us with the will of God through it all.

What believers should avoid is not poverty, misfortune and difficulty, but sin. According to the Shorter Catechism Q14, sin is any lack of God's standard and any breaking of God's law. This simple definition removes all the excuses that we use to sugarcoat our sins. I only sinned because I had no choice. I did so only reluctantly. Would this be good enough to justify us before God? No, for sin is never a matter of degree (or how far we have restrained ourselves from sinning) but the principle we hold.

We are given a completely different set of principles to live by. Unlike many who choose to do evil in order to avoid poverty, misfortune and difficulty, we should rather choose these in case

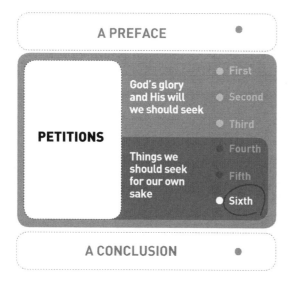

they are the very things that lead us into temptation and make us sin. Even in times of being hungry, naked, destitute, robbed, defamed and abandoned, even at the risk of losing our lives, we must be able to confess, "Lord, my soul finds its home in You!"

Yet this petition closes itself with "But deliver us from evil," reminding us of how prone we are to compromise even with the knowledge of all that is mentioned above, and for this reason, this petition makes the perfect final and desperate plea before God.

> We must use discerning wisdom to choose books only about positive and optimistic thinking!

> That's right

Keep us from being tempted to sin

Support and deliver us when we are tempted

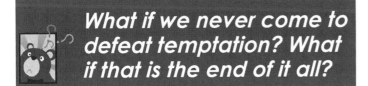

What if we never come to defeat temptation? What if that is the end of it all?

God is our Father and He permits temptation only as the correcting rod and staff. The deeper our pride and corruption is, the stronger the discipline has to be. Yet coming out of Fatherly love, God's rod and staff is never meant to end or destroy us. In Him, we are more than conquerors. (Rom 8:37-39) Even at moments of being tempted, we are as safe as the chicks under their mother's wing!

THE CONCLUSION OF THE THREE PETITIONS IN THE LATTER HALF

Directions about how we are to live our lives

This precious prayer is not given to us to ask whatever we want. These three petitions teach us what we are to ask while we live our lives on this earth. Now what is left for us is to diligently practice and actually live out what we have learned, assuring ourselves of the undergirding truth that God loves and takes care of His children.

Through the Lord's Prayer, we have covered six petitions in total. Are these six petitions enough? Are there any other things we should add to the list for our lives on this earth? The answer should be "Yes, these six are enough. Thus, no, we should not add any other things to the list." And such confidence comes from the divinity of the Teacher of this prayer. The One who is able to listen to and help us taught us this prayer. We are now only to follow the prayer in humility and gratitude.

- to take our encouragement in prayer from God only
- in our prayers to praise him ----- ascribing kingdom, power and glory to him
- we say, Amen -----
  - in testimony of our desire
  - and assurance to be heard

Q107 What doth the conclusion of the Lord's prayer teach us?

A107 The conclusion of the Lord's prayer

(which is, For thine is the kingdom, and the power, and the glory, for ever, Amen.[1])

teacheth us to take our encouragement

in prayer from God only,[2]

and in our prayers to praise him,

ascribing kingdom, power and glory to him.[3]

And, in testimony of our desire, and assurance to be heard, we say, Amen.[4,5]

1.
Matthew 6:13

And lead us not into temptation, but deliver us from evil: For thine is the kingdom, and the power, and the glory, for ever. Amen.

2.
Dan. 9:4, 7-9, 16-19

And I prayed unto the Lord my God, and made my confession, and said, O Lord, the great and dreadful God, keeping the covenant and mercy to them that love him, and to them that keep his commandments.....O Lord, righteousness belongeth unto thee, but unto us confusion of faces, as at this day; to the men of Judah, and to the inhabitants of Jerusalem, and unto all Israel, that are near, and that are far off, through all the countries whither thou hast driven them, because of their trespass that they have trespassed against thee. O Lord, to us belongeth confusion of face, to our kings, to our princes, and to our fathers, because we have sinned against thee. **To the Lord our God belong mercies and forgivenesses,** though we have rebelled against him......**O Lord, according to all thy righteousness,** I beseech thee, let thine anger and thy fury be turned away from thy city Jerusalem, thy holy mountain: because for our sins, and for the iniquities of our fathers, Jerusalem and thy people are become a reproach to all that are about us. Now therefore, O our God, hear the prayer of thy servant, and his supplications, and cause thy face to shine upon thy sanctuary that is desolate, **for the Lord's sake.** O my God, incline thine ear, and hear; open thine eyes, and behold our desolations, and the city which is called by thy name: for **we do not present our supplications** before thee for our righteousnesses, **but for thy great mercies.** O Lord, hear; O Lord, forgive; O Lord, hearken and do; **defer not, for thine own sake,** O my God: for thy city and thy people are called by thy name.

3.
1 Chronicles 29:10-13

Wherefore David blessed the Lord before all the congregation: and David said, Blessed be thou, Lord God of Israel our father, for ever and ever. **Thine, O Lord, is the greatness, and the power, and the glory, and the victory, and the majesty:** for all that is in the heaven and in the earth is thine; thine is the kingdom, O Lord, and thou art exalted as head above all. Both riches and honour come of thee, and thou reignest over all; **and in thine hand is power and might;** and in thine hand it is to make great, and to give strength unto all. Now therefore, our God, we thank thee, and praise thy glorious name.

4.
1 Corinthians 14:16

Else, when thou shalt bless with the spirit, how shall he that occupieth the room of the unlearned **say Amen** at thy giving of thanks, seeing he understandeth not what thou sayest?

5.
Revelation 22:20-21

He which testifieth these things saith, Surely I come quickly: **Amen.** Even so, come, Lord Jesus. The grace of our Lord Jesus Christ be with you all. **Amen.**

The Lord's Prayer can bring us frustration, especially when we struggle to live out what we have learned through the petitions in the Lord's Prayer, because the actual changes in our hearts and lives can come slowly (or seemingly never). "Enough is enough. This kind of prayer never works." Some may wish to give it up all together, and to those, this particular conclusion seems to shout "Not just yet!"

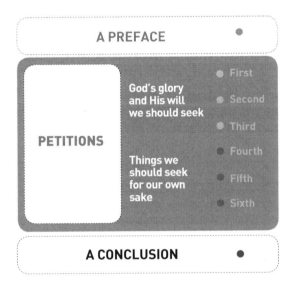

A PREFACE

PETITIONS

God's glory and His will we should seek

First
Second
Third

Things we should seek for our own sake

Fourth
Fifth
Sixth

A CONCLUSION

The conclusion of the Lord's Prayer is here to help us acknowledge and admit that 1) it is the almighty God who is always with us, 2) this God should be praised among all of us and 3) our entire being must agree to this Who-He-is with a loud Amen. And without such a conclusion, an Amen in faith, we won't be walking in a truly blessed life in God.

We should not be frustrated as we fall short of doing the will of God known to us. Rather, we should utilize moments such as these to bring ourselves to the place of humble worship and sincere prayer while saying "Lord, all belongs to You. All is in your hands—even my helplessness. You are the beginning, the end, and everything in between. You alone are my Lord."

This particular question reminds us of the following verse: *"For from him and through him and for him are all things. To him be the glory forever! Amen."* (Rom 11:36) And our response to such a proclamation should be, "Amen, let this be done just as was proclaimed!"

The Shorter Catechism as a whole can be wrapped up in this single word, Amen. Because we now know 1) what our God is like—that He is good, 2) He has begun a good work in us already, and 3) for His own glory, He will surely accomplish this good work He has begun, in confidence and trust we can say Amen.

Discussion Questions

❶ Let's say you have reached a point where you can pray the Lord's Prayer with your whole heart. How do you imagine you would look like?

❷ Share what you have come to find new through this chapter.

❸ In what sense does this chapter give us the reason to be grateful?

❹ Reflecting on the entire teaching of the Shorter Catechism, share your thoughts on what a God-glorifying and God-enjoying life looks like.

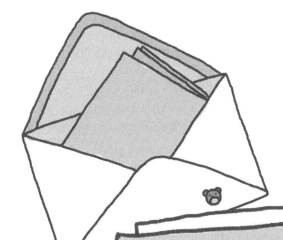

Author's note

Organized and systemized knowledge can function as the point of reference by which learners are made effortlessly able to judge and criticize. Even if not intended, that is oftentimes what comes out of the study of doctrines. Unfortunately, along the way, a number of naive judges and critics among ourselves are produced.

If a well-sharpened knife fell into the hands of robber, it would spell disaster to many. Likewise, what matters the most is a learner's character. A wellsharpened-by-doctrines knife has fallen into your hands. Please use it to sharpen yourself first. Do not cause your family and neighbors to complain, "What has happened to him? Now all he does is to judge and criticize. Is that because of THAT book of catechism?"

Use what you have learned from this book.
Yet put it into "good" use.
For if we have not love, we are only a resounding gong!

A SUMMARY OF THE SHORTER CATECHISM PART 1&2

FOR TEACHERS AND SMALL GROUP LEADERS

"What do we believe?"
"What are our duties to obey?"
They appear to be simple questions, yet we had to spend quite a time to learn these—what we believe and what duties we obey.. I hope and pray that we all have come to understand how ignorant and arrogant we are, how deep and abundant the knowledge of the Lord is, and what a joyful and grateful process getting to know God is. Now let us take a moment to summarize what we have learned so far.

As you studied, Part 2 will begin with God's commandments. It is **quite easy for us to leave what we have learned in Part 1 behind and only be focused on the duty required of us.** The God in Part 2 will be the same God in Part 1. And He will be using the same principles to come near to us as in Part 1.

gave us the Bible. In other religions, man is the one who sets out to search for the truth. Yet, in our faith, it is God who gives us it all. He gives us the faith and the strength to grow; but more than anything else, the fact that He disclosed where we should begin with our life should make us the most grateful.

Q1-2 FUNDAMENTAL PREMISE
OF THE SHORTER CATECHISM

With what question does the Shorter Catechism begin? It is quite important and worth revisiting. The first question was about the chief, the highest, the first, and the primary purpose of man. Why did this have to be the first question? Take a minute to give an answer to this question on your own.

As the major premise, Q1 and Q2 build the foundation of the entire catechism.

Q1 declares that man's purpose is found in God. Despite of the fact that numerous people may not agree with this premise, this question declares this as the truth up front. And according to Q2 it is only through the Bible that we can get to know this God. Without the Bible, we cannot accomplish the purpose given in Q1. Man may think that he is in control of getting to know God and living his own life, yet Q2 presents it clearly that this is only so in man's mind.

What the teachings of Q1 and Q2 should offer us is gratitude.

Life without a purpose is futile. Life with a purpose still could be. But the answer of Q1 of the Shorter Catechism is neither futile nor worthless. Rather, it is timeless and infinite, for it is about God, His glory, and the life that one enjoys in Him. God is the chief purpose of man. It transcends all other answers of philosophy regarding our life. That the Shorter Catechism presents man's chief purpose in God before anything else should make us grateful.

So should Q2. God did not leave us groping in the dark, but

Q3 THE MAJOR HINGE
OF THE SHORTER CATECHISM

Part 1: What we are to believe concerning God
Part 2: What duty God requires of us

Q3 divides the entire structure of the Shorter Catechism into two. While Q1-2 presents the premise, Q3 offers the overview. This over arching frame helps the learner become aware of where he is standing by enabling him to see the overall picture and the map.

Part 1 and Part 2 may appear to be from completely different perspectives, but ultimately they are the same. They are not disjointed. Proper knowledge of and belief in God are closely connected to the way we conduct our lives. Only when we come to understand who God is will we listen to what He requires of us. For it is unlikely that we come to desire to follow the commands of a stranger. The knowledge of the One we follow and love, the understanding of His desires and goals for us are prerequisites of our obedience.

Here gratitude plays the key role all over again. God sees us as personal beings. Come to know, believe, and follow, He says. Only when we come to learn, realize, and be touched by what to believe about God and we become grateful and willing to follow will we will be able to say, "What then should I do?" For we are personal beings. Not out of dutiful minds but willing hearts will we come to accept what God commands. And then we will make efforts to live accordingly. This is the whole process of our lives.

Part 2 of the Shorter Catechism is about the duty God requires of us. Yet we should aim to reach a point where we take this not as duty; rather, we are grateful to God who is not only willing but also able to raise us to such a place. This is what Q3 of the Shorter Catechism reminds us as well.

Q4-38 KEY TEACHINGS OF PART 1
OF THE SHORTER CATECHISM

The following is a summary of the key teachings of Part 1. Read closely, reminding yourself of previous teachings, and in case you fail to recall the contents, please go back to the corresponding pages.

1. Triune God (Q4-6)

Here the key point is that such a noble God has become my Father. The One that we could not even get to know not only comes to us and speaks, but also suggests sharing His love with us. That such a high God desires to have a loving relationship with such low creatures like us is the key point of our meditation on God. It is only within the Trinity that we can come to proper knowledge of Him, and this is also confirmed by the unified work of the triune God, which will be seen after Q7.

2. Everything, both in the past and in the future, is in God's decrees. (Q7-12)

In the overall structure of Part 1, Q4-6 and Q7- are distinct in that the former attempts to understand God in a cognitive way through His attributes and the latter in a personal way through

His work. It is that through His work, intention, plan, and means, as recorded in the Bible, we get to know Him more deeply. This will lead us into the knowledge of His character and His heart.

For this purpose, His creation and providence were studied in more detail.

CREATION

All things in this world were not only created according to God's will but were also good. What lies at the center of all creation was the creation of man. It is only man, which was created in God's own image, that is the key of all creation. What would be the purpose of such creation? God created man to be the ruler of all creatures. This authority must be taken with great awareness and diligence to make ourselves worthy of such a call.

PROVIDENCE

God did not put a halt to His work after creating all things, but continued with governing them. Here "that He governs" means that God works in everything we see, hear, and experience in this world. The key is that we come to acknowledge this fact despite difficulty in this world.

Some may ask, "If everything in this world belongs to God, then why is this world in such a mess?" The answer of the Bible cannot be any clearer. Everything is God's and under His sovereignty. If God does not allow it, not even a hair would be able to fall to the ground. Even the fall of man belongs to God's providence. Also the world and the Church are not separate in the sense that even non-believers are under God's sovereignty and have to obey His commandments.

The general response to the question above could be two: 1) He may not exist or is not powerful or 2) He may not love us.

What would be your answer? If the absolute God is only the living God, then this world should belong to Him; if this God is a good God, then He should not have created evil. That such a high and good God whom we have previously learned about is now working in my life regardless of how things appear to be demonstrates faith in providence. God does not work on impulse but with decrees, an unchanging plan, and He is now executing them. Therein are found creation, the fall, redemption, the after-life, and the end of eternity.

Other unresolved questions may be dealt with in the following.

3. Total Depravity (Q13-19)

Here the key is to understand what our fall means and, due to this fall, what truly has fallen to its peril. Another significant point is that even this fall belonged to God's providence. And in order for us to understand this fall properly, we need to be able to recall the teachings of creation and providence.

First we have to remind ourselves about what precious beings we were created as. Only then would we be able to fully recognize how miserable a state into which we have now fallen. Between the states into which we were created and fallen, there is an enormous gap.

The wages of sin is death. Then, by this fall, have we all come to die? On the surface, it may not look so. That is why the definition of death was so crucial at this point. Death means to be separated from God. That for man there is no state worse than being separated from God was the perspective required as we come to understand the fall.

What about providence? We should not understand man's fall as if man came to upset God's providence or be at odds with it, as if God's plan was being thwarted by our unexpected sinning against Him. "Then, is it God's will that we sin?" Such a question may surface at this point. However, this is because the concepts of God's will and God's plan are confused. It is obvious that God hates when we do what He hates. Our disobedience is not God's will, yet it can be included in His decrees. When we want to do certain things, we make plans. And these plans can include other than what we wanted in the first place. In the same way, God's decrees may include not only suffering but things beyond our understanding. Yet in the end, they will bring glory to God through His wisdom, which transcends our minds.

A misconception about sin may have played a role as well. Sin is what man commits against God. It is not that sin is something other than man, and influences him to make mistakes. This is not the right way to see it. Sin is what I commit, and its responsibility belongs to me. By attributing its responsibilities to something else, we might imagine sin to be a matter or power, but in the end, that will make us blame God, who created whatever that may be. We left God by our own will, and the responsibility for this must fall on us.

All of the above prepares for the appearance of the Redeemer.

4. The Redeemer (Q20-28)

Through this section, we have studied the grace of redemption by which God delivered us from the fall. Here the key lies in that the object of such redemption is not all humankind but only some. Moreover, the Shorter Catechism explains that only Jesus Christ can act as such a Redeemer, and He came in humanity for us. The redeeming work of Christ is described in two ways, His offices and estate. You might draw the picture or table of this for yourself.

It is worth revisiting the key point, "Why did He choose only some?" This can strike us only when we properly understand what the fall is. All had to die because of sin, yet out of His grace, God redeemed some. That all humanity had to perish out of fairness must be our focus. That He did not elect all but only some is quite natural given His attributes by which He hates/does not accept any sins and always acts justly. Also the reason He came in humanity was to sympathize with us, vanquish sin, and resurrect.

OFFICES

The offices of prophets, priests, and kings were to be filled by Christ who was to come. Being called antitypes, these offices foreshadowed the work of Christ, which will be done in the future. The people in the Old Testament, through these antitypes, placed their faith in Jesus Christ, who was to come in their future, and were saved.

ESTATE

The work of Christ is described through His humiliation and exaltation. Without being required, He voluntarily underwent all in order to let us, His children, come to know, realize, and be deeply affected by Him. It is His humiliation through which we come to realize that His work of redemption was necessary and valuable to us. Also through His exaltation, we come to be assured that only Christ is our hope and confidence, and He raises all our interests and affections to heaven.

Three offices and two estate were navigated in separate chapters, yet they must be integrated in our understanding.

5. The benefits of redemption (Q29-38)

The life after redemption is more often misconstrued than salvation. From this question forward, the work of the Holy Spirit is constantly reinforced. This is important considering that we tend to believe in error that after our salvation it is now up to us to work out our salvation. Yet as communicated in the title of this section, all are the benefits of redemption. In other words, as the result of redemption, these have been given as its benefits.

What other than benefits have we received after salvation, which has come through Christ's redemption? Nothing has been given based on my merit. Also nothing could be added to what has been already given. Everything has come for free and been done by grace. The gifts are from Christ. That God calls us to Christ without any error (effectually) is the key in the benefits of redemption.

The benefits are divided into ones in this life, at death, and after resurrection.

IN THIS LIFE, WE RECEIVE THE BENEFITS WITH GRATITUDE AND COME TO ENJOY THEM.

It is worth repeating that all are the work of the Spirit of Christ. It is so with justification, adoption, and sanctification. Among all, sanctification could appear to be a gradual growth made possible by our efforts, but even this is a benefit given to us. Such an understanding can help us avoid both the arrogance and despair.

WE MAY AVOID THE FEAR OF DEATH AS WELL.

Being still united with Christ, our souls will pass into glory immediately. There is no purgatory, no other place, no rebirth, no search for a light to enter. We will come to God and remain before Him. There is no need to fret at all.

THE TESTIMONY OF JESUS SHOULD MAKE US POSSESS THE HOPE OF RESURRECTION, WHICH IN TURN SHOULD ENCOURAGE THE ACTUAL CHANGES IN OUR LIFE.

We may not be able to imagine how the union of our soul and body will look like. Yet we can be certain that this will not only be better but perfect. And we will be openly acknowledged. Unwilling to compromise, we often attract ridicule from the people in this world, but on the judgement day, they will be openly ashamed while we are openly acknowledged. And we will also be given the perfect blessing in which we enjoy God always to eternity!

Now that we have completed the review of Part 1, it is worth noting this can be a way to systemize our faith. It is not the number of years of church experience but the sum of systematic knowledge that helps us have true faith and keep standing in it. Use this review to check up on your faith whether it rests on a solid system or not. The Shorter Catechism Map can be a measuring stick for you to find out where your systematic knowledge is strong enough or in need of improvement. Through self-examination, you can come to have either confidence about the areas where your knowledge stands strong or hope about the areas where you can improve your knowledge.

1 OPENING

The Shorter Catechism Part 2 begins with the question, "What duty does God require of man?" Interestingly there is no room for negotiation if man should obey the Creator. It is taken for granted that man (God's creature) has to obey his Creator God. And this duty given to man is not hidden in the dark, but is revealed through the rules of obedience.

These rules of obedience are called "Moral Law" and this law goes far above the rules men created for themselves, for example to settle disputes among them and keep order for society. It is also important that the "entire mankind" is bound to this Moral Law. God's will, revealed in the Moral Law, is equally applied both to believers and non-believers. Being created by God, non-believers are also held to the same accountability before God and they will also be judged by the same standard of Moral Law.

Having the above understanding regarding Moral Law is necessary as we move on to the teaching of the Ten Commandments.

2 THE PRINCIPLE UNDERGIRDING THE TEN COMMANDMENTS

God's Moral Law is embedded in the Ten Commandments. Before getting into the commandments, it must be noted that the principle undergirding the commandments of various "Dos and Don'ts" is none other than love. When it is beasts and animals we are dealing with, we may use physical discipline and reward, yet the obedience which should be exploited from those means, other than love, is not acceptable to the Giver of this Law. He demands and deserves obedience not from fear or oppression, but from loving willingness. Any obedience that does not come from loving willingness is nothing less than formality found in religion with which we cannot please either God or ourselves.

3 THE TEN COMMANDMENTS

The Ten Commandments takes almost a quarter of the entire pages of the Shorter Catechism. (In the Larger Catechism, the Ten Commandments takes up to one third in terms of pages and half in terms of number of words.) This effectively shows how significant a role the commandments were deemed to play in the eyes of the authors of these catechisms. And these expected roles of the Ten Commandments have not changed over time, but we have our own challenges today to correctly apply them into the context of our lives.

The first challenge comes with this part's massive volume of the study. As far as its volume goes, there is little to relieve this particular challenge. However, if the study is conducted with a constant reminder of the entire structure (thus the meaning and flow of each commandment), the study can be less challenging. (The map could come in handy in this perspective.)

A second challenge comes with our superficial efforts to understand the commandments. Looked at in shallow ways, for instance, "Do not murder" means very little. (How many of those who are willing to study the Ten Commandments might have murdered another human being?) It definitely takes more work for us to see the true meaning and intention of each commandment, and for that reason, having the Larger Catechism at our side can be tremendously helpful.

A third challenge comes with our sense of guilt, stirred by the rigorous demands of the commandments. Because some may feel discouraged being poor in Spirit while studying the Ten Commandments, I would like to encourage them. To ease this particular challenge, we need to encourage each other and remind each other of what comes after the Ten Commandments (the means of grace). Once again the map can be helpful.

One of two benefits can surely come from the study of the Ten Commandments, which is the given standard and way to live for Kingdom people. The study either brings us a strong desire to live according to the Law or it makes us realize how unable we are to do so, and we thus completely crumble before the Law. These benefits seem quite the opposite, yet both lead us to the Giver of the Law.

The truth is the Ten Commandments deal with everyday matters, especially from the fifth to tenth commandments. Thus using related current books or documentary films can also be helpful for us to find relativity of the commandments and take a few extra steps into the understanding and practice of the commandments.

insignificant (in our eyes) sins deserve God's wrath and punishment, yet our loving God prepared a way for us to avoid the wrath and punishment which requires us to follow His way. That requirement, which is given to us so that we may avoid well-deserved wrath and punishment, is nonetheless a gift just like all other things God gives us in this life.

4   THE MEANS OF GRACE

Through Part 1 and 2 of this catechism, we have studied what we are to learn about God and what He requires of us. What He requires of man is Moral Law, and the Ten Commandments is the summarized form of this Law. However, when these commandments are put into practice, we come to find ourselves in despair due to our complete inability to fulfill the Law on our own.

This makes the following appearance of the topic of "sin" somewhat comforting for us. As we have learned in Part 1, the mediation of Christ has gotten rid of our sins once and for all, yet we are still struggling with the "residue" of sin, which becomes a great stumbling block in our constant struggle to obey the commandments of God. Thus, every loving child of God joins the lament of Paul. "I do not understand what I do. For what I want to do I do not do, but what I hate I do." (Rom 7:15) As the solution to resolve this dilemma, the Shorter Catechism offers the "means of grace," which are the Word, sacraments and prayer. Understanding of the context (the order of their appearance) can be helpful.

2. Outward means!

These means answer our question, "Then what should be done on my end?" We should diligently use these means, for God leads us to faith and repentance through these means. These three means are the Word, sacraments, and prayer, and once again their purpose is to effectively deliver "the benefit of Christ's mediation." If recalled, these benefits, made available through Christ's mediation, are found in our redemption, calling to be His church, union with Christ, and the communion of grace—justification, sanctification, and glorious fellowship with Christ in this life, right after death, in resurrection and at judgment.

Our faith should not be merely private, but communal, and what makes our faith communal are these ordinances that are shared among believers. The following verses from the book of Acts that were used to describe the faith of the early church demonstrate this aspect well. "They devoted themselves to the apostles' teaching and to fellowship, to the breaking of bread and to prayer." (Acts 2:42-47)

1. The means to effectively deliver the benefit of redemption

What appears first as the means of grace is faith and repentance. The other outward means, the Word, sacrament and prayer follow with the encouragement for us to diligently use them as believers in this life.

Is the means of faith and repentance merely a screening process for salvation or an actual means for us to be separated from sin and more like God Himself? When taken as the latter, a God given gift for a certain purpose, we will be able to treat these outward means with a more sincere heart and attitude. Even

5   CONCLUSION

We should be able to see the connection not only between the Moral Law and the means of grace, but also among each of the means of grace. We tend to emphasize only the first part of the Shorter Catechism, but the second part is equally important, for this is where our everyday lives are connected to the doctrines of Christian faith.

> **"I believe in the sufficiency of the Bible. Thus, we don't need doctrines."**

"The Apostles' Creed is not found in the Bible. Man created it. Thus, we don't need it," said some heretics. Unfortunately, similar complaints have been made about doctrines. Yes, it is true that doctrines in and of themselves are not found in the Bible. Yet does this mean a doctrine is unbiblical? Absolutely not! "Tota scriptura(all the scriptures)" is equally important as "Sola scriptura(only the scriptures)." Teaching doctrines is same as teaching the Bible, and the following references made to doctrines in the Bible testify to that: "Proportion to his faith" (Rom 12:6) "the teachings" (1 Cor 11:2) "For what I received I passed on to you" (1 Cor 15:3) and "Guard the good deposit that was entrusted to you." (2 Tim 1:14)

Doctrines are written **by the representatives** of God's church. We cannot simply reject what the church as a whole (through her representatives) came to agree upon and document just because they were not inspired in the same way as the Bible itself or they do not fit into our personal (cultural) opinions. If there is found any error in man-made doctrines, we may initiate a discussion among churches rather than reject the whole idea of doctrine.

"There is nothing new under the sun" (Eccl 1:9), and so are the doubts and struggles believers undergo in this life. "Is the Bible really the Word of God?" "What is church? Do we really need it?" "How is the church organized and run?" or "How can we understand the evil in this world?" These questions have been asked in the past, and the answers have been written down in the form of confessions and catechisms. These are the voices from many of the faithful in the past who had the same doubts and struggles as ours, and we should pay close attention to them rather than holding on to **"chronological snobbery."**

Chronological snobbery, the uncritical acceptance of the intellectual climate common to our own age and the assumption that whatever has gone out of date is on that account discredited, was coined by C.S. Lewis, and this term well reveals the arrogant attitude we possess towards doctrine. (*Surprised by Joy* by C.S. Lewis)

No doctrines came out of futile or hollow discussion, but out of the efforts to fight against many heresies. For that reason, many of the catechisms, the most well-known ones to us, were made in the time of the Reformation and the following century. Truthfully speaking, many current discussions and questions can easily be resolved merely by the study of these historical documents. We should cherish and pay close attention to them, for it is through these efforts we come to have a greater chance to pass down a healthy church, faith, and life for the next generation.

> **Are there any other catechisms?**

THE CATECHISM OF GENEVA, A. D. 1537-1541

In the year of 1536, Calvin published the Institute and it became an instant best seller. On his way to Strasbourg, war broke out between Francis I and Charles V, so Calvin decided to make a one-night detour to Geneva. Hearing of his coming to the city of Geneva, a local reformer, Farel, invited him to stay in Geneva and threatened him with God's anger if he did not. Thus began a long, difficult, yet ultimately fruitful relationship with that city. By 1538, Calvin was asked to leave because of theological conflicts. He went to Strasbourg until the year of 1541 when the Council of Geneva requested him to return. The catechism of Geneva was born with this return to Geneva.

For more information, please see Thea B. Van Halsema's This Was John Calvin and https://calvin.edu/about/history/john-calvin.html

THE SCOTCH CONFESSION, A. D. 1560

This confession was written by John Knox and his colleagues as they were making an effort in the battle against Roman Catholics. While in exile, Knox met and had an opportunity to learn from John Calvin at the Geneva Academy. As an attempt to fight against the "false church," this confession clearly sets forth three marks of the true and faithful church, "the true preaching of the Word of God," "the right administration of the sacraments of Christ Jesus," and "ecclesiastical discipline."

For deeper understanding: John Knox and the Reformation by D.M. Lloyd-Jones & Iain H. Murray

THE BELGIC CONFESSION, A. D. 1561

The wave of reformation reached up to the region of Netherlands. There, a reformed pastor named Guido de Brès authored this particular confession out of the need for a clear and comprehensive statement of Reformed faith during the time of the Spanish inquisition in the region. At the time, he was serving an underprivileged congregation in the city called Tournai. After writing this confession, on the night of November 1, 1561, he threw his creed over the castle wall of Tournai, where the governor was staying, and for this, he was later martyred.

For more information, please see Thea Van Halsema's Three Men Came to Heidelberg and Glorious Heretic and https://www.crcna. org/welcome/beliefs/confessions/belgic-confession

THE HEIDELBERG CATECHISM, A. D. 1563

Soon after the introduction of Protestantism into the Palatinate, the controversy between Lutherans and Calvinists broke out, and it raged with great violence in Heidelberg. Frederick III, in order to put an end to religious disputes in his dominions, determined to put forth a Catechism, or Confession of Faith, and laid the duty of preparing it upon Zacharias Ursinus and Caspar Olevianus. This catechism, which came to be called the Heidelberg Catechism, soon spread to other nations in Europe and was translated into almost every spoken language. The key teaching of this catechism is that it is only through "true faith" we get to be saved and this true faith consists of "certain knowledge" and "assured confidence." This teaching came out of a context in which the congregation of the day was unsure and thus greatly confused about true faith.

For more information, please see Thea Van Halsema's Three Men Came to Heidelberg and Glorious Heretic

THE CANONS OF DORT, A. D. 1619

Time has passed and so has the intense years of the Reformation. In the early 17th century, at one of the universities in the Netherlands, a group of students came to oppose the doctrine of election and probation of Calvin. In order to settle the dispute, churches sent a theologian named Arminius to the region, but he ended up taking the same side with these students in error. So an international synod of the Reformed was convened at Dordrecht, Netherlands in 1618-19. Here it was settled that the claims of the students were in error and the doctrines related to election and probation were reaffirmed as biblical.

Out of this synod five points were affirmed, and the acronym of those points is well-known among us today as TULIP. (Total Depravity; Unconditional Election; Limited Atonement; Irresistible Grace; and Perseverance of the Saints)

"Good and faithful work, all of you who have completed the book!
We do not know what God holds in the store for all of us.
However, we will continue to serve each other and remain together,
as we bring all the glory and praise to God who has done,
does and will do all for us.
Love to all readers! :D"